## STANDARD 2.  Building Family and Community Relationships

**2a.** Knowing about and understanding diverse family and community characteristics.

**2b.** Supporting and engaging families and communities through respectful, reciprocal relationships.

**2c.** Involving families and communities in young children's development and learning.

**Chapter 1:** Families as Observers, pp. 15; Bioecological Theory, p. 09.

**Chapter 2:** Growth, p. 24; Development, pp. 25; Gender Roles, pp. 33; Ecological Factors, pp. 35; Developmental Domains, pp. 36.

**Chapter 3:** Threats to Optimum Fetal Development, pp. 56; Maternal Depression, pp. 62.

**Chapter 4:** Learning Activities, pp. 76–77.

   *Video Features*: *Attachment*, p. 92. Safety Concerns, p. 94; Positive Behavior Guidance, p. 101.

**Chapter 5:** Learning Activities, pp. 114–115; Social-Emotional Development, p. 111; Safety Concerns, p. 116;  Positive Behavior Guidance, p. 125.

**Chapter 6:**  Brain Development, p. 139;  Learning Activities, pp. 137; Safety Concerns, pp. 138–139;  Positive Behavior Guidance, p. 153.

**Chapter 7:** Learning Activities, pp. 165–166;  Brain Development, p. 168–169; Safety Concerns, p. 168;  Positive Behavior Guidance, p. 183.

**Chapter 8:** Learning Activities, pp. 196; Safety Concerns, p. 197; Positive Behavior Guidance, p. 206.

**Chapter 9:** Learning Activities, pp. 218–219; Safety Concerns, p. 219–220; Positive Behavior Guidance, p. 233.

**Chapter 10:** When to Seek Help, p. 246; Observing and Recording, pp. 247; Screening Tests, p. 248.

## STANDARD 3.  Observing, Documenting, and Assessing to Support Young Children and Families

**3a.** Understanding the goals, benefits, and uses of assessment—including its use in development of appropriate goals, curriculum, and teaching strategies for young children.

**3b.** Knowing about assessment partnerships with families and with professional colleagues to build effective learning environments.

**3c.** Knowing about and using  observation, documentation, and other appropriate assessment tools and approaches, including the use of technology in documentation, assessment, and data collection.

**3d.** Understanding and practicing responsible assessment to promote positive outcomes for each child, including the use of assistive technology for children with disabilities.

**Chapter 1:** Data Gathering, pp. 13; Families as Observers, pp. 15.

   *Video Features: Portfolio Assessment*, p. 18.

**Chapter 3:** *Video Features: Prenatal Assessment*, p. 56; *Newborn Assessment*, p. 61.

**Chapter 4:** Developmental Alerts, pp. 77.

**Chapter 5:** Developmental Alerts, pp. 115.

**Chapter 6:** Developmental Alerts, pp. 138–139.

**Chapter 7:** Developmental Alerts, pp. 166–167.

**Chapter 8:** Developmental Alerts, pp. 196–197.

**Chapter 9:** Developmental Alerts, pp. 219.

**Chapter 10:** Case Study, pp. 254.

   *Video Features: Including Children with Developmental Disabilities*, p. 242; *Assessing Children's Development*, p. 249. Is There a Problem? pp. 245; When to Seek Help, p. 246; Information Gathering, pp. 247; Diagnosis and Referral, pp. 251.

## STANDARD 4.  Using Developmentally Effective Approaches

**4a.** Understanding positive relationships and supportive interactions as the foundation of their work with young children.

**4b.** Knowing and understanding effective strategies and tools for early education, including appropriate uses of technology.

**4c.** Using a broad repertoire of developmentally appropriate teaching/learning approaches.

**4d.** Reflecting on own practice to promote positive outcomes for each child.

**Chapter 2:** Age-level expectancies or Norms, pp. 26; Brain Growth and Development, pp. 29.

   *Video Features: Brain Development in Infancy*, p. 29. Typical Growth and Development, pp. 28; Temperament, p. 32;  Developmental Domains, pp. 36.

**Chapter 4:** Brain Development, p. 86; Learning Activities, pp. 76–77;  Safety Concerns, pp. 94.

   *Video Features: Attachment*, p. 92;  Positive Behavior Guidance, p. 101.

**Chapter 5:** Learning Activities, pp. 114–115; Safety Concerns, p. 116; Positive Behavior Guidance, p. 125.

**Chapter 6:** Learning Activities, pp. 137; Safety Concerns, pp. 138–139; Positive Behavior Guidance, p. 153.

**Chapter 7:** Brain Development, p. 168–169; Learning Activities, pp. 165–166; Safety Concerns, pp. 168; Positive Behavior Guidance, p. 183.

**Chapter 8:** Learning Activities, pp. 196; Safety Concerns, pp. 197; Brain Development, p. 197–198; Positive Behavior Guidance, p. 206.

**Chapter 9:** Learning Activities, pp. 218–219; Safety Concerns, pp. 219–220.

   *Video Features: Understanding Adolescent Emotions*, p. 217. Positive Behavior Guidance, pp. 233.

**Chapter 10:** *Video Features: Children with Developmental Disabilities in the Classroom*, p. 247. Is There a Problem? pp. 245; When to Seek Help, p. 246; Screening Tests, pp. 248; IQ Tests, p. 250.

## STANDARD 5. Using Content Knowledge to Build Meaningful Curriculum

**5a.** Understanding content knowledge and resources in academic disciplines: language and literacy; the arts—music, creative movement, dance, drama, visual arts; mathematics; science, physical activity, physical education, health and safety; and social studies.

**5b.** Knowing and using the central concepts, inquiry tools, and structures of content areas or academic disciplines.

**5c.** Using own knowledge, appropriate early learning standards, and other resources to design, implement, and evaluate developmentally meaningful and challenging curriculum for each child.

**Chapter 4:** *Video Features: Early Infant Language*, p. 83; *Fine Motor Development*, p. 88. Learning Activities, pp. 76–77.

**Chapter 5:** *Video Features: Speech and Language Development*, p. 111; *Toddlers' Cognitive Development*, p. 112. Learning Activities, pp. 114–115.

**Chapter 6:** *Video Features: Preschoolers' Motor Development*, p. 133, *Preschooler's Language Development*, p. 143; *Social Skill Development*, p. 149. Learning Activities, pp. 137.

**Chapter 7:** *Video Features: Cognitive Development*, p. 163; *Cognitive Development and Concrete Operations*, p. 172. Learning Activities, pp. 165–166.

**Chapter 8:** *Video Features: Emotional Development and Bullying*, p. 194; *Middle Childhood and Cognitive Development*, p. 202. Learning Activities, pp. 196.

**Chapter 9:** *Video Features: Understanding Adolescent Emotions*, p. 217; *Technology and Learning*, p. 223. Learning Activities, pp. 218–219.

## STANDARD 6. Becoming a Professional

**6a.** Identifying and involving oneself with the early childhood field.

**6b.** Knowing about and upholding ethical standards and other early childhood professional guidelines.

**6c.** Engaging in continuous, collaborative learning to inform practice; using technology effectively with young children, with peers, and as a professional resource.

**6d.** Integrating knowledgeable, reflective, and critical perspectives on early education.

**6e.** Engaging in informed advocacy for young children and the early childhood profession.

**Chapter 3:** Promoting Health Fetal Development, pp. 50.

**Chapter 10:** Legislation Supporting Optimum Development, pp. 241; The Developmental Team, pp. 251.

**Source:** NAEYC Standards for Early Childhood Professional Preparation Programs, copyright © 2010 by the National Association for the Education of Young Children. The complete position statement can be accessed at, http://www.naeyc.org/ncate/files/ncate/NAEYC%20Initial%20and%20Advanced%20Standards%2010_2012.pdf

# DEVELOPMENTAL
# PROFILES

EIGHTH EDITION

# DEVELOPMENTAL PROFILES

## PRE-BIRTH THROUGH ADOLESCENCE

## Lynn R. Marotz, RN, Ph.D

University of Kansas

## K. Eileen Allen

Professor Emerita
University of Kansas

CENGAGE
Learning®

Australia • Brazil • Japan • Korea • Mexico • Singapore • Spain • United Kingdom • United States

**CENGAGE Learning**

*Developmental Profiles: Pre-Birth Through Adolescence*, **Eighth Edition**

**Lynn R. Marotz and K. Eileen Allen**

Product Director: Marta E. Lee-Perriard

Product Manager: Mark Kerr

Content Developer: Kate Scheinman

Product Assistant: Julia Catalano

Marketing Manager: Chris Sosa

Content Project Manager: Samen Iqbal

Art Director: Marissa Falco

Manufacturing Planner: Doug Bertke

IP Analyst: Jennifer Nonenmacher

IP Project Manager: Brittani Hall

Copy Editor: Susan McClung

Production Service/Project Manager: Teresa Christie, MPS Limited

PMG Photo Researcher: Sofia Priya Dharshini, PMG

PMG Text Researcher: Pinky Subi, PMG

Cover and Text Designer: Lisa Delgado

Cover Image Credit: KidStock/Blend RF/ Glow Images

Compositor: MPS Limited

For product information and technology assistance, contact us at **Cengage Learning Customer & Sales Support, 1-800-354-9706**

For permission to use material from this text or product, submit all requests online at **www.cengage.com/permissions**

Further permissions questions can be e-mailed to **permissionrequest@cengage.com**

Library of Congress Control Number: 2014940176

ISBN: 978-1-305-08831-3

**Cengage Learning**
20 Channel Center Street
Boston, MA 02210
USA

Cengage Learning is a leading provider of customized learning solutions with office locations around the globe, including Singapore, the United Kingdom, Australia, Mexico, Brazil, and Japan. Locate your local office at **www.cengage.com/global**

Cengage Learning products are represented in Canada by Nelson Education, Ltd.

To learn more about Cengage Learning Solutions, visit **www.cengage.com**

Purchase any of our products at your local college store or at our preferred online store **www.cengagebrain.com**

Printed in China
Print Number: 02    Print Year: 2014

# Contents in Brief

1 • Child Development Theories and Data Gathering  1

2 • Principles of Growth and Development  23

3 • Prenatal Development  46

4 • Infancy: Birth to Twelve Months  69

5 • Toddlerhood: Twelve to Twenty-Four Months  106

6 • Early Childhood: Three-, Four-, and Five-Year-Olds  129

7 • Early Childhood: Six-, Seven-, and Eight-Year-Olds  158

8 • Middle Childhood: Nine-, Ten-, Eleven-, and Twelve-Year-Olds  188

9 • Adolescence: Thirteen- to Nineteen-Year-Olds  211

10 • When and Where to Seek Help  239

APPENDIX A Developmental Checklists  257

APPENDIX B Selected Screening and Assessment Instruments  273

APPENDIX C Resources for Families and Professionals  279

# Contents

Preface   xii

About the Authors   xxi

## 1 • Child Development Theories and Data Gathering   1

**Contemporary Theories**   3
Maturational Theory   3
Psychoanalytic and Psychosocial Theory   4
Cognitive-Developmental Theory   5

**TeachSource Video Connections:** Zone of Proximal Development   8

Behaviorism and Social Learning Theory   8
Bioecological Theory   9
Maslow's Essential Needs Theory   10

**Spotlight on Brain Development:** Why Do Brain Research, and What Have We Learned?   13

**Data Gathering**   13

**TeachSource Video Connections:** Culturally Responsive Teaching   14

Teachers as Classroom Observers   14
Families as Observers   15

**Observation Methods**   15
Anecdotal Notes   16
Time or Event Sampling   16
Frequency and Duration Counts   17
Checklists and Rating Scales   17

**TeachSource Video Connections:** Assessing Children's Development   18

Portfolios   18

Summary   19
Key Terms   19
Apply What You Have Learned   19
Online Resources   20
References   21

## 2 • Principles of Growth and Development   23

**Basic Patterns and Concepts**   24
Growth   24
Development   25
Typical Growth and Development   28
Interrelatedness of Developmental Domains   28
Brain Growth and Development   29

**TeachSource Video Connections:** Brain Development in Infancy   29

**Spotlight on Brain Development:** Poverty's Toxic Effects   31

Temperament   32
Gender Identity   33

Ecological Factors   35
Transactional Patterns of Development   35
Children at Risk   35

**TeachSource Video Connections:** Children and Poverty   36

Atypical Growth and Development   36
**Developmental Domains**   36
Physical Development and Growth   37
Motor Development   37
Perceptual Development   39
Cognitive Development   39
Language Development   40
Social and Emotional Development   41

**TeachSource Video Connections:** Temperament and Personality Development   41

**Age Divisions**   41

Summary   42
Key Terms   42
Apply What You Have Learned   43
Online Resources   43
References   44

## 3 • Prenatal Development   46

**The Developmental Process**   47

**Spotlight on Brain Development:** Learning Before Birth   49

**Promoting Healthy Fetal Development**   50
Prenatal Care   50
Nutrition   51
Weight   53
Rest and Stress   54
Age and General Health   54

**TeachSource Video Connections:** Prenatal Assessment   56

**Threats to Healthy Fetal Development**   56
Alcohol   57
Smoking   58
Chemicals and Drugs   58
Maternal Infections   59
**An Infant's Arrival: Labor and Delivery**   60

**TeachSource Video Connections:** Newborn Assessment   61

**Maternal Depression**   62

Summary   64
Key Terms   64
Apply What You Have Learned   65
Online Resources   65
References   66

## 4 • Infancy: Birth to Twelve Months    69

**The Newborn (Birth to One Month)**    70

**TeachSource Video Connections:** Newborn Reflex Development    74

**TeachSource Digital Download:** Learning Activities to Promote Brain Development    76

**One to Four Months**    78

**TeachSource Video Connections:** Early Infant Learning    83

**TeachSource Digital Download:** Learning Activities to Promote Brain Development    84

**Spotlight on Brain Development:** Breast-feeding and Brain Development    86

**Four to Eight Months**    87

**TeachSource Video Connections:** Fine Motor Development    88

**TeachSource Video Connections:** Attachment    92

**TeachSource Digital Download:** Learning Activities to Promote Brain Development    92

**Eight to Twelve Months**    94

**TeachSource Video Connections:** Assessing Language Development    97

**TeachSource Digital Download:** Learning Activities to Promote Brain Development    99

**Positive Behavior Guidance**    101

Summary    102
Key Terms    103
Apply What You Have Learned    103
Online Resources    104
References    104

## 5 • Toddlerhood: Twelve to Twenty-Four Months    106

**Twelve to Twenty-Four Months**    107
**The One-Year-Old**    108

**TeachSource Video Connections:** Speech and Language Development    111

**TeachSource Video Connections:** Toddlers' Cognitive Development    112

**TeachSource Digital Download:** Learning Activities to Promote Brain Development    114

**The Two-Year-Old**    116

**TeachSource Video Connections:** Assessing Motor Development    118

**Spotlight on Brain Development:** The Brain-Autism Connection    121

**TeachSource Digital Download:** Learning Activities to Promote Brain Development    122

**Positive Behavior Guidance**    125

Summary    125
Key Terms    126
Apply What You Have Learned    126
Online Resources    127
References    127

# 6 • Early Childhood: Three-, Four-, and Five-Year-Olds    129

**Three-, Four-, and Five-Year Olds**    130
**The Three-Year-Old**    131

**TeachSource Video Connections:** The Preschooler's Motor Development    133

**TeachSource Digital Download:** Learning Activities to Promote Brain Development    137

**Spotlight on Brain Development:** The Importance of Sleep    139

**The Four-Year-Old**    140

**TeachSource Video Connections:** Preschoolers and Language Development    143

**TeachSource Digital Download:** Learning Activities to Promote Brain Development    144

**The Five-Year-Old**    146

**TeachSource Video Connections:** Social Skill Development    149

**TeachSource Digital Download:** Learning Activities to Promote Brain Development    151

**Positive Behavior Guidance**    153

Summary    154
Key Terms    154
Apply What You Have Learned    154
Online Resources    155
References    156

# 7 • Early Childhood: Six-, Seven-, and Eight-Year-Olds    158

**Six-, Seven-, and Eight-Year-Olds**    159
**The Six-Year-Old**    160

**TeachSource Video Connections:** Cognitive Development    163

**TeachSource Digital Download:** Learning Activities to Promote Brain Development    165

**TeachSource Video Connections:** Learning About Responsibility    167

**Spotlight on Brain Development:** Toxic Stress and Abnormal Brain Development    168

**The Seven-Year-Old**    169

**TeachSource Video Connections:** Cognitive Development and Concrete Operations    172

**TeachSource Digital Download:** Learning Activities to Promote Brain Development    174

**The Eight-Year-Old**    176

**TeachSource Video Connections:** Moral Development    179

**TeachSource Digital Download:** Learning Activities to Promote Brain Development    181

**Positive Behavior Guidance**    183

Summary    183
Key Terms    184
Apply What You Have Learned    184
Online Resources    185
References    185

## 8 • Middle Childhood: Nine-, Ten-, Eleven-, and Twelve-Year-Olds    188

**Nine-, Ten-, Eleven-, and Twelve-Year Olds**  189
**Nine- and Ten-Year-Olds**  190

**TeachSource Video Connections:** Emotional Development and Bullying  194

**TeachSource Digital Download:** Learning Activities to Promote Brain
Development  196

**Spotlight on Brain Development:** Physical Activity and Neurocognitive Function  197
**Eleven- and Twelve-Year-Olds**  198

**TeachSource Video Connections:** Middle Childhood and Cognitive
Development  202

**TeachSource Digital Download:** Learning Activities to Promote Brain
Development  204

**Positive Behavior Guidance**  206

Summary  206
Key Terms  207
Apply What You Have Learned  207
Online Resources  208
References  208

## 9 • Adolescence: Thirteen- to Nineteen-Year-Olds    211

**Thirteen- to Nineteen-Year-Olds**  212
**Thirteen- and Fourteen-Year-Olds (Early Adolescence)**  213

**TeachSource Video Connections:** Understanding Adolescent Emotions  217

**TeachSource Digital Download:** Learning Activities to Promote Brain
Development  218

**Spotlight on Brain Development:** Self-Control and the Adolescent Brain  221
**Fifteen and Sixteen-Year-Olds (Middle Adolescence)**  221

**TeachSource Video Connections:** Technology and Learning  223

**TeachSource Digital Download:** Learning Activities to Promote Brain
Development  225

**Seventeen- and Eighteen-Year-Olds (Late Adolescence)**  227

**TeachSource Video Connections:** Peer Influence  230

**TeachSource Digital Download:** Learning Activities to Promote Brain
Development  231

**Positive Behavior Guidance**  233

Summary  234
Key Terms  235
Apply What You Have Learned  235
Online Resources  236
References  236

# 10 • When and Where to Seek Help    239

**Public Policy and Social Attitudes**    240
  Legislation Supporting Optimum Development    241

**TeachSource Video Connections:** Including Children with Developmental
  Disabilities    242

  Early Identification and Intervention Programs    243
  Infants and Children at Medical Risk    243
  Community Screening    243

**Spotlight on Brain Development:** Premature Birth and Cognitive Development    244

**Is There a Problem?**    245
  When to Seek Help    246
**Information Gathering**    247

**TeachSource Video Connections:** Children with Developmental Disabilities in the
  Classroom    247

  Observing and Recording    247
  Screening Tests    248

**TeachSource Video Connections:** Assessing Children's Development    249

  IQ Tests: Are They Appropriate for Young Children?    250
  Achievement Tests    250
**Diagnosis and Referral**    251
  The Developmental Team    251
  Service Coordinator    252
  Referral    252

  Summary    253
  Key Terms    254
  Apply What You Have Learned    254
  Online Resources    255
  References    255

**APPENDIX A**    Developmental Checklists    257
**APPENDIX B**    Selected Screening and Assessment Instruments    273
**APPENDIX C**    Resources for Families and Professional    279

Glossary    283
Index    287

# Preface

Architectural engineers know that a structurally sound building requires a strong foundation. Similarly, early childhood teachers understand that children require a strong foundation if they are to develop to their fullest potential. The quality of children's environments, early learning opportunities, and adult support and encouragement plays an influential role in shaping the groundwork upon which all future skill acquisition is built. When adults understand children's developmental needs, capabilities, and limitations, they are able to provide effective behavioral guidance and the types of learning experiences that ultimately create a strong foundation.

*Developmental Profiles: Pre-birth Through Adolescence* is designed to be a concise, user-friendly resource for teachers, families, caregivers, practitioners, and service providers. The eighth edition has been thoroughly revised and updated, yet it maintains the authors' original purpose to provide a comprehensive yet nontechnical, easy-to-follow overview of children's development. It links contemporary research, theory, and application to the guidance of children's behavior and the promotion of developmentally appropriate learning experiences.

## Purpose and Philosophical Approach

The common practice of dividing infancy and childhood into age-related units of months and years may initially appear to distort the realities of human development. However, when describing developmental expectations, developmental progress, and delays, other systems seem to work even less well. Let it be stressed here, as it is again and again throughout the text, that *age specifications are only approximate markers derived from averages or norms*. In a way, they can be thought of as midpoints that are not intended to represent any one particular child. Rather, age expectations represent summary terms for skills that vary from child to child in form and time of acquisition. The truly important consideration in assessing a child's development is *sequence*. The essential question is not chronological age, but whether the child is moving forward step by step in each developmental area. *Developmental Profiles* has long proven itself to be an invaluable resource in addressing this issue.

As in the previous editions, the early days, weeks, and months of infancy are examined in great detail. New research findings on brain and early development clearly support the critical importance of this relatively short time span. What is now known about the infant's capacity for learning is indeed amazing given conventional wisdom, which suggests that young babies simply flounder around in a state of confusion. Far from it! With more and more infants and young children entering early education programs and receiving intervention services at ever earlier ages, it is most important that teachers and practitioners are knowledgeable about their development and ability to learn. It is also crucial that families and service providers hold appropriate expectations and be able to describe to teachers what they want and believe is best for children.

The first year of life is essential for building a foundation of learning in every developmental domain. The vast array of new and complex behaviors that toddlers and preschoolers must learn in three or four short years is also monumental. At no other period in a person's lifetime will so much be expected in so short a time. With other-than-parent child care being the norm rather than the exception, it is necessary for teachers and families to have a comprehensive understanding of how young children grow, develop, and learn. Thus, an underlying philosophy of *Developmental Profiles* continues to be partnerships with families. No matter how many hours children spend with caregivers or teachers in school each day, families still play the most significant and influential role in their lives. Families must be supported and encouraged to share their observations and concerns with teachers because this information is integral to each child's development and well-being. In turn, teachers and service providers must listen to families with focused attention and respond with genuine interest and respect.

Partnerships with families become even more critical when an infant or older child is suspected of having a developmental problem or irregularity. The *Developmental Alerts* identified for each age group can be especially useful to families, teachers, and service providers for initiating a discussion about their concerns. Let it be emphasized, however, that under no circumstances should this book or any other book be seen as an instrument for diagnosing a developmental problem. That is the job of professional clinicians and child development specialists.

Thus, the stated purposes of this text can be summed up as follows:

- To provide a concise overview of developmental principles
- To provide easily accessible information about what to expect at each developmental level
- To suggest appropriate ways for adults to facilitate learning and development
- To pinpoint warning signs of a possible developmental problem
- To suggest how and where to get help
- To describe cultural and environmental diversity in terms of its impact on the developmental process
- To emphasize the value of direct observation of children in their natural settings, whether in a classroom, early childhood program, or the child's own home
- To help adults encourage every child to achieve his or her potential, develop a positive sense of self-esteem, and feel loved and respected
- To highlight contemporary child development research

# The Intended Audience

Teachers—caregivers, families, and professionals—play an essential role in guiding children's development. It is through their ability to foster learning and self-esteem and identify challenges that interfere with developmental progress that adults can ultimately make a difference in children's lives. Thus, *Developmental Profiles* is designed for adults who care for and work with children of all ages, including:

- Students and preservice teachers.

- Teachers in home-based settings, early childhood centers, Early Start and Head Start programs, public and private schools, and before- and after-school programs; home visitors; and nonparental caregivers in the child's home.

- Allied health professionals and service providers in nursing, nutrition, audiology, social work, physical and occupational therapy, psychology, medicine, language and speech therapy, and counseling who provide services for children and their families.

- Families, the most important contributors to a child's development.

# Organization and Key Content

*Developmental Profiles* opens with a brief overview of major child development theories and principles. These chapters (1 and 2) serve as a refresher of basic concepts and provide background material on age-level expectancies for the chapters that follow. Chapter 3 is devoted to maternal practices that are essential for promoting healthy fetal development. Detailed word pictures of child and adolescent development across six developmental domains, including typical daily routines, safety alerts, developmental alerts, learning activities to promote brain development, and positive behavioral guidance are described in Chapters 4 through 9. Pages include color-coded tabs with age designations for quick, easy-to-locate reference. When and where to seek help if there are concerns about a child's developmental progress are discussed in Chapter 10. A new feature included in each chapter presents cutting-edge research on children's brain development. Developmental checklists and additional resource material of interest to families, teachers, and service providers are provided in the appendices. We believe that this format encourages vigilance in identifying delays in their earliest stage and supports adults in creating developmentally appropriate interventions and learning opportunities for children of all ages.

*Developmental Profiles* provides nontechnical, key information about the following:

- What to expect of young children and adolescents at each succeeding developmental stage

- The ways in which all areas of development are intertwined and mutually supportive

- The unique pathway that each child follows in a developmental process that is alike, yet different, among children of a similar age

- Sequences, not age, being the critical concept in evaluating developmental progress

- The use of developmental norms in teaching, observing, and assessing children and in designing individualized as well as group learning experiences

# New Content and Special Features

The eighth edition of *Developmental Profiles* continues to bring readers important content features that support understanding and practice in an easy-to-reference format:

- The **Learning Objectives** at the beginning of each chapter show students what they need to know to process and understand the information in the chapter. After completing the chapter, students should be able to demonstrate how they can use and apply their new knowledge and skills. The learning objectives are also reflected in the end-of-chapter summary.

- **Standards:** New and improved coverage of **National Association for the Education of Young Children Professional Preparation Standards (NAEYC)** standards includes a chapter-opening list of standards to help students identify where key standards are addressed in the chapter. These callouts, as well as the standards correlation chart, help students make connections between what they are learning in the textbook and the professional standards.

- **Digital Downloads:** Downloadable and often customizable, these practical and professional resources allow students to immediately implement and apply this textbook's content in the field. The student can download these tools and retain them for future use, enabling preservice teachers to begin building a library of practical, professional resources. Look for the **TeachSource Digital Downloads** label that identifies these items.

- **TeachSource videos** feature footage from the classroom to help students relate key chapter content to real-life scenarios. Critical-thinking questions provide opportunities for in-class or online discussion and reflection.

- *New* **Spotlight on Brain Development:** This feature, included in each chapter, draws attention to the latest neurocognitive research on critical issues (e.g., autism, breast-feeding, premature birth, abuse and neglect, physical activity, and adolescence) and their connections to children's brain development.

- *New* **Did You Know?** Offers interesting facts in a marginal feature to arouse students' curiosity and interest in chapter content.

- *New* **Chapter to Practice:** Field-based exercises, included in each chapter, provide opportunities for students to apply developmental concepts learned in the chapter and to critique their experiences.

- *New* **What Do You See?** Reinforces students' observational skills by asking them to answer questions based on what they see in a photograph.

- *New and expanded* **information on contemporary topics:** Additional material on brain development, children and technology, cultural awareness and sensitivity, gender identity and sexual orientation, dual-language learners, observational skills, and strategies for supporting children's transitions has been incorporated throughout the book. Updated references reflect the latest empirical research on these subjects.

- **Concise developmental profiles:** Highlight children's sequential progress across six developmental domains, from prebirth to age nineteen in a bulleted format.

- **Case Studies:** Presented at the onset of each chapter, the case studies reflect the ethnic diversity in today's schools. They set the stage for chapter content that follows and encourage students to relate what they learn to real-life situations. The *new* **Case Study Connections** located at the end of each chapter feature questions that require students to reflect on and apply what they have learned.

- **Developmental Alerts** are highlighted at each age level to aid in the early identification of potential delays, developmental problems, or both that warrant further evaluation.

- **Daily Activities and Routines** typical at each age level are offered in each chapter to help families and teachers anticipate and respond appropriately to children's developmental interests and needs.

- **Positive Behavior Guidance sections** outline effective strategies for responding to children's behavior in a constructive manner in order to promote healthy social and emotional competence.

- *New* **Learning Activities to Promote Brain Development** are now available in digital format for easy downloading. These sections offer suggestions for developmentally appropriate learning experiences that can be used to promote children's curiosity, creativity, problem-solving abilities, and skill acquisition across all domains.

- **Safety Alerts** reflect updated safety concerns associated with each developmental stage and are designed to help adults create safe environments, maintain quality supervision, and support children's safety education.

- *New* **TeachSource Digital Download** *Developmental Checklists* are provided for each age group in Appendix A. The checklists are also available in digital format and can be downloaded for teachers and families to use in monitoring children's developmental progress.

- **Screening and Assessment Instruments:** A sampling of screening tests commonly used to evaluate infants, young children, and adolescents development are identified and described in an annotated listing (Appendix B).

- **Resources:** An overview of early intervention resources is provided in Appendix C and at the end of each chapter to aid families and professionals in locating additional information and technical assistance.

# Chapter-by-Chapter Changes

Chapter 1, "Child Development Theories and Data Gathering"

- *New* and expanded descriptions of contemporary child development theory and theorists

- *New* learning objectives and summary aligned with chapter content

- *New* case study with questions for student reflection, class discussion, or both

- *New* research feature, *Spotlight on Brain Development: Why Brain Research and What Have We Learned?*

- *New TeachSource Video Connections* features: *Zone of Proximal Development and Scaffolding; Culturally Responsive Teaching; Assessing Children's Development*

- *New, Did You Know?* marginal feature: Offers facts to pique reader interest

Chapter 2, "Principles of Growth and Development"

- Expanded case study focused on diversity with *Your Turn* questions for self-reflection

- *New, What Do You See?* feature designed to reinforce students' observation skills

- *New* information on early brain development, temperament, gender identity, sexual orientation, and children at risk

- *New* research feature, *Spotlight on Brain Development: Poverty's Toxic Effects*

- *New TeachSource Video Connections* videos (*Brain Development in Infancy; Children and Poverty*)

Chapter 3, "Prenatal Development"

- *New* graphics illustrating key elements and current research data

- Increased emphasis on diversity awareness and sensitivity integrated throughout the chapter.

- *New* brain research box drawing attention to research on learning before birth
- *New What Do You See?* feature, which invites readers to make observations based on a photo
- Expanded and updated information on maternal depression and its effect on children's development, maternal practices to promote healthy fetal development, and reproductive technologies
- *New TeachSource Video Connections* videos and thought-provoking questions (*Prenatal Assessment; Newborn Assessment*)

Chapter 4, "Infancy: Birth to Twelve Months"

- Additional information on developmental changes and needs across domains and cultural differences
- *New* safety recommendations
- *New TeachSource Video Connections* videos reinforcing chapter content (*Newborn Reflex Development; Early Infant Learning; Fine Motor Development; Attachment; Assessing Language Development*)
- *New* developmentally appropriate learning experiences to promote infant brain development
- *New* brain research feature highlighting contemporary findings on breastfeeding and brain development

Chapter 5, "Toddlerhood: Twelve to Twenty-Four Months"

- Expanded information on typical development, developmental needs and interests, and cultural diversity provided throughout the chapter
- *New, TeachSource Video Connections* illustrating children's behavior in everyday situations (*Speech and Language Development; Toddlers' Cognitive Development; Assessing Motor Development*)
- *New* brain research feature presenting the latest neurocognitive findings on the brain-autism connection
- *New* chapter features, including *What Do You See?* and *Chapter to Practice*

Chapter 6, "Early Childhood: Three-, Four-, and Five-Year-Olds"

- *New* measurable objectives numbered and aligned with chapter and summary content
- Additional information on dual-language learners, diversity in milestone achievement, children's developmental interests and learning needs, media and technology, children's safety, social-emotional development, and the role of friendships
- *New TeachSource Video Connections* videos (*Preschool Motor Development; Preschoolers and Language Development; Social Skill Development*)
- *New* brain research feature on sleep and its influence on children's brain development and learning

Chapter 7, "Early Childhood: Six-, Seven-, and Eight-Year-Olds"

- *New* research findings on chronic exposure to maltreatment and toxic stress and their negative effects on children's brain development
- *New* Case Study that draws attention to cultural differences
- Expanded list of activities to promote children's brain development
- *New* information on bullying, culture, play-based learning, sleep, bullying, media safety, and the physical activity-learning link

- *New, TeachSource Video Connections* videos and thought-provoking questions (*Cognitive Development; Learning About Responsibility; Cognitive Development and Concrete Operations; Moral Development*)
- *New* descriptions of children's developmental needs and interest at each age level

Chapter 8, "Middle Childhood: Nine-, Ten-, Eleven-, and Twelve-Year-Olds"

- *New* Case Study and *Ask Yourself* questions
- *New* information on early puberty and preparing children for this important transition, language patterns, safety concerns, and eating disorders
- Expanded information on cultural differences in children's development
- *New TeachSource Video Connections* videos showcasing contemporary issues (*Emotional Development and Bullying; Middle Childhood and Cognitive Development*)
- *New Brain Research* feature describing the empirical research supporting a positive relationship between physical activity and brain development

Chapter 9, "Adolescence: Thirteen- to Nineteen-Year-Olds"

- *New* references and expanded information on adolescent development, including risky behaviors, experiences to promote brain development, and positive behavior guidance
- *New* research feature, *Spotlight on Brain Development*, provides empirical findings on adolescent brain development and behavior (self-control, impulsivity)
- *New TeachSource Video Connections* featuring video footage and content-related questions (*Understanding Adolescent Emotions; Technology and Learning; Peer Influence*)

Chapter 10, "Where and When to Seek Help"

- Updated information on legislation supporting education for all children and special intervention services
- Additional information on multiple births and medical conditions that can affect children's development, achievement testing, and cultural awareness and evaluation
- *New* brain research feature that draws attention to premature birth and its detrimental effect on children's cognitive development
- *New TeachSource Video Connections* features addressing the needs of children who have disabilities (*Including Children with Developmental Disabilities; Children with Developmental Disabilities in the Classroom; Assessing Children's Development*).

## Ancillaries

The eighth edition of this book is accompanied by an extensive package of instructor and student resources.

# For Students

## CourseMate

Cengage Learning's Education CourseMate brings course concepts to life with interactive learning, study, and exam preparation tools that support the printed textbook. Access the eBook, Digital Downloads, TeachSource Video Cases, flashcards, and other ancillaries in your Education CourseMate. Go to CengageBrain.com to register or purchase access.

## TeachSource Videos

The TeachSource videos feature footage from the classroom to help students relate key chapter content to real-life scenarios. Critical-thinking questions provide opportunities for in-class or online discussion and reflection.

# For Instructors

## CourseMate

Cengage Learning's Education CourseMate brings course concepts to life with interactive learning, study, and exam preparation tools that support the printed textbook. CourseMate includes the eBook, quizzes, Digital Downloads, Teach-Source Video Cases, flashcards, and EngagementTracker, a first-of-its-kind tool that monitors student engagement in the course. The accompanying instructor website, available through login.cengage.com, offers access to password-protected resources such as Microsoft® PowerPoint® lecture slides and the online Instructor's Manual with Test Bank. CourseMate can be bundled with the student text. Contact your Cengage sales representative for information on obtaining  access to CourseMate.

## PowerPoint Lecture Slides

These vibrant PowerPoint lecture slides for each chapter assist you with your lecture, by providing concept coverage using images, figures, and tables directly from the textbook!

## Online Instructor's Manual with Test Bank

An online Instructor's Manual accompanies this book. It contains information to assist the instructor in designing the course, including sample syllabi, discussion questions, teaching and learning activities, field experiences, learning objectives, and additional online resources. For assessment support, the updated test bank includes true/false, multiple-choice, matching, short-answer, and essay questions for each chapter.

## Cognero

Cengage Learning Testing Powered by Cognero is a flexible online system that allows you to create, edit, and manage test bank content from multiple Cengage Learning solutions; create multiple test versions in an instant; and deliver tests from your LMS, your classroom, or wherever you want.

# Acknowledgments

First and foremost, we wish to recognize Cengage Learning for their longstanding commitment to education. Their vision and dedication have contributed to an improved understanding of children and families and continue to support teachers in their efforts to help children develop to their fullest potential.

Many talented individuals were involved in bringing the eighth edition of *Developmental Profiles* to fruition. We sincerely appreciate Mark Kerr's leadership, innovation, and continued support. We are extremely grateful to Kate Scheinman, our development editor, who always responded promptly and provided invaluable guidance throughout the writing and production processes. Thank you, Kate! There are also many behind-the-scenes individuals we would like to personally thank for their innumerable contributions—the editorial, design, production, media, and marketing staff—for it is their creativity and persistent efforts that transform reams of manuscript into an attractive and functional book.

We are also grateful to all of our reviewers and want to express our sincere appreciation for their insightful critiques, suggestions, and ability to help us see issues from multiple perspectives. They include:

- Michelle Abraham, Miami University
- Sara Jane (Sally) Adler, Washtenaw Community College
- George Bortnick, Hesser College
- Karen Breitag, Lake Area Technical Institute
- Dionne Clabaugh, De Anza College
- Elizabeth Elliott, Florida Gulf Coast University
- Reva Fish, SUNY Buffalo State
- Rebecca Garte, Borough of Manhattan Community College
- Ann Guy, Lawson State Community College
- Christie Kaaland, Antioch University Seattle
- Jeannie Morgan-Campola, Rowan Cabarrus Community College
- Megan Parker Peters, Lipscomb University
- Laura Petrolle, Arizona State University
- Dave Terry, Alfred University

Finally, we would like to thank our readers for their dedication and commitment to improving the quality of life for children and families everywhere.

# ABOUT THE AUTHORS

**Lynn R. Marotz,** Ph.D., R.N., has taught undergraduate and graduate courses in the Department of Applied Behavioral Science, University of Kansas, and served as the Associate Director of the Edna A. Hill Child Development Center for over 35 years. She has worked closely with students in the Early Childhood teacher education program and offered courses in parenting, health/safety/nutrition for the young child, administration, and foundations of early childhood education.

Lynn has authored invited chapters on children's health and development, nutrition, and environmental safety in national and international publications and law books. She is also the author of *Health, Safety, and Nutrition for the Young Child* and the co-author of *Motivational Leadership,* and *By the Ages: Behavior & Development of Children Pre-birth Through Eight.* Her involvement in state policy development, health screenings, professional development training, working with families and allied health professionals, and the referral process is extensive. She has presented at international, national, and state conferences, and held appointments on national, state, and local committees and initiatives that advocate on children's and families' behalf. However, it is her daily interactions with children and their families, students, colleagues, and her beloved family that bring true insight, meaning, and balance to the material in this book.

**K. Eileen Allen,** professor emerita, was a member of the Early Childhood faculty at the University of Washington in Seattle and at the University of Kansas in Lawrence. For 31 years, she taught graduate and undergraduate courses in child development, developmental disabilities in young children, parenting, early education, and an interdisciplinary approach to early intervention and inclusion. She also trained teachers and supervised research-focused classrooms at both schools and has published seven college textbooks as well as numerous research articles and position papers in major professional journals. During her retirement, she continues to write and advocate on behalf of children and families. Her most recent book is entitled *I Like Being Old: A Guide to Making the Most of Aging.*

# chapter 1

# Child Development Theories and Data Gathering

## Learning Objectives

*After reading this chapter, you will be able to:*

**1-1** Compare and contrast the fundamental contemporary child development theories described in this chapter.

**1-2** Explain why authentic assessment is the most developmentally appropriate method for evaluating children's progress.

**1-3** Describe five methods that can be used for gathering observational data about children.

## naeyc NAEYC Standards Linked to Chapter Content

**1a and 1b:** Promoting child development and learning

**2a:** Building family and community relationships

**3b and c:** Observing, documenting, and assessing to support young children and families

Shortly after Tucker celebrated his first birthday, social workers removed him from his nineteen-year-old mother's home because of malnourishment and severe neglect. He was placed temporarily with an older couple who had long served as foster parents for many children. Several weeks after Tucker's initial placement, he was moved again to a different foster home where there were other children closer to his age. However, soon after Tucker arrived, the family decided that they no longer wanted to remain foster parents. This necessitated moving him yet again, and several additional times thereafter.

Tucker recently celebrated his fifth birthday and has been living with his current foster parents, Serena and James Martinez, for almost a year. They have two little girls of their own, ages four and six, and three additional foster children ranging in age from four to nine years. All the children are vigorous and outgoing except for Tucker, who seems to tire easily and is quite small for his age. Serena discussed her concerns with Tucker's pediatrician during his recent well-child checkup. When the

© aurenar/Shutterstock.com

nurse weighed and measured Tucker, he was only in the 30th percentile for height and weight, despite the fact that Serena says he eats far more than the other children.

Serena and James learned from their social worker that Tucker sat up, crawled, and eventually began to walk much later than most children his age. He continues to experience some motor delays, but he is working with a therapist who believes that he is making good progress. Serena and James also have noted that Tucker seldom joins in play or conversation with the other children. However, they have occasionally overheard him holding lengthy and comprehensible discussions with his imaginary friend, Honey, at times when he thinks he is alone. The talk is usually about things he fears, possibly the root of recurring bad dreams from which he often wakes up screaming. Yet, despite his problems, Tucker is a kind and lovable child. He seizes any opportunity to curl up on Serena's lap, suck his thumb, and snuggle his free hand into hers. The Martinezes have come to love Tucker as one of their own and are currently in the process of formalizing his adoption.

## Ask Yourself

- What aspects of Tucker's development pose a concern?
- In what ways are Serena and James attempting to meet Tucker's fundamental needs?

Children's development has interested philosophers and psychologists for decades (Figure 1-1). Early attempts to explain the origin of children's ideas and the processes involved in learning were derived primarily from personal observations and interpretations. Theories built solely on this information were later found to be incomplete, inconsistent, and vastly divergent in their explanations. The introduction of formalized scientific methodologies during the twentieth century enabled child development researchers to produce data that was more comprehensive, consistent, and reliable.

Figure 1-1 Children's development has been the subject of study for many decades.

Although many earlier theories were abandoned, significant differences of opinion regarding how children learned persisted among child development researchers.

It is unlikely that any one theory could ever adequately explain the complexities of human behavior. Each has contributed in some way to our understanding of children's development and reminds us that behavior is a product of multiple and complex factors. It is also important to remember that theories reflect the prevailing beliefs and conditions (e.g., social, economic, religious, and political) at a given historical point. As a result, existing children's development theories are often revisited and refined and are likely to continue changing over time.

# Contemporary Theories

A longstanding debate in the child development field has centered on whether learning is the result of heredity (innate abilities) or environment (experiences). This argument is commonly referred to as the **nature vs. nurture** controversy (Tucker-Drob, Briley, & Harden, 2013). Early philosophers, including Plato and Aristotle, believed that all behavior was biologically predetermined (nature). In other words, it was thought that children were born hardwired to think and act in specific ways. This conclusion was derived from the fact that most children learn to walk, talk, and feed themselves when they reach certain specific ages. By contrast, John Locke and other philosophers suggested that children were born with blank minds (*tabula rasa*, or clean slate) and that all behavior is learned and a product of one's environment and experiences (nurture).

Scientific advancements subsequently have criticized both theories for explaining human behavior in overly simplistic terms. Brain imaging studies, for example, have confirmed that development is not an either/or process. Rather, researchers have demonstrated that learning causes physical changes in the brain's composition and structure. These changes are the product of complex interactions that occur between genetic materials (such as brain cells and an intact neurological system) and learning opportunities in the child's environment.

Much of our current knowledge about how children learn, grow, and mature is derived from several longstanding theories: maturational, psychoanalytic and psychosocial, cognitive-developmental, behaviorism and social learning, bioecological, and essential needs. An overview of the fundamental constructs associated with each theory follows.

## Maturational Theory

Maturational theory focuses on a biological or *nature* approach to human development. All behavior is explained in terms of genetics and the biological changes that must occur before a child is able to perform certain skills; this capacity is often referred to as a stage of *biological readiness*. For example, maturational theory would argue that an infant learns to walk only when his or her neurological system has matured sufficiently to permit this activity, regardless of any other factors, including opportunity or environment.

Arnold Gesell's historic research contributed significantly to our understanding of genetic influences on children's development. He believed that all development is governed primarily by internal forces of biologic and genetic origin (Dalton, 2005; Gesell & Ilg, 1949). This led to several notable publications in which he described children's achievements by age and explained them in ways that parents could understand and put into practice.

Few scientists would disagree that genetics play a critical role in human development and, in some cases, even has a limiting effect. For example, the genes that a child inherits from his or her biological parents determine height, skin color, shoe size, hair

**nature vs. nurture** Refers to whether development is primarily due to biological–genetic forces (heredity–nature) or to external forces (environment–nurture).

**Development as a biological manifestation.** Every child differs in terms of genetic makeup and daily experiences. How would Arnold Gesell explain any differences in the way these two children perform on this counting task?

© 2016 Cengage Learning®

color, and other distinguishing features. Genes are also responsible for chromosomal abnormalities, such as those causing Down syndrome, congenital deafness, vision defects, and a host of other limiting conditions. Neuroscientists are also investigating genetic links to various personality traits (e.g., shyness, aggressiveness) as well as predispositions to certain mental health disorders (Ashare et al., 2013; Smillie, 2013).

Although most experts acknowledge that genetics are important to human development, they also do not accept it as the sole cause of behavior. Most experts believe that the maturational theory overlooks individual differences and the ways in which they influence learning experiences and outcomes. Yet it is interesting that some current educational practices, such as admission standards based on birth dates and "redshirting" a child whose birthday falls close to a predetermined cutoff date, continue to accept a maturational position.

Gesell's contributions continue to serve a functional purpose despite some of this criticism. His observations have been translated into **norms**, or benchmarks that have proven useful for assessing and monitoring children's developmental progress. More recently, they have been incorporated into several commonly used screening tools, including the Denver Developmental Screening Test and the Bayley Scales of Infant and Toddler Development. Scientists continue to update Gesell's original standards so that they more accurately reflect today's diverse population.

## Psychoanalytic and Psychosocial Theory

Psychoanalytic and psychosocial theory postulates that much of human behavior is governed by unconscious processes, some of which are present at birth and others that develop over time. Sigmund Freud, considered the originator of psychoanalytic theory, believed that children's behavior is a reflection of their inner thoughts and sexual desires. He proposed a series of stages (e.g., oral, anal, phallic, latency, and genital) and suggested that children must resolve and satisfy certain emotional conflicts fully before they can advance to the next developmental phase. The degree to which these emotions are or are not fulfilled ultimately shapes the child's basic personality, which Freud believed was established during the first five years of life.

**norms** Age-level expectancies associated with the achievement of developmental skills.

Psychosocial theory is based on the work of Erik Erikson, who expanded on Freud's ideas about personality development. He, too, believed that each developmental stage is characterized by certain conflicts that must be resolved. After a successful resolution has been achieved, a person is motivated to undertake the next developmental challenge.

However, unlike Freud, Erikson's theory acknowledges the influence of environment and social interactions. He coined the term *ego identity* to describe an individual's conscious awareness of self (who I am in relation to others) and the lifelong changes that occur as a result of social interactions. Erikson was also the first to describe development across the life span by introducing his eight universal stages of human development (Erikson, 1950). The first four stages address the early years; the remaining four cover the span from adolescence to the later years:

- **Trust vs. mistrust (0–12 months)** Establishing a sense of trust with primary caregivers
- **Autonomy vs. shame and doubt (1–3 years)** Learning to gain control over some behaviors (e.g., eating, toileting, and sleeping) and developing a sense of autonomy or independence
- **Initiative vs. guilt (3–5 years)** Using social interaction to gain control over one's everyday world
- **Industry vs. inferiority (6–12 years)** Developing a sense of competence and pride through successful accomplishments
- **Identity vs. confusion (13–20 years)** Learning about self in relationship to others
- **Intimacy vs. isolation (20–35 years)** Exploring and forming intimate relationships
- **Generativity vs. stagnation (35–55 years)** Focusing on family, career, and ways of contributing to society
- **Integrity vs. despair (60s–death)** Reflecting on one's life and forming a sense of satisfaction or dissatisfaction

Psychoanalytic and psychosocial theories have contributed to our understanding of personality and social-emotional skills and their influence on all aspects of children's development. They also have helped us to better understand the universal challenges that children face at each stage and how to create environments that support children's social and emotional needs along a developmental continuum. Although these theories are no longer as popular as they once were, they continue to foster research in areas such as caregiver consistency, attachment, morality, and sibling relationships.

## Cognitive-Developmental Theory

Jean Piaget was the first psychologist to study the qualitative and maturational changes that occur in children's cognitive development. He theorized that children were born with basic genetic capabilities that enabled them to construct knowledge and meaning through active exploration of their environment (Figure 1-2). The term **constructivism** often is used today to describe this mode of learning.

According to Piaget, children progress through four distinct stages of intellectual development, beginning in infancy and continuing into the late teens (Piaget, 1954):

- **Sensorimotor (birth–2 years)** The infant's reflexive behaviors gradually give way to intentional actions during the sensorimotor period. Children explore and discover the world around themselves primarily through their senses, and

**Did You Know**

.....Freud was the oldest of eight children and considered himself to be his mother's favorite, "darling Siggie"?

**constructivism** A learning approach in which a child forms his or her own meaning through active participation.

Figure 1-2 Jean Piaget believed that children learn best through exploration.

they begin to learn that they have the power to control some elements in their environment. For example, a toddler sees an object, picks it up, examines it while turning it around in his hands, and finally puts it into his mouth.

- **Preoperational (2–7 years)** Children begin thinking about things in their immediate environment in terms of symbols. For example, the three-year-old picks up a long stick, calls it a fishing pole, and pretends to catch a fish. This example also illustrates a second aspect of the preoperational stage (the emergence of language), which is another form of symbolic representation.
- **Concrete operational (7–11 years)** During this stage, children are developing the ability to comprehend and formulate ideas about their immediate world. Although their ideas remain quite rigid, they are beginning to think logically, to anticipate outcomes, to classify objects, and to solve problems. These emerging *schema* (Piaget's term) lead to a rudimentary understanding of abstract concepts, such as those associated with math and spatial relationships.
- **Formal operational (11–15 years)** Children are able to use complex thinking skills to visualize and manipulate ideas and experiences in their heads without having immediate access to real or concrete objects (abstract thinking). In addition, they are able to think logically, weigh consequences, and use memory for problem solving.

Piaget alleged that children's cognitive development involves far more than the passive accumulation of new information. He described cognition as an active process defined by increasingly sophisticated thought processes that emerge as children transition from one developmental stage to the next. Piaget introduced several terms to describe these changes:

- *Schemas*—Mental patterns or categories (e.g., food, objects, places, or animals) that a child begins to form and use for organizing and storing information.
- *Assimilation*—The process of incorporating new information into preexisting schemas. For example, a carrot is food, and a rabbit is an animal.
- *Accommodation*—The process of modifying preconceived schemas or forming additional schemas based on new information. For example, a carrot is a vegetable, and a rabbit is a mammal.

- *Disequilibrium*—The period of confusion, conflict, tension, or all three that results when new information does not fit within existing schemas.
- *Equilibrium*—The process of using assimilation and accommodation to alleviate intellectual conflict.

Although experts have criticized some of Piaget's ideas, his contributions continue to influence contemporary educational practices, including discovery learning, the importance of play, peer teaching, and developmentally appropriate curriculum.

Lev Vygotsky also was interested in children's cognitive development, but he considered the processes involved in its formation to be different from those proposed by Piaget. He agreed with Piaget's notion that development follows a unique pattern and that children learn through active involvement and hands-on experiences. However, Vygotsky felt strongly that social and cultural environments (e.g., values, beliefs, and practices) shaped and ultimately determined the nature of children's learning (Vygotsky, 1986). He believed that culture provided the mental framework for all thoughts and behavior, while language served as the mechanism for transmitting this information from one individual to another. For example, he explained that children initially learn how to behave in a certain way through a series of adult directives: "Don't touch," "Come here," "Eat this," "Stop that." As children begin to internalize social rules and cultural expectations and develop self-control, the nature of these directives gradually changes. Adults stop telling children what to do and shift their attention to encouraging and assisting the acquisition of new skills. Vygotsky referred to this as the Zone of Proximal Development.

Vygotsky also considered children's speech and language development a critical step in the socialization process. He believed that young children spend considerable time learning new words, thinking about their meanings, making associations, and forming an understanding about how they are to be used. Vygotsky observed that during this process, some children hold conversations with themselves as a way of thinking out loud. He referred to this stage as "self-talk," or inner speech, and suggested that the process provides children an opportunity to rehearse the meanings of words and how they function as communication tools before actually using them in social situations (Vygotsky, 1986).

Marie Montessori's ideas also have contributed to our understanding of cognitive-developmental theory. Trained as a pediatrician, she later became interested in educating children who were considered not capable of learning. She was convinced that all children had potential, but that traditional instructional methods might not always be effective. Her observations led to her belief that children learned best through a process of self-directed exploration. She designed a collection of sensory-based, self-correcting materials that required limited adult intervention. She also developed educational programs based on a philosophy that emphasized children's natural curiosity and self-directed involvement in learning experiences.

Cognitive-developmental theorists have advanced our understanding of how children learn and construct meaning. They have raised educational awareness about differences in children's rate and style of learning and the importance of individualizing instruction to address each child's unique developmental needs. Their ideas have influenced policy formation and are evident in the position statement of the National Association for the Education of Young Children (NAEYC) on developmentally appropriate practice (DAP), as well as the philosophies and activities of other early childhood organizations (NAEYC, 2009). For example, the concept and delivery of early intervention services is built on a foundation of cognitive theory. Children's cognitive development also continues to serve as a source of scientific study, particularly as it relates to curriculum, instructional methods, family involvement, social interaction, and the effects of cultural influence on children's development.

**Did You Know**

.....that Vygotsky was considered a genius of his time and often was referred to as the "Mozart of psychology"?

**Zone of Proximal Development** Vygotsky's term for tasks that initially prove too difficult for children to master by themselves but that they can perform with adult guidance or assistance.

**▶Ⅱ TeachSource** Video Connections

### Zone of Proximal Development

Adults intuitively use a variety of instructional methods to help children learn a new skill until they are able to perform it independently. Respond to the following questions after you have watched the learning video *5-11 Years: Lev Vygotsky, the Zone of Proximal Development and Scaffolding:*

1. What is the Zone of Proximal Development?
2. What role do adults play in this process?
3. What is scaffolding? How did the teacher illustrate this instructional concept in the video?

# Behaviorism and Social Learning Theory

In its modern form, behaviorism and social learning theory stem from the works of B. F. Skinner and John B. Watson, who formulated a *nurture*, or environmental, approach to learning (Skinner, 1938). They argued that development, for the most part, involves a series of learned behaviors based on an individual's positive and negative interactions with his or her environment (Figure 1-3). For example, they would suggest that reinforcing a behavior typically causes it to be repeated. In other words, telling a child that he has done a great job on his spelling test is likely to motivate him to study even harder for the next one. However, the opposite is also true: giving in to a crying child's demands for a much-wanted toy may encourage her to repeat the behavior the next time she wants something. Ignoring the child's demands eventually extinguishes the behavior because there is no reinforcement (attention).

Skinner also explained how the association between two events (stimulus-response) results in learning. For example, a toddler bumps her head (stimulus) when she stands up under the table, so she abruptly ends the activity (response). A preschooler touches a hot pan (stimulus) and is careful to avoid repeating the same behavior (response). You promise to read a favorite book to your daughter (stimulus) if she picks up her toys (response), and she does so quickly.

Albert Bandura modified several of Skinner's earlier ideas when he formulated his own theory of social learning (Bandura, 1977). He viewed behavior as a combination of environmental influences (nature) and cognitive abilities (nurture). He also believed that children learned both positive and negative behaviors through observation and modeling (imitation). However, unlike Skinner, he did not agree that reinforcement was necessary to motivate or change behavior. He believed that children learned, for example, not to hit another child or not to take away a toy after having observed another child being punished for the same act.

**Figure 1-3** Social learning theory explains development as behavioral changes that result from observation and imitation.

Families and teachers employ the principles of behavioral theory on a daily basis. They expect children to comply with requests and then reward or punish them accordingly. They model behavior that children are likely to imitate. They provide attention and encouragement, thus reinforcing the children's efforts (good or bad). Behavioral interventions also are commonly used in the treatment of behavior and developmental problems, such as aggression, feeding disorders, anger management, substance abuse, bullying, and obesity (Matson & Goldin, 2014; Cole et al., 2013; DeBar et al., 2013).

## Bioecological Theory

There is little dispute among child development experts that environment has an influential effect on development. However, Urie Bronfenbrenner, a noted American scholar and psychologist, alleged that environment played a pivotal role in this process, especially during a child's early years. He proposed his ecological model of human development based on this conviction and described environment from a multilayered, subsystem perspective: microsystems (e.g., face-to-face interactions with primary caregivers, siblings, and friends); mesosystems (e.g., school-home linkages and interactions with relatives); exosystems (e.g., mass media, parent's workplace, and social services); macrosystems (e.g., cultural values and customs, ethnicity, economic conditions, and politics); and chronosystems (e.g., changes that occur over time, such as moving to a new location, birth of a sibling, divorce, or a military deployment) (Bronfenbrenner, 1979) (Figure 1-4). Bronfenbrenner suggested that development is a product of the reciprocal interactions and relationships that an individual experiences across and within each of these subsystems. He also believed that as a result, developmental research was more insightful and meaningful when conducted in children's natural settings.

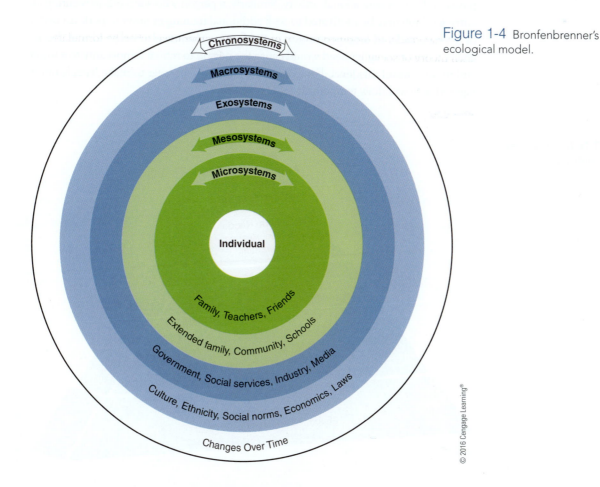

**Figure 1-4** Bronfenbrenner's ecological model.

Did You Know

.... that Urie Bronfenbrenner was a cofounder of the national Head Start program?

Bronfenbrenner later modified his original ideas to acknowledge and include the influence of biological factors. His revised bioecological model offers several unique perspectives on human development. First, it defines environment as a multilayered, interactive system and discards the notion that it can be treated as a single entity. Furthermore, it recognizes behavior as a product of the multiple, complex subsystems in which an individual participates. For example, poverty by itself might not limit a child's development if social services, high-quality schools, and a nurturing family are in place. Bronfenbrenner's revised theory also emphasized the interactive nature of environment—that not only does environment affect an individual, but also a person's behavior, age, and interactions continually change the nature of that environment.

The bioecological theory has had a significant impact on educational practices. It has raised diversity awareness, which in turn led to the development of antibias curricula, assessment procedures, play materials, and teacher education programs that reflect sensitivity and respect for individual differences. It has furthered our understanding of how environment and relationships shape a child's development and why family involvement and collaboration are essential in schools.

## Maslow's Essential Needs Theory

Abraham Maslow, an American psychologist, attempted to describe human behavior from a motivational needs perspective (Maslow, 1968). He believed that unmet physical and psychological needs drove an individual to take action to satisfy them. Only when one particular need was satisfied or fulfilled would the individual be able to move on and pursue higher goals. For example, a hungry person is driven to find food; once that hunger is satisfied, he may have the needed energy to work or to engage in a pleasurable or an educational activity. Similarly, a person who succeeds in securing an entry-level job may be motivated to seek additional training in order to perform better or to be considered for a promotion in the future. Maslow also believed that the inability to satisfy a higher need would cause the person to retreat temporarily to a lower and more comfortable level. For example, a child who is eager to make friends but is rejected may withdraw temporarily and become a loner.

Figure 1-5 Maslow's hierarchy of essential needs.

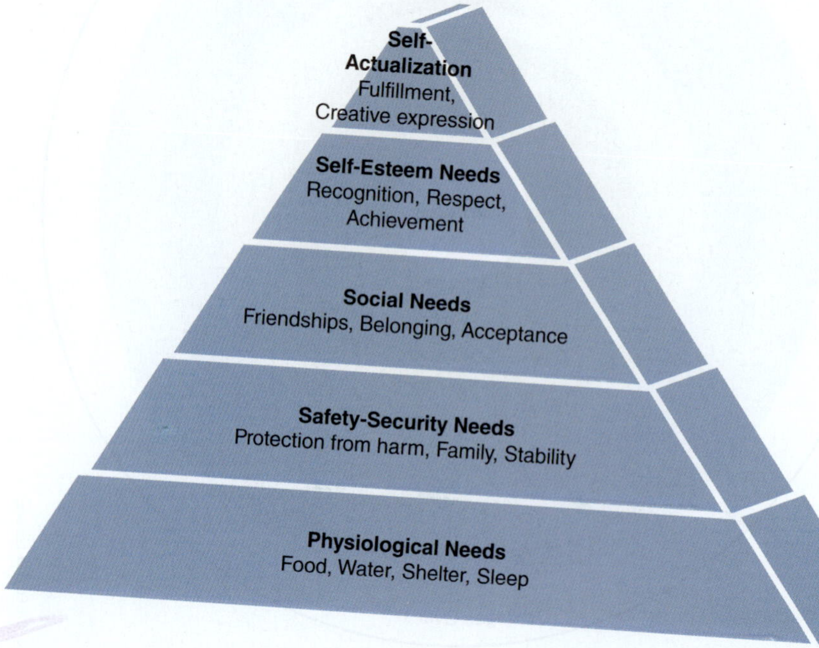
Self-Actualization
Fulfillment,
Creative expression
Self-Esteem Needs
Recognition, Respect,
Achievement
Social Needs
Friendships, Belonging, Acceptance
Safety-Security Needs
Protection from harm, Family, Stability
Physiological Needs
Food, Water, Shelter, Sleep

All children—those who are developing normally or typically and those who are gifted, have developmental disabilities, or are **at risk** for developing problems—have essential physiological and psychological needs in common. Only when these basic needs are met will a child be able to survive, thrive, and develop to his fullest potential.

Developmental psychologists have long considered the early years to be the most critical in the entire life span (Nix et al., 2013). Their assumptions have been confirmed and documented many times over by contemporary neuroscientists. During these very early years, children learn all of the many behaviors that characterize the human species—walking, talking, thinking, and socializing. Never again will the child grow as rapidly, change as dramatically, or be so totally dependent on adults to satisfy life's basic needs and opportunities for learning.

**Essential needs**—physical, psychological, and learning—are often separated for discussion purposes. However, it must be understood that they are mutually interrelated and interdependent. Meeting a child's physical needs while neglecting his or her psychological needs may lead to serious developmental problems. The opposite also is true—a child may experience difficulty in learning and getting along with others if he or she is being abused or his or her physical needs are neglected. Only when children's essential needs are being fully met will they continue to develop and become self-fulfilled, productive individuals (Elliott, 2013; Widom et al., 2013).

## Physical Needs

- Adequate shelter and protection from harm (e.g., violence, neglect, and preventable injuries)
- Sufficient food that is nutritious and appropriate to the child's age
- Clothing and shoes suitable to the climate and season
- Preventive health and dental care; access to treatment for physical and mental conditions as needed; recommended immunizations
- Personal hygiene (e.g., hand washing, brushing teeth, bathing)
- Rest and activity, in balance; opportunities for indoor and outdoor play

## Psychological Needs

- Affection and consistency: **nurturing** families and teachers who provide positive behavioral guidance
- Safety, security, and trust: familiar surroundings with family and teachers who are dependable, protective, and responsive to the child's needs
- **Reciprocal** exchanges that begin in earliest infancy; give-and-take interactions that convey trust and respect (Feldman, Bamberger, & Kanat-Maymon, 2013).
- Appropriate adult expectations of what the child can and cannot do at each stage of development
- Acceptance and positive attitudes shown toward the cultural, ethnic, language, or developmental differences (or all of them) that characterize the child and family

## Learning Needs

- Play opportunities that support early learning; freedom to explore and experiment within safe boundaries; limits that are stated clearly and maintained consistently (Curtis et al., 2013) (Figure 1-6).
- Access to **developmentally appropriate** learning experiences, environments, and play materials (Scruggs, Brigham, & Mastropieri, 2013; Copple & Bredekamp, 2009).
- Opportunities that challenge and advance a child's skill development but do not lead to excessive frustration.

**at risk** A term describing children who may be more likely to have developmental problems due to certain predisposing factors such as low birth weight (LBW), neglect, or maternal drug addiction.

**essential needs** Basic physical requirements such as food, shelter, and safety, as well as psychological needs, including love, security, and trust, which are required for survival and healthy development.

**nurturing** Refers to qualities of warmth, loving, caring, and attention to physical and emotional needs.

**reciprocal** Refers to exchanges between individuals or groups that are mutually beneficial (or hindering).

**developmentally appropriate** A term describing learning experiences that are individualized based on a child's level of skills, abilities, and interests.

Figure 1-6 Children learn continually through exploration and play.

© Photo credit.

- Treatment of errors and delays in achieving a skill as important steps in the learning process, never as reasons for criticizing or ridiculing a child.
- Adults who demonstrate in their everyday lives the appropriate behaviors expected of the child, especially in language, social interactions, and ways of handling stress. Remember that adults serve as important behavior models for children; children learn far more from what adults do than from what they say.

## Need for Respect and Self-Esteem

- A literacy-rich environment and inclusion in an active language "community" in which children can learn to communicate through sounds, gestures, signs, and, eventually, words and sentences (spoken, signed, or written).
- A supportive environment in which the child's efforts are encouraged and approved: "Thank you for picking up your crayons without being asked!"
- Respect for all accomplishments, small or large, and for errors as well as for successes: "Look at that! You laced your shoes all by yourself" (no mention of the eyelet that was missed).
- Recognition that accomplishment and the "I can do it" attitude is the major and most essential component of a child's **self-esteem**: "You did a great job of pouring the juice without spilling!"
- Sincere attention to what the child is doing well; using **descriptive praise** to help the child recognize and respect his or her own accomplishments: "You got your shoes on the right feet all by yourself!"
- Awareness of the effort and concentration that go into acquiring basic developmental skills; providing positive responses to each small step as a child works toward mastery of a complex skill, such as self-feeding with a spoon: "Right! Just a little applesauce so it stays on the spoon."

**self-esteem** Feelings about one's self-worth.

**descriptive praise** Words or actions that describe to a child specifically what she or he is doing correctly or well.

Only when children are healthy and have their basic needs satisfied can we expect them to be ready and able to learn (Marotz, 2015). Researchers continue to demonstrate the critical nature of this relationship (Lee et al., 2014). Their findings have prompted support for policy and programs that assist families in meeting children's needs for nutritious food, health care (mental, physical, and oral), safe and nurturing

## Spotlight on Brain Development

### Why Do Brain Research, and What Have We Learned?

Most of what previously was known about the brain and its role in children's development and disease was derived from observation and postmortem examinations. The introduction of noninvasive, three-dimensional computerized imaging technologies, such as positron emission tomography (PET), magnetic resonance imaging (MRI), and functional magnetic resonance imaging (fMRI), now has made it possible for scientists to study the living brain and to observe while it functions in real time. They are able to visualize in detail how an individual's brain is wired and how molecules interact to produce learning and behavior (Pugh et al., 2013; Trzaskowski et al., 2013). Scientists can detect structural and chemical changes in the brain associated with neurodevelopmental disorders (e.g., autism and attention deficit hyperactivity disorder), neurological conditions (e.g., epilepsy, Parkinson's disease, Alzheimer's, and posttraumatic stress disorder), and psychiatric disorders (e.g., depression, addiction, and schizophrenia) (Agosta, Caso, & Filippi, 2013; Gadgil et al., 2013).

Neuroimaging studies have yielded unprecedented findings that are rapidly advancing our understanding of the human brain and how it relates to learning and behavior. For example, García-Pentón et al. (2014) identified an increased plasticity in specialized language subregions of the brain in bilingual individuals. Normative changes that occur in the brain's electrical circuitry and cortical layers during adolescence have been linked to impulsive decision making and addiction (Moreno & Trainor, 2013; Romeo, 2013; Rubinstein et al., 2013; Spear, 2013). Abnormal changes in the brain's structural components have been discovered in children who are repeatedly subjected to abusive and neglectful treatment (Herrenkohl et al., 2013). Neuroscientists also have confirmed that learning rates and styles differ among individuals and that certain instructional methods are more effective for teaching second languages, reading skills, and mathematical computation (Smedt et al., 2013). These are but a sampling of the brain research discoveries that will continue to have a significant impact on practices and policy decisions in education, health care, and social justice systems.

homes, and learning opportunities. Examples include Head Start, school breakfast and lunch programs, Parents as Teachers, and Children's Health Insurance Program (CHIP). Educators also understand this critical connection and devote substantial time and effort to ensuring that children and their families obtain supportive resources.

# Data Gathering

What we know about children—how they grow and develop, how they learn, and how they interact with others—stems from firsthand observation. For decades, psychologists and educators have observed the daily activities of hundreds of infants and young children. They recorded what they saw and heard as children learned to walk, communicate, grasp basic science and math concepts, interact with peers, reason, and solve challenging problems. Their observations provided the foundation for what we now know about child development, effective teaching practices, curriculum models, and the significance of family–child relationships.

Early childhood educators continue to recognize the importance of gathering information about children's behavior and development and using it to enhance learning. Despite increasing pressures for standardized testing, documentation, and accountability issues in schools, teachers understand the value of observing children in their **naturalistic settings** (Elicker & McMullen, 2013). This approach, referred to as **authentic assessment**, is considered the most effective and appropriate method for

**naturalistic settings** Environments that are familiar and part of children's everyday experiences, such as classrooms, care arrangements, and the home.

**authentic assessment** A process of collecting and documenting information about children's developmental progress; data is gathered in children's naturalistic settings and from multiple sources.

**TeachSource** Video Connections

© 2016 Cengage Learning®

### Culturally Responsive Teaching

Children's development is shaped by an array of genetic and environmental factors. Acknowledging cultural differences is essential to recognizing and accepting children as unique individuals. Respond to the following questions after you have watched the learning video *Culturally Responsive Teaching: A Multicultural Lesson for Elementary Students*:

1. How would Urie Bronfenbrenner describe multiculturalism and its effect on children's learning?
2. Why do you think diversity should be addressed in the classroom?
3. Why is it important to remember that children are more alike than they are different?

evaluating and supporting young children's development (Rosemartin, 2013; Macy & Bagnato, 2010).

Authentic assessment involves gathering performance-based evidence in the context of everyday settings and activities. Samples of children's products, family input, and teacher observations are collected continuously and systematically to document learning. This information provides an ongoing, comprehensive picture of a child's developmental progress and reduces the potential bias that results when decisions are based on a single evaluation measure. Authentic assessment also contributes to teachers' understand of children's skills, abilities, and special needs against a background of the environmental factors that shape development (Dennis, Reuter, & Simpson, 2013; Kim, Lambert, & Burts, 2013). Authentic assessment yields results that can be used to establish learning goals, design interventions, adjust curriculum and instructional methods, and create responsive environments that effectively meet children's individual learning needs.

## Teachers as Classroom Observers

Regularly scheduled monitoring and assessment of children's developmental progress are benchmarks of high-quality schools and early childhood programs. Observing, recording, and reviewing children's performance in the classroom and during outdoor play gives teachers insight into their accomplishments, progress, strengths, and limitations. Information acquired through observational methods is also beneficial for identifying children who have special talents, developmental delays, health issues, or behavior problems. In addition, teachers can use this information to design classroom experiences and environments that are developmentally appropriate and support children's individual learning needs.

### What Do You See?

**Observing children in naturalistic environments.** Teachers have many available options to use for assessing children's development. What developmental skills is the teacher in this photo able to evaluate? What advantages does observing the children in a classroom setting offer over conducting a formal assessment?

© 2016 Cengage Learning®

The ability to conduct and interpret meaningful observations requires that teachers be familiar with children's typical development so their expectations are accurate and realistic. They also must understand that family, culture, and linguistic differences can account for variations in what children know and are able to do. With time and practice, teachers become proficient at identifying specific behaviors for observation, knowing what to look for, recording observations in an objective manner, interpreting the findings, and using the data to address children's individual needs.

## Families as Observers

Families always should be welcome in their children's classroom, whether as scheduled observers or on a drop-in basis. They have a right to know what the children are learning and to ask questions. When family members arrange for a scheduled observation, they can be given a clipboard for noting points of interest or questions that they may want to ask about learning materials, teacher responses, or what seems to please or bother the children. Teachers should arrange a follow-up meeting to learn the family's thoughts about the classroom or program, to point out the children's positive qualities, and to share any mutual concerns about the children's progress.

Figure 1-7 Family observations, information sharing, and involvement are essential to effective instruction.

© 2016 Cengage Learning®

It is important always to involve families in the assessment process and to encourage them to share observations that they have made at home (Caspe et al., 2013). This information exchange may provide teachers with unique insights into the children's special characteristics, challenges, and talents. Families know and understand their children better than anyone else and see them behaving in almost every imaginable circumstance. They are aware of their children's likes and dislikes, joys and anxieties, and positive and negative qualities. Most important, they often have goals that they want their children to achieve and care deeply about their well-being. When schools create an atmosphere that encourages families to participate and to share information and concerns, everyone—children, families, and teachers—ultimately benefits (Figure 1-7). Schools can use technology to communicate and maintain effective contact with all families. Email, videoconferencing, and a secure classroom website provide opportunities for exchanging information with families, especially those who may not be able to visit or participate on a regular basis due to conflicting work schedules, younger children to care for at home, language differences, or a host of other reasons.

# Observation Methods

Recorded observations assume many forms: anecdotal notes, running records and logs, time and event sampling, frequency and duration counts, checklists, rating scales, audio and video recordings, and portfolios. Each method is described briefly in the section that follows. Additional information on screening tests is available in Chapter 10, "When and Where to Seek Help," and Appendix B, "Selected Screening and Assessment Instruments."

# Anecdotal Notes

Several times each day, the teacher takes a minute or so to write down a few relevant thoughts about what they see occurring. These anecdotal notes can be recorded on a small notebook or pad (3 × 5 inches) carried in a pocket. The teacher makes brief, dated entries about the **discrete behaviors** observed for a given child: "Played in block area for 5 minutes without hitting another child"; "Initiated conversation with teacher"; "Seemed anxious during the test."

Anecdotal notes provide a running record, or composite picture, of the child's developmental progress in one or more **domains** over a period of time. Teachers can use this information for a variety of intended purposes, including documenting a specific behavior over time, evaluating the effectiveness of an intervention, or determining if a child's development is progressing satisfactorily. When anecdotal notes are compiled chronologically across developmental domains, they also become a valuable tool for determining placements, writing progress reports, evaluating lesson plans, establishing learning goals, and sharing relevant information with families.

# Time or Event Sampling

Sampling techniques enable a teacher to collect behavioral data on one or more children simultaneously during a given time frame or activity. For example, a teacher may be interested in learning which behaviors children use to resolve conflicts during free play: physical aggression (pa), verbal aggression (va), or cooperative problem solving (cps) skills. A simple score sheet can be developed for recording purposes, with children's names listed along one axis and the times and behavioral codes or categories identified along the other (Figure 1-8). A new sheet is dated and used for recording each day's observations.

A sampling approach often is used to obtain information about children's language development. Counts can be obtained during a live observation or from prerecorded audiotaped or videotaped sessions. An observer writes down every utterance

**Figure 1-8** Time sampling form.

| Code: pa – physical aggression  va – verbal aggression  cps – cooperative play/problem solving | | | | | | | | | | | |
|---|---|---|---|---|---|---|---|---|---|---|---|

_____ date                                                    **Activity:** Free Play

| Child | 8:30 a.m. | | | 8:40 a.m. | | | 8:50 a.m. | | | 9:00 a.m. | | |
|---|---|---|---|---|---|---|---|---|---|---|---|---|
|  | pa | va | cps | pa | va | cps | pa | va | cps | pa | va | cps |
| LaShauna |  |  |  |  |  |  |  |  |  |  |  |  |
| Jose |  |  |  |  |  |  |  |  |  |  |  |  |
| Markie |  |  |  |  |  |  |  |  |  |  |  |  |
| Winston |  |  |  |  |  |  |  |  |  |  |  |  |
|  |  |  |  |  |  |  |  |  |  |  |  |  |

**Total:** pa ___    va ___    cps ___

© Cengage Learning®

**discrete behaviors** Actions that can be observed and described clearly, such as hitting, pulling hair, or spitting.

**domains** Areas of development such as *physical, motor, social-emotional,* and *speech and language.*

exactly as the child says it. One purpose of the samplings, which are usually recorded for ten to fifteen minutes at a time over a monthlong period or so, is to track the child's speech and language progress. Another purpose is to see whether the child's language works. Is the child communicating effectively? Does the child get what he or she needs and wants by using language? No other behavior (except communicative gestures or facial grimaces) is recorded, although brief notations may be made (e.g., that other children rarely respond to the child's verbal overtures). Language samples are invaluable for monitoring developmental progress and planning individualized programs. They are also effective for recalling humorous quips or insightful statements that the child has made.

## Frequency and Duration Counts

When concerns about a specific aspect of a child's behavior arise, teachers first must determine how often the behavior occurs (frequency) or how long it continues (duration) (Figure 1-9). Observations are made and data recorded while teachers go about their daily tasks. One form of frequency count simply requires the teacher to make a tally mark every time the child engages in the specified behavior. A count might reveal that a two-year-old child who was said to cry or hit "all the time" was actually doing so only once or twice per morning, and some mornings not at all. Electronic or inexpensive digital handheld counters can be used to record behaviors that occur at a high rate. Frequency counts yield objective information that can help teachers determine if a problem indeed exists.

A duration count measures the amount of time that a child engages in a particular behavior. For example, a teacher might simply jot down the time when a child enters and leaves a learning center or activity. Another example would be penciling (unobtrusively) on a corner of a painting or collage the time that the child started and finished the project; or the teacher might note when a child's tantrum began and ended. Duration counts are helpful for deciding whether interventions are needed to increase or decrease a specific behavior.

## Checklists and Rating Scales

Checklists permit a teacher or other observer to record quickly the occurrence of certain skills or behaviors. For example, in infant centers, many firsts can be checked off: the day Josie first smiled, rolled over, or walked alone. In preschools, a checklist can be an effective method for monitoring children's skill acquisition. The date can be inserted as teachers check off when, for example, Carmella correctly identified and matched her primary colors; when Jayson built a tower of eight one-inch cubes; or when Sophia

Child's name: <u>Findley A.</u>
Week of: <u>June 4–9, 2014</u>
Observer: <u>Juanita M.</u>
Behavior observed: <u>Not attending/distracting other children</u>

Figure 1-9 Sample frequency and duration counts.

| Activity: | Mon | Tues | Wed | Thurs | Fri | Comments |
|-----------|-----|------|-----|-------|-----|----------|
| Morning circle | II | 0 | II | I | III | |
| Afternoon circle | III | II | IIII | 0 | III | |

© Cengage Learning®

## TeachSource Video Connections

### Assessing Children's Development

Adults are able to support and guide children's development when they have appropriate information about a child's progress and expected achievements. Respond to the following questions after you have watched the learning video *Portfolio Assessment: Elementary Classroom*:

1. What does portfolio assessment involve?

2. What information does it provide that may not be obtainable from other assessment methods?

3. In what ways can teachers and families use portfolio assessment results to support learning?

© 2016 Cengage Learning®

zipped up her own jacket. Teachers may wish to construct their own checklists to reflect unique program objectives. The lists, whether teacher-made or commercial, can be simple or detailed, depending on the need (see Appendix A, "Developmental Checklists").

Rating scales, like checklists, usually are designed to target specific behaviors (Figure 1-10). They provide an efficient method for recording teacher observations and later retrieving that information in a meaningful way.

## Portfolios

Representative examples of a child's work—drawings, digital photographs of a special block structure or science project, notes describing manipulative activities completed, audiotapes of conversations and language samples, and digital video of a class play or a child's attempts at learning a new skill—offer another effective method for tracking children's developmental progress (Laski, 2013; Piper, D'Angelo, & Hollan, 2013). Teachers select materials that represent a child's learning across all developmental domains and assemble them in an individual portfolio. Children also should be invited to choose items for inclusion and to review the collection from time to time. This step affords children an opportunity to explain their ideas and engage in self-assessment.

Information obtained from teacher observations and conversations with families should also be included in this collection, as they provide additional insight and meaning to the child's products.

Materials in a child's portfolio should be reviewed and updated periodically to reflect changing interests, mastery of specific skills, the need for additional instruction, or all three. Items in the child's portfolio can be used to prepare for parent conferences, illustrate discussion points, and to share with families. In addition, children's portfolios often reveal important information about the effectiveness of a curriculum or teaching method and thus can be beneficial for program improvement.

Figure 1-10 Sample rating scale form.

Child's name: <u>Findley A.</u>
Date: _____

| Task: | Not Yet | Attempts/Not always accurate | Usually accurate | Proficient | Comments (observer/date): |
|---|---|---|---|---|---|
| Identifies numbers 1–10 | | | | | |
| Arranges numbers 1–10 in correct order | | | | | |
| Counts from 1–10 with prompting | | | | | |
| Counts from 1–10 without prompting | | | | | |
| Writes numbers 1–10 | | | | | |

© Cengage Learning®

## Summary

**1-1** Current knowledge of child development is a composite of human development theories: maturational, psychoanalytic, psychosocial, cognitive-developmental, behaviorism and social learning, bioecological, and essential needs.

- All theories concur that meeting children's basic physical and psychological needs is a powerful determinant of optimum development.

- Current explanations about how children grow and develop rarely rely on any one exclusive theory. Each theory has made major contributions to our understanding of children's behavior.

- Scientists view human development as a product of biological and environmental interactions; they dismiss the nature vs. nurture question as improbable as an either/or proposition.

**1-2** Teachers and families play an important role in gathering and contributing information about children's growth and development.

- Authentic assessments provide a comprehensive understanding of children's unique interests, abilities, talents, and needs.

- The process of documenting children's behavior enables teachers to make necessary adjustments in their curricula and instructional methods to improve and support learning.

**1-3** Methods commonly used for monitoring children's developmental progress include observation, anecdotal notes, time/event sampling, frequency and duration counts, checklists, rating scales, and portfolios.

## Key Terms

nature vs. nurture **p. 3**

norms **p. 4**

constructivism **p. 5**

Zone of Proximal development **p. 7**

at risk **p. 11**

essential needs **p. 11**

nurturing **p. 11**

reciprocal **p. 11**

developmentally appropriate **p. 11**

self-esteem **p. 12**

descriptive praise **p. 12**

naturalistic settings **p. 13**

authentic assessment **p. 13**

discrete behaviors **p. 16**

domains **p. 16**

## Apply What You Have Learned

### A. Case Study Connections

*Reread the developmental sketch about Tucker at the beginning of the chapter and answer the following questions.*

1.  What conditions or circumstances may have influenced Tucker's developmental progress to date? Explain your answer based on the theories described in this chapter.

2.  Although Tucker's motor development has been somewhat delayed, he has learned to sit up, crawl, stand, walk, and eventually run. Which is more important to consider

in his case, the fact that he was older than is typical when he learned these skills, or that he has developed them in this particular order? Explain.

3. Based on the brief description of Tucker and his current foster family, what reciprocal effect(s) might you anticipate when he crawls up onto his mother's lap? How would Skinner and Bandura explain this response?

## B. Review Questions

1. What is the nature vs. nature controversy, and how does it contribute to our understanding of children's development?

2. What behaviors would children be likely to exhibit during each of the first five stages of Erikson's developmental theory (infancy–adolescence)?

3. In what ways does the maturational theory differ from the cognitive-developmental theory?

4. What is behaviorism, and how does it explain why a child might continue to refuse eating despite repeated warnings from her mother?

5. What data collection method(s) would you use to confirm or refute your suspicions about a child's ability to complete a specific task?

## C. Your Turn: Chapter to Practice

1. Use Bronfenbrenner's ecological model to diagram the environmental factors that have influenced your development. Interview a friend or colleague and repeat this exercise. In what ways are the two models similar? Different?

2. Develop five schemas for the word *apple*.

3. Select an age-specific speech-language milestone (see the section "Speech and Language Development," in Chapters 4–9). Conduct a ten-minute observation with a child of this age and record the data using anecdotal notes. Repeat the exercise (with the same child and milestone) using a time or event sampling method. Compare and contrast your experiences with each of the assessment tools. What did you like or dislike about each method?

4. Find out where developmental screenings are conducted in your community. Contact the agency and make arrangements to observe or volunteer to assist with a screening session.

# Online Resources

### Children's Defense Fund

The Children's Defense Fund is a private, nonprofit organization that serves as a national voice for children, especially those who have disabilities, live in poverty, or are of minority backgrounds. They support policy and programs designed to help children succeed in life.

### Council for Exceptional Children (CEC)

The Council for Exceptional Children (CEC) is the largest international professional organization dedicated to advocating and improving educational outcomes for persons with exceptionalities, disabilities, giftedness, or all three.

### National Center for Cultural Competence (NCCC)

The National Center for Cultural Competence (NCCC), located at the Georgetown University Center for Child and Human Development, conducts research and provides national leadership, consultation, training, assessment tools, and resource information for agency personnel, health professionals, educators, and family advocates.

## Society for Research in Child Development (SRCD)

The stated mission of the Society for Research in Child Development (SRCD) is to support, organize, and disseminate interdisciplinary, child development research findings. Their publications include *Child Development*, *Child Development Perspectives*, *Monographs*, *Social Policy Report*, and *Developments*.

# References

Agosta, F., Caso, F., & Filippi, M. (2013). Dementia and neuroimaging. *Journal of Neurology, 260*(2), 685–691.

Ashare, R., Norris, C., Wileyto, E., Cacioppo, J., & Strasser, A. (2013). Individual differences in positivity offset and negativity bias: Gender-specific associations with two serotonin receptor genes. *Personality & Individual Differences, 55*(5), 469–473.

Bandura, A. (1977). *Social learning theory*. New York: General Learning Press.

Bronfenbrenner, U. (1979). *The ecology of human development: Experiments by nature and design*. Cambridge, MA: Harvard University Press.

Caspe, M., Seltzer, A., Kennedy, J., Cappio, M., & DeLorenzo, C. (2013). Engaging families in the child assessment process. *Young Children, 68*(3), 8–14.

Cole, R., Treadwell, S., Dosani, S., & Frederickson, N. (2013). Evaluation of a short-term, cognitive-behavioral intervention for primary age children with anger-related difficulties. *School Psychology International, 34*(1), 82–100.

Copple, C., & Bredekamp, S. (2009). *Developmentally appropriate practice in early childhood programs serving children from birth through age 8*. 3rd Ed. Washington, DC: NAEYC.

Curtis, D., Brown, K., Baird, L., & Coughlin, A. (2013). Planning environments and materials that respond to young children's lively minds. *Young Children, 68*(4), 26–31.

Dalton, T. (2005). Arnold Gesell and the maturation controversy. *Integrative Psychological & Behavioral Science, 40*(4), 182–204.

DeBar, L. et al. (2013). Cognitive behavioral treatment for recurrent binge eating in adolescent girls: A pilot trial. *Cognitive & Behavioral Practice, 20*(2), 147–161.

Dennis, L., Rueter, J., & Simpson, C. (2013). Establishing a clear foundation for instructional practices. *Preventing School Failure, 57*(4), 189–195.

Elicker, J., & McMullen, M. (2013). Appropriate and meaningful assessment in family-centered programs. *Young Children, 68*(3), 22–26.

Elliott, W. (2013). The effects of economic instability on children's educational outcomes. *Children & Youth Services Review, 35*(3), 461–471.

Erikson, E. (1950). *Childhood and society*. New York: Vintage.

Feldman, R., Bamberger, E., & Kanat-Maymon, Y. (2013). Parent-specific reciprocity from infancy to adolescence shapes children's social competence and dialogical skills. *Attachment & Human Development, 15*(4), 407–423.

Gadgil, M., Peterson, E., Tregellas, J., Hepburn, S., & Rojas, D. (2013). Differences in global and local level information processing in autism: An fMRI investigation. *Psychiatry Research, 213*(2), 115–121.

García-Pentón, L., Pérez Fernández, A., Iturria-Medina, Y., Gillon-Dowens, M., & Carreiras, M. (2014). Anatomical connectivity changes in the bilingual brain. *NeuroImage, 84*(1), 495–504.

Gesell, A., & Ilg, F. (1949). *Child development*. New York: Harper.

Herrenkohl, T., Hong, S., Klika, J., Herrenkohl, R., & Russo, M. (2013). Developmental impacts of child abuse and neglect related to adult mental health, substance use, and physical health. *Journal of Family Violence, 28*(2), 191–199.

Kim, D., Lambert, R., & Burts, D. (2013). Evidence of the validity of the Teaching Strategies GOLD® Assessment Tool for English-language learners and children with disabilities. *Early Education & Development, 24*(1), 574–595.

Laski, E. (2013). Portfolio picks: An approach for developing children's metacognition. *Young Children, 68*(3), 38–43.

Lee, R., Zhai, F., Brooks-Gunn, J., Han, W., & Waldfogel, J. (2014). Head Start participation and school readiness: Evidence from the early childhood longitudinal study–birth cohort. *Developmental Psychology, 50*(1), 202–215.

Macy, M., & Bagnato, S. (2010). Keeping It "R-E-A-L" with authentic assessment. *NHSA Dialog: A Research-to-Practice Journal for the Early Intervention Field, 13*(1), 1–20.

Matson, J., & Goldin, R. (2014). Early intensive behavioral interventions: Selecting behaviors for treatment and assessing treatment effectiveness. *Research in Autism Spectrum Disorders, 8*(2), 138–142.

Moreno, M., & Trainor, M. (2013). Adolescence extended: Implications of new brain research on medicine and policy. *Acta Paediatrica, 102*(3), 226–232.

Marotz, L. (2015). *Health, safety, & nutrition for the young child*. 9th Ed. Belmont, CA: Wadsworth Cengage.

Maslow, A. (1968). *Toward a psychology of being*. 2d Ed. New York: Van Nostrand Reinhold.

National Association for the Education of Young Children (NAEYC) (2009). Position statement: Developmentally appropriate practice in early childhood programs serving children from birth through age 8. Retrieved on January 26, 2014, from http://www.naeyc.org/files/naeyc/file/positions/position%20statement%20Web.pdf.

Nix, R., Bierman, K., Domitrovich, C., & Gill, S. (2013). Promoting children's social-emotional skills in pre-school can enhance academic behavioral functioning in kindergarten: Findings from Head Start REDI. *Early Education & Development*, 24(7), 1000–1019.

Piaget, J. (1954). *The construction of reality in the child*. New York: Basic Books.

Piper, A., D'Angelo, S., & Hollan, J. (2013). Going digital: Understanding paper and photo documentation practices in early childhood education. *Proceedings of the Conference on Computer Supported Cooperative Work & Social Computing*, 1319–1328.

Pugh, K. et al. (2013). The relationship between phonological and auditory processing and brain organization in beginning readers. *Brain and Language*, 125(2), 173–183.

Romeo, R. (2013). The stress response and the adolescent brain. *Current Directions in Psychological Science*, 22(2), 140–145.

Rosemartin, D. (2013). Assessment for learning: Shifting our focus. *Kappa Delta Pi Record*, 49(1), 21–25.

Rubinstein, M., Shiffman, S., Moscicki, A., Rait, M., Sen, S., & Benowitz, N. (2013). Nicotine metabolism and addiction among adolescent smokers. *Addiction*, 108(2), 406–412.

Scruggs, T., Brigham, F., & Mastropieri, M. (2013). Common core science standards: Implications for students with learning disabilities. *Learning Disabilities Research & Practice*, 28(1), 49–57.

Skinner, B. F. (1938). *The behavior of organisms: An experimental analysis*. New York: Appleton-Century.

Smedt, B., Noël, M., Gilmore, C., & Ansari, D. (2013). How do symbolic and nonsymbolic numerical magnitude processing skills relate to individual differences in children's mathematical skills? A review of evidence from brain and behavior. *Trends in Neuroscience & Education*, 2(2), 48–55.

Smillie, L. (2013). Extraversion and reward processing. *Current Directions in Psychological Science*, 22(3), 167–172.

Spear, L. (2013). Adolescent neurodevelopment. *Journal of Adolescent Health*, 52(2), S7–S13.

Trzaskowski, M., Yang, J., Visscher, P., & Plomin, R. (2013). DNA evidence for strong genetic stability and increasing heritability of intelligence from age 7 to 12. *Molecular Psychiatry*, doi: 10.1038/mp.2012.191.

Tucker-Drob, E., Briley, D., & Harden, K. (2013). Genetic and environmental influences on cognition across development and context. *Current Directions in Psychological Science*, 22(5), 349–355.

Vygotsky, L. (1986). *Thought and language*. 2d Ed. Cambridge, MA: MIT Press.

Widom, C., Czaja, S., Wilson, H., Allwood, M., & Chauhan, P. (2013). Do the long-term consequences of neglect differ for children of different races and ethnic backgrounds? *Child Maltreatment*, 18(1), 42–55.

# chapter 2

# Principles of Growth and Development

## Learning Objectives

*After reading this chapter, you will be able to:*

**2-1** Define growth and development as separate concepts and provide at least two examples of each.

**2-2** Defend this statement: "Sequence, not age, is the important factor in evaluating a child's developmental progress."

**2-3** Identify the six major developmental domains that are the focus of this text.

### naeyc NAEYC Standards Linked to Chapter Content

**1a and 1b:** Promoting child development and learning

**2a and 2c:** Building family and community relationships

**4a:** Using developmentally effective approaches

Nina and Mitena, identical twins soon to be three years old, weighed in at a little over four pounds each at birth. Despite having being born two months early and considered to be low-birth-weight infants, both are now strong and healthy. They look alike in almost every way, with dark brown eyes, thick eyelashes, and high cheekbones. Nina and Mitena's young parents recently left with their twins and moved to a nearby state, where they would begin to attend college.

Although Nina and Mitena behave alike in many ways, there are also noticeable differences. Since early infancy, Nina has been more physically active. She slept less, ate more, sat up, crawled, and walked alone weeks before Mitena (or other babies her age, for that matter). She has also been more adventuresome in attempting new experiences, such as learning to swim and riding a tricycle. Mitena, on the other hand, was the first to smile, play peek-a-boo, and say recognizable words. She now uses complete sentences and has considerable letter, word, and number recognition skills. She likes to

© Samuel Borges Photography/Shutterstock.com

"read" to Nina and acts as her interpreter when Nina can't make herself understood. In turn, Nina is first to protect and comfort Mitena whenever she is hurt or frightened.

Soon after Nina and Mitena's parents settled into their new home, they enrolled the girls in a Head Start program conveniently located on the college campus. Initially, the girls were hesitant and slow to warm up to the other children. However, they are gradually beginning to play with several "friends" and participate in small-group activities, but still seldom venture too far from one another. Shortly after the girls arrived, their vision and hearing was tested. Mitena failed the initial screening and was referred to an eye specialist for additional evaluation. The optometrist determined that Mitena is near-sighted and requires corrective glasses.

## Ask Yourself

- From the brief descriptions of Nina and Mitena, which developmental characteristics can be attributed solely to genetic makeup?
- In what ways may environment account for differences in the girls' development?
- How do Nina and Mitena's motor skills differ?

# Basic Patterns and Concepts

Groups of children of approximately the same age, across all cultures, appear to be remarkably similar in size, shape, and developmental abilities. However, closer observation also reveals a wide range of individual differences within these groups (Figure 2-1). Both similarities and differences depend on a child's unique patterns of growth and development. What defines this complementary process of *growth and development*? Why do children experience this progression differently? Although these terms are often used interchangeably, they do not describe identical concepts.

## Growth

**Growth** refers to specific physical changes and increases in the child's size. An increase in cell numbers and enlargement of existing cells are responsible for the observable gains in a child's height, weight, **head circumference**, shoe size, length of arms and legs, body shape, and many other notable changes. Growth also lends itself to direct and fairly reliable measurement.

The growth process continues throughout the life span, although the rate varies by age. For example, growth occurs rapidly during infancy and adolescence but is typically much slower and less dramatic in the toddler and middle school years. The body continues to repair and replace its cells throughout adulthood, even into old age, although much less vigorously during these times.

Growth is a sensitive indicator of a child's overall wellness. Genetic growth parameters are set prior to birth, but it is the interaction with environmental factors that ultimately determines whether this potential will be realized. Children who have access to a nutritious diet, nurturing care, medical treatment, and opportunities for play and physical activity are most likely to achieve optimal growth. By contrast, a child exposed to poverty, abusive treatment, malnutrition, or inadequate medical care may experience delayed or stunted growth (Cook et al., 2013).

**growth** Physical changes leading to an increase in size.

**head circumference** Measurement of the head taken at its largest point (across the forehead, around the back of the head, and returning to the starting point).

# Development

**Development** refers to an increase in complexity—a change from the relatively simple to the more complex and advanced. This process involves an orderly progression along a continuum, or pathway over time. Little by little, knowledge, behaviors, and skills are learned and refined. Although the developmental sequence across domains is basically the same for all children, the rate and degree of attainment can vary greatly from child to child.

The progressive acquisition of developmental skills involves a dynamic interaction of biological and environmental factors (nature *and* nurture). Neurological, muscular, and skeletal systems must reach a certain functional maturity before a child is capable of learning a particular skill. At the same time, the social and cultural context in which a child is growing up influences what a child is likely to learn (Figure 2-2). Collectively, these factors account for the wide range of individual differences observed in children's developmental progress. For example, families in many cultures encourage their children to begin crawling and walking at an early age, whereas in other cultures, the early acquisition of motor skills is not highly valued or supported. Children living in poor, inner-urban neighborhoods may have delayed motor skills due to fewer safe opportunities for organized and spontaneous outdoor play.

Figure 2-1  Children's development includes a wide range of individual differences.

## Developmental Milestones

Major markers or points of accomplishment are referred to as *developmental milestones*, and they are useful for tracking the emergence of motor, social, cognitive, and language

Figure 2-2  Many factors play a collective role in fostering children's development.

**development** Refers to an increase in complexity, from simple to more complicated and detailed.

skills. They represent behaviors that appear in somewhat orderly steps and within fairly predictable age ranges for typically developing children. For example, almost every child begins to smile socially by ten to twelve weeks and to speak a first word or two at around twelve months. These achievements are only two of the many significant behavioral indications that a child's developmental progress is on track. When children fail to achieve one or more developmental milestones within a reasonable time frame, careful and systematic monitoring by a child development specialist or health care provider is necessary.

Sitting, walking, and talking are examples of developmental milestones that depend on biological maturation, yet these skills do not develop independently of the environment. For example, learning to walk requires muscle strength and coordination. In addition, it requires an environment that encourages practice, not only of walking as it emerges but also of the behaviors and skills that precede walking, such as rolling over, sitting up, and standing. It is also important to recognize that differences in children's biological makeup affect the ways in which they experience and respond to their environment. For example, a hearing loss may alter a child's concept of language, interest in talking, and development of linguistic skills significantly, even if he or she lives in a literacy-rich environment.

## Sequences of Development

A sequence of development is composed of predictable steps along a developmental pathway common to the majority of children. This process sometimes is referred to as **continuity**. Children must be able to roll over before they can sit, and sit before they can stand. *The critical consideration is the order in which children acquire these developmental skills, not their age in months and years.* The appropriate sequence in each developmental area is an important indication that the child is moving steadily forward along a sound developmental continuum (Figure 2-3). For example, in language development, it does not matter how many words a child speaks by two years of age. What is important is that the child has progressed from cooing and babbling to jabbering (inflected **jargon**) to syllable production. The two- or three-year-old who has progressed through these stages usually produces words and sentences within a reasonable period of time.

Some scientists explain children's development from a different point of view, believing that development occurs in a series of stages rather than as a gradual progression from simple to complex. They refer to this process as **discontinuity**. For example, rolling over, sitting up, and standing are considered distinct and abrupt steps that precede walking. It isn't necessary for a child to perfect one skill set before attempting another that may be more advanced.

In any case, developmental progress is rarely a smooth and even process. Irregularities, such as periods of **stammering** or the onset of a **food jag**, are not uncommon. Regression, or taking a step or two backward now and then, is also perfectly normal and to be expected. For example, a child who has been toilet trained for some time may begin to have accidents at times of stress, such as starting school or welcoming a new sibling into the family; an older child may resort to hitting or become verbally aggressive following a family move. Children are usually able to overcome these temporary setbacks and to move on when adults provide them with compassionate support, understanding, and direction.

## Age-Level Expectancies or Norms

Age-level expectancies can be thought of as **chronological**, or age-related, levels of development. Psychologists, including Gesell, Piaget, and Erikson, conducted hundreds of systematic observations of infants and children of various ages. Analyses of

**continuity** Developmental progress that gradually becomes increasingly refined and complex.

**jargon** Unintelligible speech; in young children, it usually includes sounds and inflections of the native language.

**discontinuity** Development that occurs in irregular periods or stages; not a smooth, continuous process.

**stammering** To speak in an interrupted or repetitive pattern; not to be confused with stuttering.

**food jag** A period when only certain foods are preferred or accepted.

**chronological** Refers to events or dates occurring in sequence over the passage of time.

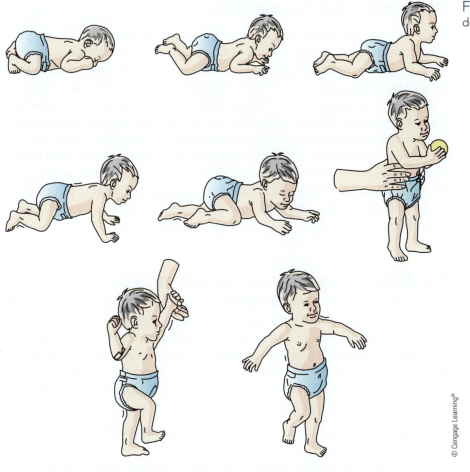

Figure 2-3 Typical motor development sequence.

their findings represent the average or typical age at which many specifically described developmental skills are acquired by most children in a given culture (Gesell & Ilg, 1949; Piaget, 1954). This average age is often referred to as the *norm*. Thus, a child's development may be described as at the norm, above the norm, or below the norm. For example, a child who begins walking at eight months is ahead of the norm (twelve to fifteen months), while a child who does not walk until twenty months is considered to be below the norm.

Age-level expectancies *always represent a range and never an exact point in time* when specific skills are most likely to be achieved. Therefore, profiles in this text (age expectancies for specific skills) always must be interpreted as approximate midpoints on a range of months (as in the example on walking, the range is from eight to twenty months, with the midpoint at fourteen months). Once again, a reminder: It is *sequence*, not age, that is the important factor in evaluating a child's progress (Bornstein, Hahn, & Wolke, 2013; Williams et al., 2013). In real life, no child is typical in every way. The range of skills and the age at which skills are acquired show great individual variation. Relevant again is the example of walking—one infant may begin at eight months and another not until twenty months (many months apart on either side of the norm). No two children grow and develop at exactly the same rate, nor do they perform in exactly the same way. For example, there are a half-dozen ways to creep and crawl. Most children, however, use what is referred to as *contralateral locomotion*, an opposite knee–hand method of getting about prior to walking. Yet, some normally walking two-year-olds never crawl, indicating a distinct variation in typical development.

## Organization and Reorganization

Development can be thought of as a series of phases. Spurts of rapid growth and development often are followed by a period of disorganization. During this time, the child works to regain confidence by practicing a new skill until it is mastered. Once this has been achieved, the child seems to recover and move into a period of reorganization. It is not uncommon for children to demonstrate behavior problems or even regression during these phases. Perhaps a new baby has become an active and engaging older infant who is now the center of family attention. At the same time, mother may expect three-year-old brother to help dress himself in the morning. He may begin to have tantrums over minor frustrations, and for the time being, revert to babyish ways and lose his hard-won bladder control. In most instances, these periods are relatively short-lived. Almost always, the three-year-old will learn more age-appropriate ways of gaining attention if given adequate adult encouragement and support.

# Typical Growth and Development

In terms of development, the words **typical** and *normal* often are used interchangeably to describe the acquisition of certain skills and behaviors according to a predictable rate and sequence. However, as previously stated, the range of typical behaviors within each developmental domain is broad and includes mild variations and simple irregularities, such as the three-year-old who stutters or the twelve-month-old who learns to walk without having crawled. The use of these terms also oversimplifies the concept. Normal or typical development implies:

- An integrated process governing change in size, **neurological** structure, and behavioral complexity.
- A cumulative or building-block process in which each new aspect of growth or development includes and builds on earlier changes; each accomplishment is necessary to the acquisition of the next set of skills.
- A continuous process of give and take (reciprocity) between the child and the environment, each changing the other in a variety of ways. For example, the four-year-old drops a glass and breaks it, and the parent scolds the child. Both events— the broken glass and the adult's displeasure—are environmental changes that the child triggered. From this experience, the child might learn to hold on more firmly next time, and this constitutes a change in both the child's and the adult's behavior—fewer broken glasses, thus less adult displeasure.

# Interrelatedness of Developmental Domains

Discussions about development usually focus on several major domains: physical, motor, perceptual, cognitive, social-emotional, and language. However, no single area develops independently of the others. Every skill a child attempts, whether simple or complex, requires a mix of developmental abilities. Social skills are a prime example. Why are some young children said to have good social skills? Often the answer is because they play well with other children and are sought out as playmates. To be a preferred playmate, a child must have many skills, all of them interrelated and interdependent. For example, a four-year-old should be able to:

- Run, jump, climb, and build with blocks (good motor skills)
- Ask for, explain, and describe what is going on (good language skills)

**typical** Refers to the achievement of certain skills according to a fairly predictable sequence, although with many individual variations.

**neurological** Refers to the brain and nervous system.

## What Do You See?

**The interplay of developmental domains** Multiple domains are actively involved in the completion of any task, from dressing oneself to putting together a puzzle. Look closely, and identify the developmental skills and domains required for this child to thread the string through the block successfully.

© 2015 Cengage Learning®

- Recognize similarities and differences among play materials and thus be able to select appropriate materials in a joint building project (good perceptual skills)
- Problem-solve, conceptualize, and plan ahead in cooperative play ventures (good cognitive skills)

Every developmental area is well represented in the preceding example, even though social development was the primary area under consideration. A significant delay in any one domain is likely to disrupt typical developmental progression in the others. For this reason, it is important to always monitor children's development across all domains.

## Brain Growth and Development

Brain maturation lays the foundation for all other aspects of a child's development. Growth and development of the fetal brain is rapid, exceedingly complex, and influenced by a combination of maternal environment and genetics (see Chapter 3, "Prenatal Development"). Healthy conditions and maternal lifestyle practices foster optimal brain formation, whereas adverse conditions can have a negative effect and place the child at lifelong risk (Johnson et al., 2013).

### ▶❙❙ TeachSource Video Connections

© 2015 Cengage Learning®

**Brain Development in Infancy**

Early brain development sets the stage for future learning and success. Adults play a critical role in fostering this early development by providing young children with enrichment opportunities, positive support, and consistent nurturing and care. Respond to the following questions after you have watched the learning video *Infancy: Brain Development*:

1. What triggers the formation of neural connections?
2. What type of learning experiences can adults provide to promote children's brain development?
3. What are "sensitive periods"?

**neural connections** Organized linkages formed between brain cells as a result of learning.

**plasticity** The brain's ability to change and reorganize its structure as a result of learning.

**pruning** The process of eliminating unused neurons and neural connections to strengthen those that the child is actively using.

A child's brain continues to grow and to be shaped through the daily interaction of genetic materials and daily experiences. Infants are born with an excess of brain cells (neurons)—an estimated 10 billion—more than adults have or will ever need! However, these neurons are relatively nonfunctional until connections are established and organized into purposeful networks. **Neural connections** are formed when chemical reactions in the brain are triggered by sensory input and learning experiences (Mueller et al., 2013). Once established, these neural connections enable brain cells to communicate with one another and to perform purposeful activities (Figure 2-4). Each time an experience is repeated, the neural connection becomes stronger. For example, consider the infant who is initially unable to feed himself, then learns to hold a cup and spoon after much practice, and eventually is able to eat a meal without giving much thought to the mechanics involved.

Children's brains continue to increase in size as neurons grow larger and neural connections become more complex. An infant's brain triples in weight by the end of the first year; a toddler's brain weighs approximately three-fourths that of an adult's. Growth is especially remarkable during the first three or four years, when the brain is most flexible and receptive to learning. This quality, known as **plasticity**, accounts for the young child's unique ability to acquire skills quickly. It explains, for example, why a four-year-old who is learning English as a second language is able to understand and converse in a significantly shorter period of time than an adult would require.

Weak or seldom-used connections are eliminated through a natural process known as **pruning** in order to make room for active cells and expanding networks. Selective pruning begins in earnest at around age 10 and peaks in early puberty. This "use it or lose it" process is ongoing throughout an individual's life, although it occurs at a slower pace with aging. It explains why an infant who is born with the capability of reproducing sounds in any language eventually learns to communicate in his or her own native language but not in any of the others; or why one child becomes an outstanding pianist while another excels at playing sports or chess.

Research has revealed an amazing relationship that exists between a child's brain development and language acquisition (Frota, Butler, & Vigario, 2014; Brown & Swanson, 2013). For example, infants not only take in the sounds of the language they

**Figure 2-4** Neural connections become stronger through repeated use.

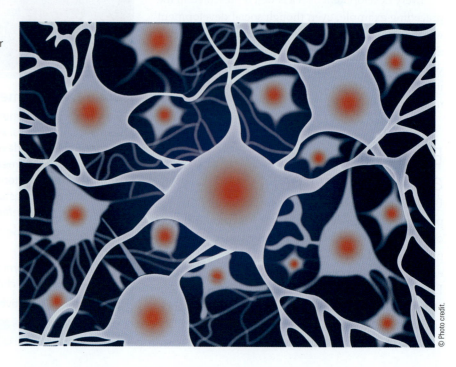

© Photo credit.

are hearing, but they also replicate them, complete with a dialect. Furthermore, the dialect is maintained without change for years to come. It is as if, in the case of language development, the brain will not easily sever connections made in the earliest months and years of life, regardless of subsequent changes in language environments.

It has long been thought that the child's brain simply continues to mature and increase in complexity as a result of ongoing experiences. However, neuroscientists used modern technologies to examine the adolescent brain and have discovered that this isn't the case. What they found was that a new layer of gray matter forms on the brain's frontal lobes during adolescence. Their discovery is especially significant because this particular region of the brain is responsible for regulating emotion, impulsivity, and decision-making processes (Arain et al., 2013). Once again, new neural connections must be established in these areas through repeated experience, refinement, and pruning before they are able to perform with any degree of consistency and adultlike sophistication. This finding helps explain why adolescents are more likely to engage in questionable behaviors and to make irrational decisions that adults often find puzzling (Geier, 2013).

Again, it is critical to remember that the interplay of genetic materials and daily experiences—positive as well as negative—determine how the brain's architectural structure ultimately forms. A positive, supportive home environment and opportunities for learning are conducive to healthy brain development. A disability may influence the way in which a child experiences and interprets everyday activities and affect the brain's structure differently. Growing up in a neglectful or abusive environment can alter a child's neural connections and wire her for instinctive survival rather than for cognitive tasks.

## Spotlight on Brain Development

### Poverty's Toxic Effects

Researchers have long focused on poverty's adverse effects on individual health outcomes, disease, and longevity. More recently, they have turned their attention to how children's neurocognitive development is affected. What scientists have learned is that growing up in an impoverished environment changes the brain's size, physical structure, and organization (Clearfield et al., 2014; Lawson et al., 2013). These deviations significantly compromise memory, attention, language, and self-regulation abilities and set children on a negative trajectory for the rest of their lives (Perkins, Finegood, & Swain, 2013; Peterson et al., 2013).

Coleman-Jensen, Nord, and Singh (2013) report that an estimated 14.5 percent of families in the United States (approximately 46 million people) lack reliable access to adequate food supplies due to poverty (Figure 2-5). Insufficient food, poor prenatal diet, and poverty-related stress are known to have a detrimental effect on fetal growth and brain development (Monk, Georgieff, & Osterholm, 2013). These children often continue to grow up in economically disadvantaged homes and thus face a higher incidence of maltreatment, lack of reading and play materials, violent neighborhoods, and unsafe, unpredictable housing. Chronic exposure to undesirable conditions and toxic stress eventually alters the way in which neural connections are established in the brain, preparing it for basic existence rather than for learning. The combined effect of early structural and learning deficits seriously limits children's development, leaves them unprepared for school, and interferes with academic achievement (Mani et al., 2013; Twardosz, 2012). It also increases children's likelihood of developing serious mental health problems later in life. Perhaps it would be more appropriate to classify poverty as a disease rather than a social problem: It affects a large segment of the population, and has observable symptoms caused by environmental factors, impairs an individual's ability to function, and can be transmitted from one person to another.

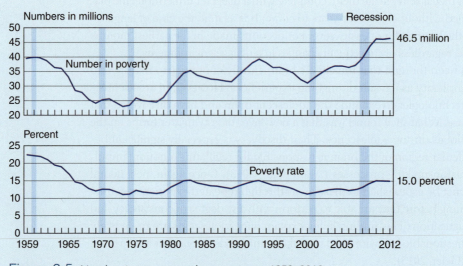

Figure 2-5   Number in poverty and poverty rate: 1959–2012.
Source: U.S. Census Bureau, Current Population Survey, 1960–2013 Annual Social and Economic Supplements.

## What are the connections?

1. What are the likely outcomes associated with chronic school failure?
2. What intervention services and assistance programs are needed to help mitigate poverty's early and cyclical nature on children's development?

# Temperament

The term *temperament* refers to the genetic component of an individual's personality (Lane et al., 2013; Cozzi et al., 2013). It describes the characteristic nature of a person's emotional responses such as the intensity, disposition or mood, focus, persistence, and ability to adapt. It accounts for individual differences in children's behavior patterns, including their activity level, alertness, irritability, soothability, restlessness, and willingness to cuddle (Figure 2-6). Thomas and Chess (1977) categorized and labeled these behaviors as the "easy" child, the "difficult" child, and the "slow-to-warm" child. They found that approximately 65 percent of children fall into one of these three categories: 40 percent of children are considered "easy," 15 percent are regarded as "slow-to-warm," and 10 percent are seen as "difficult." Subsequent studies have noted that although these behavior patterns may modify somewhat over time, they generally persist into adulthood (Soto & Oliver, 2013).

Temperament affects the way in which a child experiences everyday activities. For example, a difficult child may be hard to please and react intensely or tantrum when things don't go his way. He may find it difficult to adjust to new teachers in school and express his displeasure by acting out. By contrast, an easy child may pout for a few minutes when told she can't have an ice cream cone, but then she quickly turns her attention to the puppy playing in her neighbor's yard. A three-year-old who is slow-to-warm may require extra time to separate from his parents when they drop him off at preschool. In each case, it is easy to understand how a child's temperament influences adult expectations and responses. Parents of difficult children may take extra precautions to avoid situations that are likely to elicit an explosive response. In contrast, a smiling, easygoing toddler may invite unsolicited hugs and adult attention.

Categorical labels must be used cautiously when they are applied to children's behavior. Labeling a child as "difficult" or "slow-to-warm" may influence the expectations that an adult has for that child and end up reinforcing the very behavior in question. For example, a slow-to-warm child may evoke few displays of affection from others and so identify this as rejection, making it even more difficult for this child to act warm and outgoing.

Adult temperament must also be considered in this equation because it influences the way in which a child's behavior is perceived. For example, a short-fused parent may overreact to a curious toddler who continues to pull pots and pans from the cabinet despite an earlier warning, whereas an easygoing parent may understand that this is typical behavior and encourage the toddler's curiosity. In each case, adult temperament contributes to the contrast in perception and initial response to the toddler's behavior. Each reaction conveys an important message that continuously shapes the child's behavior (Lemery-Chalfant et al., 2013).

## Gender Identity

What does it mean to be a boy or a girl? Early in life, young children begin to develop a concept of gender and gender identity appropriate to their culture (Shutts, Roben, & Spelke, 2013). Each boy and girl develops a set of behaviors, attitudes, and commitments that are defined, directly or indirectly, as acceptable male or female attributes (Halim et al., 2013). In addition, each child plays out gender roles that reflect customary practices.

Several theories have been advanced over the years to explain children's gender identity formation. Freud's psychoanalytic theory suggested that children are initially attracted to the opposite-sex parent and later identify with the same-sex parent when they become sexually uncomfortable (Freud, 1924). Most modern theorists do not agree with this concept. The social learning theory of gender advocates that children learn male or female behaviors through observation and imitation (Bandura, 1977), but critics consider this approach overly passive and suggest that it perpetuates male and female stereotyping. Cognitive developmental theorists believe that children play an active role (e.g., observing, imitating, and experiencing) in gender concept formation (Kohlberg, 1966). However, they also acknowledge that maturation and biological differences (male/female) contribute to the ways in which children interpret and internalize gender-relevant information. Each theoretical approach has contributed to a contemporary understanding of gender and gender identity—that a child's sense of maleness or femaleness involves a complex interaction of biological, cognitive, and socialization processes, including cultural expectations, daily experiences, family values, adult role models, playmates and play opportunities, toys, and media exposure.

Children's concept of gender is formed in stages. Infants, for example, are able to distinguish the difference between male and female voices and faces. Toddlers become

© GFOW/Cengage Learning

Figure 2-6  A child's temperament can affect the nature of caregiver responses.

aware of physical differences between boys and girls and begin to show a preference for same-sex playmates. Between two and three years of age, children are able to label themselves correctly as girls or boys. Their toy selections and play often reflect gender role stereotyping (e.g., mothers feed babies, while dads go to work). Parents may begin treating children differently at this point—perhaps more tender and nurturing with girls, while reinforcing boys for their toughness and independent behaviors. Gender stability is generally achieved by three to four years of age. That is, children distinguish themselves and others as being a boy or a girl based on appearance: "Girls have long hair," "Boys have short hair"; "Girls wear pink, boys don't." However, they continue to believe that a person's gender can be changed depending on the situation (Kohlberg, 1966). For example, a girl can become a "daddy" by simply dressing up in pants, T-shirt, and a hat. Three- and four-year-olds also begin labeling toys and activities as being either for girls or boys. Gender constancy is apparent between five and seven years of age; at this point, children accept that gender is permanent and unchangeable. It is important that children's gender identity be supported at each stage because it influences all aspects of development, including self-concept, self-esteem, academic achievement, and mental health.

Children's sexual orientation is usually well established by middle childhood (Figure 2-7). Occasionally, a child may experience ideas and behaviors that do not necessarily conform to gender expectations. He or she may identify more with the opposite gender and struggle to accept (or even deny) his or her own sexuality. Scientists have explored a number of factors, including hormonal disturbances during fetal development, genetic abnormalities, environmental influences, and personal choice, in an attempt to explain this variation, but they have been unable to determine a definitive cause. It is important to understand that a child's sexual orientation cannot be changed. Children who experience gender confusion often endure considerable confusion and inner turmoil in their attempts to comprehend what is occurring. What they need most is understanding and nonjudgmental support.

**Figure 2-7** Sexual orientation is usually well established by middle childhood.

# Ecological Factors

Beginning at conception, **ecology**—the environmental influence of family and home, community, and society—affects all aspects of a child's development. The following are examples of powerful ecological factors:

- Financial resources; adequacy and availability of food and shelter (Elliott, 2013)
- Cultural values and practices
- General health and nutrition; access to prenatal and postnatal care for mother and child
- Parents' level of education, with mother's level of education being a major predictor of a child's academic achievement (Baker, 2014; Carneiro, Maghir, & Parey, 2013)
- Families' understanding of obligations and responsibilities before and after the infant's birth
- Family communication and child-rearing practices (loving or punitive, nurturing or neglectful); family stress (Carpenter & Mendez,2013)
- Family structure—single- or two-parent, blended, or extended family; grandparent with primary parenting role; same-sex parents; foster or adoptive homes

Differences in the way each of these factors are experienced ultimately results in a child being unlike any other child. For example, a child born to a single, fifteen-year-old mother living in poverty will have life experiences that differ significantly from those of a child born and raised in a family with two parents who have professional jobs.

# Transactional Patterns of Development

From birth, children influence the behavior of their adult caretakers (e.g., families and teachers). In turn, these same adults exert a great influence on children's behavior and development. For example, a calm, cuddly baby expresses her needs in a clear and pre-dictable fashion. This infant begins life with personal–social experiences that are quite different from those of a tense, colicky infant whose sleeping and eating patterns are highly irregular and often stressful for parents. This complex **transactional process** of give and take between children and their families and daily events is ongoing and continually changing, and results in developmental experiences that shape each child's unique qualities.

Infants and young children thrive when adults respond promptly and positively, at least a fair amount of the time, to appropriate things that a child says and does. Researchers have shown repeatedly that children develop healthier self-concepts as well as earlier and better language, cognitive, and social skills when they are raised by responsive adults (Gunderson et al., 2013; Bowie et al., 2013).

# Children at Risk

Some children are born into situations that may be harmful to their development or interfere with its typical progress. These children are often described as being *at risk*. Premature birth and low birth weight are two conditions known to increase a child's risk for physical impairments, learning disabilities, behavioral problems, or all three. McCoy et al. (2013), for example, noted that these children experienced a higher rate of poor memory and behavior problems than their typically developing peers. Children born to mothers outside of the "normal" age range (e.g., very young teenagers, or women in their forties) or who are significantly depressed have also been found to be at greater risk for developmental delays. Chronic exposure to domestic violence,

**ecology** In terms of children's development, refers to interactive effects between children and their family, child care situation, school, and everything in the wider community that affects their lives.

**transactional process** The give-and-take relationship between children, their primary caregivers, and daily events that influences behavior and developmental outcomes.

© 2015 Cengage Learning®

## TeachSource Video Connections

### Children and Poverty

Children have many obstacles to overcome as they grow up. One of the most challenging may be living in a family that has limited personal and financial resources. Respond to the following questions after you have watched the learning video *Students Living in Poverty:*

1. In what ways may poverty affect children's ability to be successful in school?

2. What are the consequences when children fail to achieve or to understand the value of an education?

3. What qualities does the principal bring to the school environment that students appear to find motivating?

maltreatment, or poverty has also been shown to increase a child's potential for behavior and developmental problems (Raver, Blair, & Willoughby, 2013; Widom et al., 2013). Children subjected to harsh physical punishment, such as repeated spanking, often exhibit learning problems, aggressive behaviors, and lower academic potential, expressed in statistics such as intelligence quotient (IQ) (Schwartz et al., 2013; Perkins & Graham-Bermann, 2012).

## Atypical Growth and Development

The term *atypical* describes children who have developmental differences, deviations, or marked delays—children whose development appears to be incomplete or inconsistent with typical patterns and sequences. There are many causes of atypical development, including genetic errors, poor health, inadequate nutrition, injury, and too few or poor-quality opportunities for learning.

Abnormal development in one area may or may not interfere with development in other areas. However, the child with developmental delays might perform in one or more areas of development as a much younger child does. For example, a three-year-old who is still babbling, with no recognizable words, is an example of a child with delayed development. This condition need not be disabling unless the child never develops **functional language**. The term *developmental deviation* describes an aspect of development that is different from what is expected in typical development (Figure 2-8). For example, the child born with a missing finger or a profound hearing loss has a developmental deviation. The child with a missing finger is not likely to be disabled. In contrast, the child who is deaf will experience a significant developmental disability unless early and intensive intervention is obtained.

In any event, the concepts and principles described in this chapter apply to the child with developmental differences, as well as to the child who is said to be developing typically. However, one always must be cautious not to make judgments about a child's development without first being sensitive to cultural, ethnic, socioeconomic, language, and gender variations that may account for any differences (Trawick-Smith, 2013). Most important, it also must be remembered that a child who experiences any type of developmental problem still has the same basic needs as all other children.

## Developmental Domains

A framework is needed to describe and accurately assess children's developmental progress. In this book, we focus on six major domains, or developmental areas: physical, motor, perceptual, cognitive, speech and language, and social-emotional. Each domain includes the many skills and behaviors that will be discussed in the developmental profiles that are the major focus of this book (Chapters 4–9). Although these developmental areas are separated for the purpose of this discussion, they cannot be

**functional language** Language that allows children to get what they need or want.

separated from one another in reality. Each is integrally related to, and **interdependent** with, each of the others in the overall developmental process.

Developmental profiles, or word pictures, are useful for assessing both the immediate and ongoing status of children's skills and behavior. It is important to remember that the rate of development is uneven and occasionally unpredictable across areas. For example, the language and social skills of infants and toddlers are typically less well developed than is their ability to move about. Also, children's individual achievements can vary across developmental areas: a child may walk late but talk early. Again, an important reminder: Development in any of the domains depends in large part on children having appropriate stimulation and adequately supported opportunities to learn. Additionally, the types of learning experiences that individual children encounter are highly variable and reflect cultural, socioeconomic, and family values.

**Figure 2-8** A vision impairment is an example of a developmental deviation.

## Physical Development and Growth

The physical development and growth domain governs the major tasks of infancy and childhood. Understanding the patterns and sequences of physical development is essential to being effective parents, teachers, and caregivers. Healthy growth and development, not adult pressure or coaching, is what makes new learning and behavior possible. Adult pressure cannot hurry the process and, in fact, is more likely to be counterproductive. A seven-month-old infant cannot be toilet trained; the **sphincter** muscles are not yet developed sufficiently to exert such control. Nor can the majority of kindergartners catch or kick a ball skillfully; such coordination is impossible given a five- or six-year-old's stage of physical development, yet many of us have seen a coach or family member reduce a child to tears for missing a catch or a kick.

Governed by heredity and greatly influenced by environmental conditions, physical development and growth are highly individualized processes. They are responsible for changes in body shape and proportion, as well as for overall body size. Growth, especially of the brain, occurs more rapidly during prenatal development and the first year than at any other time. Growth is also intricately related to progress in other developmental areas. It is responsible for increasing the muscle strength necessary for movement, coordinating vision and motor control, and synchronizing neurological and muscular activity in gaining bladder and bowel control. A child's growth is also closely linked to nutritional status and ethnicity (Lee et al., 2013). Thus, the state of a child's physical development serves as a fairly reliable index of general health and well-being. Physical growth also plays a direct role in determining whether children are likely to achieve their full cognitive and academic potential.

**interdependent** Affecting or influencing development in multiple domains.

**sphincter** The muscles necessary to accomplish bowel and bladder control.

## Motor Development

The child's ability to move about and control various body parts are major functions of the motor development domain. Refinements in motor development depend on brain

## What Do You See?

**Motor development**  Motor development proceeds in a fairly predictable and orderly manner. What stage is the infant in this photo exhibiting? What activities would encourage and support this phase of his motor development?

© GFOW/Cengage Learning

---

**reflexive**  Refers to movements resulting from impulses of the nervous system that cannot be controlled by the individual.

**voluntary**  Refers to movements that can be willed and purposively controlled and initiated by the individual.

**developmental sequence**  A continuum of predictable steps along a developmental pathway of skill achievement.

**cephalocaudal**  Refers to bone and muscular development that proceeds from head to toe.

**proximodistal**  Refers to bone and muscular development that begins closest to the trunk, gradually moving outward to the extremities.

**refinement**  Progressive improvement in the ability to perform fine and gross motor skills.

**gross motor**  Refers to large muscle movements such as locomotor skills (walking, skipping, or swimming) and nonlocomotive movements (sitting, pushing and pulling, or squatting).

**fine motor**  Refers to small muscle movements; also referred to as *manipulative skills;* includes the ability to stack blocks, button and zip clothing, hold and use a pencil, and brush teeth.

---

maturation, input from the *sensory system*, increased bulk and number of muscle fibers, a healthy nervous system, and opportunities for practice. This holistic approach contrasts markedly with the way that early developmentalists such as Gesell viewed the emergence of motor skills. They described motor development as a purely maturational process, governed almost entirely by instructions in the individual's genetic code (nature). Today's developmental psychologists consider such an explanation misleading and incomplete. Their research suggests, for example, that when young children show an interest in using a spoon to feed themselves, it is always accompanied by improved eye–hand coordination (to direct the spoon to the mouth), motivation (liking and wanting to eat what is in the spoon), and the drive to imitate what others are doing. In other words, the environment [that is, experience (nurture)] plays a major role in the emergence of new motor skills.

Motor activity during very early infancy is purely **reflexive** and gradually disappears as the child develops **voluntary** control over his movements. If these earliest reflexes do not phase out at appropriate times in the **developmental sequence**, that may indicate neurological problems (see Chapter 4, "Infancy"). In such cases, medical evaluation should be sought. Three principles govern motor development:

1. *Cephalocaudal*—Bone and muscular development that proceeds from head to toe. The infant first learns to control muscles that support the head and neck, then the trunk, and later, those that allow reaching. Muscles for walking develop last.

2. *Proximodistal*—Bone and muscular development that begins with improved control of muscles nearest the central portion of the body, gradually extending outward and away from the midpoint to the extremities (arms and legs). For example, control of the head and neck is achieved before the child is able to pick up an object with thumb and forefinger (pincer grasp or finger–thumb opposition).

3. *Refinement*—Muscular development that progresses from the general to the specific in both **gross motor** and **fine motor** abilities. In the refinement of a gross motor skill, for example, a two-year-old might attempt to throw a ball but achieves little distance or control. The same child, within a few short years, is likely to pitch a

ball over home plate with considerable speed and accuracy. As an instance of a fine motor skill, compare the self-feeding efforts of a toddler with those of an eight-year-old who is motivated (for whatever reason) to display good table manners.

## Perceptual Development

The increasingly complex way that a child uses information received through the senses—sight, hearing, touch, smell, taste, and body position—forms the basis of perceptual development. It might be said that perception is a significant factor that determines and orchestrates the functioning of the various senses, singly or in combination. The perceptual process also enables the individual to focus on what is relevant at a particular moment and to screen out whatever is irrelevant: Which details are important? Which differences should be noted? Which should be ignored? Perceptual development involves three important functions:

1.  *Multisensory*—Information is generally received through more than one sensory system at a time. For example, when listening to a speaker, we use sight (watching facial expressions and gestures) and sound (listening to the words) (Erdener & Burnham, 2013).
2.  *Habituation*—This term refers to a person's ability to concentrate on a specific task while ignoring everything else. For example, a child may be focused on reading a book of interest and be completely unaware of classmates' conversation or music playing in the background. In other words, the child is able to tune out things around her and devote full attention to what is most immediately important.
3.  *Sensory integration*—This process involves translating **sensory information** into functional behavior. For example, the five-year-old sees and hears a car coming and waits for it to pass before crossing the street.

The basic perceptual system is in place at birth. Through experience, learning, and maturation, it develops into a smoothly coordinated operation for processing complex information from multiple senses. As a result, children can sort shapes according to size and color and make fine discriminations or hear and distinguish the difference among initial sounds in rhyming words such as *rake*, *cake*, and *lake*. The sensory system also enables each of us to respond appropriately to different messages and signals, such as smiling in response to a smile or keeping quiet in response to a frown.

## Cognitive Development

The cognitive development domain addresses the expansion of a child's intellect or mental abilities. Cognition involves recognizing, processing, and organizing information and then using it appropriately (Charlesworth, 2014). The cognitive process includes such mental activities as discovering, interpreting, sorting, classifying, and remembering. For preschool and school-aged children, it means evaluating ideas, making judgments, solving complex problems, understanding rules and concepts, anticipating, and visualizing possibilities or consequences.

Cognitive development is an ongoing process of interaction between the child and his perceptual view of objects or events in the environment (Piaget, 1954). It is probably safe to say that neither cognitive nor perceptual development can proceed independently of each other. Cognitive skills always overlap with both perceptual and motor development. Early in the second year, the emergence of speech and language adds yet another dimension.

**Did You Know**

...the media industry incorporates basic elements of perceptual development (e.g., multisensory information, habituation, repetition, and sensory integration) to assure that cartoons and programming appeal to and hold children's attention?

**sensory information** Information received through the senses: eyes, ears, nose, mouth, touch.

**Figure 2-9** Most five-year-olds are able to express their thoughts clearly and with correct grammar.

The development of cognition begins with the primitive or reflexive behaviors that support survival and early learning in the healthy newborn. One example of very early learning is when a mother playfully sticks out her tongue several times and the baby begins to imitate her. This and other early behaviors led developmental psychologists to ponder the many striking similarities in how infants and children learn. During the 1950s, repeated observations of such similarities led Piaget to formulate his four stages of cognitive development: sensorimotor, preoperational, concrete operations, and formal operations (see Chapter 1, "Child Development Theories and Data Gathering").

## Language Development

Language is often defined as a system of symbols, spoken, written, and gestural (e.g., waving, smiling, scowling, and cowering) that enables us to communicate with one another. Normal language development is regular and sequential and depends on maturation as well as on learning opportunities. The first year of life is called the *prelinguistic* or *prelanguage phase*. The child is totally dependent on body movements and sounds, such as crying and laughing, to convey needs and feelings. This is followed during the second year by the *linguistic* or *language stage*, in which speech becomes the primary mode for communicating. Over the next three or four years, the child learns to put words together to form simple and then compound sentences that make sense to others because he has learned the appropriate grammatical constructions. Between five and seven years of age, most children have become skilled at conveying their thoughts and ideas verbally (Figure 2-9). Many children at this age have a vocabulary of 14,000 words or more, which can double or triple during middle childhood depending on a child's literacy environment.

Most children seem to understand a variety of words, concepts, and relationships long before they have the words to describe them. This ability is referred to as **receptive language**, which precedes **expressive language** (the ability to speak words to describe and explain). Speech and language development is closely related to the child's general cognitive, social, perceptual, and neuromuscular development. Language development and the rules that address how it is to be used are also influenced by the type of language that children hear in their homes, schools, and community (Hoff, 2013; Neu, 2013).

**Did You Know**

...that infants younger than two months show evidence of receptive language? They prefer and attend to repetition, sounds that rhyme, and the mother's voice.

**receptive language** Understanding words that are heard.
**expressive language** Words used to verbalize thoughts and feelings.

## Social and Emotional Development

This is a broad area that covers how children feel about themselves and their relationships with others. It refers to children's behaviors, the way they respond to play and work activities, and their attachments to family members, caregivers, teachers, and friends. Gender roles, temperament, independence, morality, trust, acceptance of rules, and social and cultural expectations are also important components of this developmental area (Bowie et al., 2013).

In describing personal and social development, it also must be remembered that children develop at different rates. Individual differences in genetic and cultural backgrounds, health status, living arrangements, family interactions, and daily experiences within the larger community continuously shape and reshape children's development. Consequently, no two children can ever be exactly alike, not in social and emotional development or in any other developmental area.

## Age Divisions

The age divisions shown in Table 2-1 and used throughout this book are commonly referred to by many child development specialists when describing significant changes within developmental areas.

Age divisions are to be used with extreme caution and great flexibility when dealing with children. They are based on the average achievements, abilities, and

**▶❚❚ TeachSource Video Connections**

© 2015 Cengage Learning®

### Temperament and Personality Development

Temperament is considered one component of an individual's personality. It influences a person's feelings and behavior. It explains, in part, why infants and toddlers differ in their emotional perceptions and responses to caregivers and the environment. Respond to the following questions after you have watched the learning video *0–2 Years: Temperament in Infants and Toddlers:*

1. What determines a child's temperament?

2. Which terms did parents in the video use to describe their child's temperament?

3. How does a child's temperament influence the transactional process of parenting?

4. How would you describe your own temperament?

5. Do you think there are cultural differences in temperament? Explain.

### Table 2-1  Common Age Divisions

| Infancy | Birth to 1 month |
| | 1–4 months |
| | 4–8 months |
| | 8–12 months |
| Toddlerhood | 12–24 months |
| | 24–36 months |
| Early childhood | 3–5 years |
| | 6–8 years |
| Middle childhood | 9–12 years |
| Adolescence | 13–14 years |
| | 15–16 years |
| | 17–19 years |

© Cengage Learning®

behaviors of large numbers of children at various stages of development. As stated again and again, there is great variation from one child to another.

The step-by-step development detailed in Chapters 4–9 speaks to the importance of understanding that it is sequential acquisition, *not* age, that indicates the developmental progress in each domain and in each child's overall development.

## Summary

**2-1** Growth and development are influenced by a child's unique genetic makeup and the quality of the everyday environment, which includes nurturing, health care, nutrition, and learning opportunities.

- The term *growth* describes physical changes that occur in a child's size.
- The term *development* refers to the acquisition of increasingly complex skills.

**2-2** Sequential acquisition, not age, is the critical factor in assessing a child's developmental progress.

- The accepted range of normalacy is broad and recognizes that each child is unique.
- A child should progress in a relatively orderly manner through each step in a given developmental area, even though it may be somewhat earlier or later than most children of a similar age.

**2-3** Each child's well-being depends on having her basic needs met and opportunities to acquire essential skills across the six developmental domains: physical, motor, perceptual, cognitive, language, and social-emotional.

- Although the six domains are separated for discussion purposes, they are interwoven and interdependent during the developmental years and throughout life.
- All children have the same basic needs for nutrients, protection, safety, attention, and nurturing, regardless of their special abilities, limitations, or challenges.

## Key Terms

growth **p. 24**

head circumference **p. 24**

development **p. 25**

continuity **p. 26**

jargon **p. 26**

discontinuity **p. 26**

stammering **p. 26**

food jag **p. 26**

chronological **p. 26**

typical **p. 28**

neurological **p. 28**

neural connections **p. 30**

plasticity **p. 30**

pruning **p. 30**

ecology **p. 35**

transactional process **p. 35**

functional language **p. 36**

interdependent **p. 37**

sphincter **p. 37**

reflexive **p. 38**

voluntary **p. 38**

developmental sequence **p. 38**

cephalocaudal **p. 38**

proximodistal **p. 38**

refinement **p. 38**

gross motor **p. 38**

fine motor **p. 38**

sensory information **p. 39**

receptive language **p. 40**

expressive language **p. 40**

# Apply What You Have Learned

## A. Case Study Connections

*Reread the developmental sketch about Nina and Mitena presented at the beginning of this chapter and answer the following questions:*

1. In what ways do Nina and Mitena differ in terms of their personal–social development? Given that they are identical twins, what factors may explain these differences?

2. According to Piaget, which stage of cognitive development are the twins, who are almost three years old, currently experiencing? Give an example of this concept from the descriptions of Nina and Mitena.

3. Should you expect Nina and Mitena to grow and develop in exactly the same way and at exactly the same rate just because they are identical twins? Explain. How would developmental theorists account for these differences (see Chapter 1)?

## B. Review Questions

1. Explain how the concepts of growth and development differ.

2. Identify and discuss three factors that contribute to atypical development.

3. Discuss the role that environment plays in children's brain development?

4. Define the term *perceptual information* and provide three examples to illustrate this concept.

5. Explain why you might not need to be concerned about a toddler who was learning to walk but now insists on only crawling.

6. What are developmental milestones, and what purpose do they serve?

## C. Your Turn: Chapter to Practice

1. Visit your local library and select twenty children's books at random. Evaluate the nature of the pictures/illustrations and narrative content in each book to determine if it perpetuates gender stereotyping. Describe your findings.

2. Visit a shopping mall or restaurant and observe parents interacting with their children for approximately an hour. In each case, record the child's behavior and the nature of the adult response. In what ways are temperament and transactional processes illustrated in each of these situations?

3. Tommy's father arrives to pick up his son from preschool and immediately becomes upset when he sees Tommy wearing a ballerina's tutu and high heels. He confronts the head teacher and wants her to explain why they have allowed his son to "dress like a girl." If you were that teacher, how would you respond to the father's question?

# Online Resources

## Centers for Disease Control and Prevention

Extensive information on children's development, developmental screening, and positive parenting is provided in lay terms and an easy-to-access format (e.g., podcasts, videos, and print materials).

### Eunice Kennedy Shriver National Institute of Child Health and Human Development

Research and information dissemination on children's development and the prevention of developmental disabilities are this organization's primary goals.

### National Center for Children in Poverty

This national center is affiliated with Columbia University. Databases, fact sheets, and community interventions for improving the lives of families and children who live in poverty are available on their website. You can also access the respected research journal *Child Care and Early Education: Research Connections*, which is published by this organization.

# References

Arain, M., Haque, M., Johal, L., Mathur, P., Nel, W., Rais, A., …, & Sharma, S. (2013). Maturation of the adolescent brain. *Neuropsychiatric Disease & Treatment*, 9, 449–461.

Baker, C. (2014). African American fathers' contributions to children's early academic achievement: Evidence from two-parent families from the Early Childhood Longitudinal Study–Birth Cohort. *Early Education and Development*, 25(1), 19–35.

Bandura, A. (1977). *Social learning theory*. Englewood Cliffs, NJ: Prentice Hall.

Bornstein, M., Hahn, C., & Wolke, D. (2013). Systems and cascades in cognitive development and academic achievement. *Child Development*, 84(1), 154–162.

Bowie, B., Carrère, S., Cooke, C., Valdivia, G., McAllister, B., & Doohan, E. (2013). The role of culture in parents' socialization of children's emotional development. *Western Journal of Nursing Research*, 35(4), 514–533.

Brown, R., & Swanson, L. (2013). Neural systems language: A formal modeling language for the systematic description, unambiguous communication, and automated digital curation of neural connectivity. *Journal of Comparative Neurology*, 521(13), 2889–2906.

Carneiro, P., Maghir, C., & Parey, M. (2013). Maternal education, home environments, and the development of children and adolescents. *Journal of European Economic Association*, 11(Suppl 1), 123–160.

Carpenter, J., & Mendez, J. (2013). Adaptive and challenged parenting among African American mothers: Parenting profiles relate to Head Start children's aggression and hyperactivity. *Early Education & Development*, 24(2), 233–252.

Charlesworth, R. (2014). *Understanding child development*. 8th Ed. Belmont, CA: Wadsworth Cengage Learning.

Clearfield, M., Bailey, L., Jenne, H., Stanger, S., & Tacke, N. (2014). Socioeconomic status affects oral and manual exploration across the first year. *Infant Mental Health Journal*, 35(1), 63–69.

Coleman-Jensen, A., Nord, M., & Singh, A. (2013). Household food security in the United States in 2012. Economic Research Report No. ERR-155. USDA. Retrieved on January 31, 2014, from http://www.ers.usda.gov/publications/err-economic-research-report/err155.aspx#.UkIMaH-E6CI.

Cook, J., Black, M., Chilton, M., Cutts, D., Ettinger de Cuba, S., Heeren, T., … & Frank, D. (2013). What are the connections? Are food insecurity's health impacts underestimated in the U.S. population? Marginal food security also predicts adverse health outcomes in young U.S. children and mothers. *Advances in Nutrition*, 4(1), 51–61.

Cozzi, P., Putnam, S., Menesini, E., Gartstein, M., Aureli, T., Calussi, P. , & Montirosso, R. (2013). Studying cross-cultural differences in temperament in toddlerhood: United States of America (US) and Italy. *Infant Behavior and Development*, 36(3), 480–483.

Elliott, W. (2013). The effects of economic instability on children's educational outcomes. *Children and Youth Services Review*, 35(3), 461–471.

Erdener, D., & Burnham, D. (2013). The relationship between auditory–visual speech perception and language-specific speech perception at the onset of reading instruction in English-speaking children. *Journal of Experimental Child Psychology*, 116(2), 120–138.

Freud, S. (1924). *The dissolution of the Oedipus complex*. Standard Edition, 19:172–179.

Frota, S., Butler, J., & Vigario, M. (2014). Infants' perception of intonation: Is it a statement or a question? *Infancy*, 19(2), 194–213.

Gesell, A., & Ilg, F. (1949). *Child development*. New York: Harper.

Geier, C. (2013). Adolescent cognitive control and reward processing: Implications for risk taking and substance use. *Hormones & Behavior*, 64(2), 333–342.

Gunderson, E., Gripshover, S., Romero, C., Sweck, C., Goldin-Meadow, S., & Levine, S. (2013). Parent praise to 1- to 3-year-olds predicts children's motivational frameworks 5 years later. *Child Development*, 84(5), 1526–1541.

Halim, M., Ruble, D., Tamis-LeMonda, C., & Shrout, P. (2013). Rigidity in gender-typed behaviors in early childhood: A longitudinal study of ethnic minority children. *Child Development*, 84(4), 1269–1284.

Hoff, E. (2013). Interpreting the early language trajectories of children from low-SES and language minority homes: Implications for closing achievement gaps. *Developmental Psychology*, 49(1), 4–14.

Johnson, S., Riley, A., Granger, D., & Riis, J. (2013). The science of early life toxic stress for pediatric practice and advocacy. *Pediatrics*, 131(2), 319–327.

Kohlberg, L. (1966). A cognitive-developmental analysis of children's sex-role concepts and attitudes. In E. E. Maccody (Ed.), *The development of sex differences*. Stanford, CA: Stanford University Press.

Lane, J., Wellman, H., Olson, S., Miller, A., Wang, L., & Tardif, T. (2013). Relations between temperament and theory of mind development in the United States and China: Biological and behavioral correlates of preschoolers' false-belief understanding. *Developmental Psychology*, 49(5), 825–836.

Lawson, G., Duda, J., Avants, B., Wu, J., & Farah, M. (2013). Associations between children's socioeconomic status and prefrontal cortical thickness. *Developmental Science*, 16(5), 641–652.

Lee, R., Zhai, F., Han, W., Brooks-Gunn, J., & Waldfogel, J. (2013). Head Start and children's nutrition, weight, and health care receipt. *Early Childhood Research Quarterly*, 28(4), 723–733.

Lemery-Chalfant, K., Kao, K., Swann, G., & Goldsmith, H. (2013). Childhood temperament: Passive gene-environment correlation, gene-environment interaction, and the hidden importance of the family environment. *Development & Psychopathology*, 25(1), 51–63.

Mani, A., Mullainathan, S., Shafir, E., & Zhao, J. (2013). Poverty impedes cognitive function. *Science*, 341(6149), 976–980.

McCoy, T., Conrad, A., Richman, L., Nopoulos, P., & Bell, E. (2013). Memory processes in learning disability subtypes of children born preterm. *Child Neuropsychology*, 19(2), 173–189.

Monk, C., Georgieff, M., & Osterholm, E. (2013). Research review: Maternal prenatal distress and poor nutrition—mutually influencing risk factors affecting infant neurocognitive development. *Journal of Child Psychology & Psychiatry*, 54(2), 115–130.

Mueller, S., Wang, D., Fox, M., Yeo, B., Sepulcre, J., Sabuncu, M., ... & Liu, H. (2013). Individual variability in functional connectivity architecture of the human brain. *Neuron*, 7(6), 586–595.

Neu, R. (2013). Development in Spanish-speaking preschool students. *Early Childhood Education Journal*, 41(3), 211–218.

Perkins, S., Finegood, E., & Swain, J. (2013). Poverty and language development: Roles of parenting and stress. *Innovations in Clinical Neuroscience*, 10(4), 10–19.

Perkins, S., & Graham-Bermann, S. (2012). Violence exposure and the development of school-related functioning: Mental health, neurocognition, and learning. *Aggression & Violent Behavior*, 17(1), 89–98.

Peterson, C., Wall, S., Jeon, H., Swanson, M., Carta, J., & Luze, G. (2013). Identification of disabilities and service receipt among preschool children living in poverty. *Journal of Special Education*, (47(1), 28–40.

Piaget, J. (1954). *The construction of reality in the child*. New York: Basic Books.

Raver, C., Blair, C., & Willoughby, M. (2013). Poverty as a predictor of 4-year-olds' executive function: New perspectives on models of differential susceptibility. *Developmental Psychology*, 49(2), 292–304.

Schwartz, D., Lansford, J., Dodge, K., Pettit, G., & Bates, J. (2013). The link between harsh home environments and negative academic trajectories is exacerbated by victimization in the elementary school peer group. *Developmental Psychology*, 49(2), 305–316.

Shutts, K., Roben, C., & Spelke, E. (2013). Children's use of social categories in thinking about people and social relationships. *Journal of Cognition and Development*, 14(1), 35–62.

Soto, C., & Oliver, J. (2013). Traits in transition: The structure of parent-reported personality traits from early childhood to early adulthood. *Journal of Personality*. Advanced online publication. doi: 10.1111/jopy.12044.

Thomas, A., & Chess, S. (1977). *Temperament and development*. New York: Brunner/Mazel.

Trawick-Smith, J. (2013). *Early childhood development: A multicultural perspective*. 6th Ed. Upper Saddle River, NJ: Pearson.

Twardosz, S. (2012). Effects of experience on the brain: The role of neuroscience in early development and education. *Early Education & Development*, 23(1), 96–119.

Widom, C., Czaja, S., Wilson, H., Allwood, M., & Chauhan, P. (2013). Do the long-term consequences of neglect differ for children of different races and ethnic backgrounds? *Child Maltreatment*, 18(1), 42–55.

Williams, M., Saunders, J., Maschette, W., & Wilson, C. (2013). Outcome and process in motor performance: A comparison of jumping by typically developing children and those with low motor proficiency. *Measurement in Physical Education & Exercise Science*, 17(2), 135–149.

## Learning Objectives

*After reading this chapter, you will be able to:*

**3-1** Describe the developmental changes that occur during the germinal, embryonic, and fetal stages of pregnancy.

**3-2** Describe at least four practices that a mother should follow throughout pregnancy to improve her chances of giving birth to a healthy infant.

**3-3** Name five teratogens and describe their preventive measures.

**3-4** Identify several changes that signal the onset of active labor.

**3-5** Define maternal depression and discuss its potential impact on infant development.

## naeyc NAEYC Standards Linked to Chapter Content

**1b:** Promoting child development and learning
**2a:** Building family and community relationships
**6e:** Becoming a professional

Anna and Miguel were elated when they learned that she was seven weeks pregnant. Six months earlier, Anna experienced a miscarriage during her third month of pregnancy. At the time, Anna's doctor advised her to stop smoking before attempting future pregnancies. Although she was not able to quit completely, she significantly reduced the number of cigarettes smoked to no more than two or three a day. Anna also has made an effort to improve her diet by eating more fruits and vegetables and eliminating all alcohol consumption. She enrolled in a beginner's yoga class and walks with Miguel on weekends to control her weight and relieve stress.

When Anna and Miguel shared their exciting news with family members, everyone had advice for preventing another miscarriage. Her mother insisted that Anna rest and avoid any type of activity, including cleaning the house and cooking. Miguel's grandmother advised Anna to eat all that she could "because now you're eating for two." She also told Anna not to drink too much milk because "it will make the baby's complexion lighter in color" and to avoid strawberries because "they can cause a red birthmark." Her sister discouraged Anna from continuing her job at the bank because she had heard that stress could cause miscarriage and affect the infant's personality. However, Anna's job provides a needed source of income. Anna appreciated everyone's well-intended suggestions, but she was convinced that everything would be okay this time around.

## Ask Yourself

- What lifestyle changes has Anna made to improve her chances of giving birth to a healthy infant? Are there other things she also might try?
- Do you think Anna should follow the advice that her friends and family have offered? Why or why not?

Each of the approximately 266 days of prenatal development (from **conception** to birth) is critical to producing a healthy newborn. **Genes** inherited from the baby's biological mother and father determine all physical characteristics, as well as many abnormalities. Studies have suggested that **temperament** may have a biological basis as well (Kandler et al., 2012). However, because it is the mother who provides everything physically essential (as well as harmful) to the growing fetus, she plays a major role in promoting its healthy development. Her personal health, nutrition, and lifestyle before and during pregnancy strongly influence the birth of a healthy infant. In addition, researchers have determined that a father's health, personal habits, and his caring support for the mother throughout the pregnancy contribute to the unborn infant's development (Deng et al., 2013; Vaiserman, 2013). Thus, it is important for every potential parent to be familiar with the patterns of normal prenatal development, as well as with practices that support and interfere with this process (Figure 3-1).

**Figure 3-1** A mother's and father's lifestyles have a direct effect on their infant's development.

## The Developmental Process

The prenatal period is commonly divided into stages. In obstetrical practice, pregnancy is described in terms of trimesters, each consisting of three calendar months:

- First trimester—Conception through the third month
- Second trimester—Fourth through the sixth month
- Third trimester—Seventh through the ninth month

Pregnancy can also be discussed in terms of fetal development (Table 3-1). This approach emphasizes the critical changes that occur week by week and encompasses three stages as well:

- Germinal
- Embryonic
- Fetal

The *germinal stage* refers to the first fourteen days of pregnancy. The union of an ovum and sperm produces a **zygote**. Cell division begins within twenty four hours and gradually forms a pinhead-size mass of specialized cells called a *blastocyst*. Around the

**conception** The joining of a single egg or ovum from the female and a single sperm from the male.

**genes** Genetic material that carries codes, or information, for all inherited characteristics.

**temperament** An individual's characteristic manner or style of response to everyday events, including degree of interest, activity level, and regulation of behavior.

**zygote** The cell formed as a result of conception; called a *zygote* for the first fourteen days.

## Table 3-1 Characteristics of Fetal Development

| 2 weeks | • Cell division results in an embryo consisting of 16 cells. |
|---|---|
| 3–8 weeks | • Structures necessary to support the developing embryo have formed: placenta, chorionic sac, amniotic fluid, and umbilical cord.<br>• Embryonic cell layers begin to specialize, developing into major internal organs and systems, as well as external structures.<br>• First bone cells appear.<br>• Less than 1 inch (2.54 cm) in length at eight weeks. |
| 12 weeks | • Weighs approximately 1–2 ounces (0.029–0.006 kg) and is nearly 3 inches (7.6 cm) in length.<br>• Sex organs develop; baby's gender can be determined.<br>• Kidneys begin to function.<br>• Arms, legs, fingers, and toes are well defined and movable.<br>• Makes facial expressions (e.g., smiles and frowns), looks around, and is able to suck and swallow. |
| 16 weeks | • Weighs about 5 ounces (0.14 kg) and is 6 inches (15.2 cm) in length.<br>• Sucks thumb.<br>• Moves about actively; mother may begin to feel baby's movement (called *quickening*).<br>• Has strong heartbeat that can be heard. |
| 20 weeks | • Weighs nearly 1 pound (0.46 kg) and has grown to approximately 11–12 inches (27.9–30.5 cm) in length (approximately half of baby's birth length).<br>• Experiences occasional hiccups.<br>• Eyelashes, eyebrows, and hair forming; eyes remain closed. |
| 24 weeks | • Weight doubles to about 1.5–2 pounds (0.68–0.90 kg) and length increases to 12–14 inches (30.5–35.6 cm).<br>• Eyes are well formed, often open; responds to light and sound.<br>• Grasp reflex develops.<br>• Skin is wrinkled, thin, and covered with soft hair called *lanugo* and a white, greasy, protective substance called *vernix caseosa*. |
| 28 weeks | • Weighs about 3–3.5 pounds (1.4–1.6 kg); grows to approximately 16–17 inches (40.6–43 cm) in length.<br>• Develops a sleep/wake pattern.<br>• Remains very active; kicks and pokes mother's ribs and abdomen.<br>• Able to survive if born prematurely, although lungs are not yet fully developed. |
| 32 weeks | • Weighs approximately 5–6 pounds (2.3–2.7 kg) and is 17–18 inches in length (43–45.7 cm).<br>• Baby takes iron and calcium from mother's diet to build up reserve stores.<br>• Becomes less active due to larger size and less room for moving about. |
| 36–38 weeks | • Weighs an average of 7–8 pounds (3.2–3.6 kg) at birth; length is approximately 19–21 inches (48–53.3 cm).<br>• Moves into final position (usually head down) in preparation for birth.<br>• Loses most of lanugo; skin still somewhat wrinkled and red.<br>• Is much less active (because there is now little room in which to move about).<br>• Body systems are more mature (especially the lungs and heart), thus increasing baby's chances of survival at birth. |

fourteenth day, this small mass attaches itself to the wall of the mother's uterus. Successful attachment (**implantation**) marks the beginning of the **embryo** and the embryonic stage. Approximately two-thirds of zygotes survive this phase and continue to develop.

The *embryonic stage* includes the third through the eighth week of a pregnancy and is a critical period for the developing fetus. Cell division continues and forms specialized cell layers that are responsible for producing all major organs and systems, including the heart, lungs, digestive system, and brain. Many of these structures will be functional near the end of this period. For example, embryonic blood begins to flow through the fetus's primitive cardiovascular system (heart and blood vessels) in the fourth to the fifth week.

During this time, other important changes also take place. When implantation is completed, a **placenta** begins to form. This organ serves four major functions:

- It supplies nutrients and hormones to the fetus.
- It removes fetal waste products throughout the pregnancy.
- It filters many harmful substances, as well as some viruses and other disease-causing organisms. (Unfortunately, many drugs can get through the placenta's filtering system.)
- It acts as a temporary immune system by supplying the fetus with the same antibodies that the mother produces against certain infectious diseases. (In most instances, the infant is protected for approximately six months following birth.)

An umbilical cord, containing two arteries and one vein, develops as the placenta forms and establishes a linkage between the fetus, its mother, and the outside world. From this point on, the fetus is affected by the mother's health and lifestyle and, via the placenta, begins to share everything that the mother experiences and takes into her body. During this early stage, the fetus is especially vulnerable if exposed to certain chemical substances, such as alcohol, cigarette smoke, medications or other drugs

**implantation** The attachment of the blastocyst to the wall of the mother's uterus; occurs around the twelfth day.

**embryo** The cell mass from the time of implantation through the eighth week of pregnancy.

**placenta** A specialized lining that forms inside the uterus during pregnancy to support and nourish the developing fetus.

## Spotlight on Brain Development

### Learning Before Birth

Until recently, scientists have only hypothesized that a certain degree of learning may take place prior to birth. Modern technologies now permit researchers to identify and measure specific fetal reactions (e.g., heart rate, brain wave activity, movement) and brain development as evidence of learning that occurs in response to external stimuli such as sound. This form of learning relies on the fetal auditory system, which matures during the second and third trimesters.

A number of contemporary studies have demonstrated a direct correlation between neural changes that occur in utero and children's subsequent language development and recognition (Moon, Lagercrantz, & Kuhl, 2013; Partanen et al., 2013). Voegtline et al. (2013) noted an increase in fetal response (e.g., heart rate and motor activity) when a resting mother began to read aloud. Researchers have also identified a strong fetal and newborn preference for their mother's voice (Muenssinger et al., 2013). Gender differences in the pattern of fetal brain development and behavioral responses have been shown in a series of experiments conducted by Hepper, Dornan, & Lynch (2013). The findings of these and additional studies underscore the critical link between prenatal brain development and a child's learning potential.

### What are the connections?

1. What role does maternal diet play in fetal brain development?
2. What additional measures can parents take to optimize their infant's brain development?

(Table 3-2), or infectious illnesses (Table 3-3) that enter the mother's body. Exposure to any of these substances can damage developing fetal organs and systems and increase the risk of irreversible birth defects.

The *fetal stage* refers to the period between the ninth week and the onset of labor and delivery (around the thirty-eighth week). Most fetal systems and structures are now formed, and this final and longest period is devoted to continued growth and maturity. By seven months, a fetus is capable of surviving birth. During the final two months, few developmental changes occur. Instead, the fetus undergoes rapid and important increases in weight and size by adding layers of fat. For example, a seven-month-old fetus who weighs 2 to 3 pounds (0.9 to 1.4 kg) will gain approximately a half-pound (0.23 kg) per week until birth. Body systems are also maturing and growing stronger, thus improving the fetus's chances of surviving outside the mother's body.

# Promoting Healthy Fetal Development

Critical aspects of fetal development take place during the earliest days of pregnancy. Because the mother may not yet know that she is pregnant, it is important that both parents follow healthy lifestyle practices throughout their reproductive years, whether they are trying to have a baby or not. Researchers have identified many practices that can improve a mother's chances of having a healthy infant, including:

- Obtaining early prenatal care
- Following a healthy diet
- Maintaining a moderate weight gain
- Obtaining adequate sleep and rest
- Avoiding excessive stress
- Having a positive emotional attitude
- Planning pregnancies when a mother is in her twenties to thirties and in good health
- Participating in daily physical activity
- Limiting exposure to teratogens such as drugs, alcohol, tobacco, and environmental chemicals
- Allowing a two-year interval between pregnancies (Kozuki et al., 2013)

Figure 3-2 Early and regular prenatal care is essential for a healthy pregnancy and infant.

## Prenatal Care

Medically supervised prenatal care is critical for ensuring the development of a healthy infant (Figure 3-2). Arrangements for this care should be made as soon as a woman suspects that she might be pregnant. Women should not rely solely on home pregnancy tests before seeking medical care because the results are not always accurate, especially during the early days and weeks. During the initial visit to a health-care provider, pregnancy can be confirmed (or refuted), immunizations can be updated, and any medical problems that the mother may have can be evaluated and treated. In addition, the parents-to-be can be counseled on practices that influence fetal development. For example, mothers may be encouraged to participate in a program of regular noncontact exercise. (So long as there are no complications to the pregnancy, regular exercise can improve weight control, circulation, muscle tone, and elimination and is believed to contribute to an easier labor and delivery.)

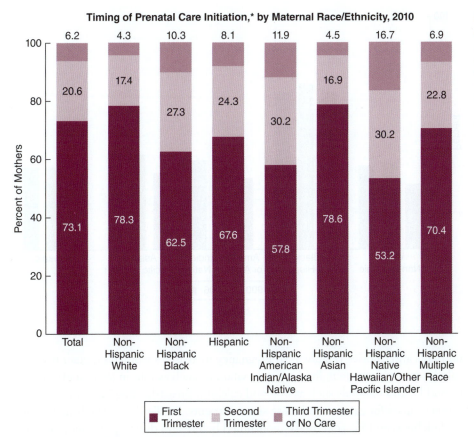

**Figure 3-3** Timing of prenatal care initiation.

Source: Centers for Disease Control and Prevention, National Center for Health Statistics. 2010 Natality Public Use File. Analysis conducted by the Maternal and Child Health Bureau. Retrieved from :http://mchb.hrsa.gov/chusa12/hsfu/pages/pc.html

*Data are from 33 states that implemented the 2003 revision of the birth certificate as of January 1, 2010, representing 67% of all US births; percentages may not total to 100 due to rounding.

At present, approximately 71 percent of women in the United States receive prenatal care during their first trimester of pregnancy (CDC, 2010) (Figure 3-3). This figure leaves considerable room for improvement and has been identified as one of the leading public health objectives in the Healthy People 2020 national agenda. A lack of prenatal care is often associated with an increased rate of medical complications, preterm births, **low birth weight (LBW)** infants, fetal death, and disabilities (Figure 3-4). Poverty is often cited as a factor in limiting a mother's access to medical care, as well as to her understanding about its importance (de Graaf, Steegers, & Bonsel, 2013). Language barriers, differences in cultural beliefs, being a teen mother, and ethnicity have been identified as other inhibiting factors (Biggs et al., 2013). Consequently, continued efforts must be made to improve mothers' awareness of government-sponsored nutrition programs such as the national Women, Infants, and Children (WIC) supplemental food program, low-cost medical insurance, and community-sponsored health clinics.

# Nutrition

A mother's nutritional status, determined by what she eats before and during pregnancy, has a significant effect on her own health, as well as on that of the developing fetus. Consuming a healthy diet lessens the risk of having a low birth weight or being a **premature infant**, two conditions commonly associated with serious developmental problems (Natalucci et al., 2013; Treyvaud et al., 2013).

It is important that pregnant women continue to follow national nutrition recommendations throughout their pregnancy to ensure an adequate intake of essential

**low birth weight (LBW)** An infant who weighs less than 5.5 pounds (2,500 grams) at the time of birth.

**premature infant** An infant born before thirty-seven weeks following conception.

Figure 3-4  Percent of infants born with low birth weight.

Source: National Center for Health Statistics, National Vital Statistics System. Retrieved on February 4, 2014 from, http://www.childstats.gov/americaschildren/health_fig.asp

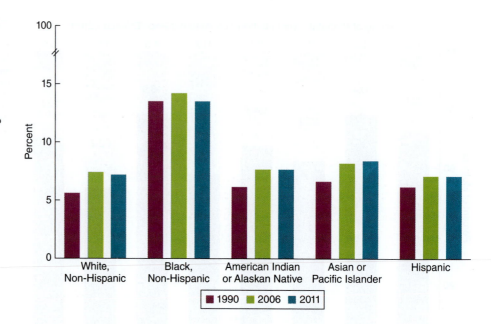

nutrients and calories (Figure 3-5). Pregnancy increases a woman's dietary need for calories (energy); protein; fluids; certain vitamins such as folacin (folic acid), $B_6$, $B_{12}$, C, and D; and minerals such as iron and calcium. Breast-feeding further increases a mother's need for calories and these same nutrients. Studies have established a critical link between folic acid intake (consumed before and during pregnancy: 400 micrograms daily for nonpregnant women, 600 micrograms daily for pregnant women) and the reduced incidence of neural tube defects (i.e., **spina bifida, anencephaly**) and **cleft lip/cleft palate** deformities (Bower, 2013; Branum, Bailey, & Singer 2013). Folic acid is a B vitamin found abundantly in many foods, especially raw, leafy green

Figure 3-5  Daily food plans for pregnant and breast-feeding mothers are available on this interactive tool.

Source: 2011 National Survey on Drug Use and Health: Summary of National Find-ings. U.S. Department of Health and Human Services. Retrieved on February 4, 2014 from, http://www.samhsa.gov/data/nsduh/2k11results/nsduhresults2011.htm#4.

**spina bifida**  A birth defect caused by a malformation of the baby's spinal column.

**anencephaly**  A birth defect resulting in malformation of the skull and brain; portions of these structures might be missing at birth.

**cleft lip/cleft palate**  Incomplete closure of the lip, palate (roof of the mouth), or both, resulting in a disfiguring deformity.

## What Do You See?

**Maternal diet and fetal development** What a mother eats and drinks in the months before and throughout pregnancy has a direct influence on her infant's development. Which food items in this photo will supply folacin? What role does this B vitamin play in fetal development?

Tetra Images/Brand X Pictures/Getty Images

vegetables, dried beans, lentils, orange juice, and fortified whole grain products such as pasta, bread, and breakfast cereal.

Although vitamin supplements are generally prescribed, they must not be considered a substitute for a nutritious diet. They lack essential protein, calories, and other important nutrients found in most foods. All these nutrients are required for healthy fetal development and also improve the absorption and utilization of vitamins and minerals taken in tablet form. Herbal preparations are not recommended due to a lack of sufficient information about their safety during pregnancy (Dante et al., 2013).

Several groups, including the U.S. Environmental Protection Agency (EPA), have advised women contemplating pregnancy, pregnant women, nursing mothers, and young children to limit their intake of certain fish and seafood varieties due to potential mercury and pesticide contamination (Driscoll et al., 2013; EPA, 2013). However, because fish are low in calories and a rich source of high-quality protein and essential fats, researchers suggest that the benefits of including them in one's diet can outweigh the potential risks. Thus, women and young children are encouraged not to avoid eating such foods, but to limit their consumption to no more than 12 ounces of seafood such as shrimp, salmon, pollock, catfish, and canned light tuna (not albacore tuna, which has a higher mercury content) per week. Fish such as shark, swordfish, tilefish, and mackerel should be avoided. Consumers also are encouraged to check with authorities before eating fish caught in local rivers and lakes to determine whether mercury or other hazardous chemical contamination is a concern.

## Weight

What is the optimum weight gain during pregnancy? Most medical practitioners agree that a woman of normal weight [i.e., having a healthy body mass index (BMI)] should ideally gain between 25 and 35 pounds (10 and 14 kg) over the nine-month period (ACOG, 2013). Gains considerably under or over this range can pose increased risks for both the mother and child during pregnancy and at birth. Jeric et al. (2013) and others have identified a strong association between insufficient maternal weight gain and infants who are born small (i.e., having substandard length and weight) for their gestational age. Excessive weight gain during pregnancy can endanger the mother's health and lead to **gestational diabetes**, hypertension (high blood pressure), and an increased rate of miscarriage. Infants born to mothers who are obese or who gain too much weight during pregnancy are often larger and at greater risk for developing conditions such as asthma, obesity, cardiovascular heart disease, and type 2 diabetes in adulthood (Patti, 2013).

Following a diet that is nutritionally adequate helps ensure optimum weight gain. Including the recommended servings of a wide variety of fruits and vegetables supplies the vitamins essential for fetal growth (vitamins A and C) and fiber to decrease constipation. Choosing low-fat dairy products and lean meats and plant proteins (e.g., dried beans, legumes, and whole grains) aids in moderating caloric intake while providing key minerals (e.g., iron and calcium) required for the infant's and mother's health. Consuming too many empty calories, such as those found in junk foods, sweets, and alcohol, can lead to increased weight gain and deprive the mother and fetus of critical nutrients found in a balanced diet.

## Rest and Stress

Pregnancy places added strain on the mother's body and often increases her sense of fatigue. Adequate nighttime sleep and occasional daytime rest periods can help ease these problems.

Pregnancy can also induce or increase emotional stress. Prolonged or excessive stress can affect the mother's health adversely by contributing to sleep and eating disorders, high blood pressure, depression, headaches, lowered resistance to infections, and backaches (Loomans et al., 2013). In addition, it has been shown to have negative effects on the fetus by reducing weight, breathing rate, heartbeat, and brain development (Painter, Roseboom, & de Rooij, 2012). A recent study conducted by Witt et al., (2014) found that women who were exposed to a stressful lifestyle prior to conception experienced a 38 percent increase in giving birth to a very low weight infant. Although it may not be possible for a pregnant woman to avoid all exposure to stress, strain, and fatigue, the ill effects often can be alleviated with proper rest, nutrition, and physical activity.

## Age and General Health

A woman's age at the time of conception is an important factor in fetal development (Figure 3-6). Numerous studies conclude that the mid-twenties to early thirties are the optimum years for childbearing. Teenage mothers experience a rate of premature births, LBW babies, infant deaths, and infants born with developmental disabilities that is nearly double that for all mothers (Malabarey et al., 2012). These problems often are attributed to inadequate prenatal care, poor nutrition and housing, substance abuse, or all three. In addition, the immaturity of a teen mother's reproductive system and her lack of basic knowledge about how best to care for her own personal needs frequently place these infants at increased risk.

Pregnancy in older women (late thirties and beyond) presents a different set of health concerns. The quality of genetic material contained in the **ova** continues to lessen as a woman ages, increasing the probability of miscarriage, infant mortality, and certain birth defects such as Down syndrome (Balasch & Gratacós, 2012; Grandel et al., 2012). In addition, it has been determined that male sperm deteriorates with age

**gestational diabetes** A form of diabetes that occurs only during pregnancy and places the fetus at increased risk; often associated with excess maternal weight gain, a family history of diabetes, and certain ethnicities (e.g., Latina, Native American, African American, Asian, Pacific Islander).

**ova** Female reproductive cells (eggs) that contain reproductive materials.

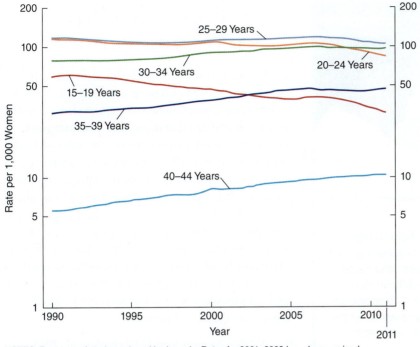

Figure 3-6 Mother's age at the time of birth.
SOURCE: CDC/NCHS, National Vital Statistics System. Retrieved on February 4, 2014 from, http://www.cdc.gov/nchs/data/nvsr/nvsr62/nvsr62_01.pdf.

NOTES: Rates are plotted on a logarithmic scale. Rates for 2001–2009 have been revised using new population estimates based on the 2010 census, and may differ from rates previously published; see Technical Notes.

**Did You Know?**

...the youngest mother recorded to give birth following natural conception was 5 1/2 years old (1939) and the oldest was 59 years (1997)? The incidence of birth complications and congenital defects is highest among mothers at both ends of the age spectrum.

and exposure to environmental contaminants and, in turn, may increase the risk of autism and other birth defects (Lampi et al., 2013). Older women are more likely to experience multiple-birth pregnancies, medical problems during pregnancy, and birthing complications. However, greater awareness of the importance of a nutritious diet, physical activity, and medical supervision has improved an older mother's chances of giving birth to a healthy infant.

Increased knowledge and improved technology also contribute to a reduction in fetal risk for mothers of all ages. Genetic counseling, ultrasound scanning **(sonogram)**, **chorionic villus sampling (CVS), amniocentesis**, and new noninvasive maternal blood tests enable medical personnel to monitor fetal growth and detect more than 800 specific genetic disorders earlier than had been possible in the past (Liao, Gronowski, & Zhao, 2014). These procedures are especially beneficial for women who are electing to delay childbearing until their late thirties and early forties.

Although the risks of pregnancy are undeniably greater for older women and teenagers, the problems often have as much to do with limited knowledge and poverty as with age. (Exceptions include chromosomal abnormalities such as Down syndrome.) Regardless of maternal age, a significant number of fetal problems are closely associated with a lack of medical care, unhealthy diet, substandard housing, substance abuse, and limited education, all often closely associated with poverty. Spacing pregnancies at least two years apart improves the mother's health and chances of carrying a subsequent pregnancy to full term (Kozuki et al., 2013).

Assisted reproductive technologies, such as in vitro fertilization, have become increasingly successful and affordable procedures for treating infertility. The most common complications associated with these techniques are **ectopic pregnancy**, premature delivery, and multiple births. Concerns regarding an increased risk of congenital deformities, intellectual disability, and autism have not been found to be statistically significant (Hansen et al., 2013).

**sonogram** A visual image of the developing fetus, created by directing high-frequency sound waves (ultrasound) at the mother's uterus; the procedure is used to determine fetal age and physical abnormalities.

**chorionic villus sampling (CVS)** A genetic-screening procedure in which a needle is inserted and cells removed from the outer layer of the placenta; performed between the eighth and twelfth weeks to detect some genetic disorders, such as Down syndrome.

**amniocentesis** Genetic-screening procedure in which a needle is inserted through the mother's abdomen into the sac of fluids surrounding the fetus to detect abnormalities such as Down syndrome or spina bifida; usually performed between the twelfth and sixteenth weeks.

**ectopic pregnancy** Pregnancy that occurs when a fertilized egg attaches itself outside the uterus, most often in one of the fallopian tubes located between the ovaries and uterus.

**▶❚❚ TeachSource** Video Connections

### Prenatal Assessment

Several procedures are available to help detect some genetic abnormalities during pregnancy. Each test has its advantages and limitations, and such tests may present the family with a difficult decision if a genetic condition is detected. Respond to the following questions after you have watched the learning video *0–2 Years: Prenatal Assessment:*

1. How is a sonogram performed, and for what purpose it is used?

2. What is an amniocentesis, and what risks are associated with this procedure?

3. How common are genetic abnormalities?

4. For a period of time, businesses offered on-the-spot sonograms in local shopping malls. Do you think this is a good idea? Why or why not?

# Threats to Healthy Fetal Development

Much is known about lifestyle practices that improve a mother's chances of having a healthy infant. However, there is also evidence to suggest that a number of environmental substances called **teratogens** can have negative consequences on the unborn child. Several are especially damaging during the earliest weeks, often before a woman realizes that she is pregnant. It is during these sensitive or critical periods that various fetal structures and major organ systems are forming rapidly and, thus, are most sensitive to the effects of any harmful substance. For example, the heart is most vulnerable between the third and sixth weeks; the palate, from the sixth to eighth weeks. Extensive research has identified a number of major teratogens, including:

- Alcohol consumption (Makelarski et al., 2013)
- Maternal smoking (Suter, Anders, & Aagaard, 2013)
- Addictive drugs (e.g., cocaine, heroin, amphetamines, marijuana) (Brown & Graves, 2013; Wendell, 2013)
- Hazardous chemicals (e.g., mercury, lead, carbon monoxide, polychlorinated biphenols [PCBs], paint solvents) (Driscoll et al., 2013)
- Pesticides and insecticides
- Some medications (Table 3-2, p. 59)
- Maternal infections (Table 3-3, p. 60)
- Radiation, such as X-rays

Researchers continue to study other potential links between environmental factors and birth defects. To date, many findings are still considered to be inconclusive, controversial, or both. Some of the factors being investigated include:

- Prolonged exposure to high temperatures (hot baths, saunas, hot tubs)
- Secondary smoke (Meeker & Benedict, 2013)
- Herbal supplements and over-the-counter medications (Dante et al., 2013)
- Electromagnetic fields such as those created by heating pads, electric blankets, and power lines (Malagoli et al., 2012)
- Aspartame and other artificial sweeteners
- Cooking smoke and consumption of grilled meats (Jedrychowski et al., 2013)
- Hazardous waste sites

The relationship between teratogen exposure and fetal damage is not always clear or direct. Several factors can influence a teratogen's harmful effect on fetal development, including the amount of exposure (dose), fetal age (timing), and genetic makeup of the mother and fetus. Thus, women who are contemplating pregnancy should avoid unnecessary contact with known teratogens that are capable of crossing the placental barrier. As noted earlier, fetal organs and body systems are especially vulnerable to these agents during the early weeks following conception. This is not to suggest that there is ever a completely safe time period. Even during the later months, fetal growth

**teratogens** Harmful agents that can cause fetal damage (e.g., malformations, neurological, and behavioral problems) during the prenatal period.

## What Do You See?

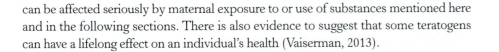

**A healthy pregnancy.** This mother is engaging in behaviors that are not conducive to healthy fetal development. What potentially harmful practices can you identify in the photo? What risks do they pose? How do they compare with information provided in this chapter?

Bubbles Photolibrary/Alamy

can be affected seriously by maternal exposure to or use of substances mentioned here and in the following sections. There is also evidence to suggest that some teratogens can have a lifelong effect on an individual's health (Vaiserman, 2013).

## Alcohol

Alcohol consumption during pregnancy is known to have serious consequences for both the mother and the developing fetus. Warnings to this effect appear on the labels of all alcoholic products. Mothers who consume alcohol during pregnancy experience a greater risk of miscarriages, stillbirths, premature infants, and LBW infants. The incidence of fetal death is also significantly higher. Because alcoholic beverages contain only calories and no nutrients, consuming them on a regular or binge basis can limit the mother's dietary intake of essential protein, vitamins, and minerals necessary for her well-being and that of her infant.

Alcohol is also a potentially toxic teratogen that can have a wide range of irreversible effects on fetal development (O'Leary et al., 2013). Because mother and infant share a common circulatory system (through the placenta and umbilical cord), both are affected by any alcohol that is consumed. However, alcohol remains in the fetal circulatory system twice as long as in that of the mother. It is especially damaging to the fetus during the critical first trimester of pregnancy when most body structures and organs, especially the brain, heart, and nervous system, are forming.

Prenatal exposure to alcohol can result in conditions commonly referred to as fetal alcohol spectrum disorders (FASDs). Heavy or binge drinking is associated with a preventable condition known as *fetal alcohol syndrome (FAS)*, which causes intellectual disabilities and growth retardation, behavior and learning problems (hyperactivity), poor motor coordination, heart defects, characteristic facial deformities (e.g., eyes set wide apart, shortened eye lids, or flattened nose), and speech impairment (Davis et al., 2013). Moderate alcohol consumption is associated with a milder form of this condition known as fetal alcohol effect (FAE). These children often exhibit a wide range of learning and behavior disorders. When alcohol is consumed later in the pregnancy, it typically interferes with proper fetal growth.

Precisely how much alcohol might be damaging to an unborn child is difficult to determine. Most likely, the relationship between alcohol and fetal damage is more complex than it might initially appear. *Thus, no amount of alcohol is considered safe to consume during pregnancy.*

## Smoking

Many pregnant women continue to smoke despite warnings issued by the U.S. surgeon general and those printed on all tobacco products (Figure 3-7). Maternal smoking has been linked to a variety of fetal malformations and birth complications (Suter, Anders, & Aagaard, 2013). Cigarette smoke contains a number of toxic substances, including nicotine, tars, ammonia, carbon monoxide, and other chemicals that cross the placental barrier and interfere with normal fetal development. Carbon monoxide reduces the amount of oxygen available to the fetus. This early oxygen deprivation seems to correlate with learning and behavior problems, especially as exposed children reach school age. Mothers who smoke during pregnancy experience a higher rate of miscarriage, premature births, stillborn infants, and LBW infants. Their infants are also three times more likely to die from sudden infant death syndrome (SIDS) and a range of acute and chronic respiratory problems (e.g., allergies, asthma, colds, croup, and bronchitis). Studies also have shown that attention deficit disorders are more common among children whose mothers smoked during pregnancy (Silva et al., 2014).

## Chemicals and Drugs

Numerous chemicals and drugs are also known to have an adverse effect on the developing fetus. These substances range from prescription and nonprescription medications

**Figure 3-7** Percent of women who smoke during pregnancy.

Source: 2011 National Survey on Drug Use and Health: Summary of National Findings. U.S. Department of Health and Human Services. Retrieved on February 4, 2014 from http://www.samhsa. gov/data/nsduh/2k11results/ nsduhresults2011.htm#4.

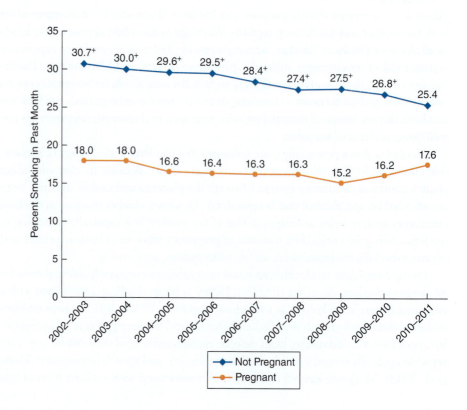

**Table 3-2** Examples of Potentially Teratogenic Drugs

- Analgesics (more than an occasional dose of aspirin or ibuprofen)
- Antibiotics (particularly tetracyclines and streptomycin)
- Anticonvulsants (such as Dilantin)
- Anticoagulants (used to thin the blood, such as Coumadin)
- Antidepressants
- Antihistamines
- Antihypertensives (used to treat high blood pressure)
- Anti-neoplastic drugs (used to treat cancers and some forms of arthritis, such as Methotrexate)
- Antiviral agents
- Hormones [such as diethylstilbesterol (DES) and progesterin]
- Large doses of vitamin A [in excess of 10,000 international units (IU); includes some acne treatments such as Accutane and Retin-A]
- Thyroid and anti-thyroid drugs
- Diet pills
- Nicotine
- Cocaine, heroin, marijuana, and methadone

© Cengage Learning®

to pesticides, fertilizers, and street drugs (Behnke & Smith, 2013; O'Leary et al., 2013) (Table 3-2). Some cause severe malformations, such as missing or malformed limbs or facial features. Others can lead to fetal death (spontaneous abortion), premature birth, or lifelong behavior and learning disabilities. Not all exposed fetuses will be affected in the same manner or to the same degree. The nature and severity of an infant's abnormalities seem to be influenced by the timing of exposure during fetal development, the amount and type of substance, the mother's general state of health, and maternal and fetal genetics. Research has not yet provided a definitive answer about which drugs and chemicals (if any) have absolutely no harmful effects on the developing fetus. Thus, women who are or may become pregnant are encouraged to check with their medical provider before using any chemical substance or medication (prescription or non-prescription). Exposure to previously discussed environmental hazards, such as high doses of radiation and X-rays, particularly in the early stages of pregnancy, also should be avoided. Furthermore, women have been advised to avoid caffeine completely during pregnancy, but adverse effects on the fetus have not been found when consumption is limited to the equivalent of one or two cups of coffee daily.

**Did You Know**

...that the supplement and herbal industries are unregulated in this country? Ingredients may not be present in amounts listed on the label and scientific evidence supporting their safety and use is often lacking.

## Maternal Infections

Although the placenta effectively filters out many infectious organisms, it does not prevent all disease-causing agents from reaching the unborn child. Some of these are known to cause fetal abnormalities (Table 3-3). Whether a fetus will be affected (and, if so, the resulting abnormality) depends on the particular disease and stage of pregnancy when the infection occurs. For example, a pregnant woman who develops rubella (German measles) during the first four to eight weeks following conception is at high risk for giving birth to an infant who may have heart problems and be deaf, blind, or both (an example of the extreme vulnerability of the fetus during its earliest weeks). *Note:* Rubella can be controlled if women who do not have natural immunity are immunized following a pregnancy or not less than three to four months prior to becoming pregnant.

**Table 3-3** Examples of Potentially Teratogenic Infectious Conditions

- Chicken pox
- Cytomegalovirus (CMV)
- Diabetes
- Fifth disease
- Herpes
- Human immunodeficiency virus (HIV)
- Mumps
- Rubella (German measles)
- Syphilis
- Toxoplasmosis

*Note*: Information about any of these infectious diseases can be found on the CDC website (*www.cdc.gov*).

© Cengage Learning®

Fortunately, only a small percentage of infants exposed to infectious agents experience abnormalities. It is still unknown why some fetuses are affected and others are not. What is reasonably certain is that pregnant women who are well nourished, have regular prenatal care, are generally healthy, and are free of addictive substances have a higher probability of giving birth to a strong and healthy infant.

# An Infant's Arrival: Labor and Delivery

For most women, childbirth is a natural process that follows months of anticipation and preparation. Several birthing options are available to families today, including birthing centers, hospitals, and home deliveries with physicians or certified nurse midwives in attendance. Although the fundamental labor and delivery process is similar for most mothers-to-be, the actual experience is often unique. Labor and delivery can occur prematurely, on time, or beyond a mother's expected due date, be long or short in duration, be considered relatively easy or difficult, and occur with or without complications.

The onset of labor is usually signaled by a number of physical changes. Approximately two weeks before labor begins, the mother may notice that she is carrying the infant lower in her abdomen. This occurs as the infant's head drops down into the birth canal in preparation for delivery and is commonly referred to as *lightening*. The mother also may note that the mild contractions (Braxton-Hicks) that she has experienced throughout her pregnancy are becoming stronger and more regular as they prepare the birth canal for delivery. When active labor begins, she may experience a small amount of bloody discharge as the mucus plug that has protected the birth canal opening for nine months becomes dislodged. Some mothers also have a leaking of amniotic fluid if the sac surrounding the fetus tears or breaks in the early stages of labor.

The normal birthing process is divided into three stages. The first and longest stage lasts approximately fourteen to seventeen hours for first-time mothers and six to eight hours for subsequent births. During this stage, contractions slowly cause the diameter of the **cervix** to expand (dilate) in preparation for delivery. Stage two lasts approximately thirty to ninety minutes and begins when the cervix is completely dilated and

**cervix** The lower portion of the uterus that opens into the vagina.

ends when the infant is delivered. Contractions become more intense and painful throughout this stage. When the infant is born, the umbilical cord is clamped, and the infant begins to function independently. Some medical researchers have suggested that clamping be delayed thirty to sixty seconds following birth, especially for low birth weight or premature infants, to reduce the incidence of anemia (Scheans, 2013). The third and final birthing stage begins after the infant arrives and ends when the placenta is delivered; this stage usually lasts only a few minutes.

The majority of births proceed normally and without complications. However, a small percentage of deliveries may require some form of medical intervention. In less than 5 percent of live births, the infant descends feet or buttocks first (rather than headfirst) into the birth canal. This situation may require a **cesarean section (C-section)** to be performed (Tully & Ball, 2013) (Figure 3-8). A C-section may also be necessary when labor does not progress, the mother's birth canal is too small, the umbilical cord prolapses, or a medical problem such as fetal distress develops. Medical intervention is sometimes used to assist the baby out of the birth canal. Forceps (a salad tong–like device) are placed around the infant's head and used to gently pull the baby out during contractions. Temporary bruises may be left on the baby's face or head, but these will fade within several days. Vacuum-assisted births are replacing the use of forceps in many hospitals today. A large plastic or rubber cap is fitted on the infant's head and suction is applied, creating gentle traction to aid the newborn's exit from the birth canal.

> ▶❚❚ **TeachSource** Video Connections
>
> © 2015 Cengage Learning®
>
> ### Newborn Assessment
>
> For nine months, the newborn relies on its mother for all essential needs—nutrients, oxygen, warmth, and protection. At birth, the infant arrives into an unfamiliar world, and the body immediately must take over many of these functions. Careful monitoring of the newborn's vital signs (such as heart rate and breathing) provides valuable information about how well she is making this transition. Respond to the following questions after you have watched the learning video
> *0–2 Years: Birth*:
>
> 1. How would you describe the newborn's appearance immediately following birth?
> 2. What is the Apgar scale, and how is the test administered?
> 3. What information does the Apgar score provide?
> 4. What does a low score indicate?

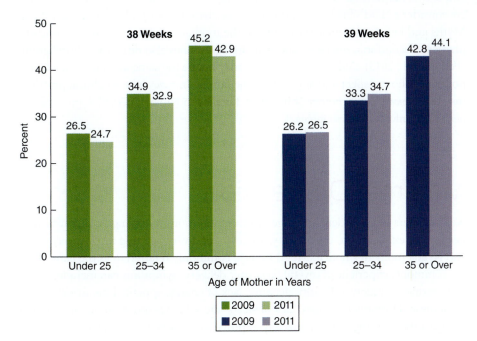

**Figure 3-8** Cesarean rate by maternal age.

Source: CDC/NCHS, National Vital Statistics System. Retrieved on February 4, 2014 from, http://www.cdc.gov/nchs/data/databriefs/db124.htm

**cesarean section (C-section)** The delivery of an infant through an incision in the mother's abdomen and uterus.

|  | 0 | 1 | 2 |
|---|---|---|---|
| **A**ppearance (skin color) | Bluish or pale | Pink, except extremities | Pink all over |
| **P**ulse | None | Fewer than 100 beats/minute | Greater than 100 beats/minute |
| **G**rimace (reflex response) | None | Makes some facial response | Strong response: cries, coughs, or sneezes |
| **A**ctivity (muscle tone) | Limp | Weak flexion of extremities | Active movement |
| **R**espiration (breathing) | None | Slow and/or irregular | Regular; strong cry |

Throughout the birth process, the infant is monitored closely for signs of distress. Heart rate is checked by using a stethoscope or ultrasound device (Doppler) or by placing a tiny electrode on the infant's head. Immediately following birth, the newborn's condition is assessed at one minute and again at five minutes, using the Apgar scoring system (Figure 3-9). The infant receives a score between 0 and 2 in each of five categories: appearance, pulse, grimace, activity, and respirations. A score of 8 or better is considered normal (Apgar, 1953). The Apgar scale provides a reliable measure of how well the infant is doing at the time, but it is not a predictor of future health or developmental problems.

Healthy mothers and infants typically are released from the hospital within one to two days following the birth. Mothers who have had a C-section or experienced health complications may remain in the hospital for several days longer. Infants born prematurely or LBW will remain hospitalized until they are healthy enough to go home.

Cultural differences can influence how a mother and her family perceive pregnancy and an infant's birth (Ma, Magnus, & Magnus, 2013). Some groups view pregnancy and delivery as normal events that require little special attention or recognition. Others consider a child's birth an experience to be shared by extended family members. Myths and beliefs about everything from the mother's diet to how she responds to physical discomforts, sexuality, and daily living routines also differ by cultural group (Ferrari et al., 2013). Although these views may not be the same as your own, it is important to show respect and support for the family. In cases where cultural practices may cause harm to the mother or her fetus, families should be directed to professional health and information resources.

# Maternal Depression

New mothers often undergo a range of mixed emotions following an infant's birth. Feelings of exhilaration, uncertainty, anxiety, and overwhelming fatigue may come and go at a moment's notice. Mood swings, commonly referred to as the *baby blues*, are commonly experienced several days after delivery. Symptoms can include weepiness, sadness, anxiety, difficulty sleeping, lack of energy, appetite loss, irritability, or all of these. Hormonal changes, lack of sleep, and added responsibilities are thought to trigger these feelings, which typically improve within several weeks. Compassionate support from family members and friends, moderate exercise, adequate rest, and a healthy diet can help ease this temporary discomfort. However, a doctor should be consulted if symptoms are severe or persist because this could be a sign of postpartum depression (PPD).

It is estimated that fewer than 10 to 15 percent of new mothers experience signs of PPD during the six months following delivery (Caplan & Whittemore, 2013; Huang et al., 2012) (Figure 3-10). Women who experience unintended pregnancy, poverty, domestic partner abuse, fetal loss, unhealthy behaviors (e.g., drinking, smoking, illicit drugs) during pregnancy, birth complications, and lack of social support are at increased risk for developing PPD (Nelson et al., 2013). Although the symptoms are similar to baby blues, they are far more serious and can include hallucinations, thoughts of harming the infant, hopelessness, and/or suicide. PPD can last three to twelve months and has been shown to interfere with the quality of maternal care and emotional attachment the mother establishes with her infant (Hayes, Goodman, & Carlson, 2013). It can also have an adverse effect on an infant's language and social-emotional development (Porritt et al., 2014).

Although PPD is a universal phenomenon, much of what is known about the disorder and its treatment is based on Western cultures. The reported rates of maternal depression are also highest among these groups. However, comparable symptoms and protective measures are described in cross-cultural literature (Huang et al., 2014; Callister, Beckstrand, & Corbett, 2010). For example, varying lengths of maternal and newborn confinement are practiced in many cultures to avoid harmful spirits and prevent illness. Somali women, for example, often wear garlic earrings following delivery to ward off the "evil eye." Women in Muslim and Arab cultures describe symptoms of PPD and attribute them to Jinn, or supernatural spirits that enter and take over the body (Hanely & Brown, 2013). As societies become increasingly diverse, it is important to understand the cultural differences that influence and shape the concept of motherhood.

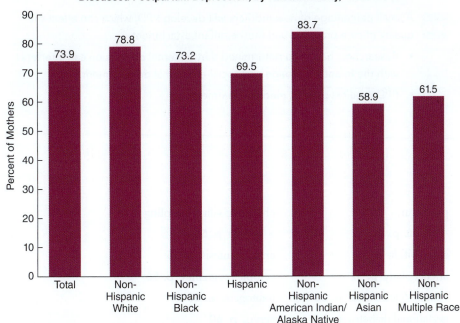

**Women with a Recent Live Birth Who Reported that a Health-Care Provider Discussed Postpartum Depression, by Race/Ethnicity,\* 2006–2008\*\***

*\*The sample of Native Hawaiians was too small to produce reliable results. \*\*Includes data from a total of 8 states and New York City; 7 states contributed all 3 years. Respondents completed surveys between 2 and 9 months postpartum.*

**Figure 3-10** Estimated incidence of postpartum depression.

Centers for Disease Control and Prevention, Pregnancy Risk Assessment Monitoring System, 2006–2008. Analysis conducted by the Maternal and Child Health Information Resource Center. Retrieved on February 4, 2014 from, http://www.mchb.hrsa.gov /whusa11/hstat/hsrmh /pages/231pds.html

# Summary

**3-1** A human pregnancy requires approximately 266 days (nine months) from conception until an infant is fully developed.

- Germinal stage—Zygote is formed; cell division begins and develops into a blastocyst.
- Embryonic stage—Embryo attaches to the uterine wall, cell division continues, the placenta develops, and all major organs and systems are formed.
- Fetal stage—Fetal systems continue to grow and mature; fetus gains weight and prepares for birth.

**3-2** The mother's general health, age, quality of diet, emotional state, and physical fitness influence healthy fetal development.

- Exposure to environmental factors (teratogens), such as certain infectious illnesses, alcohol, addictive drugs, smoking, and some medications (prescription and over-the-counter drugs) are known to have a harmful effect on fetal development.
- Mothers can take steps to improve their chances of having a healthy pregnancy and infant by obtaining routine prenatal care, maintaining good health, following a nutritious diet, gaining an appropriate amount of weight (not too much or too little), participating in daily physical activity, and maintaining a positive state of mental health.

**3-3** Substances capable of interfering with healthy fetal development include alcohol, cigarettes and secondhand smoke, addictive drugs, certain chemicals, pesticides, some medications, infectious agents, and radiation.

**3-4** Changes associated with impending delivery include lightening, contractions that increase in intensity and regularity, and bloody discharge. Some mothers also experience a leaking of amniotic fluid prior to or at the onset of labor.

**3-5** A small percentage of new mothers will develop PPD, which can affect the quality of care provided and mother-infant attachment.

- Researchers have also determined that maternal depression can interfere with the infant's language and social-emotional development.
- PPD requires prompt medical treatment.

# Key Terms

conception **p. 47**

genes **p. 47**

temperament **p. 47**

zygote **p. 47**

implantation **p. 49**

embryo **p. 49**

placenta **p. 49**

low birth weight (LBW) **p. 51**

premature
infant **p. 51**

spina bifida **p. 52**

anencephaly **p. 52**

cleft lip/cleft palate **p. 52**

gestational diabetes **p. 54**

ova **p. 54**

sonogram **p. 55**

chorionic villus sampling
(CVS) **p. 55**

amniocentesis **p. 55**

ectopic pregnancy **p. 55**

teratogens **p. 56**

cervix **p. 60**

cesarean section
(C-section) **p. 61**

# Apply What You Have Learned

## A. Case Study Connections

*Reread the developmental sketch about Anna and Miguel presented at the beginning of this chapter and answer the following questions:*

1. At what point is Anna likely to begin feeling the baby move?

2. What practices should Anna avoid during pregnancy to improve her chances of having a healthy infant?

3. What negative effects might Anna's smoking have on her pregnancy?

4. Which nutrients are especially important for Anna to include in her daily diet?

5. In what ways is Anna's Latina heritage influencing her pregnancy?

## B. Review Questions

1. Discuss three practices that promote a healthy pregnancy.

2. Describe three factors that appear to be hazardous to fetal development.

3. Identify one characteristic or change in fetal development that occurs during each month of pregnancy.

4. What role(s) does the placenta perform during pregnancy?

5. What characteristics would you expect to observe in a child who has FAS? Explain how this condition can be prevented.

## C. Your Turn: Chapter to Practice

1. Select one of the following cultural groups: Hispanic/Latina, Asian, Native American, Middle Eastern, African American, or other group of personal or local interest. Interview several mothers to learn more about their views on pregnancy, unique practices associated with pregnancy and birthing, and the role that children play in a family. Share your findings with the class.

2. Make arrangements to observe at a local WIC clinic. What services do they offer in addition to nutrition? Who is eligible to receive services? Write a brief paper summarizing your experience.

3. Organize and/or participate in a local food drive. Note how many food recipients are pregnant women and young children. What do these numbers suggest?

4. As a group, develop a one-hour class on practices to promote healthy fetal development for mothers who are pregnant or contemplating pregnancy. Make arrangements to present the class in a convenient and accessible community location.

# Online Resources

### March of Dimes

This organization is devoted to supporting families and fostering healthy infant births. Information about positive lifestyle practices for parents to follow before, during, and after pregnancy can be accessed on this site.

### Medline Plus

The National Institutes of Health (NIH) provide an abundance of information on topics related to reproduction and pregnancy.

## Office of Women's Health

Extensive information about pregnancy, prenatal care, birthing, breast-feeding, and family legislation are provided in terms that are easy to understand.

# References

American College of Obstetricians and Gynecologists (ACOG). (2013). Weight gain during pregnancy. Retrieved on February 2, 2014, from http://www.acog.org/Resources_And_Publications/Committee_Opinions/Committee_on_Obstetric_Practice/Weight_Gain_During_Pregnancy.

Apgar, V. (1953). Proposal for a new method of evaluation of the newborn infant. *Current Researches in Anesthesia & Analgesia*, 32(4), 260–267.

Balasch, J. & Gratacós, E. (2012). Delayed childbearing: Effects on fertility and the outcome of pregnancy. *Current Opinion in Obstetrics & Gynecology*, 24(3), 187–193.

Behnke, M., & Smith, V. (2013). Prenatal substance abuse: Short- and long-term effects on the exposed fetus. *Pediatrics*, 131(3), e1009–e1024. doi:10.1542/peds.2012-3931.

Biggs, M., Combellick, S., Arons, A., & Brindis, C. (2013). Educational barriers, social isolation, and stable romantic relationships among pregnant immigrant Latina teens. *Hispanic Health Care International*, 11(1), 38–46(9).

Bilder, D., Pinborough-Zimmerman, J., Bakian, A., Miller, J., Dorius, J., Nangle, B., & McMahon, W. (2013). Prenatal and perinatal factors associated with intellectual disability. *American Journal on Intellectual and Developmental Disabilities*, 118(2), 156–176.

Bower, C., (2013). Prevention of neural tube defects with folate. *Journal of Paediatrics & Child Health*, 49(1), 2–4.

Branum, A., Bailey, R., & Singer, B. (2013). Dietary supplement use and folate status during pregnancy in the United States. *Journal of Nutrition*, 143(4), 486–492.

Brown, H., & Graves, C. (2013). Smoking and marijuana use in pregnancy. *Clinical Obstetrics & Gynecology*, 56(1), 107–113.

Callister, L., Beckstrand, R., & Corbett, C. (2010). Postpartum depression and culture: Pesado Corazón. *The American Journal of Maternal/Child Nursing*, 35(5), 254–261.

Caplan, S., & Whittemore, R. (2013). Barriers to treatment engagement for depression among Latinas. *Issues in Mental Health Nursing*, 34(6), 412–424.

Centers for Disease Control and Prevention (CDC). (2010). Timing of prenatal care initiation by maternal race/ethnicity. National Center for Health Statistics. Retrieved on February 2, 2014 from http:/mchb.hrsa.gov/chusa/chusa12/hsfu/pages/pc.html.

Dante, G., Pedrielli, G., Annessi, E., & Facchinetti, F. (2013). Herb remedies during pregnancy: A systematic review of controlled clinical trials. *Journal of Maternal-Fetal and Neonatal Medicine*, 26(3), 306–312.

Davis, K., Gagnier, K., Moore, T., & Todorow, M. (2013). Cognitive aspects of fetal alcohol spectrum disorder. *Wiley Interdisciplinary Reviews: Cognitive Science*, 4(1), 81–92.

de Graaf, J., Steegers, E., & Bonsel, G. (2013). Inequalities in perinatal and maternal health. *Current Opinion in Obstetrics & Gynecology*, 25(2), 98–108.

Deng, K., Liu, Z., Lin, Y., Mu, D., Chen, X., Li, J., …, & Zhu, J. (2013). Periconceptional paternal smoking and the risk of congenital heart defects: A case-control study. *Birth Defects Research Part A: Clinical and Molecular Teratology*, 97(4), 210–216.

Driscoll, C., Mason, R., Chan, H., Jacob, D., & Pirrone, N. (2013). Mercury as a global pollutant: Sources, pathways, and effects. *Environmental Science & Technology*, 47(10), 4967–4983.

Environmental Protection Agency (EPA). (2013). *Fish consumption advisories*. Retrieved on February 3, 2014 from http://www.epa.gov/hg/advisories.htm.

Ferrari, R., Siega-Riz, A., Evenson, K., Moos, M., & Carrier, K. (2013). A qualitative study of women's perceptions of provider advice about diet and physical activity during pregnancy. *Patient Education & Counseling*, 91(3), 372–377.

Grandel, M., Borrell, A., Garcia-Posadal, R., Borobio, V., Muñoz, M., Creuss, M., …, & Balasch, J. (2012). The effect of maternal age on chromosomal anomaly rate and spectrum in recurrent miscarriage. *Human Reproduction*, 27(10), 3109–3117.

Hanely, J., & Brown, A. (2013). Cultural variations in interpretation of postnatal illness: Jinn possession amongst Muslim communities. *Community Mental Health Journal*. Published online August 17, 2013. doi 10.1007/s10597-013-9640-4.

Hansen, M., Kurinczuk, J., Milne, E., de Kerk, N., & Bower, C. (2013). Assisted reproductive technology and birth defects: A systematic review and meta-analysis. *Human Reproduction Update*, 19(4), 330–353.

Hayes, L., Goodman, S., & Carlson, E. (2013). Maternal antenatal depression and infant disorganized attachment at 12 months. *Attachment & Human Development*, 15(2), 133–153.

Hepper, P., Dornan, J., & Lynch, C. (2012). Sex differences in fetal habituation. *Developmental Science*, 15(3), 373–383.

Huang, C., Costeines, J., Kaufman, J., & Ayala, C. (2014). Parenting stress, social support, and depression for ethnic minority adolescent mothers: Impact on child development. *Journal of Child and Family Studies*, 23(2), 255–262.

Huang, Z., Lewin, A., Mitchell, S., & Zhang, J. (2012). Variations in the relationship between maternal depression, maternal sensitivity, and child attachment by race/ethnicity and nativity: Findings from a nationally representative cohort study. *Maternal & Child Health Journal*, 16(1), 40–50.

Jeric, M., Roje, D., Medic, N., Strinic, T., Mestrovic, Z., & Vulic, M. (2013). Maternal pre-pregnancy underweight and fetal growth in relation to Institute of Medicine recommendations for gestational weight gain. *Early Human Development*, 89(5), 277–281.

Jedrychowski, W., Perera, F., Tang, P., Rauh, V., Majewska, R., Mroz, W., …, & Jacek, R. (2013). The relationship between prenatal exposure to airborne polycyclic aromatic hydrocarbons (PAHs) and PAH-DNA adducts in cord blood. *Journal of Exposure Science & Environmental Epidemiology*, 23, 371–377.

Kandler, C., Held, L., Kroll, C., Bergeler, A., Riemann, R., & Angleitner, A. (2012). Genetic links between temperamental traits of the regulative theory of temperament and the Big Five: A multitrait-multimethod twin study. *Journal of Individual Differences*, 33(4), 197–204.

Kessler, R., & Bromet, E. (2013). The epidemiology of depression across cultures. *Annual Review of Public Health*, 34, 119–138.

Kozuki, N., Lee, A., Silveira, M., Victora, C., Adair, L., Humphrey, J., …, and Child Health Epidemiology Reference Group Small-for-Gestational-Age-Preterm Birth Working Group. (2013). The associations of birth intervals with small-for-gestational-age, preterm, and neonatal and infant mortality: A meta-analysis. *BMC Public Health*, 13(Suppl 3):S3 doi:10.1186/1471-2458-13-S3-S3.

Lampi, K., Hinkka-Yli-Salomäki, S., Lehti, V., Helenius, H., Gissler, M., Brown, A., & Sourander, A. (2013). Parental age and risk of autism spectrum disorders in a Finnish national birth cohort. *Journal of Autism & Developmental Disorders*, 43(11), 2526–2535.

Liao, G., Gronowski, A., & Zhao, Z. (2014). Non-invasive prenatal testing using cell-free fetal DNA in maternal circulation. *Clinica Chimica Acta*, 428(20), 44–50.

Loomans, E., van Dijk, A., Vrijkotte, T., Eijsden, M., Stronks, K, Gemke, R., & Van den Bergh, B. (2013). Psychosocial stress during pregnancy is related to adverse birth outcomes: Results from a large multi-ethnic community-based birth cohort. *European Journal of Public Health*, 23(3), 485–491.

Ma, P., Magnus, M., & Magnus, J. (2013). Perception of pregnancy-related health issues among Arab women living in the United States. *Journal of Immigrant and Minority Health*, 15(2), 273–280.

Makelarski, J., Romitti, P., Sun, L., Burns, T., Druschel, C., Suarez, L., …, & the National Birth Defects Prevention Study. (2013). Periconceptional maternal alcohol consumption and neural tube defects. *Birth Defects Research Part A: Clinical and Molecular Teratology*, 97(3), 152–160.

Malabarey, O., Balayla, J., Klam, S., Shrim, A., & Abenhaim, H. (2012). Pregnancies in young adolescent mothers: A population-based study on 37 million births. *Journal of Pediatric & Adolescent Gynecology*, 25(2), 98–102.

Malagoli, C., Crespi, C., Rodolfi, R., Signorelli, C., Poli, M., Zanichelli, P., …, & Vinceti, M. (2012). Maternal exposure to magnetic fields from high-voltage power lines and the risk of birth defects. *Bioelectromagnetics*, 33(5), 405–409.

Meeker, J., & Benedict, M. (2013). Infertility, pregnancy loss, and adverse birth outcomes in relation to maternal secondhand tobacco smoke exposure. *Current Women's Health Reviews*, 9(1), 41–49.

Moon, C., Lagercrantz, H., & Kuhl, P. (2013). Language experienced in utero affects vowel perception after birth: A two-country study. *Acta Paediatrica*, 102(2), 156–160.

Muenssinger, J., Matuz, T., Schleger, F., Kiefer-Schmidt, I., Goelz, R., Waker-Gussmann, …, & Preissl, H. (2013). Auditory habituation in the fetus and neonate: An fMEG study. *Developmental Science*, 16(2), 287–295.

Natalucci, G., Schneider, M., Werner, H., Caflisch, J., Bucher, H., Jenni, O., & Latal, B. (2013). Development of neuromotor functions in very low-birth-weight children from six to 10 years of age: Patterns of change. *Acta Paediatrica*, 102(8), 809–814.

Nelson, D., Freeman, M., Johnson, N., McIntire, D., & Leveno, K. (2013). A prospective study of postpartum depression in 17 648 parturients. *Journal of Maternal-Fetal and Neonatal Medicine*, 26(12), 1155–1161.

O'Leary, C., Taylor, C., Zubrick, S., Kurinczuk, J., & Bower, C. (2013). Prenatal alcohol exposure and educational achievement in children aged 8–9 years. *Pediatrics*, 132(2), e468–475.

Painter, R., Roseboom, T., & de Rooij, S. (2012). Long-term effects of prenatal stress and glucocorticoid exposure. *Birth Defects Research Part C: Embryo Today: Reviews*, 96(4), 315–324.

Partanen, E., Kujala, T., Näätänen, R., Liitola, A., Sambeth, A., & Huotilainen, M. (2013). Learning-induced neural plasticity of speech processing before birth. *Proceedings of the National Academy of Sciences of the United States of America*, 110(37), 15145–15150. doi: 10.1073/pnas.1302159110.

Patti, M. E. (2013). Reducing maternal weight improves offspring metabolism and alters (or modulates) methylation. *Proceedings of the National Academy of Sciences*, 110(32), 12859–12860.

Porritt, L., Zinser, M., Bachorowski, J. & Kaplan, P. (2014). Depression diagnoses and fundamental frequency-based acoustic cues in maternal infant-directed speech. *Language Learning & Development*, 10(1), 51–67.

Scheans, P. (2013). Delayed cord clamping: A collaborative practice to improve outcomes. *Neonatal Network*, 32(5), 369–373.

Silva, D., Colvin, L., Hagemann, E., & Bower, C. (2014). Environmental risk factors by gender associated with attention-deficit/hyperactivity disorder. *Pediatrics*, 133(1), e14–22. doi: 10.1542/peds.2013-1434.

Suter, M., Anders, A., & Aagaard, K. (2013). Maternal smoking as a model for environmental epigenetic changes affecting birthweight and fetal programming. *Molecular Human Reproduction*, 19(1), 1–6.

Treyvaud, K., Ure, A., Doyle, L., Lee, K., Rogers, C., Kidokoro, H., …, & Anderson, P. (2013). Psychiatric outcomes at age seven for very preterm children: Rates and predictors. *Journal of Child Psychology & Psychiatry*, 54(7), 772–779.

Tully, K., & Ball, H. (2013). Misrecognition of need: Women's experiences of and explanations for undergoing cesarean delivery. *Social Science & Medicine*, 85, 103–111. doi: 10.1016/j.socscimed.2013.02.039.

Vaiserman, A. (2013). Long-term health consequences of early-life exposure to substance abuse: An epigenetic perspective. *Journal of Developmental Origins of Health and Disease*, 4(4), 269–279.

Voegtline, K., Costigan, K., Pater, H., & DiPietro, J. (2013). Near-term fetal response to maternal spoken voice. *Infant Behavior & Development*, 36(4), 526–533.

Wendell, A. (2013). Overview and epidemiology of substance abuse in pregnancy. *Clinical Obstetrics & Gynecology*, 56(1), 91–96.

Witt, W., Cheng, E., Wisk, L., Litzelman, K., Chatterjee, D., Mandell, K., & Wakeel, F. (2014). Maternal stressful life events prior to conception and the impact on infant birth weight in the United States. *American Journal of Public Health*, 104(S1), S81–S89.

## Learning Objectives

*After reading this chapter, you will be able to:*

**4-1** Define the term *reflexive motor activity* and provide examples that are observable in newborns.

**4-2** Explain why the statement "Babies can't learn" is a myth, and describe activities that promote infants' cognitive development.

**4-3** Discuss the ways in which infants communicate with adults during each developmental stage described in this chapter.

**4-4** Describe the phenomenon known as *stranger anxiety.*

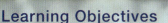 **NAEYC Standards Linked to Chapter Content**

**1a, 1b, and 1c:** Promoting child development and learning

**2a and 2c:** Building family and community relationships

**3c and 3d:** Observing, documenting, and assessing to support young children and families

**4a, 4b, 4c and 4d:** Using developmentally effective approaches

**5c:** Using content knowledge to build meaningful curriculum

Anna and Miguel beamed as they watched their infant son, Juan, sleep. Anna is grateful that her pregnancy went smoothly and that Juan is healthy despite having arrived almost two weeks early. Their family and friends tell them what a "good baby" Juan seems to be. He sleeps three to four hours between feedings, follows their every movement, is discovering his fingers and toes, and often falls asleep peacefully in his father's arms.

Juan's parents cannot believe that their son will be two months old next week. When placed on his stomach, he coos, is beginning to pick up his head, and appears to study the brightly colored geometric pictures his mother hung outside the crib. Juan also is attempting to reach for and grasp small stuffed toys that his parents offer him. Miguel enjoys reading to Juan in the evening while Anna goes for a short jog. Both parents are fascinated by how quickly Juan seems to be learning each day. Their pediatrician is also pleased with Juan's rate of growth and developmental progress.

Cultura/Liam Norris/Riser/Getty Images

Anna's maternity leave will end soon, and she finds it difficult to think about leaving Juan and returning to her job at the bank. She has arranged to work only half-time for the next two months, but her schedule will involve alternating mornings and afternoons each week. Anna and Miguel have visited a number of neighborhood child care centers but have been unable to find one that is acceptable or that will take Juan on a part-time basis. They have placed his name on several waiting lists and are hoping there will soon be an opening or that they can locate an accredited and affordable program not too far from Anna's workplace. In the meantime, Miguel's mother, who has raised four children of her own, has agreed to care for Juan temporarily until Anna returns to work full-time.

## Ask Yourself

- In what ways are Juan and his parents beginning to form a strong emotional bond with each other?
- What activities can Anna and Miguel begin doing now to encourage Juan's future language development?

# The Newborn (Birth to One Month)

The healthy newborn infant is truly amazing. Within moments of birth, he begins to adapt to an outside world that is radically different from the one experienced **in utero**. The newborn's systems for breathing, eating, eliminating, and regulating body temperature are functional and ready to take over at the time of birth. However, the infant remains completely dependent on adults for survival because these systems are still relatively immature and require time to develop fully.

The newborn's motor development (movement) is both reflexive and protective. There is no voluntary control of the body during the early weeks. Although newborn infants sleep most of the time, they do not lack awareness. They are sensitive to their environment and have unique methods of responding to it. Crying is their primary method for communicating needs and emotions. Perceptual and cognitive abilities are present, although they are primitive and relatively difficult to distinguish from one another during the initial weeks following birth (Streri et al., 2013).

**in utero** Latin term for "in the mother's uterus."

## Developmental Profiles and Growth Patterns

### Growth and Physical Characteristics

The newborn's physical characteristics are distinct from those of a slightly older infant. All infants are born with relatively light-colored skin that gradually darkens to a shade characteristic of their genetic makeup. At birth, the newborn's skin usually appears quite wrinkled. Within the first few days that follow, it becomes dry and is likely to peel, especially around the hands, ankles, and feet. Infants' skin

## Developmental Profiles and Growth Patterns *(continued)*

remains sensitive and prone to rashes and acnelike breakouts for several months. Some newborns may develop **jaundice** during the first days or weeks following birth.

The newborn's eyelids may appear swollen and closed for several days following birth, but this soon disappears. Breast and genital enlargement is common in both male and female infants and is caused by maternal hormones that have been transferred prior to birth. The infant's head may have an unusual shape as a result of the delivery process, but it gradually resumes a normal form within weeks. Hair color and amount vary; some infants are born with negligible hair, while others may have an abundance of it. Initial hair is often lost during the early weeks and replaced with new growth that may have a different texture and color. Additional physical characteristics include the following:

- Weighs approximately 6.5–9 pounds (3.0–4.1 kg) at birth; females weigh approximately 7 pounds (3.2 kg), and males weigh approximately 7.5 pounds (3.4 kg).

- Loses between 5 and 7 percent of birth weight in the days immediately following delivery.

- Gains an average of 5–6 ounces (0.14–0.17 kg) per week during the first month.

- Is approximately 18–21 inches (45.7–53.3 cm) in length at birth.

- Breathes at a rate of approximately thirty to fifty respirations per minute; breathing can be somewhat irregular in both rhythm and rate.

- Chest appears small, cylindrical, and nearly the same size as the head.

- Normal body temperature ranges from 96°F–99°F (35.6°C–37.2°C); fluctuations are normal during the early weeks, and then temperature stabilizes as the system matures and a fat layer develops beneath the skin.

- Skin is sensitive to touch, especially on the infant's hands and around the mouth.

- Head appears large in proportion to the body and accounts for nearly one-quarter of the total body length.

- Head circumference averages 12.5–14.5 inches (31.7–36.8 cm) at birth (Figure 4-1).

- "Soft" spots (called **fontanels**) are located on the top (anterior) and back (posterior) of the head (Figure 4-2).

- Tongue appears large in proportion to the mouth.

- Cries without tears.

- Eyes are extremely sensitive to light.

- Sees only outlines and shapes; is unable to focus on objects more than 8–10 inches (20.3–25.4 cm) away (AOA, 2014).

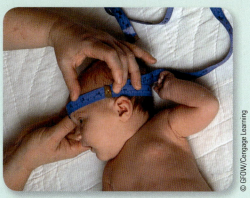

© GFOW/Cengage Learning

**Figure 4-1**  **Head circumference is measured to monitor brain growth.**

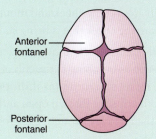

Anterior fontanel

Posterior fontanel

**Figure 4-2**  **Location of fontanels.**

## Developmental Profiles and Growth Patterns (continued)

### Motor Development

The newborn's primitive motor skills are purely reflexive movements or automatic responses that are designed for protection and survival. Sucking, for example, ensures that the infant obtains critical nutrients. During the coming weeks, the infant gradually develops some purposeful or voluntary behaviors as the central nervous system matures and several of the early reflexes begin to fade away. Any failure of reflexes to fade according to schedule may be an early indication of neurological problems (Konicarova & Bob, 2013; Futagi et al., 2013). During the first month, the typically developing infant exhibits the following behaviors:

- Engages in motor activity that is primarily reflexive (Figure 4-3):

| **Appears** | swallow,* gag,* cough,* yawn,* blink suck rooting Moro (startle) grasp stepping plantar elimination tonic neck reflex (TNR) | Landau tear* (cries with tears) | parachute palmar grasp pincer grasp | | | | |
|---|---|---|---|---|---|---|---|
| **(Age)** | (birth) | (1–4 mos) | (4–8 mos) | (8–12 mos) | (12–18 mos) | (18–24 mos) | (3–4 years) |
| **Disappears** | | grasp suck (becomes voluntary) step root tonic neck reflex (TNR) | Moro (startle) | palmar grasp plantar reflex | Landau | parachute | elimination (becomes voluntary) |

\* Permanent; present throughout person's lifetime.

Figure 4-3  **Summary of reflexes.**

- Swallowing, sucking, gagging, coughing, yawning, blinking, and elimination reflexes are present at birth.

- The rooting reflex is triggered by gently touching the sensitive skin around the cheek and mouth; the infant turns toward the cheek that is being stroked.

- The Moro (startle) reflex is set off by a sudden loud noise or touch, such as bumping of the crib or quick lowering of the infant's position (as if dropping); in this reflex, both arms are thrown open and away from the body, then quickly brought back together over the chest.

- The grasping reflex occurs when the infant tightly curls her fingers around an object placed in her hand.

- The stepping reflex involves the infant moving the feet up and down in walking-like movements when held upright with feet touching a firm surface (Figure 4-4).

© GFDW/Cengage Learning

Figure 4-4  **Stepping reflex.**

## Developmental Profiles and Growth Patterns *(continued)*

- The tonic neck reflex (TNR) occurs when the infant, in supine (face-up) position, extends the arm and leg on the same side toward which the head is turned, while the opposite arm and leg are flexed (pulled in toward the body). This is sometimes called the *fencing position* (Figure 4-5).

- The plantar reflex is initiated when pressure is placed against the ball of the infant's foot, causing the toes to curl.

- Maintains "fetal" position (with the back flexed or rounded, extremities held close to the body, and knees drawn up), especially when asleep.

- Holds hands in a fist, but does not reach for objects.

- When held in a prone (facedown) position, the infant's head falls lower than the horizontal line of the body, with hips flexed and arms and legs extending downward (Figure 4-6).

- Has good muscle tone in the upper body when supported under the arms.

- Turns head from side to side when placed in a prone position.

- **Pupils** dilate (enlarge) and constrict (become smaller) in response to light.

- Eyes do not always work together and may appear crossed at times.

- Attempts to track (follow) objects that are out of his direct line of vision; unable to coordinate eye and hand movements.

© GFOW/Cengage Learning

Figure 4-5  **The tonic neck reflex (TNR).**

Figure 4-6  **Prone suspension.**

## Perceptual-Cognitive Development

The newborn's perceptual-cognitive skills are designed to capture and hold the attention of family and caregivers and to gain some sense of the surrounding environment. Hearing is the most well developed of the senses and is nearly equivalent to that of an adult's. Newborns are able to distinguish and respond differently to various sounds; they are especially responsive to their mother's voice (Grossman, 2013). They often can be soothed with quiet sounds (cooing or humming) and movements (rocking or swaying). Newborns are also responsive to touch, with the skin around the mouth and hands being especially sensitive. Vision is present, although it is quite limited and will take several years to develop fully. Newborns see only the outline of an object (including faces) and are not able to detect any of its detail (AOA, 2013). For this reason, they are especially attracted to high-contrast (black-and-white) geometric designs. They are able to focus both eyes briefly on an object (especially a face) that is close and moving slowly (Wagner et al., 2013).

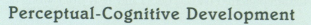

**pupil** The small, dark, central portion of the eye.

## Developmental Profiles and Growth Patterns *(continued)*

From the earliest days of life, newborns are absorbing information through all their senses and learning from what they see, hear, touch, taste, and smell. Thus, the newborn's cognitive behaviors can be characterized as being purely reflexive. They take the form of sucking, startle responses, grimacing, flailing of arms and legs, and uncontrolled eye movements, all of which overlap with perceptual responses. During the first month, the infant does the following:

- Blinks her eyes in response to a fast-approaching object.

- Follows a slowly moving object through a complete 180° arc.

- Follows an object moved vertically if it is close to his face [i.e., 10–15 inches (25.4–38.1 cm)].

- Continues looking about, even in the dark.

- Begins to study her own hand when lying in the TNR position.

- Hears as well at birth as do most adults (with the exception of quiet sounds); hearing is more acute than vision.

- Prefers to listen to his mother's voice rather than a stranger's; opens eyes and looks toward the mother.

- Often synchronizes body movements to the speech patterns of the parents or primary caregivers.

- Distinguishes some tastes; shows preference for sweet liquids.

- Has a keen sense of smell at birth; turns toward preferred (sweet) odors and away from strong or unpleasant odors (Grossman, 2013).

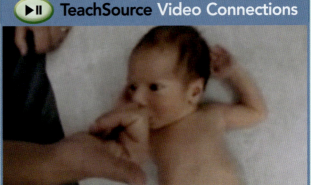

▶❚❚ **TeachSource** Video Connections

© 2016 Cengage Learning®

**Newborn Reflex Development**

Initially, newborns are not capable of purposeful movement. However, this does not suggest that they are passive individuals. Reflexes serve important protective functions and gradually give way to increasingly complex motor development. Respond to the following questions after you have watched the learning video *0–2 Years: The Newborn and Reflex Development:*

1. Which involuntary reflexes are considered to be critical for the infant's survival?

2. What does it indicate when one or more of the infant's reflexes are absent, do not fade at the correct time, or reappear later?

3. How does the infant's reflex system affect early cognitive development?

### Speech and Language Development

The beginnings of speech and language development can be identified in several of the newborn's reflexes. These include the bite–release action, which occurs when the infant's gums are rubbed; the rooting reflex; and, the sucking reflex. In addition, the newborn communicates directly and indirectly in a number of other ways:

- Communicates primarily by crying and fussing at this stage.

- Reacts to loud noises by blinking, moving, stopping a movement, shifting eyes about, or exhibiting a startle response.

- Shows a preference for certain sounds, such as quiet music and human voices, by calming down or quieting.

## Developmental Profiles and Growth Patterns *(continued)*

- Turns head to locate voices and other nearby sounds.
- Makes occasional sounds other than crying.

### Social-Emotional Development

Newborns possess a variety of built-in social skills. They are able to indicate needs and distress (by crying or fussing) and to detect some caregiver reactions (Streri, Coulon, & Guellaï, 2013). For example, an infant may become agitated, tense, or both when she senses that an adult is angry, frustrated, or hurried. The infant thrives on feelings of security and soon displays a sense of attachment to primary caregivers. The newborn exhibits the following:

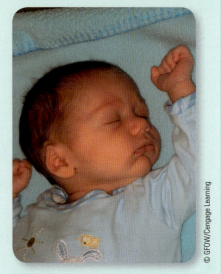

Figure 4-7 **Newborns spend most of their time sleeping.**

- Experiences a brief period of calm alertness immediately following birth; gazes at the parents and listens to their voices.
- Sleeps 17–19 hours per day; is gradually awake and responsive for longer periods (Figure 4-7).
- Likes to be held close and cuddled when awake; opens eyes and looks toward the mother.
- Shows qualities of individuality; each infant varies in how she responds or fails to respond to similar situations.
- Begins to establish an emotional attachment, or a **bonding** relationship, with the parents and primary caregivers; opens eyes; relaxes body tension.
- Develops a gradual sense of security and trust with the parents and primary caregivers; is able to sense caregiver differences and responds accordingly. For example, an infant may become tense with an adult who is unfamiliar or uncomfortable with him.

## DAILY ROUTINES

### Eating

- Takes six to ten feedings, totaling approximately 18–22 ounces (532–660 ml) per 24 hours at the beginning of this period; later, the number of feedings decreases to five to six, while the total amount consumed increases to approximately 30 ounces (887 ml).
- Drinks 2–4 ounces (59–118 ml) of breast milk or formula per feeding; takes 25–30 minutes to complete a feeding; may fall asleep toward the end.
- Expresses the need for food by crying.
- Benefits from being fed in an upright position; this practice reduces the risk of choking and of developing ear infections (Marotz, 2015).

**bonding** The establishment of a close, loving relationship between an infant and adults (usually the mother and father); sometimes called *attachment.*

## DAILY ROUTINES *(continued)*

### Toileting, Bathing, and Dressing

- Signals the need for a diaper change by crying. (If crying does not stop when diaper is changed, another cause, such as hunger or other discomfort, should be sought.)

- Enjoys bath; keeps eyes open, coos, and relaxes body tension when placed in warm water.

- Expresses displeasure (fusses, cries) when clothes are pulled over head (hence, it is best to avoid over-the-head clothes).

- Prefers to be wrapped firmly (swaddled) in a blanket; coos, stops crying, and relaxes muscle tension; swaddling seems to foster a sense of security and comfort.

- Has one to four bowel movements per day.

### Sleeping

- Begins to sleep four to six periods per 24 hours after the first few days following birth; one of these might be 5–7 hours in length.

- Cries sometimes before falling asleep (usually stops if the baby is held and rocked briefly).

- *Placing baby on her back only, and on a firm mattress, when sleeping reduces the risk of sudden infant death syndrome (SIDS). Remove all pillows, fluffy blankets, bumper pads, toys, and other soft items from the crib or sleeping area. Dress the infant lightly to avoid overheating. Pacifier use during sleep also has been shown to reduce the incidence of SIDS* (CDC, 2013).

### Play and Social Activities

- Prefers light and brightness; may fuss if turned away from a light source.

- Stares at faces in close visual range [10–12 inches (25.4–30.5 cm)].

- Signals the need for social stimulation by crying; stops when picked up or put in an infant seat close to voices and movement.

- Is content to lie on his back much of the time.

- Needs to be forewarned (e.g., touched or talked to) before being picked up to avoid being startled.

- Enjoys lots of touching and holding; however, may become fussy with too much handling or overstimulation.

- Enjoys the en face (face-to-face) position (Lavelli & Fogel, 2013).

## learning activities to promote **brain development**

Newborns begin learning from the moment they are born. Their primary mode of learning is sensory—soothing voices, gentle handling, quiet music, or familiar smells associated with nourishment. They are fascinated with faces, although they are not able to see them in detail.

## learning activities *(continued)*

### Developmentally appropriate applications for families and teachers:

- Respond with gentle and dependable attention to an infant's cries so she feels secure and begins to learn to trust. (Infants always cry for a reason; crying signals a need.) Stroking the skin gently may help soothe and relax the infant.

- Make eye contact when the infant is in an alert state. Hold your face close [10–15 inches (25.4–38 cm)] to the infant's so she can see it. Make faces, or stick out and wiggle your tongue; both are activities that infants often imitate. (Imitation is an important avenue for early learning.)

- Talk and sing to the infant often and in a normal voice during feedings, diapering, and bathing activities; vary your voice tone and rhythm of speech.

- Play quiet background music; music can have a calming effect (for caregivers also) and has been shown to improve infant feeding and sleeping patterns.

- Show delight in the baby's responsiveness: smile, laugh, and comment. (Mutual responsiveness and social turn-taking will be the bases for all teaching and learning in the months and years ahead.)

- Show the baby simple pictures (as previously noted, infants are attracted to high-contrast, black-and-white geometric designs and faces); gently move a stuffed animal or toy into the baby's visual pathway approximately 10–15 inches (25–37.5 cm) from the face to encourage visual tracking; hang toys or a mobile within the baby's visual range (and change the positioning often—novelty increases interest).

- Take cues from the infant; too much stimulation can be as distressing as too little; stop activities temporarily if the baby begins to cry, becomes fussy, or loses interest.

**TeachSource Digital Download**

## developmental **alerts**

**Did You Know**

...that suffocation is the number one cause of unintentional death among infants younger than one year?

Check with a health care provider or early childhood specialist if, by one month of age, the infant does *not*:

- Show alarm or startle responses to loud noise.

- Suck and swallow with ease.

- Increase height, weight, and head circumference.

- Grasp with equal strength in both hands.

- Make eye contact when awake and being held.

- Roll the head from side to side when placed on stomach.

- Express needs and emotions with distinctive cries and patterns of vocalizations that can be distinguished from one another.

- Stop crying or become soothed (relaxed) most times when picked up and held.

**Note:** Cultural differences may alter the timetable when some developmental skills are acquired. Expanded Developmental Alerts Checklists appear in Appendix A and also are available as digital downloads.

1 to 4
months

## safety **concerns**

Before the baby arrives, be sure to complete first aid and cardiopulmonary resuscitation (CPR) courses. Always be aware of new safety issues as the infant continues to grow and develop.

### Burns

- Never heat bottles in a microwave oven; hot spots can form in the liquid and burn the infant's mouth.
- Set the temperature of the hot water heater so that it is no higher than 120°F (49°C).
- Always check the water temperature before bathing an infant. Infants have thinner skin that burns in a matter of seconds.

### Choking

- Learn CPR.
- Always hold the infant in an upright position while feeding; do not prop bottles.

### Suffocation

- Provide a firm mattress that fits crib snugly to prevent the infant from becoming wedged in open cracks.

- *Always put infants to sleep on their back;* this practice reduces the risk of SIDS. Tuck the bottom edges of a light blanket under the bottom end of the mattress. Remove all soft items from the baby's crib (e.g., fluffy blankets, bumper pads, stuffed animals, or pillows).
- Do not use infant sleep positioners or sling carriers.
- Install smoke and carbon monoxide detectors near the infant's room.

### Transportation

- Always use an approved, rear-facing carrier installed in the vehicle's back seat whenever transporting an infant. Check the Consumer Product Safety Commission's website for safety feature recommendations and recalls; always install the carrier according to the manufacturer's guidelines.

## One to Four Months

During these early months, the wonders of infancy continue to unfold. Growth proceeds at a rapid pace. Body systems are fairly well stabilized, with temperature, breathing patterns, and heart rate becoming more regular. Motor skills improve as strength and voluntary muscle control increase. Longer periods of wakefulness encourage the infant's social-emotional development. Social responsiveness begins to appear as infants practice and enjoy using their eyes to explore the environment (Frank, Vul, & Saxe, 2012). They soon are able to maintain eye contact, smile momentarily, and imitate simple facial expressions. As social awareness develops, the infant continues to establish a sense of trust and emotional attachment to parents and primary caregivers.

Although crying remains a primary mode for communicating and gaining adult attention, more complex communication skills are beginning to emerge. Different crying patterns are used to express distinct needs (e.g., discomfort, hunger, fatigue, frustration). Infants soon find great pleasure in imitating the speech sounds and gestures of others (Oller et al., 2013). Cooing and babbling often begin around two months of age and represent an important step in the acquisition of language and give-and-take social interaction with others.

Learning occurs continuously throughout the infant's waking hours as newly acquired skills are used for exploring and gathering information about a still new and unfamiliar environment. It is important to remember that perceptual, cognitive, and motor developments are closely interrelated and nearly impossible to differentiate during these early months. However, the rate and attainment of developmental skills is also highly influenced by cultural expectations and environmental opportunities. For example, an infant confined to a crib or playpen for long hours with only limited human interaction cannot be expected to develop in a typical manner. Development across all domains is supported when infants are provided with numerous opportunities for learning (see *Learning Activities to Promote Brain Development*).

**1 to 4 months**

# Developmental Profiles and Growth Patterns

## Growth and Physical Characteristics

- Averages 20–27 inches (50.8–68.6 cm) in length; grows approximately 1 inch (2.54 cm) per month (measured with the infant lying on his back, from the top of the head to the bottom of the heels, with knees straight and feet flexed).

- Weighs an average of 8–16 pounds (3.6–7.3 kg); females weigh slightly less than males.

- Gains approximately 1/4–1/2 pound (0.11–0.22 kg) per week.

- Breathes at a rate of approximately thirty to forty breaths per minute; rate increases significantly during periods of crying or activity.

- Normal body temperature ranges from 96.4°F–99.6°F (35.7°C–37.5°C).

- Head and chest circumference are nearly equal.

- Head circumference increases approximately 3/4 inch (1.9 cm) during the first and second months and 5/8 inch (1.6 cm) during months three and four. Increases are an important indication of continued brain growth.

- Continues to breathe using abdominal muscles.

- The posterior fontanel closes by the second month; the anterior fontanel closes to approximately 1/2 inch (1.3 cm).

- The skin remains sensitive and easily irritated.

- The arms and legs are of equal length, size, and shape, and are easily flexed and extended.

- The legs may appear slightly bowed; feet appear flat, with no arch.

- Cries with tears.

- Begins moving eyes together in unison (binocular vision).

## Motor Development

- Reflexive motor behaviors change as follows (Figure 4-3):

  - The tonic neck and stepping reflexes disappear.

  - The rooting and sucking reflexes are well developed.

  - The swallowing reflex and tongue movements are still immature; baby continues to drool and is not able to move food (other than milk) to the back of the mouth.

  - The grasp reflex gradually disappears.

  - The Landau reflex appears near the middle of this period: when the baby is held in a prone (facedown) position, the head is held upright and legs are fully extended (Figure 4-8).

  - Grabs onto small objects using the entire hand (palmar grasp); however, strength is insufficient to hold onto items for long at the beginning of this period (Libertus et al., 2013).

- Holds the hands in an open or semi-open position much of the time.

## Developmental Profiles and Growth Patterns *(continued)*

**1 to 4 months**

Figure 4-8  **The Landau reflex.**

- Muscle tone and development are equal for boys and girls.
- Movements tend to be large and jerky, gradually becoming smoother and more purposeful as muscle strength and control improve.
- Raises the head and upper body on the arms when in a prone position.
- Turns the head from side to side when in a supine (face up) position; near the end of this period, can hold the head up and in line with the body.
- Shows greater activity level in upper body parts: clasps hands above the face; waves the arms about; reaches for objects.
- Begins rolling from the front to the back by turning the head to one side and allowing the trunk to follow. Near the end of this period, the infant can roll from front to back to side at will.
- Can be pulled to a sitting position, with considerable head lag and rounded back at the beginning of this period. Later, can be positioned to sit with minimal head support. By four months, most infants can sit with support, holding their heads steady and backs fairly erect; enjoys sitting in an infant seat or being held on an adult's lap.

### Perceptual-Cognitive Development

- Fixates on a moving object held at a distance of 12 inches (30.5 cm); smoother visual tracking of objects across a 180° pathway, vertically, and horizontally.
- Continues to gaze in the direction of moving objects that have disappeared.
- Exhibits some sense of size, color, and shape recognition of objects in the what Piaget refers to as **object permanence** (Piaget, 1954).

**object permanence** Piaget's sensorimotor stage in which infants understand that an object exists even when it is not in sight.

## Developmental Profiles and Growth Patterns *(continued)*

1 to 4
months

### What Do You See?

**Early motor development.** This two-month-old infant is beginning to learn about purposeful movement. What motor skills is she displaying? What other developmental abilities is she using to make this happen?

© 2016 Cengage Learning®

- Moves eyes from one object to another.

- Focuses on a small object and reaches for it; watches own hand movements intently.

- Alternates looking at an object, at one or both hands, and then back at the immediate environment—for example, recognizes her own bottle even when bottle is turned around, thus presenting a different shape (Figure 4-9).

- Ignores (does not search for) a bottle that falls out of a crib or a toy hidden under a blanket: "out of sight, out of mind." (The infant has not yet fully developed object permanence.)

- Imitates gestures that are modeled: bye-bye, patting head.

- Hits at an object closest to the right or left hand with some degree of accuracy.

- Looks in the direction of a sound source (sound localization).

- Connects sound and rhythms with movement by moving or jiggling in time to music, singing, or chanting.

© GFOW/Cengage Learning

**Figure 4-9 Recognizes familiar objects.**

- Distinguishes the parent's face from a stranger's face when other cues, such as voice, touch, or smell are also available (Streri, Coulon, & Guellaï, 2013).

## Developmental Profiles and Growth Patterns *(continued)*

- Attempts to keep a toy in motion by repeating arm or leg movements that started the toy moving in the first place.
- Begins to mouth objects (Figure 4-10).

### Speech and Language Development

- Reacts (stops whimpering, startles) to sounds, such as a voice, rattle, or doorbell. Later, will search for a sound source by turning the head and looking in the direction of a sound.
- Coordinates vocalizing, looking, and body movements in face-to-face exchanges with the parent or primary caregiver; can follow and lead to keep communication going.
- Babbles or coos when spoken to or smiled at; even infants who are deaf begin to babble (Shehata-Dieler et al., 2013).
- Coos, using single vowel sounds (e.g., *ah*, *eh*, *uh*); also imitates his own sounds and vowel sounds produced by others.
- Laughs out loud.

### Social-Emotional Development

- Imitates, maintains, terminates, and avoids interactions— for example, infants can turn at will toward or away from a person or situation.
- Reacts differently to variations in adult voices; for example, may frown or appear tense or anxious if voices are loud, angry, or unfamiliar.
- Enjoys being held and cuddled at times other than feeding and bedtime.
- Coos, gurgles, and squeals when awake.
- Smiles in response to a friendly face or voice; smiles occurring during sleep are thought to be reflexive (Kärtner, Holodynski, & Wörmann, 2013).

Figure 4-10 **Most objects end up in the infant's mouth.**

© GFOW/Cengage Learning

## What Do You **See?**

**Promoting language development** Surrounding infants with a literacy-rich environment promotes early language development, curiosity, cognitive abilities, and social skills. In what ways have these teachers created a classroom environment that supports developmentally appropriate emergent literacy?

© 2016 Cengage Learning®

## Developmental Profiles and Growth Patterns *(continued)*

- Entertains self for brief periods by playing with fingers, hands, and toes.
- Enjoys familiar routines, such as being bathed and having the diaper changed (Figure 4-11).
- Delights (as shown by squealing or laughing) in play that involves gentle tickling, laughing, and jiggling.
- Cries less often; stops crying when the parent or primary caregiver approaches.
- Recognizes and reaches out to familiar faces and objects, such as father or bottle; reacts by waving arms and squealing with excitement.

© GFOW/Cengage Learning

**1 to 4 months**

Figure 4-11 **Recognizes and reacts to familiar routines.**

© 2016 Cengage Learning®

### ▶❚❚ TeachSource Video Connections

### Early Infant Learning

It is probably true that we will never again learn as much as infants do during their first year of life! Every experience creates an opportunity for infants to acquire new information or learn something different about the world around them. Respond to the following questions after you have watched the learning video *0–2 Years: Early Learning in Infants and Toddlers:*

1. What sensory systems does the infant use to gather information for learning?
2. What behavior does the term *habituation* describe?
3. Why is it important to provide infants with a variety of different toys and activities from time to time?

**1 to 4 months**

## DAILY ROUTINES

### Eating

- Takes five to eight feedings [5–6 ounces (148–177 ml) each] per day; may eat more often if fed on demand.
- Begins fussing before anticipated feeding times; may suck on hand and become restless; does not always cry to signal the need to eat.
- Needs only a little assistance in getting the nipple to the mouth; may begin to help the caregiver by using his own hands to guide the nipple or to hold onto the bottle.
- Sucks vigorously; may choke on occasion due to the vigor and enthusiasm of sucking.
- Becomes impatient if the bottle or breast continues to be offered once hunger is satisfied.
- Requires only breast milk or formula to meet all nutrient needs; not ready to eat solid foods.

### Toileting, Bathing, and Dressing

- Enjoys bath time on most occasions; kicks, laughs, and splashes.
- Has one or two bowel movements per day; may skip a day.
- Begins to establish a regular time or pattern for bowel movements.

### Sleeping

- Averages 14–17 hours of sleep per day; often awake for two or three periods during the daytime.
- Falls asleep for the night soon after the evening feeding.
- Begins to sleep through the night; many infants do not sleep more than six hours at a stretch for several more months.
- May begin thumb-sucking during this period.
- Begins to entertain self before falling asleep: "talks," plays with hands or feet, jiggles crib.

### Play and Social Activity

- Spends waking periods engaged in physical activity: kicking, turning head from side to side, clasping hands together, grasping objects.
- Vocalizes with delight; becomes more "talkative."
- Smiles and coos when being talked and sung to; may cry when the social interaction ends.
- Appears content when awake and alone (for short periods of time).

## learning activities to promote **brain development**

Infants are becoming increasingly aware of their environment. They are learning about cause and effect through communication, movement, problem solving, and intentional behavior.

### Developmentally appropriate applications for families and teachers:

- Imitate the baby's vocalizations and faces (i.e., grunting, smacking, yawning, squinting, frowning). When the baby begins to smile, smile back and sometimes remark, "You are smiling! Happy baby!"

## learning activities *(continued)*

**1 to 4 months**

- Sing songs and read to the baby from magazines, books, or whatever interests you; it is the sound of your voice and your closeness that matter.

- Play simplified peek-a-boo (hold a cloth in front of your face, drop it, and say "peek-a-boo"); repeat if the baby shows interest.

- Gently stretch and flex the baby's arms and legs while making up an accompanying song; later, start a gentle "bicycling" or arm-swaying activity.

- Touch the baby's hand with a small toy* (soft rattles or other quiet noisemakers are especially good); encourage the baby to grasp toy.

- Walk around with the baby, touching and naming objects. Stand with the baby in front of a mirror, touching and naming facial features: "Baby's mouth, Daddy's mouth. Baby's eye, Mommy's eye."

- Position an unbreakable mirror near the crib so the baby can look and talk to herself.

- Hang brightly colored or geometric pictures (black-and-white) or objects near the baby's crib; change often to maintain the baby's interest and attention.

- Fasten small bells (securely) to the baby's booties; this helps the baby to localize sounds and learn at the same time that he has power to make things happen simply by moving about.

**TeachSource Digital Download**

*__Rule of Fist:__ Toys and other objects given to an infant should be no smaller than the baby's fist (1.5 inches; 3.8 cm) to prevent choking or swallowing.*

## developmental alerts

Check with a health-care provider or early childhood specialist if, by four months of age, the infant does *not:*

- Continue to show steady gains in height, weight, and head circumference.

- Smile in response to the smiles of others. (The social smile is a significant developmental milestone.)

- Gaze at and follow a moving object with the eyes focusing together.

- Bring the hands together over the mid-chest (a significant neurological milestone).

- Turn the head to locate sounds.

- Begin to raise the head and upper body when placed on the stomach.

- Reach for objects or familiar persons; begin to mouth objects.

- Coo or make babbling sounds.

**Note:** Cultural differences may alter the timetable when some developmental skills are acquired. Expanded Developmental Alerts Checklists appear in Appendix A and are also available as digital downloads.

**1 to 4 months**

## safety concerns

Continue to implement the safety practices described for the previous stages, and always be aware of new safety issues as the infant continues to grow and develop.

### Burns

- Do not bring hot beverages or appliances near the infant.
- Check the temperature of bottles carefully (if warming formula or breast milk) before offering them to an infant.

### Choking

- Check rattles and stuffed toys for small parts that could become loose. Purchase only toys larger than 1.5 inches (3.75 cm) in diameter and without small parts (e.g., eyes and buttons) that could become dislodged.
- Put all small items, strings, and cords out of the baby's reach.

### Falls

- Attend to the infant at all times whenever she is placed on an elevated surface (such as changing table, sofa, counter, or bed); the baby may turn over or roll unexpectedly.
- Always set the infant carrier on the floor (not on the table or countertop) and securely fasten safety straps.

### Sharp Objects

- Keep pins and other sharp objects out of the baby's reach.
- Check nursery furniture for sharp or protruding edges; purchase only furnishings and toys that comply with federal safety standards (see the "Online Resources" section at the end of this chapter).

---

**Spotlight on Brain Development**

## Breast-feeding and Brain Development

Studies have repeatedly confirmed the findings that breast milk improves children's IQ and cognitive abilities. Deoni et al. (2013) used advanced imaging procedures to scan children's brains over a period of several years. They discovered that children who had been breast-fed exclusively for three months or longer had significantly more white matter in their frontal brain lobes than children who had not been breast-fed. It is important to note that improved IQ and cognitive functioning are closely associated with an increase in white matter. Peters et al. (2013) noted sizeable differences in the reading and math scores of African American and Caucasian children. They attributed this gap to an extremely low rate of breast-feeding among African American mothers. Quigley et al. (2012) also found that incremental improvements in children's IQ and verbal performance were associated with each month an infant was breast-fed. Long-chain polyunsaturated fatty acids (PUFAs) in breast milk are known to promote brain development, attention and memory skills, and cognitive functions (Columbo et al., 2013; Innis, 2013). Some formula manufacturers are now adding PUFAs to their products based on the results of these studies. However, encouraging and supporting more mothers to breast-feed their infants so long as they are able has unquestionable, long-term benefits for children's brain potential as well as for their social-emotional development.

### What are the connections?

1. In what ways does breast milk influence early brain development?
2. What specific component in breast milk is considered beneficial for brain development?
3. What additional factors may be involved in promoting infants' early brain development?

# Four to Eight Months

Between four and eight months, infants are developing a wide range of skills and greater ability to use their bodies for purposeful activities. They seem to be busy every waking moment, manipulating and mouthing toys and other objects. They move easily from spontaneous, self-initiated activities to social activities initiated by others (Figure 4-12). They "talk" all the time, with more variety and complexity of vowel and consonant sounds. They initiate social interactions and respond to all types of cues (i.e., facial expressions, gestures, and sounds) and the comings and goings of everyone in their world. Although all infants experience the same fundamental human emotions, the ways in which they are expressed are shaped by the parenting practices in each culture. An inability to maintain social attention or eye contact may be an early indicator of autism spectrum disorder (Chawarska, Macari, & Shic, 2013; Droucker, Curtin, & Vouloumanos, 2013).

**4 to 8 months**

© 2016 Cengage Learning®

Figure 4-12 **Infants are becoming more sociable and verbal between four and eight months of age.**

## Developmental Profiles and Growth Patterns

### Growth and Physical Characteristics

- Gains approximately 1 pound (2.2 kg) per month in weight; doubles original birth weight by eight months.

- Increases length by approximately 1/2 inch (1.3 cm) per month; average length is 27.5–29 inches (69.8–73.7 cm).

- Head circumference increases by an average of 3/8 inch (0.95 cm) per month until six to seven months of age; growth then slows to approximately 3/16 inch (0.47 cm) per month. Continued gains are a sign of healthy brain growth and development.

- Takes approximately twenty-five to fifty breaths per minute, depending on activity; rate and patterns vary from infant to infant; breathing is abdominal.

- Begins to develop teeth, with upper and lower incisors erupting first.

- Color vision is now manifest (AOA, 2014).

## Developmental Profiles and Growth Patterns *(continued)*

**4 to 8 months**

- Gums may become red and swollen, accompanied by increased drooling, chewing, biting, and mouthing of objects.
- Legs often appear bowed; bowing gradually disappears as the infant grows older.
- True eye color is established.

### Motor Development

- Reflexive behaviors are changing (Figure 4-3, pg. 72).
  - The blinking reflex is well established.
  - The sucking reflex becomes voluntary.
  - The Moro reflex disappears.
  - The parachute reflex appears toward the end of this stage: when held in a prone, horizontal position and lowered suddenly, the infant throws out her arms as a protective measure (Figure 4-13).
  - The swallowing reflex (a more complex form of swallowing that involves tongue movement against the roof of the mouth) appears; this allows the infant to move solid foods from the front to the back of the mouth for swallowing.
- Reaches for objects with both arms simultaneously; later reaches with one hand or the other.
- Transfers objects from one hand to the other; still grasps objects using the entire hand (palmar grasp).
- Handles, shakes, and pounds objects; puts everything into the mouth.
- Helps to hold onto the bottle during feedings; if breast-fed, may place a hand on the breast.
- Sits alone without support, holding the head erect and the back straight, with the arms propped forward for support (Figure 4-14).
- Pulls self into a crawling position by rising up on the arms and drawing the knees up beneath the body; rocks back and forth, but generally does not move forward.
- Rolls over from front to back and back to front.

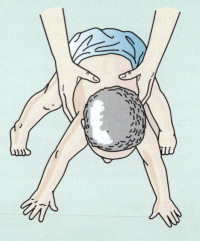

**Figure 4-13** **The parachute reflex.**

▶‖ **TeachSource Video Connections**

© 2016 Cengage Learning®

### Fine Motor Development

Motor development proceeds rapidly during the first year. Infants' motor abilities advance quickly from a reflexive stage to one that permits them to move about, explore, and manipulate their environment. Respond to the following questions after you have watched the learning video *0–2 Years: Fine Motor Development for Infants and Toddlers*:

1. What is a pincer grasp? How does a pincer grasp differ from an ulnar or a palmar grasp?
2. What purpose do improved fine motor skills and coordination serve?
3. How might cultural differences influence an infant's motor development?

## Developmental Profiles and Growth Patterns *(continued)*

Figure 4-14 **The infant sits alone with support.**

4 to 8
months

- Begins scooting backward, sometimes accidentally, when placed on the stomach; soon learns to crawl forward.
- Enjoys being placed in a standing position, especially on someone's lap; jumps in place.
- Begins to pick up objects using finger and thumb (pincer grip) near the end of this period (Figure 4-15).

### Perceptual-Cognitive Development

Figure 4-15 **The pincer grip.**

- Turns toward and locates familiar voices and sounds; this behavior can be used for informal testing of an infant's hearing.
- Focuses the eyes on small objects and reaches for them accurately with either hand.
- Uses the hands, mouth, and eyes in coordination to explore his own body, toys, and surroundings.
- Imitates actions, such as pat-a-cake, waving bye-bye, and playing peek-a-boo.
- Shows evidence of **depth perception**; tenses, pulls back, and becomes fearful of falling from high places, such as changing tables and stairs (Tsuruhara et al., 2013).
- Looks over the side of a crib or high chair for objects dropped; delights in repeatedly throwing objects overboard for an adult or older sibling to retrieve.
- Searches for a toy or food that has been partially hidden under a cloth or behind a screen; beginning to understand that objects continue to exist even when they cannot be seen. (Piaget refers to this characteristic as *object permanence*.)
- Handles and explores objects in a variety of ways: visually, turning them around, feeling all surfaces, banging, and shaking.
- Picks up an inverted object (for instance, begins to recognize a cup even when it is positioned differently) (Möhring & Frick, 2013).
- Ignores a second toy or drops a toy in one hand when presented with a new one; unable to deal with more than one toy at a time.

**depth perception** The ability to determine the relative distance of objects from the observer.

## Developmental Profiles and Growth Patterns *(continued)*

- Plays actively with small toys such as rattles or blocks.
- Bangs objects together playfully; thumps a spoon or toy on the table.
- Continues to put everything into the mouth.
- Establishes full attachment to the mother or primary caregiver(s): seeks out and prefers to be held by this adult, which coincides with a growing understanding of object permanence.

**4 to 8 months**

### Speech and Language Development

- Responds appropriately to her name and simple requests such as "Come," "Eat," and "Wave bye-bye."
- Imitates some nonspeech sounds, such as coughing, tongue clicking, and lip smacking.
- Produces a full range of vowels and some consonants: *r, s, z, th,* and *w.*
- Responds to variations in an adult's tone of voice —anger, playfulness, sadness, or frustration.
- Expresses emotions, such as pleasure, satisfaction, and anger, by making different sounds.
- "Talks" to toys and objects.
- Babbles by repeating the same syllable in a series: *ba, ba, ba.*
- Reacts differently to noises, such as a phone ringing, door slamming, toilet flushing, or dog barking; may begin to cry, whimper, or look to the parent or caregiver for reassurance.

### Social-Emotional Development

- Delights in observing surroundings; continuously watches people and activities.
- Begins to develop an awareness of self as a separate individual from others (Davidov et al., 2013).
- Becomes more outgoing and social in nature: smiles, coos, reaches out, and seeks adult attention.
- Distinguishes among and responds differently to strangers, teachers, parents, and siblings.
- Responds differently and appropriately to facial expressions: e.g., frowns and smiles.
- Imitates facial expressions, actions, and sounds (Figure 4-16).
- Remains friendly toward strangers at the beginning of this stage; later, is reluctant to be approached by or left with strangers and exhibits **stranger anxiety**. Displays considerable distress: cries, clings to the parents, and refuses to let go. Infants raised in cultures where multiple family members provide care are less likely to experience a strong reaction when parents leave.
- Enjoys being held and cuddled; indicates desire to be picked up by raising arms and vocalizing.
- Establishes a trust relationship with family members and teachers if physical and emotional needs are met consistently; by six months, begins to show preference for the primary caregiver.
- Laughs out loud.
- Becomes upset if a toy or other objects are taken away.
- Seeks attention by using body movements, verbalizations, or both.

© GFOW/Cengage Learning

**Figure 4-16  The infant delights in imitating adult made sounds.**

**stranger anxiety**  A cross-cultural phenomenon in which infants begin to show distress or fear when approached by persons other than their primary caregivers.

## DAILY ROUTINES

### Eating

- Adjusts feeding times to the family's schedule; usually takes three to four feedings per day, each 6–8 ounces (144–237 ml), depending on sleep schedule.

- *Caution:* Infants should not be allowed to drink formula or juice from a bottle or to nurse for an extended time. Extensive decay can develop when teeth are in prolonged contact with the sugars in these fluids and cause a condition known as baby bottle tooth decay (BBTD) (Leong et al., 2013). A small amount of water offered after feedings rinses the teeth and reduces the risk of BBTD.

- Shows interest in feeding activities; reaches for the cup and spoon while being fed.

- Is able to wait a half hour or more after awakening for the first morning feeding.

- Has less need for sucking.

- Begins to accept a small amount of semisolid pureed foods, such as cereal and vegetables, when placed well back on tongue (if such food is placed on the tip, the infant will push it back out).

- Closes the mouth firmly or turns the head away when hunger is satisfied.

### Toileting, Bathing, and Dressing

- Prefers being free of clothes; may fuss while being dressed.

- Splashes vigorously with both hands (and sometimes feet as well) during bath time.

- Moves hands constantly; nothing within reach is safe from being spilled, placed in the mouth, or dashed to the floor.

- Pulls off her own socks; plays with snaps, zippers, and Velcro closures on clothing.

- Has one bowel movement per day as a general rule, often at about the same time.

- Urinates often and in large quantities; female infants tend to have longer intervals between wetting.

### Sleeping

- Awakens early in the morning; usually falls asleep soon after the evening meal.

- Begins to give up the need for a late-night feeding.

- Sleeps 11–13 hours through the night.

- Takes two or three naps per day. (However, there is great variability among infants in terms of frequency and length of naps.)

### Play and Social Activity

- Enjoys lying on the back; arches back, kicks, and stretches legs upward, grasps the feet and brings them to the mouth.

- Looks at his own hands with interest and delight; may squeal or gaze at them intently.

- Plays with soft, squeaky toys and rattles; puts them in the mouth and chews on them.

- "Talks" happily to self: gurgles, growls, makes high squealing sounds.

- Differentiates between people: lively with those who are familiar, may ignore or become anxious with unfamiliar persons.

- Likes rhythmic activities: being bounced, jiggled, or swayed about gently.

**4 to 8 months**

**4 to 8 months**

© 2016 Cengage Learning®

▶❚❚  **TeachSource** Video Connections

## Attachment

Attachment is a special emotional bond formed between parents and infants through a process of give-and-take interactions. It develops as infants and parents begin to synchronize their response patterns. Studies have shown that attachment helps infants build a sense of trust and is essential for future social-emotional development. Respond to the following questions after you have watched the learning video *0–2 Years: Attachment in Infants and Toddlers:*

**1.** What can parents do to foster the attachment process?
**2.** What is a reciprocal relationship, and what purpose does it serve?
**3.** Why do infants develop stranger anxiety?
**4.** How can families and teachers help infants get through this phase?

## learning activities to promote **brain development**

Infants need a safe environment where they are free to move about, explore, and practice newly emerging motor skills. Talking, singing, and reading to infants promote important language and brain development.

### Developmentally appropriate applications for families and teachers:

- Gradually elaborate on earlier activities: imitate the baby's sounds, facial expressions, and body movements; name body parts; look in the mirror together and make faces; read, talk, and sing to the baby throughout the day.

- Provide toys, rattles, and household items that make noise as the baby shakes or waves them about (a set of measuring spoons or plastic keys, shaker cans, squeak toys)—but remember the *Rule of Fist*.

- Move objects slightly out of reach to encourage the baby's movement (physical activity) and eye–hand coordination (Thoermer et al., 2013).

## learning activities *(continued)*

- Read aloud and often to the baby—even the evening newspaper or your favorite magazine will do. Infants will not understand what you are saying, but they begin to learn about word sounds, voice inflections, facial expressions, and that reading is an enjoyable experience.

- Repeat the infant's name during all kinds of activities so that he or she begins to recognize it: "*Ethan* has a big smile," "*Stella's* eyes are wide open." "*Tyrel* looks sleepy."

- Play, dance, and move around with the baby to music on the radio, television, or a CD; vary the tempo and movement: gentle jiggling, dancing, or turning in circles; dance in front of the mirror, describing movements to the infant.

- Sing all types of songs to the baby—silly songs, lullabies, popular tunes; encourage the infant to "sing" along and to imitate your movements (Sievers et al., 2013).

- Allow plenty of time for the baby's bath. This activity provides important opportunities for reinforcing learning across developmental areas, including movement, sensory experiences, language, social interaction, and relaxation.

- Play "This little piggy," "Where's baby's (nose, eye, hand . . .)," and other simple games invented on the spot, such as taking turns at shaking rattles, gently rubbing foreheads, or clapping hands.

- Encourage the baby to touch and explore different textures. Cut small squares from a variety of fabrics (e.g., rough, smooth, soft, ridged, woven, silky); or crinkle up sheets of different types of paper (e.g., typing, construction, gift wrap, newspaper, and aluminum foil).

**TeachSource Digital Download**

**4 to 8 months**

## developmental **alerts**

Check with a health-care provider or early childhood specialist if, by eight months of age, the infant does *not*:

- Show an even, steady increase in weight, height, and head size (growth that is too slow or too rapid is cause for concern).

- Explore her own hands and objects placed in her hands.

- Hold and shake a rattle.

- Smile, babble, and laugh out loud.

- Search for hidden objects.

- Begin to pick up objects using a pincer grip.

- Have an interest in playing games such as pat-a-cake and peek-a-boo.

- Show interest in or respond to new or unusual sounds.

- Reach for and grasp objects.

- Sit alone.

- Begin to eat some solid (pureed) foods.

**Note:** Cultural differences may alter the timetable when some developmental skills are acquired. Expanded Developmental Alerts Checklists appear in Appendix A and are also available as digital downloads.

## safety concerns

Continue to implement the safety practices described for the previous stages, and always be aware of new safety issues as the baby continues to grow and develop.

### Burns

- Keep electrical cords out of reach and electrical outlets covered; inspect the condition of electrical cords and replace or remove them if worn or frayed.
- Take precautions to protect infants from accidentally touching hot objects (e.g., oven or fireplace doors, space heaters, candles, curling irons, burning cigarettes, and hot beverage cups).

### Falls

- Use approved safety gates to protect the baby from tumbling downstairs; gates are also useful for keeping the baby confined to an area for supervision.
- Always fasten the restraining strap when the infant is placed in a high chair, stroller, or grocery cart.

- Always raise crib sides to their maximum height and lock them when the baby is in bed.

### Poisons

- Use safety latches on cabinet doors and drawers where potentially poisonous substances (i.e., medications, cleaning supplies, cosmetics, or garden chemicals) are stored.

### Strangulation

- Never fasten teethers or pacifiers on a cord or around the infant's neck; avoid clothing with drawstrings.
- Remove crib gyms and mobiles after the baby reaches five months or begins pushing up on hands and knees.
- Use a wireless baby monitor; make sure that all cords are out of reach.

8 to 12 months

# Eight to Twelve Months

Between eight and twelve months of age, the infant is gearing up for two major developmental events—walking and talking. These milestones usually begin around the infant's first birthday, although cultural background may influence the acquisition rate and nature of these early skills (Lobo & Galloway, 2013; Størvold & Bratber, 2013). For example, early walking is often valued in Western cultures, and parents spend considerable time encouraging this behavior. In contrast, infants raised in many South American and African societies are often carried in slings or on their mother's back and, consequently, learn to walk several months later. Delayed walking is also associated with certain medical conditions, chromosomal abnormalities, and autism spectrum disorders, and the child should be evaluated if this behavior is observed (Lloyd, MacDonald, & Lord, 2013). During this stage, the infant also is becoming increasingly skilled at manipulating small objects and spends a great deal of time picking up and releasing toys or whatever else is at hand.

Infants at this age are also becoming extremely sociable. They find ways to be the center of attention and to win approval and applause from family and friends (Figure 4-17). When applause is forthcoming, the infant joins in with delight. The ability to imitate improves, serving two purposes: to extend social interactions and to help the child learn many new skills and behaviors in the months of rapid development that lie ahead (Hilbrink et al., 2013; Patel & Gaylord, 2013). However, it is important to remember that individual attention is not highly valued in all cultures. As a result, infants in some environments may not be encouraged or reinforced for their attention-getting efforts and gradually will be socialized to blend into the group.

Figure 4-17 The infant enjoys adult attention.

© GFOW/Cengage Learning

# Developmental Profiles and Growth Patterns

## Growth and Physical Characteristics

- Grows at a slower rate than during the previous months; averages an increase of 1/2 inch (1.3 cm) in length per month. Length is approximately 1 1/2 times the birth length by the first birthday.

- Weight increases by approximately 1 pound (0.5 kg) per month; birth weight nearly triples by one year of age: infants weigh an average of 21 pounds (9.6 kg).

- Respiration rates vary with activity: typically twenty to forty-five breaths per minute.

- Body temperature ranges from 96.4°F–99.6°F (35.7°C–37.5°C); environmental conditions, weather, activity, and clothing affect variations in temperature.

- The circumferences of the head and chest remain equal.

- The anterior fontanel begins to close.

- Approximately four upper and four lower incisors and two lower molars erupt.

- The arms and hands are more developed than the feet and legs (cephalocaudal development); hands appear large in proportion to other body parts.

- The legs may continue to appear bowed.

- The feet appear flat because the arch has not yet developed fully.

- Visual acuity is approximately 20/100; can see distant objects [15–20 feet (4.6–6 m) away] and point to them.

- Both eyes work in unison (true binocular coordination).

**8 to 12 months**

## Motor Development

- Reaches with one hand leading to grasp an offered object or toy (Nelson, Campbell, & Michel, 2013).

- Manipulates objects, transferring them from one hand to the other.

- Explores new objects by poking with one finger.

- Uses a deliberate pincer grip to pick up small objects, toys, and finger foods.

- Stacks objects; also places objects inside one another.

- Releases objects or toys by dropping or throwing; cannot intentionally put an object down.

- Begins pulling self to a standing position.

- Begins to stand alone, leaning on furniture for support; moves or "cruises" around obstacles by side-stepping (Adolph et al., 2012).

- Maintains good balance when sitting; can shift positions without falling.

- Creeps on hands and knees; crawls up and down stairs.

- Walks with adult support, holding onto adult's hand; may begin to walk alone.

## Perceptual-Cognitive Development

- Watches people, objects, and activities in the immediate environment.

- Shows awareness of distant objects (15–20 feet away) by pointing at them.

- Responds to hearing tests (voice localization); however, loses interest quickly and therefore, it may be difficult to test the infant for this informally.

- Begins to understand the meaning of some words (receptive language) (Bergelson & Swingley, 2013).

- Follows simple instructions, such as "Wave bye-bye" or "Clap your hands."

- Reaches for toys that are visible but out of reach.

## Developmental Profiles and Growth Patterns *(continued)*

**8 to 12 months**

- Puts everything into mouth (Figure 4-18).
- Continues to drop the first item when other toys or items are offered.
- Recognizes the reversal of an object: a cup that is upside down is still a cup (Frick & Möhring, 2013).
- Imitates activities, such as hitting two blocks together or playing pat-a-cake.
- Drops toys intentionally and repeatedly; looks in the direction of a fallen object; delights in having an adult or sibling pick up an object, only to throw it overboard again.
- Shows the appropriate use of everyday items: pretends to drink from a cup, puts on a necklace, hugs a doll, brushes hair, makes a stuffed animal "walk."
- Shows some sense of spatial relationships: puts a block in a cup and takes it out when requested to do so (Loucks & Sommerville, 2012).
- Begins to show an understanding of causality—for example, hands a music box back to an adult when the music stops to have it rewound.

Figure 4-18 **Safety becomes an important issue as the infant gains mobility.**

© 2016 Cengage Learning®

### What Do You See?

**Integration of developmental domains** The achievement of even simple tasks requires the collaborative efforts of multiple developmental skills. Look closely at the little boy in this picture. What developmental domains are involved in his effort to pick up this cup?

© 2016 Cengage Learning®

## Developmental Profiles and Growth Patterns *(continued)*

- Shows some awareness of the functional relationship of objects; puts a spoon in mouth, uses a brush to smooth hair, turns the pages of a book.

- Searches for a completely hidden toy or object by the end of this period.

### Speech and Language Development

- Babbles or jabbers deliberately to initiate social interaction; may shout to attract attention, listen, and then shout again if no one responds.

- Nods head to indicate "no" and might occasionally do so for "yes."

- Responds by looking for the source of the voice when her name is called.

- Babbles in sentence-like sequences, "*ma ma ma ma*," "*ba ba ba*"; followed later by jargon (syllables and sounds common to many languages, uttered with language-like inflection).

- Waves bye-bye; claps hands when asked.

- Says "*da-da*" and "*ma-ma*" (or equivalents in other languages).

- Imitates sounds similar to those that the infant already has learned to make; also imitates motor noises, tongue clicking, lip smacking, and coughing (Salomo & Liszkowski, 2013).

- Enjoys rhymes and simple songs; vocalizes and dances to music.

- Hands a toy or an object to an adult when appropriate gestures accompany the request.

### Social-Emotional Development

- Continues to exhibit a definite fear of strangers (stranger anxiety); clings to or hides behind the parent or primary caregiver; may begin to resist being away from familiar adults (separation anxiety) (Brooker et al., 2013) (Figure 4-19). Infants raised in extended families may not exhibit the same reaction.

- Wants an adult to be in constant sight; may cry and search the room when no one is immediately visible.

---

▶❚❚ **TeachSource Video Connections**

© 2016 Cengage Learning®

**Assessing Language Development**

Language provides a means for expressing pleasure, wants, and needs. Encouraging and supporting early language development creates important neural connections in the infant's brain that are critical for future vocabulary, writing, and reading skills. Respond to the following questions after you have watched the learning video *Observing and Monitoring Language Development in Infants: The Importance of Assessment:*

1. Why is it important to assess an infant's language development several times during the year?

2. At approximately what age can you expect an infant to begin understanding and responding to requests?

3. What prelinguistic skills did the infants in this video (in the main feature) display?

4. What language-promoting activities would you encourage parents to implement at home, based on what you observed in the video?

---

**8 to 12 months**

## Developmental Profiles and Growth Patterns *(continued)*

**Did You Know**

...that stranger anxiety is a universally observed phenomenon that occurs across cultures and genders? Cultural differences in child-rearing practices and temperament influence the degree of anxiety that children may experience.

Figure 4-19 **The infant shows fear of adults other than primary caregivers (stranger anxiety).**

**8 to 12 months**

- Enjoys being nearby and included in daily activities of family members and teachers; is becoming more sociable and outgoing.
- Enjoys novel experiences and opportunities to examine new objects.
- Shows a need to be picked up and held by extending arms upward, crying, or clinging to an adult's legs.
- Begins to exhibit assertiveness by resisting a caregiver's requests; may kick, scream, toss toys, or throw self on the floor.
- Offers toys and objects to others.
- Often becomes attached to a favorite toy or blanket, and cries when it is missing.
- Looks up and smiles at a person who is speaking upon hearing his name.
- Repeats behaviors that get attention; jabbers continuously.
- Carries out simple directions and requests; understands the meaning of "No," "Yes," "Come here," and other common phrases.

## DAILY ROUTINES

### Eating

- Eats three meals per day, plus mid-morning or mid-afternoon snacks such as juice, fruit, crackers, and cereal. Enjoys eating with family members; usually has a good appetite.
- Begins to refuse bottle; shows greater interest in drinking from a cup.
- Learns to drink from a cup; wants to hold it alone; will even tilt the head backward to get the last drop.
- Begins to eat finger foods; may remove food from mouth, look at it, and put it back in.
- Develops certain food likes and dislikes.

## DAILY ROUTINES *(continued)*

- Is continuously active during feedings; the infant's hands may be so busy that a toy is needed for each hand to prevent a cup or dish from being overturned or food grabbed and tossed.

### Toileting, Bathing, and Dressing

- Enjoys bath time; splashes and plays with the washcloth, soap, and water toys.
- Delights in letting water drip from a sponge or washcloth; pours water from cup to cup.
- Shows great interest in pulling off hats, shoes, and socks.
- Fusses when diaper needs changing; may pull off a soiled or wet diaper.
- Cooperates to some degree while being dressed; puts the arms in armholes when asked, may even extend the legs to have pants put on.
- Has one or two bowel movements per day.
- Remains dry after nap on occasion.

### Sleeping

- Goes to bed willingly but may not fall asleep immediately; plays or walks around in crib before eventually falling asleep.
- Sleeps until early morning.
- Plays alone and quietly for 15–30 minutes after awakening; may begin to make demanding noises, signaling the need to be up and about.
- Plays actively in the crib when awake; the crib sides must be up and securely fastened at all times.
- Takes one afternoon nap most days; length varies from infant to infant.

### Play and Social Activities

- Enjoys large motor activities: pulling to a standing position, cruising, standing alone, creeping.
- Places things on the head, such as a basket, bowl, or cup; finds this very funny and expects others to notice and laugh.
- Puts objects in and out of each other: pans that nest, toys in and out of a box.
- Enjoys hiding behind chairs to play "Where's baby?"
- Throws things on the floor and expects them to be returned.
- Shows interest in opening and closing doors and cupboards.
- Hands an object to an adult upon request; expects to have it returned immediately.
- Responds to "no-no" by stopping the activity. Later in this period, the infant might smile, laugh, and resume the inappropriate behavior, thus turning it into a game.

**8 to 12 months**

## learning activities to promote **brain development**

Infants now enjoy activities that involve movement, imitation, reciprocal actions, and repetition. Music, stories read aloud, rhyming, and back-and-forth conversation reinforce early cognitive, language, and social development.

## learning activities *(continued)*

### Developmentally appropriate applications for families and teachers:

- Continue to elaborate on previously suggested activities; sing, read, talk, play simple games (rolling a ball, stacking objects), and encourage the infant's efforts.

- Always follow the infant's lead whenever she initiates a new response or invents a new version of a familiar game (the roots of creativity).

- Provide safe floor space close to the parent or caregiver; learning to sit, crawl, stand, and explore are an infant's major tasks during these months.

- Look at photo albums together and talk about everyday happenings in the baby's life.

- Read from sturdy, brightly colored picture books, allowing the baby to help hold the book and turn pages. Point to pictures and label the object to help infants begin to make associations; "Soft brown kitten," "Happy puppy," "Big red pail."

- Talk about activities as they are unfolding, naming and emphasizing key words: "Let's *wash your hands* before you eat." "Here is the *soap*," "Let's get your hands all *wet*."

- Give the baby simple instructions: "Pat Mommy's head," "Point to baby's nose," "Find Daddy's ear."

- Allow adequate time for a response; if the infant seems interested but does not respond, demonstrate the request.

- Accept the infant's newly invented game of dropping things off a high chair or out of the crib; act surprised, laugh, return dropped object, and do not scold. This is the baby's way of learning about cause and effect, gravity, and adults' patience.

- Encourage infants to fill a container with small toys, blocks, or other items and then empty it out. (The *Rule of Fist* still applies.)

- Provide push-and-pull toys, toys with wheels, and large balls to roll. (Helping to unpack canned foods and rolling them across the kitchen floor is an all-time favorite game!)

**TeachSource Digital Download**

**8 to 12 months**

## developmental **alerts**

Check with a health-care provider or early childhood specialist if, by twelve months of age, the infant does *not:*

- Blink when fast-moving objects approach the eyes.
- Begin to develop teeth.
- Imitate simple sounds.
- Follow simple verbal requests: "Come," "Bye-bye."
- Pull self to a standing position.
- Transfer objects from hand to hand.
- Show any anxiety toward strangers by crying or refusing to be held.
- Interact playfully with parents, caregivers, and siblings.

## developmental **alerts** *(continued)*

- Feed self; hold a bottle or cup; pick up and eat finger foods.
- Creep or crawl on hands and knees.

**Note:** Cultural differences may alter the timetable when some developmental skills are acquired. Expanded Developmental Alerts Checklists appear in Appendix A and are also available as digital downloads.

## safety **concerns**

8 to 12 months

Continue to implement the safety practices described for the previous stages, and always be aware of new safety issues as the baby continues to grow and develop.

### Choking
- Cut finger foods into small pieces (1/4 inch [0.63 cm] or smaller). Avoid sticky foods (e.g., raisins, caramels, or peanut butter) and hard foods (e.g., raw vegetables, hard candies, or nuts).
- Keep small objects such as buttons, dry pet food, coins, pen tops, and small batteries out of reach; keep garbage cans closed tightly. Any item that can fit through a toilet paper tube is too small for young children to play with.

### Drowning
- Remove unsupervised water sources, including bath water, outdoor fountains, pet dishes, and wading pools. Place safety devices on toilet lids.
- Enclose pools with fences and latched gates; install alarms on windows and doors. Never leave a young child unsupervised in a pool or bathtub, even briefly to answer the telephone.

### Falls
- Always strap infants into high chairs, grocery carts, and strollers and on changing tables. Never allow them to stand up in or on these objects (unless you are holding onto the infant).
- Keep the crib sides up and locked at all times.
- Pad the sharp corners and edges of furniture and cabinet doors.
- Place safety gates across stairs.

### Strangulation
- Purchase clothing, such as jackets, with elastic instead of pull strings in the hoods.
- Fasten cords on all blinds and curtains up high and out of a child's reach.

### Suffocation
- Keep plastic bags and wrappings out of the baby's reach; knot and discard them immediately.
- Remove lids from airtight containers such as plastic storage tubs and toy chests.

## positive behavior guidance

There are several things that adults must understand about infants' behavior: they depend on adults to satisfy all their basic needs; crying is their primary mode of communication; they cannot be spoiled; and they should not be punished. Because caring for an infant can be stressful at times, it is important that adults take care of themselves, learn self-control, and practice anger management skills.

### Newborns
- Always respond to their cries with love, gentle handling, and calming words to build feelings of trust and security.

## One to four months

- Help infants learn to soothe and quiet themselves: hold, cuddle, or rock them gently; wrap them well in a blanket; massage their skin; offer a pacifier (some infants prefer their thumbs).

## Four to eight months

- Maintain consistent eating and sleeping schedules to reduce crying and fussiness.
- Create a safe environment so mobile infants don't get into items or situations that they shouldn't.
- Convey a sense of calm when responding to a fussy infant.

## Eight to twelve months

- Introduce the word "No" (spoken gently) to correct infants when they are doing something that could result in harm. If necessary, pick up and move the infant to a safe area until corrective measures can be taken, but do not punish him.
- Give attention when an infant is behaving appropriately: "You rolled the ball really far," "You came when Daddy asked."

# Summary

**4-1**  Newborns have almost no intentional or purposeful control over their motor abilities; thus, these actions are referred to as *reflexive movements*, which include:

- Swallowing, sucking, gagging, coughing, yawning, blinking, and elimination
- Rooting, in which the infant turns when skin around check is touched
- Moro (startle), in which the infant throws open the arms when surprised by loud noise
- Grasping, in which the infant tightly curls her fingers around an object
- Stepping, in which walking-like movements occur when the infant's feet touch a firm surface.

**4-2**  The first year marks one of the most important stages of brain development:

- Infants are learning continuously about the people and environment around them.
- Learning opportunities increase the number and strength of neural connections in the infant's brain.
- Learning is influenced by genetics, culture, environment, and adult expectations.

**4-3**  Initially, infants communicate through crying, eye contact, social smiling, and muscle tension (or relaxation). Later, infants begin to coo and babble, imitate adult expressions, respond to name and simple commands, and produce simple word sequences (i.e., "*ma ma ma*" or "*da da da*").

**4-4**  Infants begin to exhibit "stranger anxiety" at around nine and ten months of age; this is a normal developmental phenomenon. Observable behaviors include considerable distress and anxiety, crying, clinging, and reluctance to let a primary caregiver out of sight.

# Key Terms

in utero **p. 70**

jaundice **p.71**

fontanels **p. 71**

pupil **p.73**

bonding **p. 75**

object permanence **p.80**

depth perception **p. 89**

stranger anxiety **p. 90**

# Apply What You Have Learned

## A. Case Study Connections

*Reread the developmental sketch about Juan and his parents, Anna and Miguel, presented at the beginning of this chapter and answer the following questions:*

1. What changes can Juan's parents expect to occur in his motor development by the time he is seven months old?

2. Would you expect Juan to experience stranger anxiety if his parents don't enroll him in an early childhood program until he turns seven or eight months? Explain.

3. How would you respond to Juan's parents if they expressed concern about his lack of interest in pulling himself to a standing position or taking any steps by his first birthday?

## B. Review Questions

1. Explain why a ten-month-old infant might begin fussing and refusing to be left with a familiar babysitter.

2. Identify and discuss three informal methods for determining whether a newborn's hearing is functional.

3. Identify three newborn reflexes that typically disappear by one year of age. Why should you be concerned if they do not fade according to schedule?

4. What are some things that families and teachers can do with infants to promote early literacy skills?

5. Identify three perceptual-cognitive skills that appear during late infancy (8–12 months) and provide a behavioral example that illustrates each.

## C. Your Turn: Chapter to Practice

1. Arrange to visit four or five child care programs (e.g., centers, homes) that accept infants in your community. Before you go, research and learn about the features typically associated with high-quality programs (these are posted on many early childhood professional organization websites). Briefly summarize your observations and personal reaction to each site. If you were the parent of a six-month-old, how would you describe this experience?

2. Prepare a list of five developmentally appropriate activities for infants; each activity should involve and reinforce at least two different forms of learning (visual, auditory, tactile, or hand-eye coordination).

3. Read and compile a list of ten storybooks that you would recommend parents read to infants. Identify and describe the features that make each book an appealing and developmentally appropriate choice.

## Online Resources

### Child Care Aware®

Formerly known as the National Association of Child Care Resource and Referral Agencies (NACCRRA), this organization provides helpful information for child care providers and parents/families. Families can access guidelines to help them identify quality care programs in their area. Providers will find a host of administrative information and tools for running a child care program.

### Early Head Start National Resource Center

The Early Head Start National Resource Center, operated by Zero to Three, serves as a depository for timely information, professional expertise, and technical assistance to Early Head Start educators and families. Webcasts, podcasts, and a quarterly newsletter can be accessed from this site.

### HealthyChildren.org

The American Academy of Pediatrics supports this website and offers professional information on a variety of children's health, safety, and nutrition topics. The *Ages & Stages, Hot Topics, Search,* and *Ask a Pediatrician* sections are current and especially useful.

### Safe to Sleep

The Safe to Sleep campaign is an ongoing national effort to raise awareness about SIDS prevention. Facts about SIDS, preventive measures, and campaign resources are available on this site.

## References

Adolph, K., Cole, W., Komati, M., Garciaguirre, J., Badaly, D., Lingeman, J., …, & Sotsky, R. (2012). How do you learn to walk? Thousands of steps and dozens of falls per day. *Psychological Science*, 23(11), 1387−1394.

American Optometric Association (AOA). (2014). Infant vision: Birth to 24 months of age. Retrieved on February 5, 2014 from http://www.aoa.org/patients-and-public/good-vision-throughout-life /childrens-vision/infant-vision-birth-to-24-months-of-age.

Bergelson, E., & Swingley, D. (2013). The acquisition of abstract words by young infants. *Cognition*, 127(3), 391−397.

Brooker, R., Buss, K., Lemery-Chalfant, K., Aksan, N., Davidson, R., & Goldsmith, H. (2013). The development of stranger fear in infancy and toddlerhood: Normative development, individual differences, antecedents, and outcomes. *Developmental Science*, 16(6), 864−878.

Centers for Disease Control & Prevention (CDC). (2013). Sudden infant death syndrome. Retrieved on February 5, 2014 from http://www.cdc.gov/features/sidsawarenessmonth.

Chawarska, K., Macari, S., & Shic, F. (2013). Decreased spontaneous attention to social scenes in 6-month-old infants later diagnosed with autism spectrum disorders. *Biological Psychiatry*, 74(3), 195−203.

Columbo, J., Carlson, S., Cheatham, C., Shaddy, D., Kerling, E., Thodosoff, J., …, & Brez, C. (2013). Long-term effects of LCPUFA supplementation on childhood cognitive outcomes. *American Journal of Clinical Nutrition*, 98(2), 403−412.

Davidov, M., Zahn-Waxler, C., Roth-Hanania, R., & Knafo, A. (2013). Concern for others in the first year of life: Theory, evidence, and avenues for research. *Child Development Perspectives*, 7(2), 126−131.

Deoni, S., Dean, D., Piryatinsky, I., O'Muircheartaigh, J., Waskiewicz, N., Lehman, K., …, & Dirks, H. (2013). Breastfeeding and early white matter development: A cross-sectional study. *NeuroImage*, 82, 77−86.

Drucker, D., Curtin, S., & Vouloumanos, A. (2013). Linking infant-directed speech and face preferences to language outcomes in infants at risk for autism spectrum disorder. *Journal of Speech, Language, and Hearing Research*, 56(2), 567−576.

Frank, M., Vul, E., & Saxe, R. (2012). Measuring the development of social attention using free-viewing. *Infancy*, 17(4), 355−375.

Frick, A., & Möhring, W. (2013). Mental object rotation and motor development in 8- and 10-month-old infants. *Journal of Experimental Child Psychology*, 115(4), 708−720.

Futagi, Y., Yanagihara, K., Mogami, Y., & Ikeda, T. (2013). The Babkin reflex in infants: Clinical significance and neural mechanism. *Pediatric Neurology*, 49(3), 149–155.

Grossman, T. (2013). Mapping prefrontal cortex functions in human infancy. *Infancy*, 18(3), 303–324.

Hilbrink, E., Sakkalou, E., Ellis-Davies, K., Fowler, N., & Gattis, M. (2013). Selective and faithful imitation at 12 and 15 months. *Developmental Science*, 16(6), 828–840.

Innis, S. (2013). Maternal nutrition, genetics, and human milk lipids. *Current Nutrition Reports*, 2(3), 151–158.

Kärtner, J. Holodynski, M., & Wörmann, V. (2013). Parental ethnotheories, social practice, and the culture-specific development of social smiling in infants. *Mind, Culture, and Activity*, 20(1), 79–95.

Konicarova, J., & Bob, P. (2013). Asymmetric tonic neck reflex and symptoms of attention deficit and hyperactivity disorder in children. *International Journal of Neuroscience*, 5(1), 766–769.

Lavelli, M., & Fogel, A. (2013). Interdyad differences in early mother–infant face-to-face communication: Real-time dynamics and developmental pathways. *Developmental Psychology*, 49(12), 2257–2271.

Leong, P., Gussy, M., Barrow, S., de Silva-Sanigorski, A., & Waters, E. (2013). A systematic review of risk factors during first year of life for early childhood caries. *International Journal of Paediatric Dentistry*, 23(4), 235–250.

Libertus, K., Givson, J., Hidayatallah, N., Hirtle, J., Adcock, R., & Needham, A. (2013). Size matters: How age and reaching experiences shape infants' preferences for different-sized objects. *Infant Behavior and Development*, 36(2), 189–198.

Lloyd, M., MacDonald, M., & Lord, C. (2013). Motor skills of toddlers with autism spectrum disorders. *Autism*, 17(2), 133–146.

Lobo, M., & Galloway, J. (2013). Enhanced handling and positioning in early infancy advances development throughout the first year. *Child Development*, 83(4), 1290–1302.

Loucks, J., & Sommerville, J. (2012). The role of motor experience in understanding action function: The case of the precision grasp. *Child Development*, 83(3), 801–809.

Marotz, L. (2015). *Health, safety, and nutrition for the young child*. Belmont, CA: Wadsworth Cengage Learning.

Möhring, W., & Frick, A. (2013). Touching up mental rotation: Effects of manual experience on 6-month-old infants' mental object rotation. *Child Development*, 84(5), 1554–1565.

Nelson, E., Campbell, J., & Michel, G. (2013). Unimanual to bimanual: Tracking the development of handedness from 6 to 24 months. *Infant Behavior and Development*, 36(2), 181–188.

Oller, D., Buder, E., Ramsdell, H., Warlaumont, A., Chorna, L., & Bakeman, R. (2013). Functional flexibility of infant vocalization and the emergence of language. *Proceedings of the National Academy of Sciences of the United States of America*, 110(6), 6318–6323.

Patel, S., & Gaylord, S. (2013). Generalization of deferred imitation in 6-, 9-, and 12-month-old infants using visual and auditory contexts. *Infant Behavior & Development*, 36(1), 25–31.

Peters, K., Huang, J., Vaughn, M., & Witko, C. (2013). Does breastfeeding contribute to the racial gap in reading and math test scores? *Annals of Epidemiology*, 23(10), 646–651.

Piaget, A. (1954). *The construction of reality in the child*. New York: Basic Books.

Quigley, M., Hockley, C., Carson, C., Kelly, Y., Renfreq, M., & Sacker, A. (2012). Breastfeeding is associated with improved child cognitive development: A population-based cohort study. *Journal of Pediatrics*, 169(1), 25–32.

Salomo, D., & Liszkowski, U. (2013). Sociocultural settings influence the emergence of prelinguistic deictic gestures. *Child Development*, 84(4), 1296–1307.

Shehata-Dieler, W., Ehrmann-Mueller, D., Wermke, P., Voit, V., Cebulla, M., & Wermke, K. (2013). Pre-speech diagnosis in hearing-impaired infants: How auditory experience affects early vocal development. *Speech, Language, and Hearing*, 16(2), 99–106(8).

Sievers, B., Polansky, L., Casey, M., & Wheatley, T. (2013). Music and movement share a dynamic structure that supports universal expressions of emotion. *Proceedings of the National Academy of Sciences of the United States of America*, 110(1), 70–75.

Størvold, G., & Bratberg, G. (2013). Age for onset of walking and prewalking strategies. *Early Human Development*, 89(9), 655–659.

Streri, A., Coulon, M., & Guellaï, B. (2013). The foundations of social cognition: Studies on face/voice integration in newborn infants. *International Journal of Behavioral Development*, 37(2), 79–83.

Streri, A., de Hevia, M., Izard, V., & Coubart, A. (2013). What do we know about neonatal cognition? *Behavioral Sciences*, 3(1), 154–169.

Thoermer, C., Woodward, A., Sodian, B., Perst, H., & Kristen, S. (2013). To get the grasp: Seven-month-olds encode and selectively reproduce goal-directed grasping. *Journal of Experimental Child Psychology*, 116(2), 499–509.

Tsuruhara, A., Kaneko, H., Kanazawa, S., Otsuka, U., Shirai, N., & Yamaguchi, M. (2013). Infants' sensitivity to vertical disparity for depth perception. *Optical Review*, 20(3), 277–281.

Wagner, J., Luyster, R., Yim, J., Tager-Flusber, H., & Nelson, C. (2013). The role of early visual attention in social development. *International Journal of Behavioral Development*, 37(2), 118–124.

# chapter 5
# Toddlerhood: Twelve to Twenty-Four Months

## Learning Objectives

*After reading this chapter, you will be able to:*

**5-1** Define the concept of egocentricity and provide an example.

**5-2** Describe the motor abilities of a typical one-year-old and two-year-old.

**5-3** Define the terms *holophrastic speech* and *telegraphic speech* and give an example of each.

**5-4** Provide two illustrations of the two-year-old's improved understanding of size and spatial relationships.

**5-5** Explain why two-year-olds are often described as picky or fussy eaters.

### naeyc NAEYC Standards Linked to Chapter Content

**1a, 1b, and 1c:** Promoting child development and learning

**2a and 2c:** Building family and community relationships

**3c and 3d:** Observing, documenting, and assessing to support young children and families

**4a, 4b, 4c, and 4d:** Using developmentally effective approaches

**5c:** Using content knowledge to build meaningful curriculum

© d13/Shutterstock.com

Alandra and her husband divorced last year, when their son, Darrius, was just eighteen months old. Darrius and his mother now live in a small apartment just a few blocks away from his grandmother's house. As a single parent, Alandra often feels overwhelmed by the burdens of working evenings at a local restaurant and caring for her now-two-year-old son. Darrius spends his mornings playing alone in his bedroom or watching television while his mother sleeps. When he tires of playing with the few toys in his room, he often heads to the kitchen and begins pulling things from the drawers and cabinets. His activity usually awakens his mother and results in a scolding and an occasional spanking. Books, magazines, and newspapers are notably absent in their apartment. Alandra has little interest in reading and prefers to get her news from television. She occasionally takes Darrius to a neighborhood park, where most of the equipment is old, in poor condition, and designed for older children.

Darrius usually ends up playing alone in the sandbox with any Styrofoam cups, plastic spoons, and sticks that he can find lying around, while his mother chats with her friends.

Darrius adores his father and spends every other weekend at his house. However, when he returns home, Alandra finds Darrius unmanageable and disobedient. She blames her ex-husband for their son's behavior problems, and they often end up arguing about it in front of Darrius. His grandmother is concerned about the effect the divorce and co-parenting arrangement may be having on Darrius's development. He utters only two or three words that anyone can understand and shows little interest in the children's books that his grandmother borrows from her neighbor. Lately, Darrius has become increasingly aggressive—hitting, yelling, and throwing objects—whenever he is frustrated. He refuses to help dress himself when asked, is defiant when told to get ready for bed, and usually runs the other way when his mother calls.

## Ask Yourself

- Do you think Alandra should be concerned about Darrius's language skills? Explain.
- What suggestions, considering the family's limited financial resources, could you offer to Alandra for encouraging Darrius's language development?
- In what ways may his environment be contributing to Darrius's problematic behavior?

# Twelve to Twenty-Four Months

Toddlers are dynamos, full of unlimited energy, enthusiasm, and curiosity. Although their rate of growth slows significantly during this stage, important developmental changes are taking place. The toddler begins this period with the limited motor, social, language, and cognitive abilities of an infant and ends it with the relatively sophisticated skills of a young child.

Toddlers' improving motor skills allow them to navigate, explore, and test their surroundings. However, this newly emerging mobility is also likely to result in frequent bumps, falls, and other injuries due to toddlers' limited control and understanding of cause and effect. Toddlers begin to show interest in books and having an adult read to them. Vocabulary is acquired at a fairly rapid pace and permits toddlers to engage in more complex thinking and communication patterns. "No" becomes a favorite word, and it is used frequently and emphatically to express wants, needs, and frustration.

Defiant behaviors, such as tantrums, hitting, biting, and negative verbalizations often increase in frequency as toddlers begin asserting their independence. Although adults may find this behavior troublesome at times, it marks the beginning of a significant developmental transition. Erik Erikson described this stage as an important step in helping children achieve a sense of **autonomy** and degree of personal control over their environment (Erikson, 1959). However, early independence is not encouraged across all cultures. For example, Asian, Latino, and many Native American children are socialized to be obedient, to submit to authority, and to show respect toward others (Luo, Tamis-LeMonda, & Song, 2013). These behaviors are believed to be vital for enabling families and groups to live and work in harmony.

**Did You Know**

...that approximately 58,000 toddlers were placed in foster care last year? More than half of these children had serious emotional problems, chronic medical conditions, developmental delays, or all three.

**autonomy** A sense of self as being separate from others.

**egocentricity** Believing that everything and everyone is there for your benefit.

**solitary play** Playing alone.

# The One-Year-Old

The ability to stand upright and toddle from place to place enables one-year-olds to begin learning about the world around them. They become talkers and doers, stopping only for much-needed meals and bedtimes. Their curiosity mounts, their skills become increasingly advanced, and their energy level seems never-ending. One-year-olds believe that everything and everyone exists for their sole benefit (Piaget & Inhelder, 1967). Eventually, this **egocentricity** or self-centeredness, gives way to a gradual respect for others. However, for now, one-year-olds are satisfied to declare everything "mine." They prefer to play alone (**solitary play**), observing and imitating the actions of other children rather than joining in.

# Developmental Profiles and Growth Patterns

## Growth and Physical Characteristics

- Grows at a considerably slower rate during this period.
- Gains approximately 2–3 inches (5.0–7.6 cm) in height per year; toddlers reach an average height of 32–35 inches (81.3–88.9 cm).
- Weighs approximately 21–27 pounds (9.6–12.3 kg); gains 1/4–1/2 pound (0.13–0.25 kg) per month; weight is now approximately triple the child's birth weight.
- Breathes at a rate of 22–30 respirations per minute; rate varies with emotional state and activity.
- Heart rate (pulse) is approximately 80–110 beats per minute.
- Head size increases slowly; the head grows approximately 1/2 inch (1.3 cm) every six months; anterior fontanel is nearly closed at eighteen months as the bones of the skull thicken.
- Chest circumference is larger than the head circumference.
- Teeth begin to erupt rapidly; six to ten new teeth appear during this period.
- Legs still may appear bowed.
- Body shape begins to change; toddlers gradually develop a more adultlike appearance but remain top-heavy; abdomen protrudes; back is swayed.
- Visual acuity is approximately 20/60.

## Motor Development

- Crawls skillfully and quickly to a desired location.
- Stands alone with the feet spread apart, legs stiffened, and arms extended for support.
- Gets to the feet unaided.
- Walks unassisted near the end of this period (most children); is still somewhat unsteady and falls often; not always able to maneuver successfully around obstacles such as furniture or toys.
- Uses furniture to lower self to floor; collapses backward into a sitting position or falls forward on hands and then sits.
- Releases an object voluntarily.
- Enjoys pushing or pulling toys while walking.
- Picks up objects and throws them repeatedly; direction becomes more deliberate.
- Attempts to run (with stiff legs); has difficulty stopping and usually just drops to the floor.

## Developmental Profiles and Growth Patterns *(continued)*

Figure 5-1 **Toddlers use whole-arm movements when drawing.**

- Crawls upstairs on all fours; goes downstairs backward in the same position.
- Sits in a small chair.
- Carries toys from place to place.
- Uses crayons and markers for scribbling; draws with whole-arm movement (Figure 5-1).
- Helps feed self; wants to hold her own spoon (often upside down) and cup; not always accurate at getting utensils into the mouth; frequent spills should be expected.
- Helps turn pages of a book during storytime.
- Stacks two to four objects with reasonable accuracy.

### Perceptual-Cognitive Development

- Enjoys object-hiding activities:
  - Early in this period, the toddler always searches in the same location for a hidden object (if the child has watched the object being hidden). Later, the child will search in several locations (Riviere & David, 2013).
  - Passes an object to the other hand when offered a second object (this is referred to as *crossing the midline*—an important neurological development; Shaheen, 2013).
  - Manages three to four objects by setting an object aside (on the lap or floor) when presented with a new one.
- Studies objects by holding and manipulating them in the hands; puts toys in mouth less often (Arterberry, Bornstein, & Blumenstyk, 2013).
- Enjoys looking at picture books (Figure 5-2).

Figure 5-2 **Toddlers enjoy looking at picture books.**

**1-year-old**

## Developmental Profiles and Growth Patterns *(continued)*

- Demonstrates an understanding of functional relationships (objects that belong together):
  - Puts a spoon in a bowl and then uses spoon, pretending to eat.
  - Pounds wooden pegs with a toy hammer.
  - Tries to make a doll stand up and "walk."
- Shows or offers a toy for another person to look at.
- Names many everyday objects.
- Shows an increasing understanding of spatial and form discrimination (puts all large pegs in a pegboard; places three geometric shapes in a large formboard or puzzle).
- Places several small items (e.g., blocks, clothespins, or cereal pieces) in a container or bottle and delights in dumping them out.
- Attempts to make mechanical objects work after watching someone else do so.
- Uses some facial expressions, but they are not always accurate representations.
- Imitates gestures.

### Speech and Language Development

- Produces considerable jargon (i.e., puts sounds and words together into speechlike [inflected] patterns).
- Uses one word to convey an entire thought (**holophrastic speech**); the meaning depends on the inflection ("me" might be used to request more cookies or express a desire to feed himself). Later, the toddler produces two-word phrases to express a complete thought (**telegraphic speech**) ("more cookie," "Daddy bye-bye").
- Follows simple directions ("Give Daddy the book"; "Come here") (Figure 5-3).
- Points to familiar persons, animals, and toys when asked.
- Understands and identifies three body parts if someone names them (**receptive language**); "Show me your nose (toe, ear)."
- Indicates a few desired objects and activities by name ("bye-bye," "cookie," "story," "blanket"); verbal request is often accompanied by an insistent gesture.
- Responds to simple questions with "Yes" or "No" and appropriate head movement.
- Produces speech that is 25 to 50 percent **intelligible** during this period.
- Locates familiar objects upon request (if the child knows their location).

Figure 5-3 **A toddler understands and responds to simple questions.**

© GFOW/Cengage Learning

---

**holophrastic speech**  Using a single word to express a complete thought.
**telegraphic speech**  Uttering two-word phrases to convey a complete thought.
**receptive language**  Understanding words that are heard.
**intelligible**  Featuring language that can be understood by others.

## Developmental Profiles and Growth Patterns *(continued)*

- Acquires and uses five to fifty words (**expressive language**); typically, these are words that refer to the names of familiar objects (e.g., animals, food, and toys); bilingual toddlers tend to have smaller total vocabularies at this point (Poulin-Dubois et al., 2013).

- Uses gestures, such as pointing or pulling, to direct adult attention.

- Enjoys rhymes and songs; tries to join in; dances and sings along.

- Seems aware of reciprocal (back-and-forth) aspects of conversational exchanges; engages in some vocal turn-taking, such as making and imitating sounds.

### Social-Emotional Development

- Remains friendly toward others, although the toddler still may be shy; usually less wary of strangers (Umemura et al., 2013).

- Becomes anxious or cries when parent or parents leave or are out of sight.

- Helps to pick up and put away toys when asked.

- Plays alone for short periods.

- Enjoys being held and read to.

- Observes and imitates adult actions during play (Shimpi, Akhtar, & Moore, 2013).

- Is eager for adult attention; likes to know that an adult is near; gives hugs and kisses.

- Recognizes self in mirror.

- Enjoys the companionship of other children but seldom engages in cooperative play; prefers to play alone.

- Begins to assert independence; often refuses to cooperate with daily routines that once were enjoyable: may resist getting dressed, putting on shoes, eating, taking a bath when asked; wants to try doing things without any adult help.

- Cries and resorts to tantrums on occasion when things go wrong or if overly tired, hungry, or frustrated (Cole, LeDonne, & Ran, 2013).

- Shows a growing curiosity about people and surroundings (approaches and talks to strangers; wanders away when left unattended; searches through cabinets).

**▶❚❚ TeachSource Video Connections**

© 2015 Cengage Learning®

### Speech and Language Development

One-year-olds are learning that language is a functional tool, useful for making requests, informing adults about their needs, and letting others know where they stand—sometimes quite emphatically! Perhaps even more significant is their level of understanding, which far exceeds their ability to use spoken language. Respond to the following questions after you have watched the learning video *0–2 Years: Observation Module for Infants and Toddlers* (focus your attention on the one-year-old in the last one-third of the clip):

1. Were you able to understand all of what the toddler was saying? Why do you think her mother was able to do so?

2. Would you consider the toddler's speech and language skills to be developmentally typical for a one-year-old?

3. What behaviors did the toddler exhibit that would suggest she is in a stage of autonomy?

---

**expressive language** Words used to verbalize thoughts and feelings.

## Developmental Profiles and Growth Patterns *(continued)*

### What Do You See?

**Toddler development** Toddlers are entering a stage of increased awareness, but they are not always ready to play cooperatively with other children. What type of play does this boy appear to be absorbed in? Is this typical? How might you expect him to react if another child tried to help him build the tower higher?

© 2015 Cengage Learning®

### ▶❚❚ TeachSource Video Connections

© 2015 Cengage Learning®

#### Toddlers' Cognitive Development

Children younger than two years learn about their world primarily through their senses. Hand one-year-olds a new toy, and they might look it over, shake it, pound it on the table, and then pop it into their mouths (if it is small enough). Two-year-olds begin to utilize a whole new set of emerging abilities for learning. Respond to the following questions after you have watched the learning video *Infants and Toddlers: Cognitive Development and Imaginative Play*:

1. What advanced cognitive skills are the two-year-olds in this video exhibiting?

2. What instructional strategies is the teacher using to foster and reinforce the children's learning?

3. Could the teacher expect to achieve the same learning outcomes if the children were one-year-olds instead of two-year-olds? Explain.

**Did You Know ?**

...that until the twentieth century, fathers ignored their children and did not participate in their care or upbringing until they had reached the age of seven?

**1-year-old**

## DAILY ROUTINES

### Eating

- Has a much smaller appetite than as an infant; lunch is often the preferred meal (Marotz, 2015).

- Goes on occasional **food jags** (willing to eat only a few preferred foods, such as peanut butter and jelly sandwiches and macaroni and cheese); sometimes described as a picky or fussy eater; neither requires nor wants a large amount of food (Weatherspoon et al., 2013; Howard et al., 2012).

- Holds food in mouth without swallowing it on occasion; this usually indicates that the child does not need or want more to eat.

- Uses a spoon with some degree of skill (if hungry and interested in eating).

- Shows good control of a cup (i.e., lifts it up, drinks from it, sets it down, and holds it with one hand).

- Helps to feed self; some toddlers of this age can feed themselves independently, while others still need some help.

### Toileting, Bathing, and Dressing

- Tries to wash self; plays with washcloth and soap.

- Helps with dressing (puts her arms in sleeves, lifts his feet to have socks put on). Likes to dress and undress self (takes off her own shoes, socks, or mittens); often puts a shirt on upside down and backward or places both feet in one pant leg.

- Lets an adult know when diaper or pants are soiled or wet.

- Begins to gain some control of bowels and bladder (intervals between wetting and soiling becoming longer, resulting in fewer accidents). Complete control is often not achieved until around age three (longer for boys).

### Sleeping

- Sleeps 10–12 hours at night. May fall asleep at dinner if the nap has been missed or if the day's activities have been vigorous. Toddlers in Western cultures often are put to bed at an early and consistent time each night (7 to 8 p.m), whereas evening bedtimes tend to be more flexible and occur later (10 or 11 p.m.) in Asian and European cultures.

- Experiences occasional difficulty falling asleep; overflow of energy is shown in behaviors such as bouncing on the bed, calling for parent, demanding a drink or trip to the bathroom, singing, and making and remaking the bed—all of which seem to be ways of gradually "winding down." A short, consistent bedtime routine and quiet story often promotes relaxation and prepares toddlers for sleep.

- Makes many requests at bedtime for stuffed toys, a book or two, or a special blanket.

### Play and Social Activity

- Develops a strong sense of property rights; "mine" is heard frequently. Sharing is difficult; often hoards toys and other items.

- Enjoys helping but often gets into trouble when left alone (e.g., smears toothpaste, tries on lip gloss, empties dresser drawers, or unrolls toilet paper).

- Enjoys being read to; especially likes rhyming stories with repetition, such as *Is Your Mama a Llama*, *One Duck Stuck*, *Five Little Monkeys*, *Bang! Bang! Toot! Toot!* and Dr. Seuss books; points to pictures and names objects.

**food jag** A phase during which a child is willing to eat only certain foods.

**1-year-old**

## DAILY ROUTINES *(continued)*

- Likes to go on walks; stops frequently to look at things (like rocks, bits of paper, and insects); squats to examine and pick up objects; easily distracted; much dawdling, with no real interest in reaching any particular destination.

- Plays alone (solitary play) most of the time, although beginning to show some interest in other children; engages in a lot of watching. Participates in some occasional **parallel play** (play alongside but not with another child). Might offer play items to another child, but there is little cooperative (purposeful) play; the exception can be children who have spent considerable time in group care (Xu, 2010).

- Seems to feel more secure and better able to settle down at bedtime if the door is left slightly ajar, with a light turned on in another room.

- Continues to nap; however, naps that are too long or too late can interfere with bedtime.

- Wakes up slowly from a nap; cannot be hurried or rushed into any activity.

## learning activities to promote **brain development**

Toddlers learn primarily through play. They need ample time to explore, manipulate, imitate, and experiment in safe environments. Simple, everyday objects and activities provide endless opportunities for learning and often prove to be the most interesting for toddlers.

### Developmentally appropriate applications for families and teachers

- Respond to the toddler's jabbering and voice inflections, both in kind (playfully) and with simple words and questions; maintain conversational turn-taking; describe what you or the child are doing (this helps children associate words with actions and objects).

- Encourage the toddler to point to familiar objects in picture books, catalogs, and magazines; name and count the objects and encourage (but do not force) the toddler to imitate you.

- Hide a toy or other familiar object in an obvious place and encourage the toddler to find it (give clues as needed).

- Provide blocks, stacking rings, shape-sorting boxes, and nesting cups; such toys promote problem-solving and hand-eye coordination.

- Encourage frequent water play; the sink is always a favorite spot when an adult is working in the kitchen. (*Caution:* Use an absorbent towel or rug to catch spills and reduce the chance of slips or falls.) A plastic bowl or dishpan filled with an inch or

---

**parallel play** Playing alongside or near another person, but not involved in that person's activity.

## learning activities *(continued)*

so of water can be equally intriguing when set on the floor; provide sponges, plastic cups, and small toys.

- Place favorite toys in different parts of the room so the toddler must crawl, cruise, or walk to reach them (thus practicing motor skills).

- Provide toys that can be pushed or pulled or a stable plastic or wooden riding toy to steer and propel with the feet; arrange safe, low places for climbing over, under, and on top of (label activities to help toddlers make connections). Avoid gender stereotypes when choosing toys (e.g., trucks are only for boys and dolls are only for girls). Offer toys that address a wide range of interests: boats, trucks, farm animals, books, art materials, dress-up clothes, garden tools, musical instruments, balls, play dishes, etc.

- Take short walks and talk about what you see (e.g., bugs, clouds, and colors); labeling reinforces language development.

- Turn off the television. Young children learn from doing, not through passive activity.

- Encourage active play to promote healthy development, reduce the risk of obesity, and help toddlers release excess energy. Have them toss or kick a soft ball back and forth, blow and chase bubbles, or pick up and drop small objects (e.g., clothespins or blocks) into a bowl or bucket placed across the room.

**TeachSource Digital Download**

## developmental alerts

Check with a health-care provider or early-childhood specialist if, by twenty-four months of age, the child does *not*:

- Attempt to talk or repeat words.

- Understand some new words.

- Respond to own name or answer simple questions with "Yes" or "No".

- Walk alone (or with very little help).

- Exhibit a variety of emotions: anger, delight, fear, and surprise.

- Show interest in pictures; point to named objects when asked.

- Recognize self in a mirror (smile at, point to, or state own name).

- Make eye contact when responding to questions or making a request (unless this is a cultural taboo).

- Attempt self-feeding (hold own cup to mouth and drink from cup).

- Want any physical contact (i.e., to be held, touched, or picked up).

**Note:** Cultural differences may alter the timetable when some developmental skills are acquired. Expanded Developmental Alerts Checklists appear in Appendix A and also are available as digital downloads.

2-year-old

## safety concerns

Continue to implement the safety practices described for the previous stages. Always be aware of new safety issues as the child continues to grow and develop.

### Burns (Thermal and Electrical)
- Cover all electrical outlets with plastic caps.
- Prevent toddlers from touching hot objects such as oven doors, space heaters, water pipes, fireplace doors, outdoor grills, and toasters.
- Keep electrical appliance cords (e.g., coffeepot or curling iron) out of toddlers' reach.
- Apply sunscreen to prevent sunburns; dress toddlers in long sleeves and a hat if they are outdoors for long periods.

### Choking
- Remove objects and toys with small pieces (less than 1 1/2 inch [3.75 cm] in diameter) such as coins, watch or calculator batteries, marbles, pen tops, beads, buttons, magnets, gum and hard candies, paper clips, latex balloons, and plastic bags.
- Cut foods into small pieces; insist that children sit down to eat; avoid foods such as popcorn, pretzels, hot dogs (unless cut crosswise and in small pieces), raw carrots, whole grapes, nuts, and hard candies.

### Water Hazards
- Eliminate unsupervised water sources: swimming or wading pools, mop buckets, fish tanks, outdoor fountains, or other water features. Purchase and use locking devices on toilet seats; *children can drown in 2 inches (5 cm) of water.*
- Install a fence, gates, locks, and an alarm system to protect toddlers from wandering into unsupervised backyard pools or hot tubs.

### Falls
- Place approved safety gates across stairwells; secure them properly to the door frame. Gates can also be used to confine toddlers to rooms where they can be supervised closely.
- Keep doors to the outside, garage, bathrooms, and stairwells locked.
- Pad sharp corners of tables and chairs.
- Eliminate tripping hazards: electrical cords, rugs, wet spills, and highly waxed floors; clear pathways of furniture and toys.

### Poisons
- Store medications (e.g., vitamins, cough syrups, ointments, and prescription drugs), automotive and garden chemicals, and cleaning supplies in a locked cabinet. (High shelves are not always safe from children who can climb.)
- Check for and remove poisonous plants from indoor and outdoor environments. (Contact a local county extension agent for more information.)

### Strangulation
- Avoid clothing with drawstrings around the head or neck.
- Limit strings on pull toys to no more than 14 inches (35 cm) in length; supervise their use closely. Remove toys, mobiles, or clothing with strings from the toddler's bed before sleeping.
- Fasten cords from curtains or window blinds so they are high and inaccessible to children.

# The Two-Year-Old

This year can be terrific, but it can also be a challenge—for the child, family, and teachers. Exasperated adults often describe a two-year-old as impossible (or other words such as *demanding, unreasonable,* or *contrary* may come to mind). However, the two-year-old's fierce determination, impulsivity, and inability to accept limits are part of normal development and seldom under the child's control (Mittal et al., 2013;

Gloeckler & Cassell, 2012) (Figure 5-4). The two-year-old faces demands that can be overwhelming at times: new skills and behaviors to be learned and remembered, needs and feelings that are difficult to express, learned responses to be perfected, and puzzling adult expectations with which to comply. However, toddlers also are gaining an emerging sense of self-confidence as their developmental skills and awareness improve. This can result in moment-to-moment struggles as they try to resolve conflicting desires for independence (autonomy) or dependence (Erikson, 1959). Is it any wonder that two-year-olds are frustrated, have difficulty making choices, and say no, even to things they really want?

Most two-year-olds are able to identify themselves as either being a girl or a boy. However, they don't consider gender to be a permanent quality; they believe that it can be changed at any time simply by wearing different clothing or desiring it to happen. The toddler's concept of gender and gender roles is being shaped continuously by media exposure, adult expectations, and peer responses.

Although this year of transition may be somewhat trying for all, many positive things also happen. Two-year-olds are noted for their frequent and spontaneous outbursts of laughter and affection. They chatter nonstop, ask seemingly endless questions, and are on the go most of their waking hours. They are able to function more ably and amiably as newly acquired skills and earlier learning are consolidated. New skills are learned quickly through trial and error, self-discovery, play, and hands-on-activities. However, the use of computers, child-oriented software, smart toys, electronic pads and game devices, DVDs, and television programming does not support this type of learning, nor does it give children any educational advantage at this age (Duch et al., 2013; Vaala & Lapierre, 2013; Linebarger & Vaala, 2010). Increased concerns have been raised about obesity, sleep disturbances, inactivity, and language and motor delays associated with media use during the early years (Pagani, Fitzpatrick, & Barnett, 2013). The American Academy of Pediatrics (AAP) and pediatricians in other countries discourage television viewing and electronic media entertainment for children younger than two years (AAP, 2013; Carson et al., 2013).

Figure 5-4 Toddlers often exhibit a strong sense of determination.

2-year-old

# Developmental Profiles and Growth Patterns

## Growth and Physical Characteristics

- Gains an average of 2–2.5 pounds (0.9–1.1 kg) per year; weighs approximately 26–32 pounds (11.8–14.5 kg) or about four times the weight at birth.

- Grows approximately 3–5 inches (7.6–12.7 cm) per year; average height is 34–38 inches (86.3–96.5 cm) tall.

- Assumes a more erect posture; the abdomen is still large and protruding and the back somewhat swayed due to weak abdominal muscles that are not developed fully.

- Respirations are slow and regular (approximately 20–35 breaths per minute).

- Body temperature continues to fluctuate with activity, emotional state, and environment.

- The brain reaches about 80 percent of its adult size.

- Eruption of teeth is nearly complete; second molars appear, for a total of twenty deciduous (or *baby*) teeth.

## Developmental Profiles and Growth Patterns *(continued)*

### Motor Development

- Walks with a more erect, heel-to-toe pattern; able to maneuver around obstacles in a pathway.
- Runs with greater confidence; has fewer falls.
- Squats for long periods while playing.
- Climbs stairs unassisted (but not with alternating feet), holding onto the railing for support.
- Balances on one foot (for a few moments), jumps up and down with both feet but might fall.
- Begins to achieve toilet training during this year (depending on the child's level of physical and neurological development), although accidents still should be expected; children will indicate readiness for toilet training (e.g., understands concepts of wet and dry, is able to pull clothing up and down, communicates needs, and understands and follows directions).
- Throws a large ball underhand without losing balance.
- Holds a cup or glass (be sure it is unbreakable) in one hand.
- Unbuttons large buttons; unzips large zippers.
- Opens doors by turning doorknobs.
- Grasps a large crayon with fist; scribbles enthusiastically on a large piece of paper (Figure 5-5).
- Climbs up on a chair, turns around, and sits down.
- Enjoys pouring, filling, and dumping activities involving such materials as sand, water, or Styrofoam peanuts.
- Stacks four to six objects on top of one another.
- Uses feet to propel wheeled riding toys.

### Perceptual-Cognitive Development

- Follows simple requests and directions: "Find your sweater," "Come here."
- Exhibits eye–hand movements that are better coordinated; puts objects

**Figure 5-5** **A two-year-old can hold a crayon in a fist and scribble.**

▶❚❚ **TeachSource** **Video Connections**

### Assessing Motor Development

Toddlers become increasingly adept at controlling their body movements. They are able to manipulate objects with improving accuracy, assist with their personal care, walk and run with confidence, and draw with large, sweeping motions. These abilities serve as the foundation for more complex skills that the child will continue to develop. Respond to the following questions after you have watched the learning video *Observing and Monitoring Physical/Motor Development in Toddlers: The Importance of Assessment:*

1. Why is it important to assess the toddler's motor skill development in a naturalistic setting?

2. What is the purpose of asking parents to complete the same questionnaire that the teachers use for assessment?

3. Identify and describe three fine motor skills that the children performed in this video. What additional activities could you plan to reinforce a toddler's continued development of these skills?

## Developmental Profiles and Growth Patterns *(continued)*

together and takes them apart; fits large pegs into a pegboard, places large puzzle pieces in the approximate area where they should go (Arterberry, Bornstein, & Blumenstyk, 2013).

- Begins to use objects for purposes other than the intended ones (e.g., may push a block around as a pretend boat, use a box as a drum, or turn a bucket into a hat).

- Completes simple classification tasks based on one dimension (separates toy dinosaurs from toy cars, blocks from markers, or red beads from blue beads); this is an important development for learning future math skills.

- Stares for long moments; seems fascinated by, or engrossed in, figuring out a situation (where a tennis ball has rolled, where the dog went, what has caused a particular noise); however, often has a short attention span.

- Sits quietly and engages in self-selected activities for longer periods (Figure 5-6).

- Shows discovery of cause and effect (squeezing the cat makes her scratch or run away; turning the door handle makes the door open).

- Knows where familiar persons should be; notes their absence; finds a hidden object by looking in the last hiding place first.

- Names objects in picture books; might pretend to pick something off the page and taste or smell it.

- Recognizes and expresses pain; can point to its location.

### Speech and Language Development

- Enjoys being read to if allowed to participate by pointing, making relevant noises, and turning pages.

2-year-old

Figure 5-6 **Toddlers are able to focus on an activity for longer periods.**

© GFOW/Cengage Learning

- Realizes that language is effective for getting others to respond to needs and preferences. Makes simple requests ("More cookies?"); refuses adult wishes, sometimes forcefully ("No!").

- Uses 50 to 300 words; vocabulary continuously increasing.

- Has broken the **linguistic code**; that is, much of a two-year-old's talk has meaning to her, but not always to adults (i.e., Lev Vygotsky's "self-talk").

- Understands significantly more language than is able to communicate verbally; most two-year-olds' have receptive language that is far more advanced than their expressive language (Beuker et al., 2013).

- Utters three- and four-word statements; uses conventional word order to form more complete sentences.

- Refers to self as "me" or sometimes "I" rather than by name ("Me go bye-bye"); has no trouble verbalizing "mine."

- Expresses negative statements by tacking on a negative word such as "no" or "not" ("Not more milk," "No bath").

**linguistic code** Verbal expression that has meaning to the child.

**2-year-old**

## Developmental Profiles and Growth Patterns *(continued)*

- Asks repeatedly, "What's that?" "Why?"
- Uses some plurals, but not always correctly ("See the gooses"); often overgeneralizes grammatical rules. Talks about objects and events not immediately present, as in "We saw peoples." (This is both a cognitive and a linguistic advance.)
- Experiences occasional stammering and other common **dysfluencies**.
- Produces speech that is as much as 65–70 percent intelligible.

### Social-Emotional Development

- Shows signs of empathy and caring (comforts another child who is hurt or frightened); at times, can be overly affectionate in offering hugs and kisses to children (sociocultural differences and expectations may influence the nature of this behavior) (Brownell, 2013; Panfile & Laible, 2012).
- Continues to use physical aggression if frustrated or angry; this response is more exaggerated for some children than for others; physical aggression usually diminishes as verbal skills improve. Children's expressions of temperament are influenced through cultural socialization and, thus, are highly variable (He et al., 2013; Slobodskayal et al., 2013).
- Often expresses frustration through temper tantrums; frequency of tantrums typically peaks during this year; cannot be reasoned with while tantrum is in progress (Daniels, Mandleco, & Luthy, 2012).
- Finds it difficult to wait or take turns; often impatient.
- Eager to "help" with household chores; imitates everyday activities (might try to toilet a stuffed animal or feed and bathe a doll).
- Is bossy at times; orders peers and adults around; makes demands and expects immediate compliance.
- Watches and imitates the play of other children but seldom joins in; content to play alone.
- Offers toys to other children but is usually possessive of playthings; still tends to hoard toys.
- Finds it difficult to make choices; wants both options at the same time.
- Shows much defiance; shouting "No!" becomes almost automatic.
- Wants everything just so; is quite ritualistic; expects routines to be carried out exactly as before and belongings to be in their usual places.

## What Do You See?

**Social development** Toddlers learn by observing and doing. What other typical social-emotional characteristics are these children exhibiting?

© 2015 Cengage Learning®

**dysfluency** Repetition of whole words or phrases, uttered without frustration and often at the beginning of a statement, such as "Let's go, let's go get some cookies."

## Spotlight on Brain Development

### The Brain-Autism Connection

Scientists have used functional neuroimaging technologies, such as magnetic resonance imaging (MRI) and diffusion tensor imaging, to study the brains of young children who have been diagnosed with autism or autism spectrum disorders (e.g., Uddin, Supekar, & Menon, 2013). Their findings have consistently revealed abnormalities in the way that early connections are formed between brain cells and critical neural networks, including those involved in children's cognitive, sensorimotor, social, and language development (e.g., Boersma et al., 2013).

Although these discoveries are universally accepted among scientists, many questions remain to be answered about the exact cause, nature, and effect these alterations may have on age-related behaviors (Lynch et al., 2013; Nair et al., 2013). For example, why are boys diagnosed with autism at a significantly higher rate than are girls (Lai et al., 2013)? How robust or strong are the associations between abnormal neural connections and social behavior? Are the observed neural alterations the cause or the result of abnormal connectivity?

As is often the case, research findings raise more questions than they initially answer. What is becoming clearer is that autism and autism spectrum syndromes are complex disorders that may not have a simple answer. Additional studies are needed to pinpoint more specifically the underlying neurobiological causes. These findings, in turn, may contribute to the development of new diagnostic tools, earlier detection methods, and intervention strategies, such as the use of stem cells, restoration of brain plasticity, new medications, and redesigned behavioral therapies, that are more effective than those currently in use (Delorme et al., 2013; Kim et al., 2013; Yuan & Shaner, 2013).

**What are the connections?**

1. What signs of abnormal development might be observed in a toddler who is potentially autistic?
2. Why is early detection so important?

## DAILY ROUTINES

### Eating

- Has fair appetite; interest in food fluctuates with periods of growth; lunch is often the preferred meal.
- Sometimes described as a picky or fussy eater; usually has strong likes and dislikes (which should be respected); may go on temporary food jags, as discussed previously (Saavedra et al., 2013).
- Prefers simple, recognizable foods; dislikes mixtures and often refuses new food items; wants familiar foods that are served in customary ways (Weatherspoon et al., 2013).
- Needs between-meal snacks, which should be of good nutritive value (fresh fruits and vegetables, cheese with whole-grain crackers, or yogurt), with junk foods limited.
- Feeds self with increasing skill, but may be "too tired" or uninterested at times.
- Has better control of a cup or glass, although frequent spills are likely to happen.
- Learns table manners through verbal instruction and by imitating those of adults and older children.

### Toileting, Bathing, and Dressing

- Enjoys bath if allowed ample playtime (must *never* be left alone when bathing); tries to wash self; may object to being washed and squirm when being dried off.
- Dislikes, even resists, having hair shampooed.

**2-year-old**

## DAILY ROUTINES *(continued)*

- Wants to brush own teeth but isn't thorough (it is important that an adult always follow up the toddler's attempts).

- Tries to help when being dressed; needs simple, manageable clothing; can usually undress self without much effort (Figure 5-7).

- Shows signs of readiness for bowel training (some children may have already mastered bowel control); uses appropriate words; becomes upset when pants are soiled and may run to the bathroom or hide.

- Stays dry for longer periods of time, which is one sign of readiness for toilet training; other signs include interest in watching others use the toilet, holding a doll or stuffed animal over the toilet, clutching at diaper or pants, willingness to sit on potty for a few moments, expressing discomfort about being wet or soiled (Zero to Three, 2012).

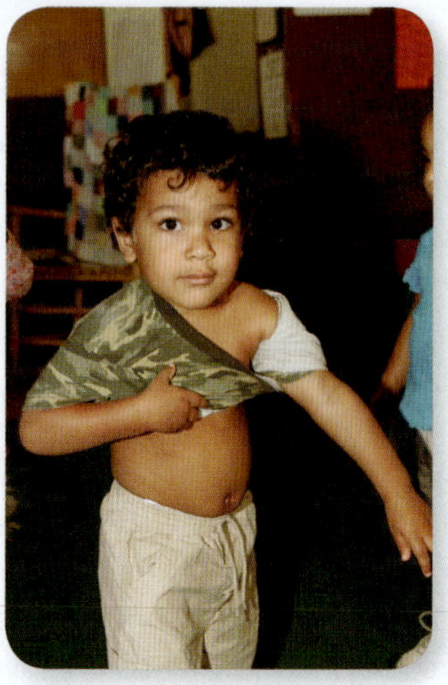

**Figure 5-7** Toddlers often insist on dressing themselves, but they still need some adult help.

© GFOW/Cengage Learning

### Sleeping

- Sleeps between nine and twelve hours at nighttime.

- Still requires an afternoon nap; needs time to wake up slowly.

- Resists going to bed; however, usually complies if given ample warning and can depend on a familiar bedtime routine (with a story, talk time, or a special toy) (Williams, Zimmerman, & Bell, 2013).

- Takes awhile to fall asleep, especially if overly tired; might sing, talk to herself, bounce on the bed, call for parents, and make and remake the bed (again, these are ways of winding down).

### Play and Social Activity

- Enjoys dressing up and imitating family activities (wearing father's hat makes the child a "daddy"; putting on high-heeled shoes makes the child a "mommy").

- Likes to be around other children but does not always play well with them (observes intently, imitating other children's actions [parallel play] but is unlikely to join in).

- Displays extreme negativism toward parents and caregivers at times—an early step toward establishing independence; shouts "No!" or runs when asked to pick up toys, get ready for bed, or come to the dinner table.

- Pretends to have an imaginary friend as a constant companion.

- Explores everything in the environment, including other children; might shove or push other children as if to test their reaction.

## learning activities to promote **brain development**

Two-year-olds' interests are driven by movement, language, enthusiasm, and curiosity. Do things together and provide opportunities that strengthen existing skills and help children to develop new ones.

## learning activities *(continued)*

### Developmentally appropriate applications for families and teachers

2-year-old

- Play games, such as large Lotto and picture dominoes, that encourage children to match colors, animals, facial expressions, and everyday objects.

- Offer manipulative materials to foster problem solving and hand–eye coordination: large beads for stringing; brightly colored cubes; puzzles; large, plastic, interlocking bricks; nesting toys.

- Provide toy replicas of farm and zoo animals, families, dishes and cooking and eating utensils, cars, trucks, and planes for sorting and imaginative play.

- Read to the child regularly; provide colorful picture books for naming objects and describing everyday events; use simple, illustrated storybooks (one line per page) so the child can learn to "tell" the story; ask the child to turn the pages.

- Share nursery rhymes, simple finger plays, and action songs; respond to, imitate, and make up simple games based on the child's spontaneous rhyming or chanting.

- Set out (and keep a close eye on) washable paints, markers, chalk, large crayons, and large paper for the toddler's artistic expression.

- Encourage make-believe activities: save empty cereal and cracker boxes, plastic juice containers with intact labels, and recyclable bags for a pretend store; set out dress-up clothes and an unbreakable mirror; or give the child plastic gardening supplies.

- Provide wagons; large trucks and cars that can be loaded, pushed, or sat upon; a doll carriage or stroller; a rocking boat; or beanbags and rings for tossing.

- Create opportunities for musical enjoyment: encourage children to play musical instruments, invent and sing songs, dance, wave around scarves or crepe paper streamers to musical rhythms, or pretend to be animals.

- Play games that involve sorting simple objects: laundry (towels in one pile, socks in another); colored blocks (red in one stack, blue in the other).

- Let children help with household chores: dusting furniture, "washing" the car, sweeping the sidewalk, or "painting" with a brush and water.

- Go for walks; collect items to use for an art project; organize a parade; or play "I Spy" ("a brown dog," "a blue house," "something red").

**TeachSource Digital Download**

## developmental alerts

Check with a health-care provider or early childhood specialist if, by the third birthday, the child does *not*:

- Eat a fairly well-rounded diet, even though amounts are limited.

- Walk confidently with few stumbles or falls; climb steps with help.

- Avoid bumping into objects.

- Carry out simple, two-step directions: "Come to Daddy and bring your book"; express desires; ask questions.

## developmental **alerts** (continued)

- Point to and name familiar objects; use two- or three-word sentences.
- Enjoy being read to; help to hold a book; name and point to objects.
- Show interest in playing with other children (watching, and perhaps imitating).
- Indicate a beginning interest in toilet training (runs to the bathroom, pulls pants down, and uses appropriate words).
- Sort familiar objects according to a single characteristic, such as type, color, shape, or size.
- Make eye contact when making a request or responding to questions (unless this is a cultural taboo). Failing to make eye contact may be an early sign of autism.

**Note:** Cultural differences may alter the timetable when some developmental skills are acquired. Expanded Developmental Alerts Checklists appear in Appendix A and are also available as digital downloads.

2-year-old

## safety **concerns**

Continue to implement the safety practices described for previous stages. Always be aware of new safety issues as the child continues to grow and develop.

### Burns
- Set the temperature of the hot water heater no higher than 120°F (49°C).
- Purchase and use protective devices on bathtub and sink faucets.
- Keep hot liquids and cooking tools out of reach.

### Choking
- Continue to cut food into small pieces; insist that children sit down to eat; avoid popcorn, hot dogs (unless cut crosswise in small pieces), raw carrots, whole grapes, nuts, and hard candies.

### Water
- Supervise any accessible water source (e.g., wading pools, fish tanks, garden ponds or fountains, bathtubs). *Children can drown in 2 inches (5 cm) of water. Never leave children unattended.*

### Play Environment
- Fasten bookcases, filing cabinets, dressers, and shelves securely to a wall or floor to prevent them from tipping over.
- Place toys and books on lower shelves so they are accessible.

- Keep the doors to the outside and stairwells locked.
- Cover electrical outlets and remove unnecessary electrical cords.

### Poisons
- Store all medicines (including vitamins and nonprescription drugs), automotive and garden chemicals, and cleaning supplies in a locked cabinet. (High shelves are not safe from children who can climb.)
- Check for and remove poisonous plants from indoor and outdoor environments.

### Strangulation
- Avoid dress-up clothing that could become entangled around a child's neck (e.g., neckties and clothes with drawstrings).

### Vehicles
- Never leave children alone in a car.
- Always securely fasten a child in a properly installed car safety seat.
- Insist that children hold an adult's hand when exiting a vehicle and walking where other cars are nearby.

# positive behavior guidance

Adults are responsible for protecting toddlers from harm and teaching them about social and cultural expectations. Toddlers understand the world only from their own self-centered perspective, and they must learn gradually, through trial and error, how they are supposed to behave and fit in with society. This process requires ongoing adult guidance, patience, and nurturing support.

2-year-old

## One-year-olds

- Acknowledge and encourage children's efforts, even if they aren't perfect: "I am proud of you for trying to put on your own shoe."
- Minimize the need for rules by childproofing the environment.
- Maintain predictable routines and schedules so that children can anticipate what to expect.
- Set limits that are reasonable, developmentally appropriate, and necessary to protect children's safety.
- Provide short explanations and guide a child's actions: "Gentle touches" (take the child's hand and pet the dog); "No hitting" (pick the child up and move her to another area; distract or redirect the child's attention by offering another toy or activity).
- Enforce limits consistently so that the child understands your expectations.
- Ignore simple misbehaviors unless they are likely to cause someone harm.

## Two-year-olds

- Give children your undivided attention and let them know when they are behaving appropriately.
- Recognize that children will forget and repeat undesirable behaviors.
- Accept the toddler's intense desire for autonomy. Whenever appropriate, offer a choice instead of insisting that he do things your way: for instance, ask "Do you want to wear the red shirt or the blue shirt?" or "Would you like to read a story or put a puzzle together after you put on your pajamas?"
- Choose your battles. Remember that toddlers may misbehave simply to get your attention. Ignore a negative behavior, so long as it doesn't cause harm to the child or to others. When the child is behaving appropriately, be sure to give him the attention that he is seeking.
- Set a positive example. Toddlers imitate the way that they see others behaving.

# Summary

**5-1** One-year-olds have limited awareness and concern for others. They are self-absorbed, believe in their own self-importance, and consider adults to be there to satisfy their every demand and desire.

**5-2** Rapid changes occur in the motor development of one-year-olds. They learn how to walk unassisted, crawl up and down stairs, carry and manipulate objects, stack blocks, and help to feed themselves. Two-year-olds continue to perfect and elaborate on these skills: their locomotion is more deliberate and directional, they run and climb stairs unassisted, stack blocks higher, and learn to navigate riding toys.

- Toddlers' limited understanding of cause and effect, ability to judge size and distance, and grasp of functionality place them at high risk for unintentional injury.

continued on following page

## Summary

**5-3** Toddlers' language skills progress from using a single word to convey a complete thought to using two or three words.

- Expressive language remains limited; receptive language is considerably more advanced.
- The toddler is beginning to grasp the concept of language and how it can be used for communication purposes: naming objects, making requests, and expressing wants and needs.

**5-4** Two-year-olds are beginning to understand the concepts of size, shape, and position. They attempt simple puzzles, place objects in a container, begin to stack blocks and arrange items by size, etc.

**5-5** Appetite wanes during the toddler years due to a slower rate of growth. Toddlers need less food (and fewer calories) per pound of body weight than they required as an infant.

## Key Terms

autonomy **p. 107**

egocentricity **p. 108**

solitary play **p. 108**

holophrastic speech **p. 110**

telegraphic speech **p. 110**

receptive language **p. 110**

intelligible **p. 110**

expressive language **p. 111**

food jags **p. 113**

parallel play **p. 114**

linguistic code **p. 119**

dysfluency **p. 120**

## Apply What You Have Learned

### A. Case Study Connections

*Reread the developmental sketch about Darrius and his family presented at the beginning of this chapter and answer the following questions.*

1. What language skills would you expect a typically developing two-year-old to have?

2. Do you consider Darrius's displays of anger and aggression to be typical or atypical of a toddler? Explain.

3. From a developmental perspective, explain why Darrius continues to get into his mother's kitchen cabinets and dresser drawers despite repeated warnings to stop.

4. Because Alandra sleeps in the morning while Darrius is playing, what special precautions should she take in their apartment to ensure his safety?

### B. Review Questions

1. Describe two activities that would promote a two-year-old's developmental skills in each of the following areas: self-care, motor, and language.

2. Why are toddlers more likely to experience tantrums? In what ways would you expect to see a one-year-old begin asserting his autonomy?

3. Why are toddlers at high risk for unintentional injury? What steps must adults take to reduce this risk?

4.  What is holophrastic speech? Provide three examples to illustrate this form of speech. At what age are children most likely to exhibit holophrastic speech?

5.  Describe three activities designed to help two-year-olds learn about the concept of size.

## C. Your Turn: Chapter to Practice

1.  Visit the children's section of your local library. Select and briefly annotate ten to fifteen books that you would recommend for parents to read to their toddlers.

2.  Make arrangements to observe an early intervention toddler classroom. Focus your observation on one toddler and use the milestones in this chapter to assess the level of development. Write up a brief description of the child's development across domains.

3.  Observe a toddler classroom for approximately 30 minutes. Note how the teacher handles incidences of troublesome behavior. What strategies were used, and were they effective? What suggestions would you have for managing the situations differently based on the information in this chapter?

4.  Develop a series of four or five activities that would reinforce and advance a toddler's manipulative and cognitive skills.

# Online Resources

## Centers for Disease Control and Prevention (CDC)

The Centers for Disease Control and Prevention (CDC) offers an extensive parent information site (enter "Parent Information" into the search box) that addresses developmental milestones, safety tips, diseases, parenting advice, parent videos, and links to additional information resources.

## Child Development Institute

Child development topics, health and safety concerns, activities to reinforce learning, and behavior guidance tips can be accessed on this site.

## National Autism Resource and Information Center

On this website, families, educators, health-care professionals, employers, and community workers will find information to help them work effectively with individuals of all ages who experience autism.

## Zero to Three

This national nonprofit organization has as its mission the promotion of infant and toddler health and development through funded research, advocacy for policies that benefit young children, and the dissemination of information for parents and educators.

# References

American Academy of Pediatrics (AAP). (2013). Children, adolescents, and the media. *Pediatrics*, 132(5), 958–961.

Arterberry, M., Bornstein, M., & Blumenstyk, J. (2013). Categorization of two-dimensional and three-dimensional stimuli by 18-month-old infants. *Infant Behavior & Development*, 36(4), 786–795.

Boersma, M., Kemner, C., de Reus, M., Collin, G., Snijders, T., Hoffman, D., …, & van den Heuvel, M. (2013). Disrupted functional brain networks in autistic toddlers. *Brain Connectivity*, 3(1), 41–49.

Brownell, C. (2013). Early development of prosocial behavior: Current perspectives. *Infancy*, 18(1), 1–9.

Beuker, K., Rommelse, N., Donders, R., & Buitelaar, J. (2013). Development of early communication skills in the first two years of life. *Infant Behavior & Development*, 36(1), 71–83.

Carson, V., Tremblay, M., Spence, J., Timmons, B., & Janssen, I. (2013). The Canadian Sedentary Behaviour Guidelines for the early years (zero to four years of age) and screen time among children from Kingston, Ontario. *Paediatrics Child Health*, 18(1), 25–28.

Cole, P., LeDonne, E., & Tan, P. (2013). A longitudinal examination of maternal emotions in relation to young children's developing self-regulation. *Parenting, Science and Practice*, 13(2), 113–132.

Daniels, E., Mandleco, B., & Luthy, K. (2012). Assessment, management, and prevention of childhood temper tantrums. *Journal of the American Academy of Nurse Practitioners*, 24(10), 569–573.

Delorme, R., Ey, E., Toro, R., Leboyer, M., Gillberg, C., & Bourgeron, T. (2013). Progress toward treatments for synaptic defects in autism. *Nature Medicine*, 19, 685–694.

Duch, H., Fisher, E., Ensari, I., Font, M., Harrington, A., Taromino, C., …, & Rodriguez, C. (2013). Association of screen time use and language development in Hispanic toddlers: A cross-sectional and longitudinal study. *Clinical Pediatrics*, 52(9), 857–865.

Erikson, E. (1959). Identity and the life cycle. *Psychological Issues*, *1(1)*, 1–171.

Gloeckler, L., & Cassell, J. (2012). Teacher practices with toddlers during social problem-solving opportunities. *Early Childhood Education Journal*, 40(4), 251–257.

He, J., Qiu, P., Park, K., Xu, Q., & Potegal, M. (2013). Young Chinese children's anger and distress: Emotion category and intensity identified by the time course of behavior. *International Journal of Behavioral Development*, 37(4), 349–356.

Howard, A., Mallan, K., Byrne, R., Magarey, A., & Daniles, L. (2012). Toddlers' food preferences. The impact of novel food exposure, maternal preferences, and food neophobia. *Appetite*, 59(3), 818–825.

Kim, K., Jung, Y., Sullivan, G., Chung, L., & Park, I. (2013). Cellular reprogramming: A novel tool for investigating autism spectrum disorders. *Trends in Molecular Medicine*, 18(8), 463–471.

Lai, M., Lombardo, M., Suckling, J., Ruigrok, A., Chakrabarti, B., Ecker, C., …, & Bullmore, E. (2013). Biological sex affects the neurobiology of autism. *Brain*, 136(9), 2799–2815.

Linebarger, D., & Vaala, S. (2010). Screen media and language development in infants and toddlers: An ecological perspective. *Developmental Review*, 30(2), 176–202.

Luo, R., Tamis-LeMonda, C., & Song, L. (2013). Chinese parents' goals and practices in early childhood. *Early Childhood Research Quarterly*, 28(4), 843–857.

Lynch, C., Uddin, L., Supekar, K., Khouzam, A., Phillips, J., & Menon, V. (2013). Default mode network in childhood autism: Posteromedial cortex heterogeneity and relationship with social deficits. *Biological Psychiatry*, 74(3), 212–219.

Marotz, L. (2015). *Health, safety, and nutrition for the young child*. 9th Ed. Belmont, CA: Wadsworth Cengage Learning.

Mittal, R., Russell, B., Britner, P., & Peake, P. (2013). Delay of gratification in two- and three-year-olds: Associations with attachment, personality, and temperament. *Journal of Child & Family Studies*, 22(4), 479–489.

Nair, A., Treiber, J., Shukla, D., Shih, P., & Müller, R. (2013). Impaired thalamocortical connectivity in autism spectrum disorder: A study of functional and anatomical connectivity. *Brain*, 136(6), 1942–1955.

Pagani, L., Fitzpatrick, C., & Barnett, T. (2013). Early childhood television viewing and kindergarten entry readiness. *Pediatric Research*, 74(3), 350–355.

Panfile, T., & Laible, D. (2012). Attachment security and child's empathy: The mediating role of emotion regulation. *Merrill-Palmer Quarterly*, 58(1), 1–21.

Piaget, J., & Inhelder, B. (1967). *The child's conception of space*. New York: Norton.

Poulin-Dubois, D., Bialystok, E., Blaye, A., Polonia, A., & Yott, J. (2013). Lexical access and vocabulary development in very young bilinguals. *International Journal of Bilingualism*, 17(1), 57–70.

Riviere, J., & David, E. (2013). Perceptual–motor constraints on decision making: The case of the manual search behavior for hidden objects in toddlers. *Journal of Experimental Child Psychology*, 115(1), 42–52.

Saavedra, J., Deming, D., Dattilo, A., & Reidy, K. (2103). Lessons from the Feeding Infants and Toddlers Study in North America: What children eat, and implications for obesity prevention. *Annals of Nutrition & Metabolism*, 62(suppl 3), 27–36.

Shaheen, S. (2013). Motor assessment in pediatric neuropsychology: Relationships to executive function. *Applied Neuropsychology: Child*, 2(2), 116–124.

Shimpi, P., Akhtar, N., & Moore, C. (2013). Toddlers' imitative learning in interactive and observational contexts: The role of age and familiarity of the model. *Journal of Experimental Child Psychology*, 116(2), 309–323.

Slobodskayal, H., Gartstein, M., Nakagawa, A., & Putnam, S. (2013). Early temperament in Japan, the United States, and Russia: Do cross-cultural differences decrease with age? *Journal of Cross-Cultural Psychology*, 44(3), 438–460.

Uddin, L., Supekar, K., & Menon, V. (2013). Reconceptualizing functional brain connectivity in autism from a developmental perspective. *Frontiers in Human Neuroscience*, 7, 458, doi: 10.3389/fnhum.2013.00458.

Umemura, T., Jacobvitz, D., Messina, S., & Hazen, N. (2013). Do toddlers prefer the primary caregiver or the parent with whom they feel more secure? The role of toddler emotion. *Infant Behavior & Development*, 36(1), 102–114.

Vaala, S., & Lapierre, M. (2013). Marketing genius: The impact of educational claims and cues on parents' reactions to infant/toddler DVDs. *Journal of Consumer Affairs*, doi:10.1111/joca.12023.

Weatherspoon, L., Venkatesh, S., Horodynski, M., Stommel, M., & Brophy-Herb, H. (2013). Food patterns and mealtime behaviors in low-income mothers and toddlers. *Journal of Community Health Nursing*, 30(1), 1–15.

Williams, J., Zimmerman, F., & Bell, J. (2013). Norms and trends of sleep time among U.S. children and adolescents. *JAMA Pediatrics*, 167(1), 55–60.

Xu, Y. (2010), Children's social play sequence: Parten's classic theory revisited. *Early Child Development & Care*, 180(4), 489–498.

Yuan, S., & Shaner, M. (2013). Bioengineered stem cells in neural development and neurodegeneration research. *Ageing Research Reviews*, 12(3), 739–748.

Zero to Three. (2012). Learning to use the toilet. Retrieved on February 7, 2014, from http://www.zerotothree.org/child-development/early-development/all-about-potty-training.html.

# chapter 6

# Early Childhood: Three-, Four-, and Five-Year-Olds

## Learning Objectives

*After reading this chapter, you will be able to:*

**6-1** Describe the changes that occur in children's cognitive development between three, four, and five years of age.

**6-2** Discuss the preschooler's desire for adult attention and trace the ways that this need changes as children become more independent.

**6-3** Identify at least eight ways that adults can support the preschool-child's language development.

**6-4** Describe the food preferences, eating habits, and calorie needs of typical three-, four-, and five-year-olds.

### naeyc NAEYC Standards Linked to Chapter Content

**1a, 1b, and 1c:** Promoting child development and learning

**2a and 2c:** Building family and community relationships

**3c and 3d:** Observing, documenting, and assessing to support young children and families

**4a, 4b, 4c, and 4d:** Using developmentally effective approaches to connect with children and families

**5c:** Using content knowledge to build meaningful curriculum

Hasina's interest in resuming her education was sparked after she attended a recruiting program sponsored by the local community college. When Hasina discovered there was space for her four-year-old daughter, Munisa, at the child care center on campus, she was even more determined. Hasina knows that Munisa's language and social development are delayed and believes that she will benefit from having more opportunities to interact with children her own age.

Each morning, Hasina drops Munisa off at the child care center while she attends classes and works in the school cafeteria. However, Munisa has been slow to adjust to her new school. She often prefers to play alone, seldom stays involved in any activity for more than a few minutes, and insists on carrying her security blanket wherever she goes.

© Andresr/Shutterstock.com

Despite her busy schedule, Hasina sets aside time in the evenings to play with Munisa. They talk about things that she has done in school that day and sometimes work together on puzzles or art projects. Before Munisa heads to bed, they always sit quietly and read a story together. Hasina is becoming increasingly confident in her ability to encourage Munisa's development ever since attending a parent education class at the college. She now realizes how simple, everyday things she does with her daughter help to foster her brain development. Hasina thinks she would enjoy working with young children and is seriously considering becoming an early childhood teacher.

## Ask Yourself

- Would you consider Munisa's personal-social development appropriate for her age?
- In what ways is Hasina encouraging Munisa's language and literacy development?
- What signs of stress is Munisa displaying as she tries to adjust to a new experience?

# Three-, Four-, and Five-Year Olds

Three-, four-, and five-year-olds are typically full of energy, eagerness, and curiosity (Figure 6-1). They seem to be constantly on the move, engrossing themselves totally in whatever captures their interest at the moment. During these preschool years, children are perfecting their motor skills. They exhibit creativity and imagination in everything they do, from their artwork and storytelling to dramatic play. Vocabulary and intellectual skills are expanding rapidly, enabling children to express ideas, solve problems, and plan ahead. Grammatical errors and mispronunciations remain fairly common, however, especially among children who are dual-language learners (Cooperson, Bedore, & Peña, 2013). For this reason, caution must be exercised when determining if a child who is bilingual may have a language impairment or delay (Bloom & Paradis, 2013; Michael-Luna, 2013).

Preschool-age children are becoming more aware of concepts such as death and gender, but their immature cognitive abilities limit a comprehensive understanding. Children younger than five may acknowledge that someone or something has died but express hope that death can be reversed (Gaab, Owens, & MacLeod, 2013; Vlok & de Witt, 2012). By age seven, they understand death as universal—that it happens to everyone—and, shortly thereafter, children are able to accept that all body functions cease at the time of death. Children's understanding of gender undergoes similar cognitive changes. Most five-year-olds are not only able to identify themselves as being either a boy or girl, but they also believe that gender can be changed temporarily by wearing different outfits or acting out different roles (Hamlin et al., 2013).

Preschool children strongly believe in their own opinions but, at the same time, they begin to understand that others have needs and feelings too. They are learning self-control, distinguishing right from wrong, tolerance, and how to make better choices (Taylor et al., 2013a). They are eager to gain independence, yet they need reassurance that an adult is nearby to give assistance, to comfort, to mediate, or to rescue if need be.

# The Three-Year-Old

Three-year-olds tend to be more peaceful, relaxed, and cooperative. Conflicts with adults that grew out of the two-year-old's struggle for independence are now fewer and less intense. Three-year-olds experience fewer emotional outbursts, are more likely to comply with adult requests most of the time, and are able to delay their need gratification longer than before. However, there are distinct cultural differences in the expression of these behaviors and the importance given to developing compliance at a young age (Li-Grining, 2013; Wanless et al., 2013). Three-year-olds are also becoming more aware and accepting of others, and thus are able to participate in group play. They take obvious delight in themselves and life in general and show an irrepressible urge to discover everything they can about the world around them.

Figure 6-1 Children are exceptionally curious and inquisitive at this age.

## Developmental Profiles and Growth Patterns

### Growth and Physical Characteristics

- Growth is steady, although it is slower than during the first two years.
- Height increases 2–3 inches (5–7.6 cm) per year; average height is 38–40 inches (96.5–101.6 cm), nearly double the child's birth length.
- Adult height can be predicted from measurements at three years of age; males are approximately 53 percent of their adult height; females are 57 percent.
- Gains an average of 3–5 pounds (1.4–2.3 kg) per year; weight averages 30–38 pounds (13.6–17.2 kg).
- Heart rate (pulse) averages 90–110 beats per minute.
- Respiratory rate is 20–30 breaths per minute, depending on activity level.
- Body temperature averages 96°F–99.4°F (35.5°C–37.4°C); temperature varies with exertion, illness, and stress.
- Legs grow more rapidly in length than do the arms, giving the three-year-old a taller, thinner, adultlike appearance.
- Head and chest circumference are nearly equal.
- Neck appears to lengthen as "baby fat" disappears.
- Posture is more erect; the abdomen no longer protrudes.
- Has a full set of baby teeth (20 teeth).
- Needs to consume approximately 1,500 calories daily.
- Visual acuity is approximately 20/40, using the Snellen eye chart.

### Motor Development

- Walks up and down stairs unassisted, using alternating feet; might jump from bottom step, landing on both feet.
- Balances momentarily on one foot.

**3-year-old**

## Developmental Profiles and Growth Patterns *(continued)*

- Kicks a large ball.
- Feeds self; needs minimal assistance.
- Jumps in place.
- Pedals a small tricycle or riding toy.
- Catches a large bouncing ball with both arms extended.
- Enjoys swinging on a swing (not too high or too fast); laughs and asks to be pushed.
- Shows improved control of crayons or markers; uses vertical, horizontal, and circular strokes.
- Holds a crayon or marker between first two fingers and thumb (**tripod grasp**), not in a fist as earlier (Figure 6-2).
- Turns the pages of a book one at a time.
- Enjoys building with blocks.
- Builds a tower of eight or more blocks.
- Plays with clay; pounds, rolls, and squeezes it with enthusiasm.
- Begins to show **hand dominance**.
- Carries a container of liquid, such as a cup of milk or bowl of water, without much spilling; pours liquid from a pitcher into another container.
- Manipulates large buttons and zippers on clothing.
- Washes and dries hands; brushes own teeth, but not thoroughly.
- Achieves complete bladder control, for the most part, during this time.

**Figure 6-2** **Three-year-olds now can hold a marker or pencil in a tripod grasp.**

© 2015 Cengage Learning®

## Perceptual-Cognitive Development

- Listens attentively to age-appropriate stories.
- Makes relevant comments during stories, especially those that relate to home, family, and familiar events.
- Spends considerable time looking at books; may pretend to read to others by explaining the pictures.
- Requests stories with riddles, guessing, and suspense.
- Points with a fair degree of accuracy to correct pictures when given sound-alike words (*keys–cheese; fish–dish; sand–band; cat–bat*).
- Plays realistically.
- Feeds a doll, puts it down for a nap, covers it up to stay warm (Figure 6-3).
- Hooks a truck and trailer together, loads the truck, and drives it away while making "motor" noises.
- Experiments with things to see how they work; takes objects apart and reassembles them into new "inventions."

---

**tripod grasp**   A hand position whereby an object, such as a pencil, is held between the thumb and first and second fingers.
**hand dominance**   Preference for using one hand over the other; most individuals are said to be either right-handed or left-handed.

## Developmental Profiles and Growth Patterns *(continued)*

- Places eight to ten pegs in a pegboard, or six round and six square blocks in a form board.

- Attempts to draw; copies circles, squares, and some letters, but imperfectly.

- Identifies a triangle, a circle, and a square; can point to the correct shape when asked.

- Sorts objects logically on the basis of one dimension, such as color, shape, or size; usually chooses color or size as a basis for classification (all red beads in one pile, green beads in another) (Fitzpatrick & Pagani, 2012).

- Shows understanding of basic size-shape comparisons much of the time; will indicate which is bigger when shown a tennis ball and a soccer ball; also understands the concept of "smaller of the two."

- Names and matches, at minimum, primary colors (red, yellow, and blue).

- Arranges cubes in a horizontal line; also positions cubes to form a bridge.

- Counts objects out loud.

- Points to a picture that has "more" (cars, planes, or kittens) (Odic et al., 2013).

- Shows some understanding of duration of time by using phrases such as "all the time," "all day," or "for two days"; but some confusion remains: "I didn't take a nap tomorrow."

- Uses objects symbolically in play (a block of wood might be a truck, a ramp, or a bat) (Yates & Marcelo, 2014).

**Figure 6-3** At this stage, the child begins to engage in realistic make-believe play.

### ▶❙❙ TeachSource Video Connections

**The Preschooler's Motor Development**

Three-year-olds have mastered most basic gross motor skills and now will concentrate their efforts on improving strength, accuracy, and coordination. Respond to the following questions after you have watched the learning video entitled *2–5 Years: Gross Motor Development for Early Childhood*:

1. What gross motor skills did the children display in the opening scenes of this video?

2. What gross motor skills would you expect a typically developing three-year-old to be capable of performing?

3. What indoor and outdoor activities could you plan to help three-year-olds practice and improve their gross motor skills?

## Speech and Language Development

- Talks about objects, events, and people not present: "Jasmine has a big dog at her house."

- Talks about the actions of others: "Daddy's mowing the grass."

- Adds information to what has just been said: "Yeah, and then he grabbed it back."

- Answers simple questions appropriately.

**3-year-old**

## Developmental Profiles and Growth Patterns *(continued)*

- Asks many questions, particularly about the location and identity of objects and people (Figure 6-4).

- Uses an increasing number of speech forms that keep conversation going: "Why can't I?" "Where are we going now?" This characteristic is more common among children in Western cultures and less so in others (Gauvain, Munroe, & Beebe, 2013).

- Calls attention to self, objects, or events in the environment: "Watch my helicopter fly."

- Encourages the behavior of others: "Let's run through the sprinkler. You first."

- Joins in social interaction rituals: "Hi," "Bye," "Please," "Let's go."

- Comments about objects and ongoing events: "There's a horse"; "The truck's pulling a boat."

- Vocabulary has increased; now uses 300 to 1,000 words.

- Recites nursery rhymes; sings songs.

- Uses understandable speech most of the time.

- Produces expanded noun phrases: "big brown dog."

- Produces verbs with *ing* endings; uses -*s* to indicate more than one; often puts -*s* on already pluralized forms (*geeses, mices, deers*).

- Indicates negatives by inserting "no" or "not" before a simple noun or verb phrase ("Not baby").

- Answers "What are you doing?" "What is this?" and "Where?" questions dealing with familiar objects and events.

### Social-Emotional Development

- Seems to understand taking turns, but is not always willing to do so (Figure 6-5).

- Laughs frequently; is friendly and eager to please.

- Has occasional nightmares and fears about the dark, monsters, fire, or being left behind.

- Joins in simple games and group activities, sometimes hesitantly.

- Talks to self often.

Figure 6-4  **Children ask many questions!**

Figure 6-5  **Learning to play well with others takes time and practice.**

## Developmental Profiles and Growth Patterns *(continued)*

- Identifies self as a "boy" or "girl" (Goble et al., 2012).

- Observes other children playing; might join in for a short time; often imitates and plays parallel to other children.

- Defends toys and possessions; may be aggressive at times, grabbing a toy, hitting another child, or hiding toys.

- Engages in make-believe play alone and with other children (Yates & Marcelo, 2014; Howe, Abuhatoum, & Chang-Kredl, 2013).

- Shows affection toward children who are younger or a child who is hurt.

- Sits and listens to stories up to 10 minutes at a time; does not bother other children who are listening to the story; becomes upset if disturbed or interrupted.

- May continue to have a special blanket, stuffed animal, or toy for comfort.

## What Do You See?

**Social inclusion** Learning to be part of a group requires special skills. What typical social-emotional behaviors are these three-year-olds exhibiting? What skills must young children develop in order to play and work together cooperatively?

© 2015 Cengage Learning®

## DAILY ROUTINES

### Eating

- Has fair appetite; prefers small servings. Dislikes many cooked vegetables; eats almost everything else; should not be forced to eat refused foods (Marotz, 2015).

- Feeds self independently if hungry. Uses spoon in semi-adult fashion; may spear food with a fork or occasionally resort to eating with hands.

- Eats slowly at times; plays with food when not hungry.

- Pours milk and juice with fewer spills; serves individual portions from a serving dish with some adult prompting; "Fill it up to the line"; "Take only two spoonfuls."

- Drinks a great deal of milk. (However, be sure that children do not consume milk to the exclusion of other much-needed foods.)

**3-year-old**

## DAILY ROUTINES *(continued)*

### Toileting, Bathing, and Dressing

- Helps wash self in a bathtub but is not always thorough; often resists getting out of the tub.
- Brushes own teeth, but adults should continue to monitor the child's brushing technique.
- Manages most of own toilet needs during the daytime. (Boys, especially, may continue to have daytime accidents, resulting in wet pants.)
- Some children sleep through the night without wetting the bed; others are in transition—they may stay dry at night for days or weeks, and then regress to night-wetting for several weeks.
- Is better at undressing than dressing, although is capable of putting on some articles of clothing.
- Manipulates zippers, large buttons, and snaps with increasing dexterity and skill.

### Sleeping

- Sleeps 10–12 hours most nights; often wakes up early in the morning.
- Begins to give up afternoon naps; however, continues to benefit from a midday quiet time.
- Prepares for bed independently most of the time; has given up many bedtime rituals, but still needs a bedtime story or song and tucking-in.
- Has dreams that may cause the child to awaken; this is a common phase that usually passes. Maintain a consistent bedtime schedule and routine; read a story, play a quiet game, engage in storytelling; leave a hall light on.
- May occasionally get up and wander at night; quiet firmness may be needed to coax the child back into bed.

### Play and Social Activity

- Wants to be included in everything; the "me too" age.
- Joins in spontaneous group play for short periods; very social; beginning to play cooperatively more often.
- Argues or quarrels with other children on occasion; adults should allow children an opportunity to try to settle their own disagreements before intervening, unless physical harm is threatened.
- Dresses up and participates in dramatic play reflecting everyday activities. Some children still exhibit strong **gender** and role stereotypes: "Boys can't be nurses"; "Only girls can be dancers" (Goble et al., 2012).
- Responds well to options rather than to commands: "Do you want to put your pajamas on before or after the story?"
- Continues to find sharing difficult, but seems to understand the concept.

> **Did You Know**
>
> ...that you will spend approximately one-third of your lifetime sleeping if you get the recommended 8 hours of sleep each night? Your brain isn't taking a vacation during this time, though. It continues to work and process information while you sleep.

---

**gender**  Reference to being either male or female.

## learning activities to promote **brain development**

**3-year-old**

Three-year-olds are eager to learn, to be helpful, and to test their improving motor skills. Now is an ideal time to engage children in activities that foster language development, imagination, physical activity, and self-confidence.

### Developmentally appropriate applications for families and teachers

- Limit children's video and television viewing to no more than two hours a day. All content should be developmentally appropriate; young children understand media as reality, not as fiction or entertainment. Active play promotes learning and decreases the risk of obesity.

- Encourage children to create new uses for safe household items and discards: a blanket stretched over a table to create a cave or tent; spoons for pretend cooking; discarded mail for playing post office; a hose with a trickle of water for washing a tricycle or wagon; a plastic milk carton for a floating boat; a paintbrush and water for "painting" outdoor structures.

- Provide more complex manipulative materials: parquetry blocks; pegboards with multicolored pegs; various items to count, sort, and match; construction sets with medium-size, interlocking pieces.

- Offer nontoxic art and craft materials that encourage experimentation: crayons, washable markers, chalk, play dough, round-tipped scissors, papers, glue, paints, and large brushes (supervision is required).

- Keep a plentiful supply of books about animals, families, everyday events, alphabet and counting activities, and poems and rhymes on hand; continue daily reading sessions. Ask children to retell stories using puppets, or have them create their own story ending.

- Make regular trips to the library; allow plenty of time for children to make their own book selections. Include some nonfiction books on topics that interest children, such as animals, the ocean, and planets.

- Spend time together outdoors: encourage active games—kick, hit, or throw balls; catch bugs; jump rope; fly kites, and play tag or hide-and-seek. Children should participate in at least 60 minutes of adult-led and 60 minutes of unstructured physical activity every day.

- Provide wheeled riding toys, wheelbarrow and garden tools, doll strollers, or shopping carts to build eye–hand–foot coordination (e.g., steering and maneuvering).

- Take children on walks, *at the child's pace*; allow ample time for children to explore, examine, and collect rocks, bugs, leaves, and seed pods; name and talk about things along the way. Plan walks around a theme: sounds, textures, colors, counting, etc.

- Assign simple responsibilities for children to complete. Involve them in retrieving or putting away toys, classroom supplies, or clothing. Let them help to set the dinner table, put away groceries, wash the car, fill the dog's water bowl, or rake leaves.

**TeachSource Digital Download**

**3-year-old**

## developmental alerts

Check with a health-care provider or early childhood specialist if, by the fourth birthday, the child does *not*:

- Have intelligible speech most of the time; have children's hearing checked if there is any reason for concern.
- Understand and follow simple commands and directions.
- State own name and age.
- Play near or with other children.
- Use three- to four-word sentences.
- Ask questions and maintain eye contact.
- Stay with an activity for 3–4 minutes; play alone for several minutes at a time.
- Jump in place without falling.
- Balance on one foot, at least briefly.
- Help with dressing self.
- Engage in pretend play, using common objects for imaginative purposes.
- Maintain eye contact (unless this is a cultural taboo); the inability to do so may be a sign of an autism spectrum disorder.

**Note:** Cultural differences may alter the timetable when some developmental skills are acquired. Expanded Developmental Alerts Checklists appear in Appendix A and are also available as digital downloads.

## safety concerns

Continue to implement the safety practices described for the previous stages. Always be aware of new safety issues as the child continues to grow and develop.

### Burns
- Keep hot items out of children's reach.
- Place lighted candles, matches, and cigarette lighters where they are inaccessible.
- Monitor children carefully when grills, fireplaces, candles, or fireworks are lit.

### Choking
- Avoid foods that can cause choking, such as popcorn, nuts, raw carrots, and hard candies; serve grapes and hot dogs only if they are cut into small pieces.
- Serve all foods in small, bite-size pieces and insist that children sit quietly while eating.
- Supervise children closely when they are eating items with sticks, such as a lollipop or popsicle.

### Drowning
- Continue to supervise children closely when around any source of water; always empty wading pools when not in use.
- Fence in permanent pools; use pool alarm; keep gates closed and riding toys away from pool area.
- Learn cardiopulmonary resuscitation (CPR)!

### Falls
- Insist that children wear sturdy, flat-soled shoes to prevent injuries when running and playing, especially outdoors. Shoes with hard or slippery soles, sandals, and slip-ons increase the risk of tripping and falling.

### Poisons
- Avoid the use of pesticides and chemicals on grass where children

## safety **concerns** *(continued)*

play; residues can get on hands and into sandboxes.

- Store hazardous substances, such as cleaning supplies, lawn chemicals, and medications, in locked cabinets.

### Traffic

- Insist on holding the child's hand when walking in parking lots or crossing streets.
- Always buckle the child securely into an appropriate car seat.

---

**Spotlight** **on Brain Development**

## The Importance of Sleep

Why do humans and animals sleep? What purpose does sleep serve? Scientists have long been intrigued by these questions but have had few answers until recently. What they are beginning to learn is that sleep offers surprising health benefits, whereas insufficient sleep can have detrimental consequences, especially for young children. Deficient sleep in adults has been shown to increase the risk of obesity, diabetes, cardiovascular heart disease, high blood pressure, and certain psychiatric disorders. Children are more likely to experience behavior and cognitive problems when they lack adequate sleep (Scharf et al., 2013).

Sleep problems are not uncommon during the preschool years. An estimated 25–30 percent of children will experience some form of temporary sleep disturbance. However, the behaviors that parents perceive as being problematic are highly influenced by cultural differences in sleep patterns and practices (Mindell et al., 2013). Young children's heightened awareness of their surroundings, limited understanding, and hectic lifestyles often contribute to late bedtimes and interrupted sleep patterns. Television viewing and access to computers and electronic media, especially in the hours prior to bedtime, are also known to compromise the quality of children's sleep. Most children eventually outgrow occasional periods of troubled sleep and go on to establish healthy sleeping habits. However, children who have autism, developmental syndromes (e.g., Asperger's, Down, and Williams), and certain medical conditions (e.g., anemia, eczema, obesity, and snoring) may experience serious, prolonged sleep disorders that require medical treatment (Ashworth et al., 2013; Buckhalt, 2013; Camfferman et al., 2013).

Although empirical studies have contributed to an understanding of the health benefits associated with high-quality sleep, it may be the effects on children's brain development that prove to be of even greater significance. Numerous studies have documented sleep's physiological impact on neurocognitive processing and memory (Huber & Born, 2014; Piosczyk et al., 2013). They have shown that sleep improves memory by enabling the brain to consolidate and organize information that it has received throughout the day. Chronic sleep deprivation interferes with this process (neural plasticity) and limits short-term memory, which in turn impedes cognitive function and lowers IQ scores (Yorbik et al., 2014; Bernier et al., 2013; Kurdziel, Duclos, & Spencer, 2013). Furthermore, scientists have identified a positive association between adequate sleep and an increase in gray matter volume in children's brains (Taki et al., 2012). Gray matter is responsible for processing and transmitting sensory impulses involved in emotions, memory, vision and hearing, muscle control, thought, and decision making.

The findings of these and similar studies reinforce the critical importance of making sure that children obtain adequate sleep for good health and optimal brain development. Concerns about a child's sleep problems always should be discussed with a health-care provider.

### What are the connections?

1. What factors may be interfering with children's ability to get sufficient sleep?
2. What potential effects can a lack of sleep have on a person's health and cognitive function?
3. Why is sleep deprivation in young children a major public health concern?

**4-year-old**

# The Four-Year-Old

Tireless bundles of energy, brimming over ideas, overflowing with chatter and activity—these are the characteristics typical of most four-year-olds. Bouts of stubbornness and arguments between children and adults can be frequent as children test limits and work to achieve greater independence. Many are loud, boisterous, even belligerent; they try adults' patience with nonsense talk and silly jokes, constant chatter, and endless questions. At the same time, they have many lovable qualities. They are enthusiastic, eager to be helpful, imaginative, and able to plan ahead to some extent: "When we get home, I'll make you a picture."

Although today's children are growing up in environments dominated by digital and electronic technologies—not just television, but also handheld games, computers, software, cell phones, Internet, videos, "smart" toys, and webcams—evidence supporting their contribution to children's learning remains limited. There are also concerns about the amount of sedentary time that children are spending with these devices and their limiting effect on imagination and creativity. What we do know is that young children learn best through face-to-face social interaction with other children and hands-on manipulation and experimentation with real objects. However, scientists are finding that well-designed media can support some forms of learning when used in moderation and in conjunction with traditional educational experiences (Castles et al., 2013; Plowman & McPake, 2013). Positive outcomes also have been demonstrated when children who have developmental delays, disabilities, or both use specially designed software and devices to reinforce learning (Case-Smith, 2013; Ploog et al., 2013).

# Developmental Profiles and Growth Patterns

## Growth and Physical Characteristics

- Gains approximately 4–5 pounds (1.8–2.3 kg) per year; weighs an average of 32–40 pounds (14.5–18.2 kg).
- Grows 2–2.5 inches (5.0–6.4 cm) in height per year; is approximately 40–45 inches (101.6–114 cm) tall.
- Heart rate (pulse) averages 90–110 beats per minute.
- Respiratory rate ranges from 20–30 breaths per minute, varying with activity and emotional state.
- Body temperature ranges from 98°F–99.4°F (36.6°C–37.4°C).
- Requires approximately 1,700 calories daily.
- Hears well; hearing acuity can be assessed by the child's correct usage of sounds and language, as well as by her appropriate responses to questions and instructions.
- Visual acuity is approximately 20/30, as measured on the Snellen eye chart.

## Motor Development

- Walks a straight line (tape or chalk line on the floor).
- Hops on one foot.
- Pedals and steers a wheeled toy with confidence; turns corners and avoids obstacles and oncoming "traffic."
- Climbs ladders, trees, and playground equipment.
- Jumps over objects 5 or 6 inches (12.5 to 15 cm) high; lands with both feet together.

## Developmental Profiles and Growth Patterns *(continued)*

- Runs, starts, stops, and moves around obstacles with ease.
- Throws a ball overhand; distance and aim are improving.
- Builds a tower with ten or more blocks.
- Forms shapes and objects out of clay: cookies, snakes, simple animals, etc.
- Reproduces some shapes and letters (Figure 6-6).
- Holds a crayon or marker by using a tripod grasp.
- Paints and draws with purpose; might have an idea in mind but often has trouble implementing it, so calls the creation something else.
- Hammers nails and pegs with greater accuracy.
- Threads small wooden beads on a string.

Figure 6-6 **Four-year-olds are able to reproduce some shapes and letters.**

### Perceptual-Cognitive Development

- Stacks at least five graduated cubes from largest to smallest; builds a pyramid of six blocks. Early spatial and assembly abilities have a positive correlation with future math skills.
- Indicates whether paired words sound the same (*sheet–feet*, *ball–wall*) or different (*ship–sheet*, *stop–start*).
- Names eighteen to twenty uppercase letters near the end of this year; some children may be able to print several letters and write their own name; may recognize some printed words (especially those that have a special meaning for them).
- Shows interest in reading; near the end of this period, a few children may begin to read simple words in books, such as alphabet books, with only a few words per page and many pictures (Robinson, Einav, & Fox, 2013).
- Selects and enjoys stories about how things grow and operate.
- Delights in wordplay, creating silly language.
- Understands the concepts of "tallest," "biggest," "same," and "more"; selects the picture that has the "most houses" or the "biggest dogs."
- Rote counts to twenty or more; has limited understanding of what numbers represent.
- Understands the sequence of daily events: "When we get up in the morning, we get dressed, have breakfast, brush our teeth, and go to school."
- Sorts, classifies, and patterns objects with various attributes, such as smallest to biggest; color and shape; or things that float or sink (Nguyen, 2012).
- Recognizes and identifies missing puzzle parts (of a person, car, or animal) when looking at the picture.

### Speech and Language Development

- Uses the prepositions *on*, *in*, and *under* correctly for the most part.
- Uses possessives consistently (*hers*, *theirs*, *baby's*).
- Answers "Whose?" "Who?" "Why?" and "How many?" (Nip & Green, 2013).
- Produces elaborate sentence structures: "The cat ran under the house before I could see what color it was" (Salomo, Lieven, & Tomasello, 2013).
- Uses almost entirely intelligible speech.

**4-year-old**

> **Did You Know**
>
> …that children younger than four years have no long-term memory due to immature brain development? Their inability to recall early experiences is referred to as *infantile amnesia*.

4-year-old

## Developmental Profiles and Growth Patterns *(continued)*

### What Do You See?

**Concept and classification development** Four-year-olds are beginning to grasp the meaning of relationships. What cognitive abilities are these children using to sort the objects by color? What additional types of learning could this activity be used to reinforce?

- Begins to use the past tense of verbs correctly: "Mommy closed the door," "Daddy went to work" (Washington, 2013).
- Refers to activities, events, objects, and people that are not present.
- Changes tone of voice and sentence structure to adapt to the listener's level of understanding: To baby brother, "Milk all gone?" To mother, "Did Ethan finish all of his milk?"
- States first and last name, gender, siblings' names, and sometimes home telephone number.
- Answers appropriately when asked what to do if tired, cold, or hungry.
- Recites and sings simple songs and rhymes.

## Social-Emotional Development

- Is outgoing and friendly (cultural differences may reinforce or not encourage this behavior); can be overly enthusiastic at times.
- Changes moods rapidly and unpredictably; may laugh one minute, cry the next; tantrum over minor frustrations (e.g., a block structure that will not balance, difficulty tying a shoe); sulk over being left out or having a request denied.
- Holds conversations and shares strong emotions with imaginary playmates or companions; having an invisible friend is fairly common (Lev Vygotsky's self-talk) (Taylor et al., 2013b).
- Establishes close relationships with playmates; beginning to have "best" friends (Figure 6-7).
- Boasts, exaggerates, and bends the truth with made-up stories or claims of boldness; tests the limits with "bathroom" or forbidden talk.
- Cooperates with others more often now; participates in group activities, role-playing, and make-believe activities (Ramani & Brownell, 2014).

**Figure 6-7** A four-year-old may have a "best" friend at this stage.

## Developmental Profiles and Growth Patterns *(continued)*

- Shows pride in accomplishments; seeks frequent adult approval.

- May tattle on other children and appear selfish at times; still has trouble understanding turn-taking in some situations (Ingram & Bering, 2010).

- Insists on trying to do things independently but can become so frustrated as to verge on tantrums when problems arise (paint that drips, paper airplane that will not fold correctly).

- Relies (most of the time) on verbal rather than physical aggression; may yell angrily rather than hit to make a point; threatens: "You can't come to my birthday party if I can't play with you."

- Uses name-calling and taunting as ways of excluding other children: "You're such a baby."

**4-year-old**

### ▶❚❚ TeachSource Video Connections

© 2015 Cengage Learning®

### Preschoolers and Language Development

Four-year-olds chatter endlessly and have much to say. They are learning how to use language for thinking, problem solving, and communicating their ideas to others. The ways in which children develop and use written and spoken language are highly influenced by cultural patterns. Respond to the following questions after you have watched the learning video *2–5 Years: Language Development for Early Childhood*:

1. What language development does the term *overregularization* describe?

2. What changes do most four-year-olds experience in the language development?

3. What grammatical irregularities did you note in four-year-old Caroline's description of recent bowling and putt-putt golf experiences?

4. Would you consider her grammatical usage typical for a four-year-old? Explain.

## DAILY ROUTINES

### Eating

- Experiences periodic fluctuations in appetite; hungry and eager to eat at one meal, uninterested in eating at the next.

- Develops dislikes of certain foods and may refuse them to the point of tears if pushed (such pressure can cause serious adult–child conflict).

4-year-old

## DAILY ROUTINES *(continued)*

- Is able to use all eating utensils; quite skilled at spreading jelly or butter on bread or cutting soft foods such as bananas with a table knife.
- Talks while eating; eating and talking often get in each other's way; talking usually takes precedence over eating.
- Shows interest in helping with meal preparations (dumping premeasured ingredients, washing vegetables, setting the table).

### Toileting, Bathing, and Dressing

- Takes care of own toileting needs; often demands privacy in the bathroom.
- Performs bathing and toothbrushing tasks with improved skill and attention; still needs some adult assistance and routine (subtle) inspection.
- Dresses self; can lace own shoes, fasten buttons, zip up jacket. Becomes frustrated if problems arise while getting dressed, yet stubbornly refuses adult help, even if it is needed.
- Likes to help with household tasks; is able to help sort and fold clean clothes, put clothes away, hang up towels, and pick up room; however, is easily distracted.

### Sleeping

- Averages 10–12 hours of sleep at night, although the amount of sleep required varies from child to child; still may take an afternoon nap.
- Bedtime is usually not a problem if cues, rather than orders, signal the time (when the story is finished, when the clock hands are in a certain position).
- Fear of the dark at night is relatively common for some children; a hallway light left on may be helpful.
- If children get up to use the bathroom, they may require help in settling back down to sleep.

### Play and Social Activities

- Playmates are important; plays cooperatively most of the time; can be bossy.
- Takes turns; shares (most of the time); wants to be with other children every waking moment.
- Needs (and seeks out) adult approval and attention; might comment, "Look what I did," "See my boat."
- Understands and needs limits (but not too constraining); will abide by rules most of the time.
- Brags about possessions; shows off; boasts about family members. These behaviors are more typical in Western cultures and not always evident in others.

## learning activities to promote **brain development**

Four-year-olds enjoy moving about, talking, engaging in make-believe, reading, and trying new things. Everyday learning experiences, a healthy diet, and ample opportunities for physical activity are important for continued brain development.

## learning activities *(continued)*

### Developmentally appropriate applications for families and teachers

- Join in simple board and card games (picture lotto, Candy Land) that depend on chance, not strategy; emphasis should be on attending, taking turns, and playing, not winning. (Learning to be a good sport does not come until much later.)

- Provide puzzles with five to twenty pieces (the number depends on the child), counting and alphabet games, matching games such as more detailed matching and dominos games.

- Offer a variety of basic science and math materials: ruler, compass, magnifying glass, small scales, plastic eyedroppers; encourage activities such as collecting leaves, raising worms or ants, or sprouting seeds.

- Appreciate (and sometimes join in) the child's spontaneous rhyming, chanting, silly name-calling, jokes, and riddles.

- Continue daily read-aloud times; encourage children to supply words or phrases, to guess what comes next, to retell the story (or parts of it) by telling what happened first, what happened last; introduce the idea of looking things up in a simple picture dictionary or encyclopedia. Go to the library regularly, allowing the child ample time to choose books.

- Encourage children's artistic interests: collect and paint rocks, turn household items and boxes into musical instruments, make a batch of homemade play dough, put on a puppet show, or dance to music.

- Participate in 30–60 minutes of vigorous physical activity with your child each day: go for a walk; play in the park; ride bikes; provide balls for kicking, throwing, and hitting; enroll in swim, tumbling, or dance classes; play in the sprinkler or "swim" in an inflatable pool *(always requires an adult present)*.

**TeachSource Digital Download**

**4-year-old**

## developmental **alerts**

Check with a health-care provider or early childhood specialist if, by the fifth birthday, the child does *not*:

- State own first and last name.

- Speak in three- and four-word sentences.

- Identify and draw simple shapes: circle, square, triangle.

- Catch a large ball when bounced (if children fail repeatedly, their vision should be checked).

- Speak and be understood by strangers (if there is a problem, have children's hearing checked to rule out a hearing loss).

- Have good control of posture and movement.

- Hop on one foot.

- Show interest in and respond to surroundings; ask questions, stop to look at and pick up small objects.

## developmental **alerts** *(continued)*

- Respond to statements without constantly asking to have them repeated.
- Dress self with minimal adult assistance; manage buttons and zippers.
- Take care of own toilet needs; have good bowel and bladder control with infrequent accidents.

**Note:** Cultural differences may alter the timetable when some developmental skills are acquired. Expanded Developmental Alerts Checklists appear in Appendix A and are also available as digital downloads.

5-year-old

## safety **concerns**

Continue to implement the safety practices described for the previous stages. Always be aware of new safety issues as the child continues to grow and develop.

### Burns
- Teach children the dangers of fire.
- Make sure smoke and carbon monoxide detectors are operational.
- Use cooking opportunities to help children learn appropriate safety practices.

### Dangerous Objects
- Keep all chemicals, cleaning supplies, personal care products, medications, guns, and dangerous tools in locked storage; curiosity peaks during this stage.

### Falls
- Always insist that children wear a bike helmet and pads when biking or skating.
- Rethink the use of trampolines; many children sustain serious harm, including head and spinal cord injuries (AAP, 2012).

### Personal Safety
- Teach children their full name, telephone number, what to do if they are approached by a stranger or become lost, and how to dial 911. Increased independence may cause children to wander too far from parents and teachers.

### Toys
- When purchasing toys, evaluate their safety (e.g., rounded edges, not easily broken, nontoxic, nonflammable, no protruding wires, no electrical connections, and no loud noises).
- Avoid toys with small parts if there are younger children in the home or a school setting.

### Suffocation
- Remove doors from an old freezer or refrigerator before disposing of it.
- Select toy boxes with removable lids or use open containers to prevent children from being trapped by a fallen top. Remove the lids from large plastic storage bins.

# The Five-Year-Old

More in control of themselves, both physically and emotionally, most five-year-olds are in a period of relative calm and are becoming increasingly self-confident and reliable. Their world is expanding beyond home, family, and school. Friends, friendships, and group activities involving both girls and boys are becoming more important at this age (Leman et al., 2013). However, sharing and turn-taking continue to be difficult.

Five-year-olds expect others to share but are often unwilling to do so themselves; fairness is seen only from the child's own perspective.

Five-year-olds devote much of their time and attention to the practice and mastery of skills across all developmental areas (Figure 6-8). They are exceedingly curious, energetic, and often fearless. They initiate and engage in conversations, identify numbers and grasp their meaning, enjoy tackling challenges and solving problems, and begin learning how to read and write. They have a robust level of self-confidence but are unable to comprehend fully the inherent dangers or consequences of their actions. As a result, five-year-olds experience a high rate of unintentional injuries (Marotz, 2015; Karazsia & Kirschman, 2013). Safe-

Figure 6-8 Practice leads to mastery.

guarding children's well-being continues to be of extreme importance. Adults must be on the alert, supervise children closely, and take measures to protect them from harm. However, it is important not to create environments or situations that prevent children from learning self-protection skills or inhibit a child's sense of curiosity, competence, and self-esteem.

# Developmental Profiles and Growth Patterns

## Growth and Physical Characteristics

- Gains 4–5 pounds (1.8–2.3 kg) per year; weighs an average of 38–45 pounds (17.3–20.5 kg).
- Grows an average of 2–2.5 inches (5.1–6.4 cm) per year; is approximately 42–46 inches (106.7–116.8 cm) tall.
- Heart rate (pulse) is approximately 90–110 beats per minute.
- Respiratory rate ranges from 20–30 breaths per minute, depending on activity and emotional status.
- Body temperature is stabilized at 98°F–99.4°F.
- Head size is approximately that of an adult's.
- Begins to lose baby (deciduous) teeth (Figure 6-9).
- Body is adultlike in proportion.
- Requires approximately 1,800 calories daily.
- Visual acuity is approximately 20/20 on the Snellen eye chart.
- Visual tracking and **binocular vision** are well developed.

Figure 6-9 **Five-year-olds may begin losing their "baby" teeth.**

## Motor Development

- Can walk backward, toe to heel.
- Walks unassisted up and down stairs, alternating feet.
- Learns to turn somersaults (should be taught the right way to avoid injury).

**binocular vision** Both eyes working together to send a single image to the brain.

## Developmental Profiles and Growth Patterns *(continued)*

- Touches toes without flexing the knees.
- Can walk a balance beam.
- Learns to skip using alternate feet.
- Catches a bounced ball thrown from 3 feet (91.4 cm) away.
- Rides a tricycle or wheeled toy with speed and skillful steering; some children can learn to ride bicycles, usually with training wheels.
- Jumps or hops forward ten times in a row without falling.
- Balances on either foot for 10 seconds with good control.
- Builds three-dimensional structures with small cubes by copying from a picture or model.
- Reproduces many shapes and letters (square, triangle, *A, I, O, U, C, H, L, T*).
- Demonstrates fair control of a pencil or marker; begins to color within the lines.
- Cuts on the lines with scissors (but not perfectly) (Figure 6-10).
- Establishes hand dominance for the most part.

**Figure 6-10** Five-year-olds are able to cut along a straight line.

© GFOW/Cengage Learning

### Perceptual-Cognitive Development

- Forms a rectangle from two triangular pieces.
- Builds steps with a set of small blocks.
- Understands and demonstrates the concept of *same* shape, *same* size.
- Sorts objects on the basis of two dimensions, such as color and form.
- Sorts a variety of objects so that all things in the group have a single common feature (classification skill: all are food items or boats or animals; Godwin, Marlen, & Fisher, 2013). A child's conceptualization of categories may be highly influenced by cultural factors.
- Understands the concepts of smallest and shortest; places objects in order from shortest to tallest and smallest to largest.
- Identifies objects with specified serial positions: first, second, last.
- Rote counts to 20 and above; many children can count to 100 (Hachey, 2013; Purpura & Lonigan, 2013).
- Recognizes numerals from 1 to 10.
- Understands the concepts of *more* and *less than:* "Which bowl has less water?"
- Understands the terms *dark, light,* and *early:* "I got up early, before anyone else. It was still dark."
- Relates clock time to daily schedule: "Time to go to bed when the little hand points to 8."
- Shows interest in telling time; some children can tell time on the hour: five o'clock, two o'clock.
- Knows what a calendar is for.
- Recognizes and identifies a penny, nickel, and dime; beginning to count and show interest in saving money.

**Did You Know ?**

...that children will have heard between 3 and 11 million words by the time they enter kindergarten? Growing up in a literacy-rich environment increases word exposure and vocabulary size.

## Developmental Profiles and Growth Patterns *(continued)*

- Knows the alphabet; many children can name uppercase and lowercase letters and some letter sounds.

- Understands the concept of *half*; can say how many pieces an object has when it has been cut in half.

- Asks innumerable questions: "Why?" "What?" "Where?" "When?"

- Eager to learn new things.

### Speech and Language Development

- Has a vocabulary of 1,500 words or more.

- Tells a familiar story while looking at pictures in a book.

- Uses functional definitions (a ball is to bounce; a bed is to sleep in; a book is to read).

- Identifies and names four to eight colors.

- Recognizes the humor in simple jokes; makes up jokes and riddles.

- Produces sentences with five to seven words; much longer sentences are not unusual.

- States own birthday, name of hometown, and names of family members.

### ▶❚❚ TeachSource Video Connections

**Social Skill Development**

Five-year-olds are imaginative, engaging, and social by nature. They usually get along well with other children, preferring to play with one or two friends at a time. However, they also can become bossy when things do not go their way. Respond to the following questions after you have watched the learning video *Preschool: Social Development, Cooperative Learning, and Play:*

1. What social skills must a child have to engage successfully in cooperative or constructive play groups?

2. In what ways can teachers encourage children's development of positive social skills?

3. What skills do children acquire as a result of group participation that cannot be gained from solitary play?

*5-year-old*

© 2015 Cengage Learning®

- Answers the telephone appropriately; calls an adult to the telephone or takes a brief message.

- Produces speech that is almost entirely intelligible.

- Uses *would, could,* and *should* appropriately.

- Uses the past tense of irregular verbs consistently (*went, caught, swam*).

- Uses past-tense inflection (*-ed*) appropriately to mark regular verbs (*jumped, rained, washed*).

### Social-Emotional Development

- Enjoys friendships; often has one or two special playmates (Leman et al., 2013; Nurmsoo, Einav, & Hood, 2012).

- Shares toys, takes turns, and plays cooperatively (with occasional lapses); is often quite generous.

- Participates in group play and shared activities with other children; suggests imaginative and elaborate play ideas.

- Is usually affectionate and caring, especially toward younger or injured children and animals (Taylor et al., 2013a).

- Follows directions and carries out assignments most of the time; generally does what the parent or teacher requests.

## Developmental Profiles and Growth Patterns *(continued)*

- Continues to need adult comfort and reassurance, but might be less open in seeking and accepting comfort.
- Has better self-control; experiences fewer dramatic swings of emotion.
- Likes to tell jokes, entertain, and make people laugh.
- Takes pride in accomplishments; boasts at times and seeks adult acknowledgment and approval.

5-year-old

### What Do You **See?**

**Friendships** Five-year-olds are quite sociable and enjoy spending time with friends. What social-emotional qualities have these boys developed to make this relationship possible? What other developmental skills are involved?

© GFOW/Cengage Learning

## DAILY ROUTINES

### Eating

- Has a good appetite, but not at every meal.
- Likes familiar foods; prefers most vegetables raw rather than cooked.
- Often adopts the food dislikes of family members, teachers, peers, or all three.
- Can "make" breakfast (pours cereal, gets out milk and juice) and lunch (spreads peanut butter and jam on bread).

### Toileting, Bathing, and Dressing

- Takes full responsibility for her own toileting needs; might put off going to the bathroom until an accident occurs or is barely avoided.
- Bathes fairly independently but may need some help getting started.
- Dresses self completely; learning to tie shoes; sometimes aware when clothing is on wrong side out or backward.
- Careless with clothes at times; leaves them scattered about and forgets where they were left; needs many reminders to pick them up.
- Uses a tissue for blowing his nose, but often does a careless or incomplete job; forgets to throw the tissue away; needs a reminder to wash hands afterward.

## DAILY ROUTINES (continued)

### Sleeping

- Manages all routines associated with getting ready for bed independently; can help with a younger brother's or sister's bedtime routine.

- Averages 10 or 11 hours of sleep per night. Some five-year-olds still may nap or rest quietly in the afternoon.

- Dreams and nightmares are common.

- Delays going to sleep if the day has been especially exciting or if long-anticipated events are scheduled for the next day.

### Play and Social Activities

- Carries out family chores and routines; is usually helpful and cooperative.

- Knows the "right" way to do something and often has the "right" answers to questions; seems somewhat opinionated and rigid in beliefs at times.

- Remains attached to home and family; willing to have an adventure but wants it to begin and end at home; fearful that parents may leave or not return.

- Plays well with other children most times, but three might be a crowd: two five-year-olds often exclude the third.

- Shows affection and is protective toward younger siblings; may feel overburdened at times if the younger child demands too much attention.

**5-year-old**

## learning activities to promote brain development

Five-year-olds are ready to take on more challenge and responsibility. They are drawn to activities that require problem solving, creative or artistic expression, or working with other children or adults.

### Developmentally appropriate applications for families and teachers

- Provide inexpensive materials (newsprint, old magazines, wallpaper books, paint samples, or fabric scraps) for cutting, pasting, painting, coloring, and folding; turn a cardboard box into a loom for weaving; offer easy sewing activities and smaller beads for stringing; gather wood scraps, glue, and tools for simple carpentry projects.

- Collect props and dress-up clothes that allow more detailed pretend play (e.g., family roles or occupations); visit and talk about community activities—house construction, post office and mail deliveries, a farmers' market; encourage play with puppets; assist in creating a stage. (A large cardboard box works well.)

- Continue to read aloud regularly and frequently; expose children to books on a wide variety of topics.

- Encourage children's increasing interest in paper-and-pencil, number-, letter-, and word-recognition games that they often invent, but may need adult help to play.

## learning activities *(continued)*

- Plan cooking experiences that involve children: washing and peeling vegetables; cutting out cookies; measuring, mixing, and stirring.

- Set up improvised target games that promote eye–hand coordination (beanbag toss, bowling, ring toss, horseshoes, or basketball with a low hoop); ensure opportunities for vigorous play (with wheeled toys; jungle gyms and parallel bars; digging, raking, sweeping, and hauling).

- Create an indoor or outdoor treasure hunt. Write the names of simple objects on a piece of paper (e.g., stone, leaf, bug, paper, toy, brush, and book) for children to find; alternatively, draw or cut pictures from a magazine. Talk about the characteristics of "treasures" that children have found: sizes, textures, colors, and function.

**TeachSource Digital Download**

## developmental **alerts**

Check with a health-care provider or early childhood specialist if, by the sixth birthday, the child does *not*:

- Alternate feet when walking up and down stairs.
- Speak in a moderate voice—not too loud, too soft, too high, or too low.
- Follow simple three-step directions in stated order: "Please go to the cupboard, get a cup, and bring it to me."
- Use four to five words in acceptable sentence structure.
- Cut on a line with scissors.
- Sit still and listen to an entire short story (5–7 minutes).
- Maintain eye contact when spoken to (unless this is a cultural taboo).
- Play well with other children; listen, take turns, and offer assistance.
- Perform most self-grooming tasks independently (brush teeth, wash hands and face).

**Note:** Cultural differences may alter the timetable when some developmental skills are acquired. Expanded Developmental Alerts Checklists appear in Appendix A and are also available as digital downloads.

## safety **concerns**

Continue to implement the safety practices described for the previous stages. Always be aware of new safety issues as the child continues to grow and develop.

### Falls

- Monitor parks and play areas for potential hazards—broken glass, sharp objects, defective structures, holes, inadequate cushioning material under play equipment, etc.

### Toys

- Refrain from purchasing toys that make loud noises, involve projectiles, or require electricity; battery-operated toys are safer.

## safety concerns *(continued)*

### Traffic

- Teach street safety, especially to children who walk to and from school; review safety practices often.
- Use recommended car seats and safety restraints appropriate for the child's increasing weight and height.

### Personal Safety

- *Never* leave children alone in a vehicle for any length of time; temperatures (hot or cold) inside a closed vehicle can become deadly in a matter of minutes. Unattended children also may be targeted by potential kidnappers.
- Teach children to run away and seek adult help if approached by a stranger. Tell them to yell, "You're not my mommy (daddy)." Establish a code word to help children recognize a trusted adult.
- Teach children how to swim and about water safety rules.

### Poisoning

- Use only nontoxic art supplies; check product labels carefully (see the Consumer Product Safety Commission website for product information and safety recalls).
- Remind children to always check with an adult before putting items possibly not meant for eating (such as pills or berries found growing on plants) in their mouth.

5-year-old

## positive behavior guidance

Adults play an essential role in helping preschool-age children develop self-control. They must set behavioral expectations that are developmentally realistic for children, state them in positive terms, and enforce them consistently. It is also important that adults provide unconditional love and serve as positive role models for children.

### Three-year-olds

- Set limits and use short, simple statements to explain why they are necessary.
- Acknowledge children when they are behaving appropriately. "That was nice of you to share your crayons."
- Remain calm and patient; keep your own anger and frustration under control.
- Redirect the child's activity: if the child is throwing sand, ask him to help you sweep the sand back into the sandbox.

### Four-year-olds

- Offer choices: "Do you want to wear your sandals or sneakers?"
- Explain natural consequences to help children understand the outcomes of their actions: "If you spill the paint, there won't be any left for our picture." "If you bump into the other children with your bike, you will need to leave the area."
- Provide simple directions and warnings so that children know what to expect next: "Lunch will be served in a few minutes, so we need to begin picking up the toys."

### Five-year-olds

- Involve children in problem solving: "Which toy do you think your brother would like?" "Where should we look for your jacket?"
- Remove children from an activity if inappropriate behavior continues and give them time by themselves to think about their actions.
- Include children in setting rules to increase compliance: "What should we do if someone pushes another child?"

# Summary

**6-1** Preschoolers undergo remarkable advancements in their cognitive abilities:

- Three-year-olds listen, imitate, and understand basic concepts (e.g., bigger, smaller, more, less, etc.)
- Four-year-olds recognize letters and numbers and begin to understand their meaning, classify objects, answer questions correctly, and make up stories.
- Five-year-olds have grasped more advanced concepts such as telling time, understanding a calendar, expressing complex thoughts, and classifying objects based on more than one dimension.

**6-2** Preschool-age children want and continue to need a great deal of adult support, reassurance, and approval, although this becomes less significant as they move out of the preschool and into the primary school years.

**6-3** Adults serve an important role in promoting children's early language skills through interactive conversation, reading stories, singing songs, asking questions, and encouraging storytelling.

**6-4** Eating patterns change during the preschool years. Three-year-olds are learning to use utensils and require some adult assistance during meals; four-year-olds are able to manage most eating skills with minimal help, are easily distracted, and enjoy helping with food preparations; five-year-olds typically have a good appetite and have developed an awareness and interest in food options.

## Key Terms

tripod grasp **p. 132**      gender **p. 136**

hand dominance **p. 132**      binocular vision **p. 147**

## Apply What You Have Learned

### A. Case Study Connections

*Reread the developmental sketch about Hasina and Munisa presented at the beginning of this chapter and answer the following questions.*

1. Assuming that Munisa's motor development is progressing typically, what skills would you expect to observe?

2. What social behaviors would be characteristic of a four-year-old?

3. How would you respond to Hasina if she asked, "How much responsibility can I expect Munisa to assume for her own personal care at this age?"

4. In addition to reading bedtime stories, what other types of activities might Hasina engage in with Munisa to further her language development?

### B. Review Questions

1. Describe three motor skills that appear between three and five years of age.

2. Describe three major speech and language skills that appear between three and five years of age (in the order in which they should develop).

3.  What self-help skills would you expect a typically developing four-year-old to be capable of performing?

4.  Should a teacher be concerned about a four-year-old who exhibits frequent mood swings or often tattles? Why or why not?

5.  Describe how a teacher might use a cooking activity to promote five-year-olds' perceptual-cognitive development.

## C.  Your Turn: Chapter to Practice

1.  Interview the parent of a preschool-age child. Ask the parent what behavior(s) he finds most challenging or troublesome to handle. What seems to trigger the behavior(s)? How does the parent manage the behavior(s), and is the approach effective in achieving the desired outcome?

2.  Develop an activity that teaches a three-year-old the concepts of *small, smaller,* and *smallest,* and present it to several children. Were you successful in teaching the concepts? What would you change if you were to repeat the learning activity at another time?

3.  Interview the parent of a preschool-age child who has special developmental needs. What specific concerns does the parent have about the child's developmental progress? What short- and long-term goals does the parent hope the child can achieve? Conduct a second interview with a parent of a preschool-age child who is developmentally advanced for her age and ask the same questions. In what ways are the parents' objectives similar and different?

# Online Resources

## Canadian Paediatric Society
The Canadian Paediatric Society is a national advocacy association comprised of pediatricians. Their goal is to promote quality health care for all children through professional development and public education. Information about children's development, safety, learning activities, and behavior guidance can be found under the "For Parents" tab.

## Council for Exceptional Children (CEC)
The Council for Exceptional Children (CEC) is the largest international professional organization dedicated to advocating and improving educational outcomes for persons with exceptionalities, disabilities, or giftedness.

## Society for Research on Child Development (SRCD)
The Society for Research on Child Development (SRCD) has a longstanding history of supporting and disseminating interdisciplinary child development research. It publishes three journals that are distributed worldwide; *Child Development, Child Development Perspectives,* and *Monographs.*

## U.S. Consumer Product Safety Commission (CPSC) (*Safety Education: Safety Guides*)
The CPSC provides excellent safety guidelines that address a variety of topics especially relevant for young children—from toys and furniture to clothing and pool safety. Up-to-date product recalls are also provided.

# References

American Academy of Pediatrics (AAP). (2012). Trampoline safety in childhood and adolescence. *Pediatrics*, 130(4), 774–779; also available online at http://pediatrics.aappublications.org/content/early/2012/09/19/peds.2012-2082.full.pdf.

Ashworth, A., Hill, C., Karmiloff-Smith, A., & Dimitriou, D. (2013). Cross syndrome comparison of sleep problems in children with Down syndrome and Williams syndrome. *Research in Developmental Disabilities*, 34(5), 1572–1580.

Bernier, A., Beauchamp, M., Bouvette-Turcot, A., Carlson, S., & Carrier, J. (2013). Sleep and cognition in preschool years: Specific links to executive functioning. *Child Development*, 84(5), 1542–1553.

Bloom, E., & Paradis, J. (2013). Past tense production by English second language learners with and without language impairment. *Journal of Speech, Language, and Hearing Research*, 56(1), 281–294.

Buckhalt, J. (2013). Sleep and cognitive functioning in children with disabilities. *Exceptional Children*, 79(4), 391–405.

Camfferman, D., Kennedy, J., Gold, M., Simpson, C., & Lushington, K. (2013). Psychophysiology and cognitive neuroscience of sleep and sleep disorders. *International Journal of Psychophysiology*, 89(2), 265–272.

Case-Smith, J. (2013). Systematic review of interventions to promote social-emotional development in young children with or at risk for disability. *American Journal of Occupational Therapy*, 67(4), 395–404.

Castles, A., McLean, G., Bavin, E., Bretherton, L., Carlin, J., Prior, M., …, & Reilly, S. (2013). Computer use and letter knowledge in preschool children: A population-based study. *Journal of Paediatrics and Child Health*, 49(3), 193–198.

Cooperson, S., Bedore, L., & Peña, E. (2013). The relationship of phonological skills to language skills in Spanish-English-speaking bilingual children. *Clinical Linguistics & Phonetics*, 27(5), 371–389.

Fitzpatrick, C., & Pagani, L. (2012). Toddler working memory skills predict kindergarten school readiness. *Intelligence*, 40(2), 205–212.

Gaab, E., Owens, G., MacLeod, R. (2013). Caregivers' estimations of their children's perceptions of death as a biological concept. *Death Studies*, 37(8), 693–703.

Gauvain, M., Munroe, R., & Beebe, H. (2013). Children's questions in cross-cultural perspective: A four-culture study. *Journal of Cross-Cultural Psychology*, 44(7), 1148–1165.

Goble, P., Martin, C., Hanish, L., & Fabes, R. (2012). Children's gender-typed activity choices across preschool social contexts. *Sex Roles*, 67(7–8), 435–451.

Godwin, K., Marlen, B., & Fisher, A. (2013). Development of category-based reasoning in 4–7-year-old children: The influence of label co-occurrence and kinship knowledge. *Journal of Experimental Child Psychology*, 115(1), 74–90.

Hachey, A. (2013). The early childhood mathematics education revolution. *Early Education & Development*, 24(4), 419–430.

Halim, M., Ruble, D., Tamis-LeMonda, C., & Shrout, P. (2013). Rigidity in gender-typed behaviors in early childhood: A longitudinal study of ethnic minority children. *Child Development*, 84(4), 1269–1284.

Howe, N., Abuhatoum, S., & Chang-Kredl, S. (2013). Everything's upside down. We'll call it upside down valley! Siblings' creative play themes, object use, and language during pretend play. *Early Education & Development*, 25(3), 1–18, doi:10.1080/10409289.2013.773254.

Huber, R., & Born, J. (2014). Sleep, synaptic connectivity, and hippocampal memory during early development. *Trends in Cognitive Sciences*, 18(3), 141–152.

Ingram, G., & Bering, J. (2010). Children's tattling: The reporting of everyday norm violations in preschool settings. *Child Development*, 81(3), 945–957.

Karazsia, B., & Kirschman, K. (2013). Evidence-based assessment of childhood injuries and physical risk-taking behaviors. *Journal of Pediatric Psychology*, 38(8), 829–845.

Kurdziel, L., Duclos, K., & Spencer, R. (2013). Sleep spindles in midday naps enhance learning in preschool children. *Proceedings of the National Academy of Sciences of the United States of America*, 110(43), 17267–17272.

Leman, P., Ben-Hmeda, M., Cox, J., Loucas, C., Seltzer-Eade, S., & Hine, B. (2013). Normativity and friendship choices among ethnic majority- and minority-group children. *International Journal of Behavioral Development*, 37(3), 202–210.

Li-Grining, C. (2013). The role of cultural factors in the development of Latino preschoolers' self-regulation. *Child Development Perspectives*, 6(3), 210–217.

Marotz, L. (2015). *Health, safety, and nutrition for the young child*. 9th Ed. Belmont, CA: Wadsworth Cengage Learning.

Michael-Luna, S. (2013). What linguistically diverse parents know and how it can help early childhood educators: A case study of a dual-language preschool community. *Early Childhood Education Journal*, 41(6), 447–455.

Mindell, J., Sadeh, A., Kwon, R., & Goh, D. (2013). Cross-cultural differences in the sleep of preschool children. *Sleep Medicine*, 14(12), 1283–1289.

Nguyen, S. (2012). Inductive selectivity in children's cross-classified concepts. *Child Development*, 83(5), 1748–1761.

Nip, I., & Green, J. (2013). Increases in cognitive and linguistic processing primarily account for increases in speaking rate with age. *Child Development*, 84(4), 1324–1337.

Nurmsoo, E., Einav, S., & Hood, B. (2012). Best friends: Children use mutual gaze to identify friendships in others. *Developmental Science*, 15(3), 417−425.

Odic, D., Pietroski, P., Hunter, T., Lidz, J., & Halberda, J. (2013). Young children's understanding of "more" and discrimination of number and surface area. *Journal of Experimental Psychology: Learning, Memory, and Cognition*, 39(2), 451−461.

Piosczyk, H., Holz, J., Feige, B., Spiegelhalder, K., Weber, F., Landmann, N., ..., & Nissen, C. (2013). The effect of sleep-specific brain activity versus reduced stimulus interference on declarative memory consolidation. *Journal of Sleep Research*, 22(4), 406−413.

Ploog, B., Scharf, A., Nelson, D., & Brooks, P. (2013). Use of computer-assisted technologies (CAT) to enhance social, communicative, and language development in children with autism spectrum disorders. *Journal of Autism & Developmental Disorders*, 43(2), 301−322.

Plowman, L., & McPake, J. (2013). Seven myths about young children and technology. *Childhood Education*, 89(1), 27−33.

Purpura, D. & Lonigan, C. (2013). Informal numeracy skills: The structure and relations among numbering, relations, and arithmetic operations in preschool. *American Educational Research Journal*, 50(1), 178−209.

Ramani, G., & Brownell, C. (2014). Preschoolers' cooperative problem solving: Integrating play and problem solving. *Journal of Early Childhood Research*, 12(1), 92−108.

Robinson, E., Einav, S., & Fox, A. (2013). Reading to learn: Prereaders' and early readers' trust in text as a source of knowledge. *Developmental Psychology*, 49(3), 505−513.

Salomo, D., Lieven, E., & Tomasello, M. (2013). Children's ability to answer different types of questions. *Journal of Child Language*, 40(2), 469−491.

Scharf, R., Demmer, R., Silver, E., & Stein, R. (2013). Nighttime sleep duration and externalizing behaviors of preschool children. *Journal of Developmental & Behavioral Pediatrics*, 34(6), 384−391.

Taki, Y., Hashizume, H., Thyreau, B., Sassa, Y., Takeuchi, H., Wu, K., ..., & Kawashima, R. (2012). Sleep duration during weekdays affects hippocampal gray matter volume in healthy children. *NeuroImage*, 60(1), 471−475.

Taylor, Z., Eisenberg, N., Spinrad, T., Eggum, N., & Sulik, M. (2013a). The relations of ego-resiliency and emotion socialization to the development of empathy and prosocial behavior across early childhood. *Emotion*, 13(5), 822−831.

Taylor, M., Sachet, A., Maring, B., & Mannering, A. (2013b). The assessment of elaborated role-play in young children: Invisible friends, personified objects, and pretend identities. *Social Development*, 22(1), 75−93.

Vlok, M., & de Witt, M. (2012). Naïve theory of biology: The pre-school child's explanation of death. *Early Child Development & Care*, 182(12), 1645−1659.

Wanless, S., McClelland, M., Lan, X., Son, S., Cameron, C., Morrison, F., ..., & Sung, M. (2013). Gender differences in behavioral regulation in four societies: The United States, Taiwan, South Korea, and China. *Early Childhood Research Quarterly*, 28(3), 621−633.

Washington, K., (2013). The association between expressive grammar intervention and social and emergent literacy outcomes for preschoolers with SLI. *American Journal of Speech-Language Pathology*, 22(1), 113−125.

Yates, T., & Marcelo, A. (2014). Through race-colored glasses: Preschoolers' pretend play and teachers' ratings of preschooler adjustment. *Early Childhood Research Quarterly*, 29(1), 1−11.

Yorbik, O., Mutlu, C., Koc, D., & Nutluer, T. (2014). Possible negative effects of snoring and increased sleep fragmentation on developmental status of preschool children. *Sleep and Biological Rhythms*, 12(1), 30−36.

# chapter 7
# Early Childhood: Six-, Seven-, and Eight-Year-Olds

## Learning Objectives

*After reading this chapter, you will be able to:*

**7-1** Describe at least two sensory learning experiences that would be developmentally appropriate for six-, seven-, and eight-year-olds.

**7-2** Explain why behavior problems and emotional outbursts may reappear during this developmental stage.

**7-3** Compare and contrast the speech and language skills of six- and eight-year-olds.

**7-4** Explain and demonstrate Piaget's concept of conservation.

**7-5** Discuss the role of friendships in children's development.

### naeyc NAEYC Standards Linked to Chapter Content

**1a, 1b, and 1c:** Promoting child development and learning

**2a and 2c:** Building family and community relationships

**3c and 3d:** Observing, documenting, and assessing to support young children and families

**4a, 4b, 4c, and 4d:** Using developmentally effective approaches

**5c:** Using content knowledge to build meaningful curriculum

For weeks, Huang has asked his mother repeatedly when school will begin. Soon to turn seven, he is eagerly anticipating the start of first grade, riding on a school bus, and eating lunch in the school cafeteria. Huang recently met his new teacher, Mr. Chen, during an open house held at the school and is excited about having a "man teacher." His mother, Bao-yu, has been concerned about Huang since his father's death and thinks that he will benefit from having a male role model back in his life.

Huang is happy that his best friend, Lin, will be in the same class this year. Unlike Huang, who is an only child, Lin is the youngest of four siblings. Lin's parents work long hours and seldom show any interest in his school activities or homework. They view their primary role to be that of caretakers and believe that teachers are responsible for helping their son to learn. Lin struggles to write his name, has difficulty sorting objects by category, and is unable

© Denis Kuvaev/Shutterstock.com

158

to recognize and order numbers consistently. The kindergarten teacher was reluctant to advance Lin to the first grade, but Mr. Chen assured her that he would devote extra time to help the boy succeed. Mr. Chen is aware that Lin's family speaks little English at home and has limited resources.

Huang thinks it is "pretty neat" that he will go to school all day like his mother, who plans to finish her associate's degree in accounting this spring. She is proud of her son's progress in school and works with him at home so that he continues to do well. Huang's advanced reading and writing skills are apparent in the imaginative stories that he composes on the computer when he and his mother visit their local library. When he is finished, Huang often seeks out his "favorite" librarian so he can read his story to her. Huang also is excited about learning to tell time and repeatedly wants his mother to ask him what time it is.

## Ask Yourself

- What environmental factors may help to explain why Huang and Lin are performing differently in school?
- What steps is Huang's mother taking to support his literacy development?

# Six-, Seven-, and Eight-Year-Olds

The period following the preschool years is especially remarkable. Children are in a stage of developmental integration—organizing and combining various developmental skills to accomplish increasingly complex tasks. At this age, both boys and girls are becoming more competent at managing their own personal needs—washing, dressing, toileting, eating, getting up, and getting ready for school. They observe family rules regarding mealtimes, television, chores, and the need for privacy. They can be trusted to run errands and carry out simple responsibilities at home and school without frequent reminders. In other words, children are in control of themselves and their immediate world. Above all, six-, seven-, and eight-year-olds are ready and eager to attend school, even though they may be somewhat apprehensive when the time actually arrives. Going to school creates anxieties about things such as arriving on time, remembering to bring back assigned homework, having a new teacher, being accepted and making new friends, taking tests, or walking home alone (Eggum-Wilkens et al., 2013; Grills-Taquechel et al., 2013).

Learning to read is one of the most complex perceptual tasks children will encounter during this developmental stage (Gordon & Browne, 2014; Piaget, 1926) (Figure 7-1). Recognizing visual letter symbols and associating them with their spoken sounds is an important component of **emerging literacy**. It also means that children must learn to combine letters to form words and to put these words together to form intelligible thoughts that can be read or spoken (Ding, Richardson, & Schnell, 2013). Complex as the task is, most children become relatively adept at reading between six and eight years of age; for some, the skill soon is taken for granted.

**Sensory** activities continue to be an effective method for promoting children's learning. This approach encourages children to manipulate a variety of materials—blocks; puzzles; paints, glue, paper, and found materials; sand, water, and dirt; musical instruments; and measurement devices. It can also include project-based activities that reinforce learning across all developmental domains and actively engage children

### Did You Know

...that a small percentage of parents are choosing to "red shirt" or delay their children's school entry to give them additional time to mature and gain an academic or competitive athletic advantage?

**emerging literacy** Early experiences, such as being read and talked to, naming objects, and identifying letters, that prepare a child for later reading, writing, and language development.

**sensory** Refers to the five senses: hearing, seeing, touching, smelling, and tasting.

© 2015 Cengage Learning®

**Figure 7-1** Learning to read is one of the most complex perceptual tasks that children will undertake during this developmental stage.

in experiences such as cooking, gardening, carpentry, science, and dramatic play. The National Association for the Education of Young Children (NAEYC) strongly endorses a play-based, **hands-on learning** approach with six-, seven-, and eight-year-olds, as well as with younger children. This philosophy is clearly stated in the organization's *Developmentally Appropriate Practice in Early Childhood Programs Serving Children from Birth through Age 8* (NAEYC, 2009). Particularly noteworthy are the subsections entitled "Principles of Child Development and Learning that Inform Practice" and "Guidelines for Developmentally Appropriate Practice" that outline the rationale for individualizing children's educational opportunities. Above all, this position statement acknowledges that each child is a unique individual whose developmental abilities, family and cultural heritage, needs, and learning style differ from those of other children. Similar recommendations that emphasize the importance of individualizing learning have been adopted by other early childhood professional organizations, including family child care and school-age programs.

Play-based learning remains an important instructional method for fostering children's cognitive and social skill development in the early grades (Weisberg, Hirsh-Pasek, & Golinkoff, 2013; Hedges & Cullen, 2012). For the most part, six-, seven-, and eight-year-olds play well with other children, especially if the group is not too large. There is keen interest in making friends, being a friend, and having friends. At the same time, there also can be quarreling, bossing, and excluding: "If you play with Lynette, then you're not *my* friend." Some children show considerable aggression, but it often tends to be verbal, aimed at hurting feelings rather than at causing physical harm.

Friends are usually playmates whom the child has ready access to in the neighborhood and at school. Friends are often defined as someone who is "fun," "pretty," "strong," "nice," or "awesome." Friendships at this age are established easily and abandoned readily; few are stable or long-lasting (House et al., 2013).

Throughout the primary school years, many children seem almost driven by the need to do everything right, yet they enjoy being challenged and completing tasks. They like to build models, do craft projects, play computer and board games, and participate in organized activities. Most children enjoy these early school years. They become comfortable with themselves, their families, and their teachers.

**hands-on learning** A curriculum approach that involves children as active participants, encouraging them to manipulate, investigate, experiment, and solve problems.

# The Six-Year-Old

Exciting adventures begin to open up to six-year-olds as their coordination improves and their size and strength increase. Children need ample opportunities for vigorous play each day to promote their physical development, decrease the risk for obesity, and channel excess energy. However, new challenges often are met with a mixture of enthusiasm and frustration. Six-year-olds typically have difficulty making choices and, at times, are overwhelmed by unfamiliar situations. At the same time, changes in their cognitive abilities enable them to see rules as useful for understanding everyday events and the behavior of others.

For many children, this period also marks the beginning of formal, subject-oriented schooling. It should be noted that highly structured academic activities (e.g., worksheets, drills, and memorization) are considered developmentally inappropriate at this age by many early childhood educators (Bulunuz, 2013; Ransom & Manning, 2013). Behavior problems and signs of stress or tension such as tics, nail-biting, hair-twisting, bed-wetting, or sleeping difficulties may flare up as children encounter new challenges and struggles. Generally, these pass as children become familiar with expectations and the responsibilities associated with going to school. Despite the turmoil and trying times, most six-year-olds experience an abundance of happy times marked by a lively curiosity, an eagerness to learn, an endearing sense of humor, and exuberant outbursts of affection and good will (Figure 7-2).

**Figure 7-2**  Six-year-olds are curious and eager to learn.

# Developmental Profiles and Growth Patterns

## Growth and Physical Characteristics

- Continues to grow slowly but steadily.
- Gains 2–3 inches (5–7.5 cm) in height each year: girls are an average of 42–46 inches (105–115 cm) tall; boys are an average of 44–47 inches (110–117.5 cm).
- Adds 5–7 pounds (2.3–3.2 kg) in weight per year: girls weigh approximately 38–47 pounds (19.1–22.3 kg); boys weigh approximately 42–49 pounds (17.3–21.4 kg). Increased muscle mass accounts for a significant portion of weight gain.
- Heart rate (80 beats per minute) and respiratory rates (18–28 breaths per minute) are similar to those of adults; both rates vary with activity.
- Appears lanky as the long bones in arms and legs begin a phase of rapid growth.
- Loses baby **(deciduous) teeth**; permanent (secondary) teeth erupt, beginning with the two upper front teeth; girls tend to lose teeth at an earlier age than do boys.
- Has a visual acuity of approximately 20/20; children testing 20/40 or less should have a thorough professional evaluation (Ma, Yang, & Hwang, 2013; Neely, 2013).
- Farsightedness is not uncommon and may be outgrown as children mature.
- Develops more adultlike facial features and overall physical appearance.
- Requires approximately 1,600 to 1,700 calories per day.

## Motor Development

- Has increased muscle strength; boys are typically stronger than girls of a similar size.
- Gains greater control over large and fine motor skills; movements are becoming more precise and deliberate, although some clumsiness persists.
- Enjoys vigorous physical activity (running, jumping, climbing, and throwing).
- Moves constantly, even when trying to sit still.

**deciduous teeth**  The initial set of teeth that eventually fall out; often referred to as *baby teeth*.

**6-year-old**

## Developmental Profiles and Growth Patterns *(continued)*

### What Do You See?

**Physical activity** Active play is natural for most children. What motor skills are these girls using? What benefits do children get from being physically active each day? How could the activities in this picture be modified for a child who has limited physical mobility?

© 2015 Cengage Learning®

- Has increased dexterity and eye–hand coordination along with improved motor functioning, which make it easier for children to learn how to ride a bicycle (without training wheels), swim, swing a bat, or kick a ball.
- Enjoys art projects (likes to paint, model with clay, "make things," draw and color, put things together, and work with wood).
- Writes numbers and letters with varying degrees of precision and interest; may reverse or confuse certain letters (such as *b/d, p/g, g/q, or t/f*).
- Traces around hand and other objects.
- Folds and cuts paper into simple shapes.
- Ties own shoes (but this task is still a struggle for some children).

### Perceptual-Cognitive Development

- Shows increased attention span; works at tasks for longer periods of time, although concentrated effort is not always consistent.
- Understands concepts such as simple time markers (e.g., today, tomorrow, and yesterday) or uncomplicated concepts of motion (cars go faster than bicycles).
- Identifies seasons and major holidays and the activities associated with each.
- Enjoys challenges: puzzles, counting and sorting activities, paper-and-pencil mazes, and games that involve counting or matching letters and words with pictures.
- Recognizes some words by sight; attempts to sound out words (some children may be reading well by this time).
- Identifies familiar coins (i.e., pennies, nickels, dimes, and quarters).
- Includes at least six body parts when drawing a person.
- Names and correctly holds up the right and left hands fairly consistently; identifies the smallest of two shapes and the longer of two lines.

## Developmental Profiles and Growth Patterns *(continued)*

- Clings to certain beliefs involving magic or fantasy (the Tooth Fairy swapping a coin for a tooth; the Easter Bunny hiding eggs; blowing out birthday candles and making a wish).

- Has limited understanding of death and dying (believes that it can be reversed or that he has caused it to happen; often expresses fear that parents might die, especially the mother) (Legare et al., 2012; Vlok & de Witt, 2012).

### Speech and Language Development

- Talks nonstop (this behavior may not be encouraged in all cultures); sometimes described as a "chatterbox."

- Acquires language pattern reflective of her cultural background.

- Carries on adultlike conversations; asks many questions.

- Learns as many as 5 to 10 new words each day; vocabulary consists of approximately 10,000 to 14,000 words.

- Uses appropriate verb tenses, word order, and sentence structure.

- Uses language rather than tantrums or physical aggression to express displeasure: "That's mine! Give it back, or I'm telling."

- Talks self through the required steps in simple problem-solving situations (although the logic may be irregular and unclear to adults).

- Imitates slang and profanity; finds "bathroom" or "forbidden" talk extremely funny.

- Delights in telling jokes and riddles; often the humor is far from subtle (Figure 7-3).

- Enjoys being read to and making up stories.

- Is capable of learning more than one language; does so spontaneously in a bilingual or multilingual family (Granena & Long, 2013; Nicolay & Poncelet, 2013).

▶❚❚ **TeachSource Video Connections**

### Cognitive Development

Advances in children's cognitive abilities, including improved memory capacity, information processing, and abstract thinking, begin to open new opportunities for complex learning. Respond to the following questions after you have watched the learning video *Kindergarten Children's Observations about a 100 Chart*:

1. What learning strategies did the teacher use to help children grasp the meaning of numbers?

2. What cognitive and speech-language skills were involved in the children's ability to describe the numbers chart?

3. In what ways did the classroom environment reflect an understanding of the typical six-year-old's developmental needs?

Figure 7-3  **The six-year-old finds humor in almost everything.**

**6-year-old**

### Social-Emotional Development

- Experiences sudden mood swings: can be "best friends" with someone one minute and "worst of enemies" the next; loving one day, uncooperative and irritable the next; especially unpredictable toward the mother or primary caregiver.

- Becomes less dependent on family members as the friendship circle begins to expand; still needs familial closeness, security, and nurturing, yet has urges to break away and "grow up" (Piaget, 1929).

- Craves and seeks adult approval, reassurance, and praise; anxious to please; may complain excessively about minor hurts or other children's behavior to gain attention.

- Continues to be self-centered (egocentric); still sees and interprets events almost entirely from own perspective (i.e., views everything and everyone as existing for the child's own benefit).

- Easily disappointed and frustrated by self-perceived failure.

- Has difficulty composing and soothing self; dislikes being corrected or losing at games; might sulk, cry, refuse to play, or reinvent rules to suit own purposes.

- Is enthusiastic and inquisitive about surroundings and everyday events.

- Shows little or no understanding of ethical behavior or moral standards; often fibs, cheats, or takes items belonging to others without meaning to cause harm.

- Knows when she has been "bad"; values of "good" and "bad" are based on school, family, and cultural expectations and rules.

- May become increasingly fearful of thunderstorms, the dark, unidentified noises, dogs, and other animals (Burnham, Lomax, & Hooper, 2013).

## DAILY ROUTINES

### Eating

- Has a healthy appetite most of the time; often takes helpings larger than is able to finish. May skip an occasional meal; usually makes up for it later, though.

- Has strong food preferences and definite dislikes; willingness to try new foods is unpredictable.

- Uses table manners that often do not meet adult standards; may revert to eating with fingers on occasion; puts too much food into the mouth at one time; continues to spill milk or drop food in his lap.

- Has difficulty using a table knife for cutting and a fork for anything but spearing food.

- Finds it difficult to sit quietly through an entire meal; wiggles and squirms, gets off (or "falls" off) a chair, drops utensils, or needs to go to the bathroom.

### Personal Care and Dressing

- Balks at having to take a bath; finds many excuses for delaying or avoiding a bath entirely.

- Manages toileting routines without much adult help; sometimes is in a hurry or waits too long so that "accidents" happen.

- Reverts to occasional accidental soiling or wetting of pants, especially during new experiences, such as in the first weeks of school or when under stress.

## DAILY ROUTINES *(continued)*

- Sleeps through most nights without having to get up to use the bathroom. *Note:* Some children, especially boys, may not maintain a dry bed for another year or so.

- Performs self-care routines such as hand-washing, bathing, and toothbrushing in a hurry; not always careful or thorough; still needs frequent supervision and demonstrations to make sure that routines are carried out properly.

- Expresses interest in selecting own clothes; still needs some guidance in determining occasion and seasonal appropriateness.

- Drops clothing on the floor or bed, loses shoes around the house, and flings jacket down; often forgets where items were left (Figure 7-4).

### Sleeping

- Requires 9–11 hours of uninterrupted sleep.

- Sleeps through the night; some children continue to experience nightmares and sleep disturbances (Zisenwine et al., 2013).

- Sometimes requests a night-light, special blanket, or favorite stuffed toy (may want all three).

- Finds numerous ways to avoid bedtime; when finally in bed, falls asleep quickly.

- Amuses self with books, toys, television, or coloring if awake before the rest of the family.

### Play and Social Activities

- Has strong sense of self, which is evident in terms of preferences and dislikes; uncompromising about wants and needs. (These often do not coincide with adult plans or requests.)

- Is possessive about toys, books, family, and friends, but is able to share on some occasions.

- Forms a close, friendly relationship with one or two other children (often slightly older); play involves working together toward specific goals.

- Becomes intolerant of being told what to do; may revert to tantrums on occasion.

- Seeks teachers' attention, praise, and reassurance; now views the teacher (rather than the parent) as the ultimate source of "truth."

**Figure 7-4** The six-year-old is often forgetful when it comes to caring for clothes.

## learning activities to promote **brain development**

Six-year-olds are naturally curious and eager to learn. They enjoy imaginative play, art, math, science, outdoor activities, and projects that involve building, sorting, and matching. Learning to read and write is also of special interest.

**6-year-old**

## Developmentally appropriate applications for families and teachers

- Provide materials for drawing, cutting, pasting, and painting.

- Offer paper-and-pencil games (dot-to-dot, number-to-number, word search, hidden objects; copying and tracing activities).

- Provide (and frequently join in) simple card games (such as Hearts, Uno, and Flinch) and board games (e.g., Scrabble Junior, Candy Land, checkers, and dominos), especially those in which competitiveness is minimal.

- Keep a plentiful supply of books and magazines on hand for children to look at, as well as for adults to read with children; encourage children to make up and tell their own stories. Make weekly trips to the library.

- Share children's interest in collecting objects (e.g., seashells, colored stones, or bugs); help them to group, label, and display objects.

- Teach children what to do if they become lost or are approached by a stranger.

- Provide an assortment of dress-up clothes for boys and girls; use children's interests and familiar community workers as a guide for role-playing.

- Encourage simple carpentry and construction activities; provide wood scraps (along with hammer, glue, and small nails), blocks, empty boxes, cars, trucks, planes, and plastic zoo and farm animals. Avoid battery-driven and mechanical toys that offer little involvement (hence limited learning) once their novelty has worn off.

- Encourage at least 60 minutes a day of vigorous physical activity (e.g., bicycling; skating; swimming; gardening; throwing, catching, batting, and kicking balls; and walking). Limit time spent on computer and electronic games, which encourage sedentary behavior and reduce children's active play (a major cause of obesity).

- Involve children in cooking activities; use these opportunities to build language, math, science, and problem-solving skills.

**TeachSource Digital Download**

## developmental alerts

Check with a health-care provider or early childhood specialist if, by the seventh birthday, the child does *not*:

- Show signs of ongoing growth (increases in height and weight); continue to display improved mastery of motor skills, such as running, jumping, climbing, balancing, and throwing or catching a ball.

- Show some interest in reading and trying to reproduce letters, especially own name.

## developmental alerts *(continued)*

- Follow simple, multiple-step directions: "Finish your book, put it on the shelf, and then get your coat on."

- Understand basic concepts, such as largest, larger, biggest, next, first, and before.

- Follow through with instructions and complete simple tasks (putting dishes in the sink, picking up clothes, or finishing a puzzle). *Note:* All children forget. Task incompletion is not a problem unless a child *repeatedly* leaves tasks unfinished.

- Begin to develop alternatives to the excessive use of inappropriate behavior to get his way.

- Develop a steady decrease in tension-type behavior that may be associated with the start of school or participation in an organized activity (repeated grimacing or facial tics, eye twitching, grinding of teeth, nail-biting, regressive soiling or wetting, aggression, frequent stomachaches, difficulty sleeping, or refusing to go to school).

**Note:** Cultural differences may alter the timetable when some developmental skills are acquired. Expanded Developmental Alerts Checklists appear in Appendix A and are also available as digital downloads.

▶❚❚ **TeachSource** Video Connections

### Learning About Responsibility

When children are involved in classroom and household responsibilities, they learn important things about themselves and group involvement. They also develop skills that will help them to be successful as they grow up. Respond to the following questions after you have watched the learning video *School Age: Guidance:*

1. Why is it important to assign children tasks to complete on a one-time or routine basis?

2. What do children learn as a result of having responsibilities?

3. What challenges might a child who has never had any responsibilities be likely to experience in school?

**6-year-old**

Continue to implement the safety practices described for the previous stages. Always be aware of new safety issues as the child continues to grow and develop.

### Burns
- Keep matches and lighters in locked storage.

### Falls
- Make sure that clothing fits properly; skirts and pants that are too long can cause a child to trip or become entangled in play equipment. Remind children to keep shoes tied or Velcro straps fastened.
- Require children to wear helmets and other appropriate protective gear whenever they ride bikes, skateboards, or scooters.

### Equipment
- Store machinery and sharp instruments in a safe place, out of children's reach.
- Teach children proper use of scissors, knives, hammers, and kitchen equipment.
- Set parental controls on televisions (V-chip) and computers to protect children from unwanted content.

### Personal
- Teach children that it is inappropriate for anyone to touch their private parts without permission. Talk with them about how to get help if this occurs, and whom they should tell.
- Let children know that they always should tell an adult if they are being bullied.
- Reinforce children's resilience skills (e.g., communication, problem-solving, and conflict resolution).

### Traffic
- Review the safety rules to follow in and around motor vehicles, such as when crossing streets or riding a bicycle. Teach children to dismount and walk their bike across the street only at an intersection.
- Discuss appropriate behavior on buses if your child rides one to school.
- Insist that children always wear a seatbelt when riding in motor vehicles.

### Water
- Enroll children in swimming lessons and teach them the correct safety rules to follow around pools. Have proper rescue equipment accessible.
- Never leave children unattended near water.

**Spotlight on Brain Development**

## Toxic Stress and Abnormal Brain Development

The toxic effects of childhood maltreatment (e.g., abuse and neglect) on children's academic performance, physical and mental health, and adult potential have been studied extensively. In the past, the negative manifestations of such treatment were simply attributed to social conditions that shaped children's behavior in abnormal ways. Only recently have scientists been able to understand and explain these outcomes in terms of actual chemical and structural alterations that occur in the brain. They have discovered that early exposure to other forms of chronic stress, including dysfunctional parenting, neighborhood violence, corporal punishment, poverty, war, and bullying, also produces similar effects (Theall et al. 2013).

*Toxic stress* is a term used in the literature to describe the damaging nature of prolonged, negative physical, psychological, and emotional experiences on children's brain and developmental progress. The Adverse Childhood Experiences (ACE) Study is one of the most extensive studies to establish a strong link between toxic stress exposure during childhood and adverse effects on adult well-being. This collaborative study was conducted by the Centers for Disease Control and Prevention (CDC) and Kaiser-Permanente during 1995–1997, 2008, and 2011. More than 60 percent of the approximately 17,000 study participants reported experiencing maltreatment or dysfunctional family interactions before the age of eighteen (CDC, 2013). Physical examination and a self-administered survey revealed that adult subjects who experienced toxic stress as children subsequently developed a variety of health disorders, including substance abuse, heart disease, depression, autoimmune diseases, and premature death. Smaller-scale studies have confirmed similar findings (Herrenkohl et al., 2013; Hosang et al., 2013). Scientists have also identified significant cognitive and behavioral impairments associated with childhood exposure to toxic stress (Frodl & O'Keane, 2013; Haight et al., 2013; Samplin et al., 2013; Widom et al., 2013).

It is clear that toxic stress interferes with many aspects of children's development and also challenges their adult health and productivity. Chronic and excessive exposure to stress wires children's brains for basic survival and hinders their ability to learn (Frankenhuis & de Weerth, 2013). Policies and practices that support the early identification of children who live in challenging environments are imperative if the long-term, detrimental consequences of toxic stress are to be limited. Mentoring programs that teach essential coping and resilience skills (e.g., communication, problem solving, and conflict resolution), build positive self-esteem, and involve families in the context of culture and community are also fundamental to promoting children's healthy development.

### What are the connections?

1. What is toxic stress?
2. Why should teachers be concerned about children who are subjected to maltreatment or who live in dysfunctional or disadvantaged situations?
3. What legal responsibilities are teachers in your state mandated to perform in situations where they believe that maltreatment may be occurring?

# The Seven-Year-Old

Seven-year-olds are becoming more aware of themselves as individuals. They work hard at being responsible, being "good," and doing things "right" (Figure 7-5). They tend to take themselves seriously—too seriously at times. When they fail to live up to their own self-imposed expectations, they may sulk, become overly frustrated, or withdraw. It is as if children at seven are trying to think things through and to integrate what they already know with the flood of new experiences coming their way (Grills-Taquechel et al., 2013). Worrying about what might or might not come to pass is also typical; for example, anticipating yet dreading second grade can create anxiety. Maybe the work will be too hard; maybe the teacher won't be nice; or maybe the other kids won't be friendly.

Figure 7-5 Seven-year-olds take pride in doing everything right.

At the same time, children of this age have many positive traits. They are becoming more reasonable to deal with, cooperative, and willing to share. They are better listeners and are able to understand and follow through with requests for the most part. They stay on task longer and strive mightily to do everything perfectly (which only increases their worry load). Overwhelming efforts to cope with these conflicts may lead to unpredictable outbursts and mood swings. These complicated emotions require parents and teachers to exercise considerable patience and tolerance with seven-year-olds and to help them set expectations that are realistic and achievable.

7-year-old

# Developmental Profiles and Growth Patterns

## Growth and Physical Characteristics

- Grows slowly and steadily during this year; some girls may overtake boys in height.

- Increases in weight tend to be relatively small; a gain of 6 pounds (2.7 kg) per year is typical. Seven-year-olds weigh approximately 50–55 pounds (22.7–25 kg).

- Adds an average of 2.5 inches (6.25 cm) in height per year. Girls are approximately 44–44.5 inches (110–116.3 cm) tall; boys are approximately 46–49.5 inches (115–124 cm) tall.

- Muscle mass is fairly equal for boys and girls.

- Develops a longer, leaner, adultlike appearance; posture is more erect; the arms and legs continue to lengthen.

- Experiences swings in energy level; fluctuates between spurts of high energy and intervals of temporary fatigue.

- Continues to experience frequent respiratory infections and other minor illnesses; however, these episodes occur less often than at age six.

- Eyeballs continue to change shape and size; children's eyes should be checked periodically to ensure good vision.

- Hair often grows darker in color.

- Permanent teeth continue to replace baby teeth.

## Motor Development

- Exhibits large and fine motor control that is more precisely tuned: balances on either foot; runs up and down stairs with alternating feet; throws and catches smaller balls; practices batting balls; manipulates a computer mouse, knitting needles, or paintbrush with greater accuracy (Figure 7-6).

- Approaches more challenging physical activities, such as climbing up or jumping down from high places, with caution.

- Practices a new motor skill over and over until mastered, and then abandons it to work on something else.

Figure 7-6 **The seven-year-old can manipulate objects with improved skill and accuracy.**

- Finds the floor more comfortable than furniture when reading, playing games, or watching television; legs are often in constant motion.

- Uses a knife and fork appropriately, but inconsistently.

- Holds a pencil in a tight grasp near the tip; rests head on forearm, lowers head almost to the tabletop when doing pencil-and-paper tasks.

- Produces letters and numbers in a deliberate and confident fashion (characters are increasingly precise and uniform in size and shape; may run out of room on the line or page when writing).

## Developmental Profiles and Growth Patterns *(continued)*

### Perceptual-Cognitive Development

- Understands the concepts of space and time in ways that are both logical and more practical (a year is "a long time"; 100 miles is "far away") (Burny, Balcke, & Desoete, 2012; Casasanto, Fotakopoulou, & Boroditsky, 2010).

- Begins to grasp Jean Piaget's concepts of **conservation;** for example, the shape of a container does not necessarily reflect the quantity that it can hold (Figure 7-7). (Children now are entering Piaget's stage of *concrete operations.*)

- Gains a better understanding of cause and effect: "If I'm late for school again, I'll be in big trouble"; "Ice cubes will melt if they get too warm."

**Figure 7-7** **Children are beginning to understand that two differently shaped containers can hold the same amount of liquid.**

- Tells time by the clock and understands calendar time—days, months, years, and seasons; children who have difficulty learning these concepts may struggle with math as well (Muldoon et al., 2013).

- Plans ahead: "I'm saving this cookie for later tonight."

- Shows marked fascination with magic tricks; enjoys putting on shows for family and friends.

- Finds reading easier; many seven-year-olds read for their own enjoyment and delight in retelling story details.

- Has better reading than spelling skills.

- Understands numbers and estimation; can do simple addition and subtraction computations and begin to conceptualize and solve number and word problems mentally.

- Enjoys counting and saving money.

- Continues to reverse some letters and substitute sounds on occasion; this is typical development and does not indicate a reading or learning disability.

### Speech and Language Development

- Engages in storytelling; likes to write short stories and tell imaginative tales.

- Uses adultlike sentence structure and language in conversation; patterns reflect cultural and geographical differences and early literacy exposure.

- Becomes more precise and elaborate in the use of language; includes more descriptive adjectives and adverbs in conversation and written stories.

- Uses gestures to illustrate conversations.

- Criticizes own performance: "I didn't draw that right," "Her picture is better than mine."

**Did You Know**

...that many studies have shown that children who are physically active each day tend to perform better academically, have higher grades, and experience fewer behavior problems?

**conservation** The stage in children's cognitive development in which they understand that an object's physical qualities (e.g., weight and mass) remain the same despite changes in its appearance; for example, flattening a ball of play-dough does not affect its weight.

## Developmental Profiles and Growth Patterns *(continued)*

- Engages in verbal exaggeration: "I ate ten hot dogs at the picnic."
- Explains events in terms of own preferences or needs: "It didn't rain yesterday because I was going on a picnic."
- Describes personal experiences in great detail: "First we parked the car, then we hiked up this long trail, then we sat down on a broken tree near a lake and ate...."
- Understands and carries out multiple-step instructions (with up to five steps); may need to have directions repeated because she didn't listen to the entire request the first time.
- Enjoys writing email messages and simple notes to friends.

### Social-Emotional Development

- Is cooperative and affectionate toward adults and less frequently annoyed with them; sees humor in everyday happenings and is more outgoing.
- Likes to be the "teacher's helper"; is eager for the teacher's attention and approval, but less obvious about seeking it than when they were younger.
- Seeks out friendships; friends are important, but the child can find plenty to do if no one is available.
- Is beginning to develop empathy for others' feelings, motives, and actions.

**▶❚❚ TeachSource Video Connections**

### Cognitive Development and Concrete Operations

Children are developing an increasingly sophisticated understanding of how things work, their causes and effects, and how various manipulations can alter the outcome. These cognitive advances pique children's curiosity and interest in undertaking new activities. Respond to the following questions after you have watched the learning video entitled *5–11 Years: Piaget's Concrete Operational Stage:*

1. Which cognitive abilities make it possible for seven-year-olds to understand the concepts of size and volume as described in Piaget's theory of conservation?

2. Which changes in children's cognitive skills are evident during Piaget's concrete operational stage?

3. In what ways do these newly emerging cognitive abilities influence children's development in other domains, such as motor, speech and language, and social-emotional?

4. Do all children experience this stage of cognitive development? How might cultural or developmental differences influence this process?

- Quarrels less often, although squabbles and tattling continue to occur in both one-on-one and group play; may decide to play or work alone if frustrated.
- Complains that family decisions are unjust; that a particular sibling may get to do more or is given more.
- Blames others for own mistakes; makes up alibis for personal shortcomings: "I could have made a better one, but my teacher didn't give me enough time."
- Prefers same-gender playmates; more likely to play in groups.
- Worries about not being liked; feelings easily hurt; might cry, be embarrassed, or state adamantly, "I will never play with you again," when criticized.
- Takes responsibilities seriously; can be trusted to carry out directions and commitments; worries about being late for school or not getting work done on time.

## DAILY ROUTINES

### Eating

- Eats most foods; is better about sampling unfamiliar foods or taking small tastes of disliked foods, but still may refuse a few strong "hates."
- Shows interest in food; likes to help with grocery shopping and meal preparation.
- Eats with improved table manners, although adults may consider them far from perfect; spills milk less often and has fewer other accidents due to silliness, impulse, or haste to finish.
- Uses eating utensils with relative ease; seldom eats with fingers; some children still have trouble cutting meat.
- Is distracted sometimes during mealtimes by conversations and things going on elsewhere; at other times, is focused on eating and finishing up quickly.

### Personal Care and Dressing

- Manages own bath or shower with minimal assistance; is often reluctant to begin bathing; however, once started, seems to relax and enjoy the experience.
- Dresses self, although slow and distracted at times; can speed up the process when time becomes critical or there is something else that they want to do.
- Buttons and zips own clothes; ties own shoes; not always careful or precise (i.e., buttons askew, zipper undone, or shoelaces soon dragging).
- Shows little interest in clothes; wears whatever is laid out or available.
- Shows more interest in combing or brushing own hair.
- Has achieved complete bowel and bladder control; individual rhythm is well established; may resist having bowel movements at school.
- Less likely to get up during the night to use the toilet.

### Sleeping

- Averages 10–11 hours of sleep at night; insufficient sleep makes it difficult to get up in the morning and contributes to poor academic performance and behavior problems (Buckhalt, 2013; Kelly, Kelly, & Sacker, 2013; Astill et al., 2012).
- Sleeps soundly, with few if any bad dreams; instead, often dreams about participating in exploits and adventures.
- Gets ready for bed independently most nights, but still enjoys being tucked in or read to.
- Wakes up early most mornings by self; may remain in bed and occupy time with toys, counting savings in a piggy bank, looking at a baseball card collection, reading, and so forth.

### Play and Social Activities

- Participates in organized group activities (such as Boys' and Girls' Clubs, Cub Scouts and Brownies, 4-H, or swim and soccer teams).
- Dislikes missing school or social events; wants to keep up with friends and classmates.
- Has interest in creative arts, music, dancing, or drama; participates with a friend or alone.
- Engages in favorite play activities such as bicycle riding, climbing activities, basketball, soccer, skating, jumping rope, and computer games.
- Likes to play competitive board and card games, but may bend the rules when losing.
- Turns activities into challenges. "Let's see who can throw rocks the farthest." "I can run to the corner faster than you can."

7-year-old

7-year-old

## learning activities to promote **brain development**

Seven-year-olds use their basic skills and understanding to tackle new challenges. They enjoy reading complex stories, sharing what they know with others, and using their creativity to compose stories and plays. Active games and outdoor play provide opportunities for releasing excess energy, practicing motor skills, and learning how to interact cooperatively with other children.

### Developmentally appropriate applications for families and teachers

- Take trips to the library for children's storytime and dramatic play activities, as well as for checking out books.

- Sign up for free or low-cost community offerings of interest to the child (e.g., art, theater, science, swimming, T-ball, tumbling, yoga, or zoo and museum programs).

- Utilize the outdoors for learning; take family "collecting walks" in a park, on the beach, or around the neighborhood; support children's interests in photographing, collecting, and organizing found treasures (Figure 7-8).

© GFOW/Cengage Learning

**Figure 7-8** **The outdoors provides a wealth of learning opportunities.**

- Provide several small tools and equipment (such as for carpentry or gardening implements; science materials for growing a potato vine or maintaining an ant farm; a small aquarium).

- Gather materials for art projects, building models, or conducting science experiments (e.g., pieces of wood, Styrofoam, various weights and textures of cardboard and paper, beads, fabric, ribbon, yarn, and so forth).

- Offer dress-up clothes and props for planning and staging "original" shows; encourage children to write their own stories or songs, and attend their "performances."

- Assemble a box of discarded small appliances (such as a clock, hair dryer, radio, electric can opener, or mixer—with *cords removed*) and tools for taking them apart.

- Provide a dollhouse, farm or zoo set, space station, or airport, complete with small-scale people, animals, and equipment.

## learning activities (continued)

- Set out different-sized containers (plastic, metal, or glass [if closely supervised]). Add water to each container and encourage children to create musical notes by tapping on the various containers.

**TeachSource Digital Download**

7-year-old

## developmental alerts

Check with a health-care provider or early childhood specialist if, by the eighth birthday, the child does *not*:

- Attend to the task at hand; show longer periods of sitting quietly, listening, and responding appropriately.

- Follow through on simple instructions.

- Go to school willingly most days (of concern are excessive complaints about stomachaches or headaches when getting ready for school).

- Make friends (observe closely to see whether the child plays alone most of the time or withdraws consistently from contact with other children).

- Sleep soundly most nights. (Frequent or recurring nightmares are usually rare at this age.)

- See or hear well most of the time; frequent squinting, excessive rubbing of the eyes, or asking to have statements repeated requires professional evaluation.

- Handle stressful situations without undue emotional upset (i.e., excessive crying, sleeping or eating disturbances, withdrawal, and frequent anxiety).

- Assume responsibility for personal care (e.g., dressing, bathing, and feeding self) most of the time.

- Show improved fine motor skills: draw basic shapes, reproduce letters and numbers, cut along straight and curved lines.

**Note:** Cultural differences may alter the timetable when some developmental skills are acquired. Expanded Developmental Alerts Checklists appear in Appendix A and are also available as digital downloads.

## safety concerns

Continue to implement the safety practices described for the previous stages. Be aware of new safety issues as the child continues to grow and develop.

### Firearms

- Store unloaded guns in a locked cabinet, with ammunition kept in a different locked location. Teach children never to pick up or even touch a gun and to report immediately to an adult if they find one. Check with the families of your children's friends to determine whether guns are present and properly stored in their house.

### Play Environments

- Review rules for safe play and the use of playground equipment when away from home. Be aware of your child's friends and the types of play in which they tend to engage. Remind children to wash their hands after playing, especially after touching any animals.

### Tools/Equipment

- Do not let children use power mowers or other motorized yard equipment (e.g., weed eaters or hedge trimmers); keep children away when equipment is in use.

### Water

- Continue to supervise children at all times when they are in a pool, lake, or around any body of water.
- Teach children to swim and to follow water safety rules. Insist that they wear approved flotation vests when in or around large bodies of water (while fishing, boating, or skiing).

**8-year-old**

# The Eight-Year-Old

Eight-year-olds display a great enthusiasm for life. Energy is concentrated on improving skills that they already possess and enhancing what they already know. Eight-year-olds, once again, experience strong feelings of independence and are eager to make decisions about their own plans and friends. Interests and attention are increasingly devoted to peers and team or group activities rather than to family, teachers, or siblings. However, eight-year-olds continue to need adult guidance and to feel the love and security of family despite their increased reliance on peers for gratification. Sometime near midyear, boys and girls begin to go their separate ways and to form new interests in same-gender groups.

A small percentage of children may begin to engage in aggressive, intimidating, or **bullying** behaviors. Their targets are often peers who are perceived as loners, likely to react or retaliate, lacking in self-confidence, having special needs, or unable to stand up for themselves (Bejerot et al., 2013). Occasional incidences of name-calling, threatening, or hitting are not uncommon at this age, but it is important that they be addressed. However, a pattern of intentional and hurtful behavior that escalates as children approach adolescence distinguishes bullying from typical developmental expectations.

Researchers continue to study why some children have more difficulty controlling aggressive behavior than do others. Their findings suggest that bullies typically fall into two categories. The first group includes children who use their physical strength to intimidate others and have a tendency to be self-assured, impulsive, angry, and lacking in empathy and moral engagement (Wolke et al., 2013; Pozzoli, Gini, & Vieno, 2012). In addition, these children are known to frequently play violent video games, live in a household where an authoritarian parenting style is used, experience frequent parent-child conflict, or all three (Dittrick et al., 2013; Georgiou & Stavrinides, 2013). The second group consists of children who tend to be passive and are less likely to initiate bullying, but are willing to join in after it has begun. These children often possess poor social skills and low self-esteem and may themselves be victims of abuse or neglect. They also have difficulty knowing how to initiate appropriate social interaction and how to control their own impulsive behaviors.

Schools and communities have implemented a number of anti-bullying programs to reduce intimidating behaviors, increase empathy and kindness, and prevent the immediate and long-term effects of bullying on children's development. These initiatives are aimed at increasing children's resilience by promoting positive social, communication, and anger management skills; boosting self-esteem; and reducing harassing behaviors (Holt et al., 2013). Prevention efforts are also focusing on the victims, helping them to develop empowering behaviors such as walking away, avoiding bullies, problem solving, informing an adult, and using peaceful conflict resolution (Lindsay et al., 2013; Sapouna & Wolke, 2013).

**Did You Know**

…that approximately 40–80 percent of school-age children report being bullied at some point? Studies have found a strong association between repeated bullying and an increased risk of depression and suicide.

**bullying** Verbal and physical behavior that is hurtful, intentional, and repeatedly directed toward a person or child who is viewed as weaker.

# Developmental Profiles and Growth Patterns

## Growth and Physical Characteristics

- Continues to gain 5–7 pounds (2.3–3.2 kg) per year; an eight-year-old weighs approximately 55–61 pounds (25–27.7 kg). Girls typically weigh less than boys.

- Grows slowly and steadily in height, averaging 2.5 inches (6.25 cm) per year; girls are generally taller [46–49 inches (115–122.5 cm)] than boys [48–52 inches (120–130 cm)].

- Develops a more mature body shape and appearance; arms and legs grow longer, creating an image that is tall and lanky.

- Has nearly 20/20 vision (normal); periodic vision checks assure that children's visual acuity is developing properly.

- Some girls may begin to develop breasts and pubic hair and experience menses (Mensah et al., 2013).

- May have mood swings associated with early hormonal changes.

- Is generally healthy and experiences fewer illnesses than when younger.

8-year-old

## Motor Development

- Enjoys vigorous activity; likes to dance, inline skate, swim, wrestle, ride bikes, play basketball, jump rope, and fly kites (Figure 7-9).

- Seeks out opportunities to participate in team activities and games such as soccer, baseball, and kickball.

- Exhibits significant improvement in agility, balance, speed, and strength.

- Develops improved eye–hand coordination; copies words and numbers from a blackboard with increasing speed and accuracy; is able to learn cursive writing and to play a musical instrument.

- Possesses seemingly endless energy.

© GFOW/Cengage Learning

**Figure 7-9** The typical eight-year-old enjoys good health and vigorous activity.

## Perceptual-Cognitive Development

- Collects objects; organizes and displays items according to more complex systems; bargains and trades with friends to obtain additional pieces.

- Saves money for small purchases; eagerly develops plans to earn cash from odd jobs; studies catalogs and magazines for ideas of items to purchase.

- Begins taking an interest in what others think and do; understands that there are distant countries and differences of opinion and cultures.

- Accepts challenges and responsibilities with enthusiasm; delights in being asked to perform tasks, both at home and in school; is interested in being rewarded for efforts.

- Likes to read and work independently; spends considerable time planning and making lists.

- Understands perspective (i.e., shadow, distance, and shape); drawings reflect greater detail and more realistic portrayal of objects.

## Developmental Profiles and Growth Patterns *(continued)*

- Grasps the basic principles of conservation. (A tall, narrow jar might look different from one that is short and wide, but they both can hold the same amount of liquid.)

- Uses more sophisticated logic to understand everyday events; for example, is systematic in looking for a misplaced jacket, backpack, or toy.

- Adds and subtracts multiple-digit numbers; learning simple multiplication and division.

- Looks forward to school and is disappointed when ill or unable to attend.

### Speech and Language Development

**8-year-old**

- Delights in telling jokes and riddles.

- Understands and carries out multiple-step instructions (with up to five steps); may need to have directions repeated because they did not listen to the entire request.

- Reads with ease and understanding.

- Composes and sends imaginative and detailed messages to friends and family via email, texting, or webcam (Figure 7-10).

- Uses language to criticize and compliment others; repeats slang and curse words.

- Understands and follows the rules of grammar in conversation and written form.

- Is intrigued with learning secret word codes and using code language.

- Converses fluently with adults; able to think and talk about the past and future: "What time is my swim meet next week?" "Where did we go on vacation last summer?"

© GFOW/Cengage Learning

**Figure 7-10** Eight-year-olds can compose messages and tell stories with competence and imaginative detail.

### Social-Emotional Development

- Begins to form opinions about moral values and attitudes; declares things either right or wrong (based on family and cultural principles) (Cushman et al., 2013).

- Plays with two or three "best friends," most often of the same age and gender; makes friends easily (Stone et al., 2013).

- Enjoys spending some time alone; the need for privacy should be respected.

- Seems less critical of own performance but is easily frustrated and upset when unable to complete a task or when the product does not meet expectations.

## Developmental Profiles and Growth Patterns *(continued)*

### What Do You See?

**Friendships** Having a few "best friends" is important for eight-year-olds. What social-emotional qualities have these boys now developed that make mutual friendships possible?

8-year-old

- Participates in team games and activities; group membership and peer acceptance are becoming more important.

- Continues to blame others or makes up alibis to explain own shortcomings or mistakes.

- Enjoys talking on the telephone or communicating with friends and family via email, texting, or Skype.

- Understands and respects the fact that some children are more talented in certain areas such as drawing, sports, reading, art, or music.

- Enjoys performing for adults and challenging them in games; is proud of accomplishments and eager for adult recognition and approval. This behavior is less likely to be displayed in cultures where attention to self is discouraged; parent acknowledgment may be expressed quietly or nonverbally through eye contact or a smile.

- Exhibits spur-of-the-moment mood swings, happy one minute, obstinate and rude the next; can be overly sensitive and dramatic.

### ▶❚❚ TeachSource Video Connections

### Moral Development

As children mature, they begin to develop a greater understanding of social expectations, the consequences of their choices, and the ability to "know better." Respond to the following questions after you have watched the learning video *5–11 Years: Moral Development in Middle Childhood:*

1. Why are six-, seven-, and eight-year-olds only able to view a person's behavior as being either "right" or "wrong"?

2. What is guilt?

3. How would a child in the preconventional stage of moral development respond to another child who takes an extra cookie at lunchtime and hides it in his pocket? How might the response differ if the child were in the conventional stage?

© 2015 Cengage Learning®

## DAILY ROUTINES

### Eating

- Looks forward to meals; boys are often hungry and will consume more than girls. Serving nutrient-dense foods (such as fruits, vegetables, whole grains, low-fat dairy, and lean meat) and limiting calorie-dense items (like candy, cookies, chips, soft drinks, and French fries) meets critical growth requirements and reduces the risk of **obesity** (Marotz, 2015). Calorie intake needs to be balanced with physical activity to prevent excessive weight gain.

- Is willing to try new foods and some of those previously refused; likes to make some decisions about foods to be served and eaten.

- Takes pride in using good table manners, especially when eating out or when company is present; at home, manners are of less concern.

- Finishes meals quickly to resume previous activities; may stuff mouth with too much food or not chew food thoroughly in order to hurry through eating.

### Personal Care and Dressing

- Develops a pattern for bowel and bladder functions; usually has good control but may need to urinate more frequently when under stress.

- Hurries through hand-washing; dirt often ends up on the towel rather than washed down the drain.

- Enjoys bath and playing in water; easily sidetracked when supposed to be getting ready to bathe; some children are able to prepare their own bath or shower.

- Takes greater interest in appearance, selecting and coordinating own outfits, brushing hair, and looking good.

- Helps care for own clothes; hangs clothes up most times, helps with laundry by folding and returning items to dresser.

- Ties own shoes skillfully, but often too busy to be bothered.

### Sleeping

- Sleeps soundly through the night (requires 10–11 hours); efforts to delay bedtime might suggest that less sleep is needed.

- Begins to question the established bedtime; wants to stay up later; becomes easily distracted and involved in other activities while getting ready for bed.

- Sometimes wakes early and gets dressed while family members are still sleeping.

### Play and Social Activities

- Enjoys competitive activities and sports (e.g., soccer, baseball, swimming, or gymnastics); eager to join a team, but just as eager to quit if there is too much forced competition.

- Begins to adopt a know-it-all attitude toward the end of the eighth year; becomes bossy or argumentative with peers (and adults) at times; this behavior is more commonly noted not only in Western cultures, but it also may be observed in others.

- Likes to play board, electronic, computer, and card games; often interprets rules to improve his chances of winning.

- Seeks acceptance from peers; begins to imitate the clothing fads, hairstyles, behavior, and language of admired peers.

8-year-old

**obesity** Although no uniform definition exists, experts usually consider a child whose height-weight ratio (otherwise known as body mass index, or BMI) exceeds the 85th percentile for his age to be overweight, and obese if it is greater than the 95th percentile.

## learning activities to promote **brain development**

Eight-year-olds need many independent opportunities to explore their unique interests—writing, math, science, music, art, sports, dance, and theater—and to practice and advance the knowledge and skills that they already have acquired. They enjoy helping adults and take pride in completing assigned tasks.

### Developmentally appropriate applications for families and teachers

- Provide (and join in) games that require a moderate degree of strategy (e.g., chess, checkers, dominoes, card games, magic sets, and educational computer games).

- Encourage creativity; provide materials for painting, crafts, cooking, gardening, or building projects.

- Make frequent trips to the library; provide books to read, as well as stories on CDs and DVDs.

- Arrange opportunities for children to participate in noncompetitive activities—swimming, dancing, tumbling, skating, basketball, karate, bowling, or playing a musical instrument; this is a time for exploring many interests and developing new skills; seldom is there a long-term commitment to any particular activity.

- Assign routine tasks, such as feeding the dog, folding laundry, dusting furniture, bringing in the mail, watering plants, or setting the dinner table, to foster a sense of responsibility and self-esteem.

- Create a family-tree photo album. Have children take pictures of family members with a cell phone or still camera; create an album (in electronic or print format), and encourage children to write a few sentences about each person.

- Have fun with music. Help children make instruments from common household objects or discarded items: a cereal-box guitar (with rubber-band "strings"), shakers (a margarine container filled with small pebbles or cereal that can be eaten later), coffee can drums, paper-towel kazoos, etc.

- Provide children with sentence starters and ask them to complete the thought: "When it rains outside I like to…"; "If I could be any animal I would be a…"; "The color blue makes me think about…."

**TeachSource Digital Download**

8-year-old

## developmental **alerts**

Check with a health-care provider or early childhood specialist if, by the ninth birthday, the child does *not*:

- Exhibit a good appetite and continue to grow (height and weight). (Some children, especially girls, may begin to show early signs of an eating disorder at this point.) Medical evaluation should be sought for excessive weight gains or losses.

- Experience fewer illnesses and sleep well.

- Show improved motor skills in terms of agility, speed, and balance.

## developmental alerts *(continued)*

- Understand abstract concepts and use complex thought processes to solve problems.
- Look forward to school and the challenge of learning on most days.
- Follow through on multiple-step instructions.
- Express ideas clearly and fluently.
- Form friendships with other children and participate in group activities.

**Note:** Cultural differences may alter the timetable when some developmental skills are acquired. Expanded Developmental Alerts Checklists appear in Appendix A and are also available as digital downloads.

**8-year-old**

## safety concerns

Continue to implement the safety practices described for the previous stages. Be aware of new safety issues as the child continues to grow and develop.

### Animals

- Remind children to respect animals (not to approach unfamiliar animals and to refrain from yelling or making sudden movements).
- Teach children to recognize poisonous snakes and to leave them alone.
- Insist on thorough hand-washing after touching any animal to avoid illness.

### Backpacks

- Provide backpacks with dual shoulder straps to prevent injury; load the heaviest items against the child's back; packs should weigh less than 20 percent of the child's body weight. Wheeled backpacks are preferable.

### Media

- Monitor children's computer use; remove electronic equipment (e.g., computers and video game consoles) from children's bedrooms and place them within view; set parental controls (security) to block access to unwanted Internet sites; establish a family email account for children to use and monitor it closely.
- Talk to children about not giving out personal information to protect their online safety; have them use a nickname when online.
- Know what television programs and movies children are watching, what music they are listening to, and what video games they are playing (both at home and at friends' houses).

### Toys

- Supervise the use of more advanced toys, such as chemistry or woodworking sets and those that involve motors, electricity, or propellants.
- Require children to wear a helmet and appropriate protective gear when biking, skating, roller-blading, skateboarding, or playing baseball or softball.

### Water

- Require children to wear a life jacket whenever fishing, boating, skiing, or participating in other water sports.

## positive behavior guidance

Although six-, seven-, and eight-year-olds begin to question and test limits, they also need and want rules that are easy to understand, provide structure, and are enforced consistently. They must be allowed to develop increasing independence, but only with continued adult supervision.

### Six-, seven-, and eight-year-olds

- Adults serve as role models for children by displaying positive behavioral responses and self-control. Set a good example: take a deep breath, maintain eye contact, and respond in a calm, nonthreatening manner. If necessary, remove yourself from a stressful situation momentarily until you regain your composure.

- State expectations clearly and in terms that children can understand; enforce them consistently.

- Establish rules in positive terms so that they teach children how to behave appropriately rather than emphasizing behaviors that are deemed unacceptable: "We always go down the slide on our bottoms, feet first," "Hands must be washed before we can eat."

- Acknowledge the child's feelings and frustrations. Listen to her explanations, even though you may not agree with what is said.

- Help children learn effective problem solving, communication, and conflict resolution skills.

- Use logical consequences or withhold privileges when rules have been broken: "I can't let you go to Laura's house because you didn't clean up your room when I asked."

- Acknowledge children's appropriate behavior, such as saying, "You really were a big help by putting away the groceries."

- Limit the use of time out; if necessary, use it to help children regain their composure. Briefly explain why this action is being taken and send children to their room or a quiet area; this allows them time to think about their misbehavior and to regain emotional control.

- Ignore behaviors that, while inappropriate, are not likely to cause harm to the child or to others. When children end the undesirable behavior, be sure to give them some form of attention or acknowledgment.

8-year-old

# Summary

**7-1** The transition to formal schooling marks a distinctive change for many children. New experiences and opportunities generally are met with a combination of enthusiasm and improving abilities, as well as periodic reluctance and frustration.

- Children continue to learn best through hands-on experiences with actual materials. They are eager to learn and able to accomplish many complex skills, including reading, writing, telling time, counting money, and following detailed instructions during this stage.

**7-2** Children often set high expectations for themselves and then falter when they find that they cannot meet these standards.

- Frustration may be vented through mood swings, unpredictable outbursts, complaints, alibis, and physical aggression on occasion.

- These behaviors tend to decrease in frequency and intensity as children mature and develop better self-control.

continued on following page

## Summary

**7-3** Children's vocabulary expands rapidly during this stage, and their ability to articulate ideas becomes more complex.

**7-4** Cognitive maturation enables children to grasp and understand the meaning of increasingly complex concepts, such as numbers, volume, money, distance, and time.

**7-5** Friends and friendships gradually assume a greater importance for children as they approach age eight. They make friends easily, establish friendships that are longer lasting, and become less dependent on family members to meet their social needs. However, family remains important.

## Key Terms

emerging literacy **p. 159**        deciduous teeth **p. 161**        obesity **p. 180**

sensory **p. 159**        conservation **p. 171**

hands-on learning **p. 160**        bullying **p. 176**

## Apply What You Have Learned

### A. Case Study Connections

*Reread the developmental sketch about Huang and Lin presented at the beginning of this chapter and answer the following questions:*

1. Which initial forms of screening would you arrange for Lin to ensure that his learning delays were not being caused by a health-related condition?

2. Which motor skills would you expect Huang to exhibit if his development was typical for a seven-year-old?

3. Is it appropriate for Huang's mother to encourage his participation in a local youth soccer league? Explain your answer from a developmental perspective.

### B. Review Questions

1. Compare and contrast the cognitive skills of the typical six-year-old and eight-year-old.

2. Should you be concerned about a seven-year-old who weighs 75 pounds? Explain.

3. What classroom activities can a teacher plan to reinforce eight-year-olds' interest in reading and writing?

4. Describe three perceptual skills that indicate a readiness to begin reading.

5. Identify three reasonable expectations for a six-year-old in terms of home routine.

### C. Your Turn: Chapter to Practice

1. Interview at least five children who are seven or eight years old. Find out if they ever feel afraid at school. How often do they feel this way? What makes them afraid? Do they tell anyone about what they are experiencing? Summarize and comment on your findings.

2. Make arrangements to observe a first- or second-grade classroom. Describe what steps the teacher has taken to address ethnic and cultural diversity. What additional suggestions would you offer?

3. Visit a local retail store where children's toys are sold. Identify two toys that you think would appeal to a six-year-old. Briefly describe each toy and explain what qualities make it a safe and developmentally appropriate choice.

4. Conduct a 15-minute observation while kindergarten children are playing outdoors during recess. What types of behavior problems did you note during this time? How did the supervising teacher handle each situation, and was the approach effective? Would you have responded differently? If so, explain how.

# Online Resources

## Healthy Youth
This CDC site offers comprehensive information on a range of topics that include children's well-being, school health, nutrition, physical activity, statistics, funding opportunities, and media resources.

## National Center for Cultural Competence
This award-winning site is sponsored by the Georgetown University Center for Child and Human Development. Extensive resource material on cultural, linguistic, and family diversity is provided (also available in Spanish).

## National Military Family Association
This nonprofit organization addresses issues of importance to military families and teachers who work with their children, including children's mental health and stress management.

## Stopbullying.gov
The U.S. Department of Health and Human Services has posted information about bullying and cyberbullying at this website, including definitions, access to state bullying laws, and prevention resource materials for families, children, educators, and community organizations.

# References

Astill, R., Van der Heijden, K., Van Ijzendoorn, M., & Van Someren, E. (2012). Sleep, cognition, and behavioral problems in school-age children: A century of research meta-analyzed. *Psychological Bulletin*, 138(6), 1109–1138.

Bejerot, S., Plenty, S., Humble, A., & Humble, M. (2013). Poor motor skills: A risk marker for bully victimization. *Aggressive Behavior*, 39(6), 453–461.

Buckhalt, J. (2013). Sleep and cognitive functioning in children with disabilities. *Exceptional Children*, 79(4), 391–405.

Bulunuz, M. (2013). Teaching science through play in kindergarten: Does integrated play and science instruction build understanding? *European Early Childhood Education Research Journal*, 21(2), 226–249.

Burnham, J., Lomax, R., & Hooper, L. (2013). Gender, age, and racial differences in self-reported fears among school-aged youth. *Journal of Child & Family Studies*, 22(2), 268–278.

Burny, E., Valcke, M., & Desoete, A. (2012). An underestimated topic in children with mathematics difficulties. *Journal of Learning Disabilities*, 45(4), 351–360.

Casasanto, D., Fotakopoulou, O., & Boroditsky, L. (2010). Space and time in the child's mind: Evidence for a cross-dimensional asymmetry. *Cognitive Science*, 34(3), 387–405.

Centers for Disease Control and Prevention (CDC). (2013). Adverse Childhood Experiences (ACE) Study. Retrieved on February 10, 2014 from http://www.cdc.gov/ace/.

Cushman, F., Sheketoff, R., Wharton, S., & Carey, S. (2013). The development of intent-based judgment. *Cognition*, 127(1), 6–21.

Ding, C., Richardson, L., & Schnell, T. (2013). A developmental perspective on word literacy from kindergarten through the second grade. *Journal of Educational Research*, 106(2), 132–145.

Dittrick, C., Beran, T., Mishna, F., Hetherington, R., & Shariff, S. (2013). Do children who bully their peers also play violent video games? A Canadian national study. *Journal of School Violence*, 12(4), 297–318.

Eggum-Wilkens, N., Valiente, C., Swanson, J., & Lemery-Chalfant, K. (2013). Children's shyness, popularity, school liking, cooperative participation, and internalizing problems in the early school years, *Early Childhood Research Quarterly*, 29(1), 85–94.

Frankenhuis, W., & de Weerth, C. (2013). Does early-life exposure to stress shape or impair cognition? *Current Directions in Psychological Science*, 22(5), 407–412.

Frodl, T., & O'Keane, V. (2013). How does the brain deal with cumulative stress? A review with focus on developmental stress, HPA axis function, and hippocampal structure in humans. *Neurobiology of Disease*, 52, 24–37.

Georgiou, S., & Stavrinides, P. (2013). Parenting at home and bullying in school. *Social Psychology of Education*, 16(2), 165–179.

Gordon, A., & Browne, K. (2014). *Beginnings and beyond: Foundations in early childhood education*, 9th Ed. Belmont, CA: Wadsworth Cengage Learning.

Granena, G., & Long, M. (2013). Age of onset, length of residence, language aptitude, and ultimate L2 attainment in three linguistic domains. *Second Language Research*, 29(3), 311–343.

Grills-Taquechel, A., Fletcher, J., Vaughn, S., Denton, C., & Taylor, P. (2013). Anxiety and inattention as predictors of achievement in early elementary school children. *Anxiety, Stress, & Coping: An International Journal*, 26(4), 391–410.

Haight, W., Kayama, M., Kincaid, T., Evans, K., & Kim, N. (2013). The elementary-school functioning of children with maltreatment histories and mild cognitive or behavioral disabilities: A mixed methods inquiry. *Children and Youth Services Review*, 35(3), 420–428.

Hedges, H., & Cullen, J. (2012). Participatory learning theories: A framework for early childhood pedagogy. *Early Child Development and Care*, 182(7), 921–940.

Herrenkohl, T., Hong, S., Klika, J., Herrenkohl, R., & Russo, M. (2013). Developmental impacts of child abuse and neglect related to adult mental health, substance use, and physical health. *Journal of Family Violence*, 28(2), 191–199.

Holt, M., Razynski, K., Frey, K., Hymel, S., & Limber, S. (2013). School and community-based approaches for preventing bullying. *Journal of School Violence*, 12(3), 238–252.

Hosang, G., Johnson, S., Kiecolt-Glaser, J., Gregorio, M., Lambert, D., Bechtel, M., …, & Glaser, R. (2013). Gender-specific association of child abuse and adult cardiovascular disease in a sample of patients with basal cell carcinoma. *Child Abuse & Neglect*, 37(6), 374–379.

House, B., Henrich, J., Sarnecka, B., & Silk, J. (2013). The development of contingent reciprocity in children. *Evolution & Human Behavior*, 34(2), 86–93.

Kelly, Y., Kelly, J., & Sacker, A. (2013). Time for bed: associations with cognitive performance in 7-year-old children: a longitudinal population-based study. *Journal of Epidemiology & Community Health*, 67(11), 926–931.

Legare, C., Evans, M., Rosengren, K., & Harris, P. (2012). The coexistence of natural and supernatural explanations across cultures and development. *Child Development*, 83(3), 779–793.

Lindsay, S., McPherson, A., Aslam, H., McKeever, P., & Wright, V. (2013). Exploring children's perceptions of two school-based social inclusion programs: A pilot study. *Child & Youth Care Forum*, 42(1), 1–18.

Ma, D., Yang, H., & Hwang, J. (2013). Reliability and validity of an automated computerized visual acuity and stereoacuity test in children using an interactive video game. *American Journal of Ophthalmology*, 156(1), 195–201.

Marotz, L. (2015). *Health, safety, and nutrition for the young child*, 9th Ed. Belmont, CA: Wadsworth Cengage Learning.

Mensah, F., Bayer, J., Wake, M., Carlin, J., Allen, N., & Patton, G. (2013). Early puberty and childhood social and behavioral adjustment. *Journal of Adolescent Health*, 53(1), 118–124.

Muldoon, K., Towse, J., Simms, V., Perra, O., & Menzies, V. (2013). A longitudinal analysis of estimation, counting skills, and mathematical ability across the first school year. *Developmental Psychology*, 49(2), 250–257.

National Association for the Education of Young Children (NAEYC). (2009). Developmentally appropriate practice in early childhood programs serving children from birth through age 8. Retrieved on February 9, 2014 from http://www.naeyc.org/files/naeyc/file/positions/PSDAP.pdf.

Neely, D. (2013). Advances in vision screening should lead to early diagnosis, treatment of preventable blindness in children. *AAP News*, 34(5), 14; doi: 10.1542/aapnews.2013345-14.

Nicolay, A., & Poncelet, M. (2013). Cognitive abilities underlying second-language vocabulary acquisition in an early second-language immersion education context: A longitudinal study. *Journal of Experimental Child Psychology*, 115(4), 655–671.

Piaget, J. (1926). *The language and thought of the child*. New York: Harcourt, Brace, & World.

Piaget, J. (1929). *The child's conception of the world*. New York: Harcourt Brace.

Pozzoli, T., Gini, G., & Vieno, A. (2012). Individual and class moral disengagement in bullying among elementary school children. *Aggressive Behavior*, 38(5), 378–388.

Ransom, M., & Manning, M. (2013). Teaching strategies: Worksheets, worksheets, worksheets. *Childhood Education*, 89(3), 188–190.

Samplin, E., Ikuta, T., Malhotra, A., & DeRosse, P. (2013). Sex differences in resilience to childhood maltreatment: Effects of trauma history on hippocampal volume, general cognition, and sub-clinical psychosis in healthy adults. *Journal of Psychiatric Research, 47*(9), 1174–1179.

Sapouna, M., & Wolke, D. (2013). Resilience to bullying victimization: The role of individual, family, and peer characteristics. *Child Abuse & Neglect, 37*(11), 997–1006.

Stone, L., Giletta, M., Brendgen, M., Otten, R., Engels, R., & Janssens, J. (2013). Friendship similarities in internalizing problems in early childhood. *Early Childhood Research Quarterly, 28*(2), 210–217.

Theall, K., Brett, Z., Shirtcliff, E., Dunn, E., & Drury, S. (2013). Neighborhood disorder and telomeres: Connecting children's exposure to community level stress and cellular response. *Social Science & Medicine, 85*, 50–58.

Vlok, M., & de Witt, M. (2012). Naïve theory of biology: The pre-school child's explanation of death. *Early Childhood Development & Care, 182*(112), 1645–1659.

Weisberg, D., Hirsh-Pasek, K., & Golinkoff, R. (2013). Guided play: Where curricular goals meet a playful pedagogy. *Mind, Brain, & Education, 7*(2), 104–112.

Widom, C., Czajal, S., Wilson, H., Allwood, M., & Chauhan, P. (2013). Do the long-term consequences of neglect differ for children of different races and ethnic backgrounds? *Child Maltreatment, 18*(1), 42–55.

Wolke, D., Copeland, W., Angold, A., & Costello, E. (2013). Impact of bullying in childhood on adult health, wealth, crime, and social outcomes. *Psychological Science, 24*(10), 1958–1970.

Zisenwine, T., Kaplan, M., Kushnir, J., & Sadeh, A. (2013). Nighttime fears and fantasy-reality differentiation in preschool children. *Child Psychiatry & Human Development, 44*(1), 186–199.

# chapter 8

# Middle Childhood: Nine-, Ten-, Eleven-, and Twelve-Year-Olds

## Learning Objectives

*After reading this chapter, you will be able to:*

**8-1** Provide examples of the physical changes that occur during early puberty.

**8-2** Define the concept of friendship from a nine- and a ten-year-old's perspective.

**8-3** Plan developmentally appropriate activities for nine- to ten-year-olds and eleven- to twelve-year-olds.

**8-4** Compare and contrast the language development of nine- and ten-year-olds with that of eleven- and twelve-year-olds.

### naeyc NAEYC Standards Linked to Chapter Content

**1a, 1b, and 1c:** Promoting child development and learning

**2a and 2c:** Building family and community relationships

**3c and 3d:** Observing, documenting, and assessing to support young children and families

**4a, 4b, 4c, and 4d:** Using developmentally effective approaches

**5c:** Using content knowledge to build meaningful curriculum

Mason's mother recently remarried after spending several years as a single parent. Mason, who will soon turn twelve, thinks it is "awesome to have a man in the family again." He and his new stepfather spend many hours together, attending sporting events, camping in the mountains, going on long bike rides, and building model airplanes. Mason enjoys school, especially his math and computer classes, and has many "best friends." His teacher considers Mason a model student and appreciates his hard work and offers to help around the classroom.

Mason has been adjusting slowly to the idea of having a stepsister. Emma, a caring and talkative nine-year-old, is somewhat less enthusiastic than Mason about school. During the last parent–teacher conference, Emma's teachers expressed concern about her inability to remain seated and focused on assignments for longer than five or ten minutes at a time. Her stepmother has made similar observations

© urbanlight/Shutterstock.com

at home. Emma seems to have difficulty following multistep directions and is often quite disorganized. She "forgets" to feed the dog, that she was asked to set the dinner table, and when her homework assignments are due. She has few friends and prefers to play alone in her room, or with her new step-brother and his friends. However, Mason finds it annoying when Emma tags along and frequently begs his mother to make her stop.

## Ask Yourself

- How would you describe a typical eleven-year-old's development based on this scenario?
- Would you refer Emma to an early childhood specialist for evaluation if you were her teacher? Why?

# Nine-, Ten-, Eleven-, and Twelve-Year Olds

The stretch of years from age eight to early adolescence is usually an enjoyable and relatively peaceful time for all concerned. Spontaneous behavior is gradually channeled into more goal-directed efforts as children begin making the transition from a state of dependence to one of greater independence. Although they are no longer young children, preteens are also not yet capable adults. This tension can lead to increased doubts, loss of self-esteem, and questions about how they should fit in.

The middle years are also marked by a hunger for knowledge and understanding. Most children have adjusted to being at school for six or more hours each day. The stresses, strains, and frustrations of learning to read, write, do basic arithmetic, and follow directions are long forgotten. Language usage becomes more sophisticated and adultlike. During this period, children also develop an increasingly complex ability to think in the abstract, understand cause and effect, and use **logic** to solve problems and figure out how things work. They comprehend that things really are the same in spite of serving different purposes—a shovel can be used not only for digging, but also for prying the lid off of a paint can; a broom can be used for sweeping or playing hockey; a mixing bowl can be used to draw a perfect circle.

Near the end of this stage, many children begin to undergo early physical and developmental changes associated with puberty. The

**Figure 8-1** Children grow and develop at very different rates.

onset and extent of these changes vary from child to child and also reflect the influence of genetic, ethnic, and cultural differences (Figure 8-1). Early hormonal changes have been noted in some girls and boys who are as young as eight or nine years of age and has raised questions about what effects this may have on children's social and emotional development (Mensah et al., 2013). Researchers also are trying to determine why puberty is occurring earlier and have identified childhood obesity as a major risk factor (Lee & Styne, 2013).

**logic** A process of reasoning based on a series of facts or events.

It is important that parents take time to prepare children for the changes that they will begin to experience as they approach puberty (e.g., enlarging breasts, menstruation, facial and pubic hair, spontaneous erections, deepening voice, moodiness, and modesty) so that they are not confused or frightened by what is occurring. These discussions should include information about changes that both genders undergo to help children understand that puberty is universal. The American Academy of Pediatrics (AAP), Canadian Paediatric Society, and similar health organizations have posted information on their websites to help parents address the topic of puberty with children. Although sex education is taught in some schools, children may find the information intimidating and be uncomfortable asking questions in the presence of their peers. Reassuring children that these developmental changes are normal and that they can count on parents to answer their questions is crucial in making this a healthy transition.

Middle childhood is also a time when some children may begin to experiment with new behaviors, such as wearing alternative clothing and hairstyles, quitting a longtime sport or favorite musical instrument, forming associations with a "different crowd," or dieting. Families may find these changes distressing, but they are part of an important developmental process that shapes self-identity and helps children determine what ultimately is right for them. A small percentage of children may also begin to experiment with substances such as legal or illegal drugs, tobacco, alcohol, or inhalants, which can pose a serious threat to their well-being and may require professional intervention and treatment (Castellanos-Ryan et al., 2013; Scholes-Balog et al., 2013).

Although children's ideas about gender identity and behavior are relatively set by middle childhood, some male–female contrasts become more evident during this stage (Gifford-Smith & Brownell, 2013). Boys' ideas about what is masculine remain quite rigid and tend to follow a more stereotypical path (e.g., football, baseball, or competitive video games) (Chalabaev et al., 2013). In contrast, girls may be completely at ease with their femininity and also begin to branch out and explore a broad range of activities, such as hunting, fishing, carpentry, cross-country running, and team sports. However, there is little tolerance for crossing gender lines, especially when it comes to boys who hang around with girls, exhibit "unmanly" behavior, or dress in feminine-type clothing (Halim et al., 2013). It must also be remembered that a child's ethnic and cultural heritage continues to be a strong determinant in shaping gender behavior and role expectations.

Despite frequent protests and rejections, children still want and need their family's continued trust and support. It is important that families and teachers maintain an ongoing dialogue with children about subjects such as personal health, substance abuse (i.e., drugs, alcohol, and smoking), and sex education (i.e., typical development, pregnancy, and protection from sexually transmitted diseases) because many of these decisions have serious, long-term consequences (Anderson, 2014; Colby et al., 2013; Branstetter & Furman, 2013). When adults treat these issues in an open and nonthreatening manner, it conveys understanding and compassion to children. It also fosters their sense of self-esteem and enhances the likelihood that children will continue to seek adult input in the future.

## Nine- and Ten-Year-Olds

Most nine- and ten-year-olds have entered a phase of relative contentment— sometimes described as the calm before the storm of adolescence. Although nine-year-olds may still display some emotional highs and lows, these outbursts gradually mellow by age 10. Home and family continue to provide a source of security and comfort for most children. Hugs and kisses are still offered as signs of affection for family members.

Most nine- and ten-year-olds also find school enjoyable. They eagerly anticipate classes and meeting with friends and are disappointed if they must miss out on school activities. Teachers are respected and their attention is highly coveted. Small home-made gifts and offers of assistance are made in the hope of pleasing one's teachers. Although children's attention span is longer, they still require frequent opportunities to move about in the classroom and to release restless energy during vigorous outdoor play (Niemann et al., 2013).

## What Do You See?

**Physical development** Nine- and ten-year-olds enjoy and seek out challenge. What developmental advancements make it possible for this girl to do what she is doing?

© GFOW/Cengage Learning

# Developmental Profiles and Growth Patterns

## Growth and Physical Characteristics

- Grows at a slow and irregular rate; girls begin to experience growth spurts that are far more dramatic than those of boys; boys are more alike in size and smaller than most girls.

- Assumes a slimmer shape as fat accumulations begin to shift.

- Appears awkward as various body parts grow at different rates; the lower half of body grows faster; the arms and legs appear long and out of proportion.

- Brain increases significantly in size, almost reaching adult proportions by age 10.

- Gains approximately 2 inches (5 cm) in height each year; increases are usually greater during growth spurts.

- Adds approximately 6 1/2 pounds (14.3 kg) per year.

- Loses remaining baby teeth; overcrowding might occur when larger, permanent teeth erupt into a still-small jaw.

- Begins to experience early prepubertal changes. Some girls may begin to develop budding breasts, appearance of pubic hair, rounding of hips, accentuated waistline; darkening of hair color; boys are less likely to undergo any observable sexual changes for another year or two.

# Developmental Profiles and Growth Patterns *(continued)*

## Motor Development

- Throws a ball with accuracy; writes, sketches, and performs other fine motor skills with improved coordination. This period is marked by continued refinement of fine motor skills, especially notable among girls (Ruitenberg, Abrahamse, & Verwey, 2013).

- Uses arms, legs, hands, and feet with ease and improved precision; boys tend to excel in large motor activities requiring strength and speed (Rudroff et al., 2013).

- Runs, climbs, skips rope, swims, rides bikes, and skates with skill and confidence.

- Enjoys team sports, but still may need to develop some of the necessary complex skills.

- Likes to use hands for arts and crafts, cooking, woodworking, needlework, painting, building models, or taking apart objects such as a clock or telephone.

- Includes considerable detail in drawings.

- Takes great joy and pride in writing and perfecting handwriting skills.

## Perceptual-Cognitive Development

- Develops the ability to reason based more on experience and logic than on **intuition** (Piaget's stage of **concrete operational thought**): "If I hurry and walk the dog, I can play with my friends." Still sees some situations as either/or, with "yes" or "no" answers, but is beginning to think in less concrete, more creative ways (Lange-Küttner & Ebersbach, 2013; Piaget, 1928). Understands abstract concepts if real (concrete) objects can be seen and manipulated: "If I eat one cookie now, only two will be left for later."

- Likes challenges in arithmetic, but does not always understand mathematical relationships involved in complex operations such as multiplication or division.

- Learns best through hands-on learning; prefers to research information in books or online, conduct science experiments, build

Figure 8-2 **Hands-on involvement optimizes learning.**

ECE Library

models, or put on a play rather than listen to teachers' lectures that produce the same information (Figure 8-2).

- Enjoys time at school; finds it difficult to sit still for periods longer than 30 minutes; forgets all about school as soon as it is over.

- Uses reading and writing skills for activities outside of school (e.g., compiling shopping lists, composing scripts for puppet shows, drawing and labeling neighborhood maps, texting or sending email).

- Shows improved understanding of cause and effect.

- Continues to master concepts of time, weight, volume, and distance (Muftuler et al., 2012).

**intuition**  A thought or idea based on a feeling or hunch.
**concrete operational thought**  Piaget's third stage of cognitive development; the period when the concepts of conservation and classification are understood.

## Developmental Profiles and Growth Patterns *(continued)*

- Traces events based on recall; is able to think in reverse, following a series of occurrences back to their beginnings.
- Prefers reading books that are longer, contain greater detail and description, and provide complex plots.

### Speech and Language Development

- Talks, often nonstop and for no specific reason; sometimes talks simply to gain attention; may be reserved in the classroom, but boisterous and talkative at other times.
- Expresses feelings and emotions effectively through words.
- Understands and uses language as a system for communicating with others.
- Uses slang expressions commonly expressed by peers in conversation (e.g., "sweet," "seriously," "awesome," "hey, dude").
- Recognizes that some words have double meanings (e.g., "far out," "cool haircut," "wicked", or "chill").
- Finds humor in using illogical metaphors (plays on words) in jokes and riddles (Figure 8-3).
- Shows advanced understanding of grammatical sequences; recognizes when a sentence is not grammatically correct.

### Social-Emotional Development

- Enjoys being with friends; seeks out friendships based on common interests and proximity (neighborhood children or classmates); is often verbally critical of the opposite gender ("Boys are too rough," "Girls are babies") (McDonald et al., 2013; Quinn & Oldmeadow, 2013).
- Has several "good" friends and an "enemy" or two; friends and friendships often change from day to day.

**Did You Know**

…that researchers have identified cultural differences in the timing and methods used to teach children about numerical concepts, values, and manipulations (e.g., adding, subtracting, multiplying, and division) that appear to give Asian children an advantage in mathematics over their Western counterparts?

Figure 8-3  **Nine- and ten-year-olds delight in telling jokes and riddles.**

© Creatista/Shutterstock.com

## Developmental Profiles and Growth Patterns *(continued)*

- Begins to show more interest in rules and basing games on realistic play; rules should be kept simple so everyone enjoys playing (Figure 8-4). Likes to win and is not always a good loser.

- Responds with name-calling and teasing when provoked; less likely to use physical aggression than previously; also understands that such behavior can affect others' feelings. Still relies on adults occasionally to settle some disputes.

- Begins to develop moral reasoning; adopts social customs and moral values; for example, understands honesty, right from wrong, fairness, good and bad, and respect (Mares & Braun, 2013; Knight & Carlo, 2012).

**Figure 8-4** Children begin to develop the concepts of fairness, honesty, and distinguishing right from wrong during this stage.

ECE Library

- Develops strong attachments to teachers, coaches, and club leaders; may see them as heroes; often goes out of her way to please and gain their attention.

- Acts with considerable confidence; knows everything and can do no wrong.

- Takes criticism as a personal attack; feelings get hurt easily; has difficulty at times dealing with failure and frustration.

---

▶❚❚  **TeachSource Video Connections**

© 2015 Cengage Learning®

### Emotional Development and Bullying

Although most grade-school children achieve reasonable control of their emotions, a small percentage may engage in aggressive, antisocial behavior that is intentional. Respond to the following questions after you have watched the learning video *School Age: Emotional Development:*

1. Why is it important that teachers and families discuss the issue of bullying with children?

2. What consequences are associated with being bullied?

3. Why might some children who are bullied be reluctant to tell an adult?

## DAILY ROUTINES

### Eating

- Experiences fluctuating appetite depending on the amount and vigor of activity; consumes more food with increased activity; prefers to eat when hungry rather than at prescribed times.

- Eats at any time of day, yet often is still hungry at mealtime; is more receptive to trying new foods. Many children also enjoy cooking and helping with meal preparations. Prefers certain favorite foods, usually pizza, French fries, tacos, ice cream, and cookies; has few dislikes, but is less fond of cooked vegetables (often prefers them raw).

- Battles over posture and table manners (e.g., elbows on the table; slouched in chair; or a fisted grasp of forks and spoons) but usually displays good manners when eating out or at a friend's house.

### Personal Care and Dressing

- Shows limited interest in personal hygiene; often needs reminders to bathe, wash hair, brush teeth, and put on clean clothes.

- Requires coaxing to bathe but, after a bath is started, may not want to get out of the tub or shower.

- Takes some interest in his appearance; wants to dress and look like friends; school clothes take on an important role in self-identification.

- Manages own toileting needs without reminders; seldom gets up at night unless too much liquid is consumed before bedtime.

### Sleeping

- Seems unaware of fatigue and the need for sleep.

- Requires 9–10 hours of sleep to function throughout the day. Wakes up in time for school without much coaxing if getting enough sleep. Sleep is essential for the consolidation of information and long-term memory. Insufficient sleep interferes with learning and has also been linked to increased weight gain (McNeil, Doucet, & Chaput, 2013; Stickgold, 2013).

- Girls may have more bedtime rituals and take longer to fall asleep than do boys.

- Nightmares and fear of the dark may redevelop; some children experience sleepwalking, waking up in the middle of the night, or bed-wetting. Parents should not criticize children who develop these problems, and if they persist, seek professional help.

### Play and Social Activities

- Maintains activity level that fluctuates between extremes of high intensity and almost nonexistent activity; may virtually collapse following periods of intense play.

- Spends free time reading magazines, playing computer games, watching videos, listening to music, texting, and talking with friends.

- Forms and joins clubs with secret codes, languages, and signs.

- Offers to help with simple household chores such as dusting and sweeping, vacuuming, putting away groceries, and washing the car.

- Develops new hobbies or collections based on special interests.

**9 and 10 year olds**

## Learning Activities to Promote **Brain Development**

Nine- and ten-year-olds are ready and eager for new challenges that involve learning and applying developmental skills. Reading, writing, experimenting, adventure, and competitive games are among their favorite activities. They also enjoy crafts and doing things with their hands, such as building, drawing, and assembling collections.

### Developmentally appropriate applications for families and teachers

- Take advantage of educational opportunities in the community. Plan outings to the beach, farmers' market, library, museums, zoo, park, aquarium, garden center, cabinet-maker, pet shop, or grocery store.

- Encourage children to appreciate diversity by learning about the customs and celebrations of other cultures. Obtain library books, visit websites, invite guests, locate musical instruments, attend celebrations, and prepare ethnic foods for children to taste. Teach children to be accepting and avoid prejudice through your own actions and words.

- Gather sports equipment such as balls, bats, nets, and rackets; encourage children to organize and participate in group activities.

- Provide space, seeds, and tools for planting and maintaining a garden.

- Assemble materials and provide basic instructions for conducting science experiments; science activity suggestions can be found in many good books at the public library or on child-oriented websites.

- Nurture children's interest in reading, writing, and friendships by locating pen pals in another state or country: encourage children to correspond (via letter, email, Skype); read books about where a pen pal lives; locate the state or country on a map.

- Encourage children to participate in at least 60 minutes of vigorous physical activity daily for healthy development; plan some activities that all family members can do together.

- Maintain open communication with children. Spend time together, talk about their interests and friends, and be supportive.

**TeachSource Digital Download**

## developmental **alerts**

Check with a health-care provider or early childhood specialist if, by the eleventh birthday, the child does *not*:

- Continue to grow at a rate appropriate for the child's gender.

- Show continued improvement of fine motor skills.

- Make or keep friends.

- Enjoy going to school and show interest in learning most days. (If this does not happen, have children's hearing and vision tested; vision and hearing problems affect children's ability to learn and maintain their interest in learning.)

- Approach new situations with reasonable confidence; show a willingness to try.

9 and 10
year olds

## developmental **alerts** *(continued)*

- Handle failure and frustration in a constructive manner; learn from mistakes.
- Sleep through the night or experiences prolonged problems with bed-wetting, nightmares, or sleepwalking.

**Note:** Cultural differences may alter the timetable when some developmental skills are acquired. Expanded Developmental Alerts Checklists appear in Appendix A and are also available as digital downloads.

## safety **concerns**

Continue to implement the safety practices described for the previous stages. Always be aware of new safety issues as the child continues to grow and develop.

### Media Exposure

- Be aware of online websites (and content) that children visit. Teach them Internet safety rules and the importance of not giving out personal information (e.g., name, address, telephone number, or birth date) online. Set security controls to block websites that you don't want children to access.
- Know what music children listen to, what video games they play, and what movies they watch, to determine whether they are being exposed to violence, sex, or the drug culture.

### Firearms

- Educate children about the dangers of guns and other weapons. Stress the importance of not touching firearms and always alerting an adult if one is found.

- Store firearms and ammunition separately and keep in locked storage; never leave loaded firearms unattended.

### Traffic

- Insist that children wear seat belts on every motor trip.
- Review safe practices for crossing streets, getting in and out of parked cars, riding a bicycle, skateboarding, and otherwise acting responsibly around traffic.
- Make sure that children always wear helmets and appropriate protective gear when engaged in sports activities.

### Water

- Provide and require children to wear approved flotation devices whenever fishing, skiing, or boating.
- Teach basic water safety and continue to supervise water-related activities.

**Spotlight** **on Brain Development**

## Physical Activity and Neurocognitive Function

Children and adults in the United States and worldwide are facing serious health risks associated with being overweight or obese. The World Health Organization (WHO) estimates that more than 1.4 billion adults and 40 million children younger than 5 years of age are overweight (WHO, 2013). Scientists have identified increasingly sedentary lifestyles as a primary cause of this epidemic and encourage persons of all ages to engage in some form of physical activity each day. Although there are signs that the obesity rate may be stabilizing and even declining in some regions of the United States, it remains a significant public health concern.

Physical exercise is known to be an effective weight control measure. However, scientists are also learning that it has a positive outcome on brain plasticity and neurocognition (Booth et al., 2014; Hötting & Röder, 2013). Children who were enrolled in vigorous exercise regimes have shown statistically significant improvements in math and literacy scores (Gao et al., 2013; Krafft et al., 2014). O'Dea and Mugridge (2013) found similar results among children who came from disadvantaged homes. Their findings are especially notable because they demonstrate that low-cost exercise programs, including Kinect and Wii games, can be an effective and low-cost intervention for reducing socioeconomic disparities in children's academic achievements. Voss et al. (2013) have also shown that exercise continues to influence the brain's structure and plasticity throughout the lifespan and may help to lower the risk of developing Alzheimer's disease.

Several preliminary studies have been undertaken to determine if exercise has similar effects on the social and cognitive behaviors of children who experience attention deficit hyperactivity disorder (ADHD). Verret et al., (2013) observed that children with ADHD exhibited better motor and behavioral control after participating in a ten-week program of moderately intense physical activity. Other studies have confirmed a positive relationship between exercise and improved neurocognitive functioning in children with ADHD (Pontifex et al., 2013; Wigal et al., 2013).

Evidence supporting the beneficial effects of exercise on health and brain function is substantial. School-age children, especially those who experience ADHD, obesity, socioeconomic disadvantage, or all three may stand to gain the most from participation in physical activity. For these reasons, it is important that school provide physical education activities as part of the daily curriculum and that teachers and families make daily exercise a priority for all children, as well as for themselves.

### What are the connections?

1. Why do you think populations have become more sedentary?
2. In what ways can teachers incorporate more physical activity across the curriculum?
3. Why is it important that children learn to enjoy and engage in physical activity while they are young?

# Eleven- and Twelve-Year-Olds

For the most part, eleven- and twelve-year-olds are endearing individuals. They are curious, energetic, helpful, and usually happy (Figure 8-5). They willingly assist with chores around the house, sometimes even volunteering before being asked. Their language, motor, and cognitive skills are reaching adult levels of sophistication. By age twelve, children have developed a sense of confidence in their capabilities and approach tasks with renewed interest. Their emotional stability is generally smoother, and they encounter fewer conflicts with family and peers (King, Lenua, & Monahan, 2013).

Eleven- and twelve-year-olds are energetic and enjoy participating in organized sports and physical activities. In general, their health is good, and they begin to understand that a healthy lifestyle is not only important but also requires dedicated awareness and effort. However,

Figure 8-5 Eleven- and twelve-year-olds are curious, energetic, and confident.

© GFOW/Cengage Learning

eleven- and twelve-year-olds also see themselves as invincible. Few children think about or believe they will ever experience serious health conditions such as sexually transmitted diseases (STDs), lung cancer, diabetes, or heart disease, despite engaging in risky behaviors (e.g., smoking, following a sedentary lifestyle, or eating a high-fat diet) (Martinengo, 2013; Santelli et al., 2013).

# Developmental Profiles and Growth Patterns

**11 and 12 year olds**

## Growth and Physical Characteristics

- Triples birth length by the end of this period. Height and weight vary significantly from child to child; body shape and proportion are influenced by heredity and environment.

- Girls are first to experience a prepuberty growth spurt, growing taller and weighing more than boys at this age; may add as much as 3.5 inches (8.75 cm) and 20 pounds (44 kg) in one year. This period of rapid growth ends around age twelve to thirteen for girls; boys' growth rate is much slower and doesn't begin to accelerate until the early teens (Marcovecchio & Chiarelli, 2013).

- Bodily changes mark approaching puberty (e.g., widening hips and budding breasts (girls), enlarging testes and penis [boys], appearance of pubic hair) (Mouritsen et al., 2013).

- Menstruation begins if it has not already started; some girls have vaginal discharge sooner; some may be upset if not progressing at the same rate as other girls.

- Spontaneous erections are common among eleven- and twelve-year-old boys; pictures, physical activity, talk, and daydreams can trigger these events; some begin to have nocturnal emissions (involuntary discharge of seminal fluid at night).

- Gains in muscle mass and strength, especially boys; girls often reach their maximum muscle strength by age twelve.

- Stands more erect; increases in bone size and length cause shoulders, collarbone, rib cage, and shoulder blades to appear more prominent.

- Complaints of headaches and blurred vision are not uncommon if children are experiencing vision problems; the added strain of schoolwork (smaller print, computer use, longer periods of reading and writing) may cause some children to request an eye examination.

## Motor Development

- Displays movements that are smoother and more coordinated; however, rapid growth spurts can cause temporary clumsiness.

- Enjoys participating in activities such as dancing, karate, soccer, gymnastics, swimming, and organized games in which improved skills can be used and tested.

- Concentrates efforts on continued refinement of fine motor abilities through a variety of activities (e.g., model-building, rocket construction, drawing, woodworking,

Figure 8-6 **Improved fine motor skills enable children to attempt and be successful at new activities.**

cooking, sewing, arts and crafts, writing letters, or playing a musical instrument); now has perfected most fundamental gross motor skills (Figure 8-6).

## Developmental Profiles and Growth Patterns *(continued)*

**11 and 12 year olds**

- Requires outlets for release of excess energy that builds during the school day; enjoys team sports, riding bikes, playing in the park, taking dance lessons, going for a walk with friends, shooting hoops, playing soccer.

- Has an abundance of energy but also fatigues quickly.

- Uses improved strength to run faster, throw balls farther, jump higher, kick or bat balls more accurately, and wrestle with friends.

### Perceptual-Cognitive Development

- Begins thinking in more **abstract** terms; expanded memory ability enables improved long-term recall; now remembers stored information, so no longer needs to rely solely on experiencing an event to understand it (Santamaria et al., 2013).

- Succeeds in sequencing, ordering, and classifying objects as a result of improved long-term memory capacity; these skills are essential for solving complex science and mathematical problems (Hemphill & Hill, 2013).

- Accepts the idea that problems can have multiple solutions; often works through problems by talking aloud to oneself. Develops solutions or responses based on logic.

- Enjoys challenges, problem solving, researching, and testing possible solutions; researches encyclopedias, the Internet, and dictionaries for information (Figure 8-7).

- Exhibits a longer attention span; is generally able to stay focused and complete school assignments and other tasks in a timely fashion.

- Develops detailed plans and lists to reach a desired goal.

- Performs many routine tasks without having to give them much thought; increased memory sophistication makes automatic responses possible.

- Shows more complex understanding of cause and effect; learns from mistakes; identifies factors that may have contributed to or caused an event (e.g., combining baking soda with vinegar releases a gas; attaching a longer tail helps a kite fly higher in strong winds).

### Speech and Language Development

- Completes the majority of language development by the end of this stage; only subtle refinements are still necessary during the next few years.

ECE Library

**Figure 8-7** **Researching and solving problems is fun for children at this age.**

---

**abstract** The ability to think and use concepts; an idea or theory.

## Developmental Profiles and Growth Patterns *(continued)*

### What Do You See?

**Interest in learning** Advanced cognitive skills and expanding interests make children eager to learn. Why are each of these children likely to learn something different from this project, even though they have worked on it together? How do children learn best at this age?

© iStockphoto.com/Christopher Futcher

**11 and 12 year olds**

- Talks and argues, often nonstop, with anyone who will listen; this behavior is more apparent in Western cultures (and among children who are acculturated into Western cultures), whereas it is considered unacceptable in others.

- Uses longer and more complex sentence structures in written and oral communications.

- Masters increasingly complex vocabulary; adds 4,000–5,000 new words each year; uses vocabulary skillfully to weave elaborate stories and precise descriptions.

- Becomes a thoughtful listener.

- Understands that word statements can have implied (intended) meanings. (When your mother asks, "Is your homework done?" she might really mean that you had better stop playing, gather up your books, and get started.)

- Grasps concepts of irony and sarcasm; has a good sense of humor and enjoys telling jokes, riddles, and rhymes to entertain others (Massaro, Valle, & Marchetti, 2013).

- Masters several language styles, shifting back and forth based on the occasion: uses a more formal style when talking with teachers, a more casual style with parents, and a style that often includes slang and code words when conversing with friends or other peers (Mills, Watkins, & Washington, 2013).

### Social-Emotional Development

- Organizes group games and activities, but may modify rules while the game is in progress.

- Views self-image as very important; typically defines self in terms of appearance, possessions, friends, or activities; may also make comparisons to much admired adults (Gupta et al., 2013; Thomas & Bowker, 2013).

- Becomes increasingly self-conscious and self-focused; understands the need to assume responsibility for his or her own behavior and that there are consequences associated with one's choices and actions.

- Forms complex relationships with same-gendered friends; boys and girls begin to go their separate ways during this point in development.

- Begins to think and talk about occupational interests and career plans; daydreams and fantasizes about the future.

## Developmental Profiles and Growth Patterns *(continued)*

**11 and 12 year olds**

- Develops a critical and idealistic view of the world; realizes that the world is larger than one's own neighborhood; expresses interest in other cultures, foods, languages, and customs.

- Adopts the dress, hairstyles, and mannerisms of peers, sports figures, and celebrities; researches and reads about popular personalities online.

- Recognizes that loyalty, honesty, trustworthiness, and being a considerate listener are prerequisites to becoming a good friend; may spend more time now with peers than with family members (Spencer et al., 2013).

- Handles frustration with fewer emotional outbursts; is able to express what is emotionally troubling; accompanies words with facial expressions and gestures for emphasis.

### ▶❙❙ TeachSource Video Connections

© 2015 Cengage Learning®

### Middle Childhood and Cognitive Development

Most of the developmental skills that children will need as they approach adolescence are now in place. Eleven- and twelve-year-olds are able to think abstractly, make judgments based on logic, and face challenges with a reasonable degree of competence and self-confidence. Respond to the following questions after you have watched the learning video *5–11 Years: Observation Module for Middle Childhood:*

1. What cognitive skills are the children using to arrive at their responses to the conservation demonstration and to the question, "What did you do last night"?

2. What qualities did the first two children in the video clip use to describe themselves? Were they consistent with gender expectations?

3. Were you surprised by the responses of the first two children in the video clip to the questions about gender differences? What do you think accounted for the contrast in their answers?

4. What signs of stress or tension did you note while the first two children were being interviewed? If you were a teacher, how might you use this feedback?

## DAILY ROUTINES

### Eating

- Eats nonstop and is always hungry; boys in particular may consume astonishing amounts and combinations of foods (Figure 8-8). Boys require approximately 2,500 calories daily; girls need 2,200 calories daily.

- Has few dislikes; is willing to eat less preferred foods now and then; shows interest in trying foods from other cultures.

- Needs a large snack upon arriving home from school; searches the cabinets and refrigerator for anything to eat. Having access to nutritious foods encourages healthy eating habits.

- Makes some connection between eating (calories) and gaining or losing weight, especially girls. Boys and girls

**11 and 12 year olds**

Figure 8-8  **Eleven- and twelve-year-old children seem to be constantly hungry and able to eat at almost any time.**

ECE Library

may begin talking about dieting and weight control to address concerns about body image, ways to improve athletic abilities, or both. Preadolescents should be monitored closely for signs of a developing eating disorder (Wang et al., 2013).

### Personal Care and Dressing

- Cares for most personal needs without any adult assistance.

- Bathes often and willingly; keeps clean; often prefers showers.

- Still needs the occasional reminder to wash hands.

- Brushes and flosses teeth regularly; believes that a bright smile is important for appearance. Dental checkups are recommended every six months to monitor rapidly erupting permanent teeth and to treat existing cavities; many children already have several decayed teeth or dental fillings (Creske et al., 2013).

- Takes pride in appearance; likes to wear what is fashionable or what friends are wearing.

### Sleeping

- Requires plenty of uninterrupted sleep (8 ½ to 9 hours); growth spurts and active play often leave children feeling tired. Growth and appetite-regulating hormones are released while children are sleeping.

- Heads to bed without much resistance, but now wants to stay up longer on weeknights and even later on weekends and nonschool days.

- Sleeps less soundly than previously; may wake up early and read or finish homework before getting up.

- Bad dreams still trouble some eleven- and twelve-year-olds.

### Play and Social Activities

- Shows less interest in frivolous play; prefers goal-directed activities (e.g., money-making schemes, competing on a swim team, writing newsletters, and attending summer camp).

- Gets involved in organized youth groups such as sports teams, 4-H, or Scouts, or just spends time alone with a friend or two; never without something to do.

- Likes animals; offers to care for and train pets.

**11 and 12 year olds**

## DAILY ROUTINES (continued)

- Reads enthusiastically; enjoys listening to music, attending movies, watching the news, surfing on the computer, and playing video games.
- Enjoys and participates in outdoor activities such as skateboarding, inline skating, basketball, tennis, hockey, riding bikes, or walking with friends.
- Prefers to attend movies, theater, or sport performances with friends (and without parents) on occasion.

## Learning Activities to Promote Brain Development

Eleven- and twelve-year-olds are notoriously high-energy and curious. They seem interested in trying everything and often need guidance in focusing their attention on one activity at a time. They thrive on activities that lead to a sense of accomplishment, including competitive sports, complex board games, crafts, collecting items, building models, and earning money. They are intrigued with technology and electronic gadgets and can easily spend hours on the Internet or playing video games unless an adult limits their involvement.

### Developmentally appropriate applications for families and teachers

- Continue to maintain open communication with children. Spend time together, know what is going on in their lives, and be supportive (not judgmental). Provide children with information about their personal health (on topics such as sexuality, drugs and alcohol, pregnancy, and sexually transmitted diseases) and the importance of making sound decisions. Encourage them to come to you with their questions and problems.
- Encourage children's interest in reading; take them to the library or bookstore.
- Read and discuss newspaper and magazine articles together; suggest that children create their own newsletter.
- Help children develop a sense of responsibility by assigning tasks that they can perform on a regular basis (e.g., caring for a pet, reading stories to a younger sibling, folding laundry, loading the dishwasher, washing dishes, and sweeping the garage).
- Gather a variety of large cardboard boxes, paints, and other materials; challenge children to design a structure (e.g., a store, library, train, castle, farm, or space station).
- Help children stage a play; invite them to write the script, design scenery, construct simple props, and rehearse.
- Offer to help children plan and organize a pet show, bike parade, scavenger hunt, or neighborhood fundraiser.
- Locate free or low-cost opportunities to join organized group or sporting activities; these are often available through local parks and recreation departments, YMCA/YWCAs, church youth groups, and after-school programs.
- Provide children with a variety of art materials (e.g., paints, crayons, markers, paper, old magazines and catalogs, cloth scraps); encourage children to collect natural materials such as leaves, pebbles, interesting twigs, seed pods, feathers, and grasses to use for collages.

**TeachSource Digital Download**

## developmental alerts

Check with a health-care provider or early childhood specialist if, by the thirteenth birthday, the child does *not:*

- Have movements that are smooth and coordinated.

- Have energy sufficient for playing, riding bikes, or engaging in other desired activities.

- Stay focused on tasks at hand.

- Understand basic cause-and-effect relationships.

- Handle criticism and frustration with a reasonable response (physical aggression and excessive crying could be an indication of underlying problems).

- Exhibit a healthy appetite. (Frequent skipping of meals is not typical for this age group and may be an early sign of an eating disorder; excessive eating also should be monitored.)

- Make and keep friends.

**Note:** Cultural differences may alter the timetable when some developmental skills are acquired. Expanded Developmental Alerts Checklists appear in Appendix A and are also available as digital downloads.

11 and 12 year olds

## safety concerns

Continue to implement the safety practices described for the previous stages. Always be aware of new safety issues as the child continues to grow and develop.

### Machinery
- Teach children how to operate small appliances and equipment safely.
- Provide basic first aid instruction or enroll children in a local first aid training course.

### Media Exposure
- Monitor children's online activities (e.g., websites, social networking, and chat rooms) for inappropriate content and correspondence. A new teen craze called "planking" involves posing (face down, arms at sides) on various surfaces (e.g, between two structures or on a high balcony railing), taking a photo, and posting it on social media; several deaths involving this activity have been reported.
- Reinforce the importance of online safety: not giving out personal information, not responding to marketers, and setting browsers to delete cookies automatically.
- Talk with children about **cyberbullying** and **sexting**; let them know it is inappropriate (and illegal in some states) to engage in this activity and to inform you if they ever receive these types of messages, whether or not they are about themselves.
- Limit the amount of time children spend online (unless related to schoolwork) or playing video games. Children need to be active; too much sedentary activity increases the risk of obesity and interferes with other learning opportunities.

### Sports
- Make sure that proper protective equipment is available and worn; check its condition periodically.
- Make sure that an adult is supervising any competition; check the safety of area, equipment, and practices.
- Meet and talk with team coaches; know what they expect of children, how they interact with children, and steps that they take to protect children's safety.

**cyberbullying** Sending hurtful, threatening, or harassing messages via the Internet or cell phone.

**sexting** Sending sexually explicit messages or pictures of yourself or friends via a cell phone.

## safety concerns *(continued)*

### Substance Abuse

- Be aware of warning signs associated with "huffing" (inhaling) hazardous vapors from common household products such as hair spray, polish remover, aerosol paints, ammonia, and gasoline. Note any unusual odor on the child's breath or clothing, slurred speech, jitteriness, poor appetite, bloodshot eyes, or reddened areas around the nose or mouth.
- Discuss the hazards of prescription and nonprescription drug abuse and underage drinking.

## positive behavior guidance

The years between nine and twelve mark the end of childhood and the approach of adolescence. It is during these years that adults need to change their disciplinary style so that children begin to assume gradual responsibility for their own behavior and parents become less controlling.

### Nine-, ten-, eleven-, and twelve-year-olds

- Focus on children's positive behaviors and let them know often that you appreciate their efforts to behave in a responsible manner.
- Involve children in setting appropriate limits and expectations and enforce them consistently. Children are more likely to abide by rules if they have helped to develop them.
- Take time to hear children's side of the story before passing judgment. Let children know that you understand how they feel; however, doing so doesn't necessarily suggest that you accept their behavior.
- Provide unconditional love. Everyone makes mistakes from time to time, and children are still in the process of learning to make sound decisions.
- Maintain an open dialogue with children and encourage them to talk about their concerns and feelings.
- Help children develop and use problem-solving and conflict-resolution skills to make responsible choices.
- Use consequences to reinforce compliance with behavioral expectations: performing poorly on a math test because the child "forgot" to bring his book home the night before (**natural consequence**); not being allowed to attend a movie with friends because she was late coming home the previous time (**logical consequence**).

## Summary

**8-1**  Growth patterns during this stage are irregular and inconsistent.
- Girls tend to grow more than do boys, although there are significant differences among individuals.
- Some girls begin to experience prepubertal changes.

**8-2**  Friendships are becoming increasingly important.
- Peers begin to serve as important role models and information sources, although family ties are still needed and valued.
- Boys and girls begin to go their separate ways and to establish friendships with same-gendered peers.

continued on following page

**natural consequence**  An outcome that occurs as a result of a certain behavior.
**logical consequence**  A planned response that is implemented in response to misbehavior.

# Summary

**8-3**  Nine- to twelve-year-olds possess many advanced skills that enable them to engage in more complex activities. They are industrious, eager to learn, and able to follow detailed instructions. They enjoy physical challenges, sports-related activities, projects that involve designing and building objects, and artistic adventures.

**8-4**  Nine- and ten-year-olds have a reasonable grasp of language and understand its power for expressing ideas, concerns, and desires. They are quite talkative and able to carry on meaningful conversations. Eleven- and twelve-year-olds have achieved adultlike fluency and conversational skills. They are good listeners, express convincing opinions, and are able to adapt their language style to the setting.

## Key Terms

logic **p. 189**

intuition **p. 192**

concrete operational
   thought **p. 192**

abstract **p. 200**

cyberbullying **p. 205**

sexting **p. 205**

natural consequence **p. 206**

logical consequence **p. 206**

## Apply What You Have Learned

### A.  Case Study Connections

*Reread the developmental sketch about Mason and Emma presented at the beginning of this chapter and answer the following questions:*

1.  What physical characteristics would you expect to observe in the typical eleven-year-old?

2.  Would it be developmentally appropriate to expect most eleven-year-olds to like school? Why do you agree or disagree with this statement?

3.  From a developmental perspective, do you think Mason's reactions to having his sister tag along are typical or atypical? Explain.

4.  Would you consider Emma's development to be typical for a nine-year-old? Explain.

### B.  Review Questions

1.  What gender differences are nine-year-olds likely to exhibit in their social-emotional development?

2.  How do nine- and eleven-year-olds differ in their ability to think abstractly?

3.  What physical changes are ten-year-olds likely to experience?

4.  Describe the cognitive abilities typical of most eleven- and twelve-year-olds.

5.  Identify three qualities that are needed to make and keep friends.

### C.  Your Turn: Chapter to Practice

1.  Volunteer to mentor children (between 9 and 11 years old) in an after-school program. What strengths and limitations did the children bring to the program? What aspects did you find most challenging?

2.  Watch several television programs designed for the preteen audience. Describe the language, behavior, and themes portrayed in each show. What was your

overall reaction to the type of shows that preteens are presented with? Would you recommend them to families? Explain why or why not.

3. Arrange to observe children (between 9 and 12 years old) during their school lunch hour. Describe the nature of their interactions and conversation topics. How closely did their behaviors follow the developmental milestones described in this chapter?

4. Interview four or five children between the ages of 9 and 10 or 11 and 12 years. Ask them to name their favorite popular songs. Locate and listen to the lyrics of several of these songs, and comment on your findings.

# Online Resources

## American Psychological Association

Easy-to-understand explanations and guidelines for building children's resilience can be found at the American Psychological Association's website. The *Resilience Guide for Parents and Teachers* outlines strategies for helping children (e.g., those in preschool, elementary, and middle and high school) cope with a variety of difficult experiences. Information is also provided in Spanish.

## Child and Adolescent Mental Health

This section of the National Institute of Mental Health site includes a video and an in-depth description about adolescent brain development. Fact sheets and additional resources on various mental health disorders can also be retrieved.

## ConnectSafely

Extensive safety information and resources that address social media, video-gaming, and mobile safety are provided at this site for parents, teens, children, and educators.

## YourChild

This award-winning website, sponsored by the University of Michigan Health System, provides evidence-based information and media resources on a comprehensive list of child development, safety, and behavioral topics. Links to additional materials and professional organizations are also provided. Educators and families of children who have special needs will find the section on "Sexuality and Youth with Disabilities" informative.

# References

Anderson, N. (2014). A racial/ethnic comparison of teen sexual attitudes and behavior. *Health Behavior and Policy Review*, 1(1), 16–27.

Booth, J., Leary, S., Joinson, C., Ness, A., Tomporowski, P., Boyle, J., & Reilly, J. (2014). Associations between objectively measured physical activity and academic attainment in adolescents from a UK cohort. *British Journal of Sports Medicine*, 48(3), 265–270.

Branstetter, S., & Furman, W. (2013). Buffering effect of parental monitoring knowledge and parent-adolescent relationships on consequences of adolescent substance use. *Journal of Child and Family Studies*, 22(2), 192–198.

Castellanos-Ryan, N., Parent, S., Vitaro, F., Tremblay, R., & Séguin, J. (2013). Pubertal development, personality, and substance use: A 10-year longitudinal study from childhood to adolescence. *Journal of Abnormal Psychology*, 122(3), 782–796.

Chalabaev, A., Sarrazin, P., Fontayne, P., Boiché, J., & Clément-Guillotin, C. (2013). The influence of sex stereotypes and gender roles on participation and performance in sport and exercise: Review and future directions. *Psychology of Sport & Exercise*, 14(2), 136–144.

Colby, M., Hecht, M., Miller-Day, M., Krieger, J., Syvertsen, A., Graham, J., & Pettigrew, J. (2013). Adapting school-based substance use prevention curriculum through cultural grounding: A review and exemplar of adaptation processes for rural schools. *American Journal of Community Psychology*, 51(1–2), 190–205.

Creske, M., Modeste, N., Hopp, J., Rajaram, S., & Cort, D. (2013). How do diet and body mass index impact dental caries in Hispanic elementary school children? *Journal of Dental Hygiene*, 87(1), 38–46.

Gao, Z., Hannan, P., Xiang, Pl, Stodden, D., & Valdez, V. (2013). Video game–based exercise, Latino children's physical health, and academic achievement. *American Journal of Preventive Medicine*, 44(3), S240–S246.

Gifford-Smith, M., & Brownell, C. (2013). Childhood peer relationships: Social acceptance, friendships, and peer networks. *Journal of School Psychology*, 41(4), 235–284.

Gupta, T., Way, N., McGill, R., Hughes, D., Santos, C., Jia, Y., …, & Deng, H. (2013). Gender-typed behaviors in friendships and well-being: A cross-cultural study of Chinese and American boys. *Journal of Research on Adolescence*, 23(1), 57–68.

Halim, M., Ruble, D., Tamis-LeMonda, C., Zosuls, K., Lurye, L., & Greulich, F. (2013). Pink frilly dresses and the avoidance of all things "girly": Children's appearance rigidity and cognitive theories of gender development. *Developmental Psychology*, doi:10.1037/a0034906.

Hemphill, D., & Hill, J. (2013). Tested in and placed in: Are sixth-grade boys and girls completing early challenge math coursework before they are ready? *Creative Education*, 4(8), 521–527.

Hötting, K., & Röder, B. (2013). Beneficial effects of physical exercise on neuroplasticity and cognition. *Neuroscience & Biobehavioral Reviews*, 37(9), 2243–2257.

King, K., Lenua, L., & Monahan, K. (2013). Individual differences in the development of self-regulation during pre-adolescence: Connections to context and adjustment. *Journal of Abnormal Child Psychology*, 41(1), 57–69.

Knight, G., & Carlo, G. (2012). Prosocial development among Mexican American youth. *Child Development Perspectives*, 6(3), 258–263.

Krafft, C., Schwarz, N., Chi, L., Weinberger, A., Schaeffer, D., Pierce, J., …, & McDowell, J. (2014). An 8-month randomized controlled exercise trial alters brain activation during cognitive tasks in overweight children. *Obesity*, 22(1), 232–242.

Lange-Küttner, C., & Ebersbach, M. (2013). Girls in detail, boys in shape: Gender differences when drawing cubes in depth. *British Journal of Psychology*, 104(3), 413–437.

Lee, Y., & Styne, D. (2013). Influences on the onset and tempo of puberty in human beings and implications for adolescent psychological development. *Hormones & Behavior*, 64(2), 250–261.

Marcovecchio, M., & Chiarelli, F. (2013). Obesity and growth during childhood and puberty. *World Review of Nutrition and Dietetics*, 106, 135–141.

Mares, M., & Braun, M. (2103). Effects of conflict in tween sitcoms on U.S. students' moral reasoning about social exclusion. *Journal of Children and Media*, 7(4), 428–445.

Martinengo, M. (2013). Preadolescents and adolescents' relationship with food and food quality. *Journal of Nutritional Ecology and Food Research*, 1(1), 45–50(6).

Massaro, D., Valle, A., & Marchetti, A. (2013). Irony and second-order false belief in children: What changes when mothers rather than siblings speak? *European Journal of Developmental Psychology*, 10(3), 301–317.

McDonald, K., Dashiell-Aje, E., Menzer, M., Rubin, K., Oh, W., & Bowker, J. (2013). Contributions of racial and sociobehavioral homophily to friendship stability and quality among same-race and cross-race friends. *Journal of Early Adolescence*, 33(7), 897–919.

McNeil, J., Doucet, E., & Chaput, J. (2013). Inadequate sleep as a contributor to obesity and type 2 diabetes. *Canadian Journal of Diabetes*, 37(2), 103–108.

Mensah, F., Bayer, J., Wake, M., Carlin, J., Allen, N., & Patton, G. (2013). Early puberty and childhood social and behavioral adjustment. *Journal of Adolescent Health*, 53(1), 118–124.

Mills, M., Watkins, R., & Washington, J. (2013). Structural and dialectal characteristics of the fictional and personal narratives of school-age African American children. *Language, Speech, & Hearing Services in Schools*, 44(2), 211–223.

Mouritsen, A., Aksglaede, L., Soerensen, K., Hagen, C., Petersen, J., Main, K., & Juul, A. (2013). The pubertal transition in 179 healthy Danish children: Associations between pubarche, adrenarche, gonadarche, and body composition. *European Journal of Endocrinology*, 168(2), 129–136.

Muftuler, L., Davis, E., Buss, C., Solodkin, A., Su, M., Head, K., …, & Sandman, C. (2012). Development of white matter pathways in typically developing preadolescent children. *Brain Research*, 23, 33–43.

Niemann, C., Wener, M., Voelcker-Rehage, C., Holzweg, M., Arafat, A., & Budde, H. (2013). Influence of acute and chronic physical activity on cognitive performance and saliva testosterone in preadolescent school children. *Mental Health and Physical Activity*, 6(3), 197–204.

O'Dea, J., & Mudridge, A. (2013). Nutritional quality of breakfast and physical activity independently predict the literacy and numeracy scores of children after adjusting for socioeconomic status. *Health Education Research*, 27(6), 975–985.

Pontifex, M., Saliba, B., Raine, L., Picchietti, D., & Hillman, C. (2013). Exercise improves behavioral, neurocognitive, and scholastic performance in children with attention-deficit/hyperactivity disorder. *Journal of Pediatrics*, 162(3), 543–551.

Quinn, S., & Oldmeadow, J. (2013). Is the igeneration a "we" generation? Social networking use among 9- to 13-year-olds and belonging. *British Journal of Developmental Psychology*, 31(1), 136–142.

Rudroff, T., Kelsey, M., Melanson, E., McQueen, M., & Enoka, R. (2013). Associations between neuromuscular function and levels of physical activity differ for boys and girls during puberty. *Journal of Pediatrics*, 163(2), 349–354.

Ruitenberg, M., Abrahamse, E., & Verwey, W. (2013). Sequential motor skill in preadolescent children: The development of automaticity. *Journal of Experimental Child Psychology*, 115(4), 607–623.

Santamaria, C., Tse, P., Moreno-Rios, S., & Garcia-Madruga, J. (2013). Deductive reasoning and metalogical knowledge in preadolescence: A mental model appraisal. *Journal of Cognitive Psychology*, 25(2), 192–200.

Santelli, J., Sivaramakrishnan, K., Edelstein, Z., & Fried, L. (2013). Adolescent risk-taking, cancer risk, and life course approaches to prevention. *Journal of Adolescent Health*, 52(5), S41–S44.

Scholes-Balog, K., Hemphill, S., Reid, S., Patton, G., & Toumbourou, J. (2013). Predicting early initiation of alcohol use: A prospective study of Australian children. *Substance Use & Misuse*, 48(4), 343–352.

Spencer, S., Bowker, J., Rubin, K., Booth-LaForce, C., & Laursen, B. (2013). Similarity between friends in social information processing and associations with positive friendship quality and conflict. *Merrill-Palmer Quarterly*, 59(1), 106–134.

Stickgold, R. (2013). Early to bed: How sleep benefits children's memory. *Trends in Cognitive Sciences*, 17(6), 261–262.

Thomas, K., & Bowker, J. (2013). An investigation of desired friendships during early adolescence. *Journal of Early Adolescence*, 33(6), 867–890.

Verret, C., Guay, M., Berthiaume, C., Gardiner, P., & Béliveau, L. (2013). A physical activity program improves behavior and cognitive functions in children with ADHD. *Journal of Attention Disorders*, 16(1), 71–80.

Voss, M., Vivar, C., Kramer, A., & Praag, H. (2013). Bridging animal and human models of exercise-induced brain plasticity. *Trends in Cognitive Sciences*, 17(10), 525–544.

Wang, M., Walls, C., Peterson, K., Richmond, T., Spadano-Gasbarro, J., Greaney, M., …, & Austin, S. (2013). Dietary and physical activity factors related to eating disorder symptoms among middle school youth. *Journal of School Health*, 83(1), 14–20.

Wigal, S., Emmerson, N., Gehricke, J., & Galassetti, P. (2013). Exercise applications to childhood ADHD. *Journal of Attention Disorders*, 17(4), 279-290.

World Health Organization (WHO). (2013). Obesity and overweight. Retrieved on February 12, 2014 from http://www.who.int/mediacentre/factsheets/fs311/en/index.html.

# chapter 9

# Adolescence: Thirteen- to Nineteen-Year-Olds

## Learning Objectives

*After reading this chapter, you will be able to:*

**9-1** Identify changes that occur in the adolescent brain and explain how they affect behavior.

**9-2** Explain why thirteen- and fourteen-year-olds often experience a loss of self-confidence.

**9-3** Describe the role that friends and friendships play during middle adolescence.

**9-4** Discuss the nature of social-emotional development in late adolescence.

## naeyc NAEYC Standards Linked to Chapter Content

**1a, 1b, and 1c:** Promoting child development and learning

**2a and 2c:** Building family and community relationships

**3c and 3d:** Observing, documenting, and assessing to support young children and families

**4a, 4b, 4c, and 4d:** Using developmentally effective approaches

**5c:** Using content knowledge to build meaningful curriculum

Morena and Emilia Escobar moved to the United States with their family several months before the beginning of the current school year. Both girls had attended private schools in Argentina and speak relatively good English, which made their transition into the middle and high schools here somewhat easier. Morena, soon to be sixteen, is sociable, outgoing, and an exceptional soccer player who makes friends quickly. She enjoys learning about her new culture and participating in things that teenagers in this country typically do at her age, such as watching movies with friends, texting, shopping at the mall, talking about boys, and dating. Emilia, Morena's thirteen-year-old sister, who is an accomplished pianist and honor student, is small for her age, soft-spoken, and not as outgoing. Emilia has met several friends through her involvement on the school newspaper and governance councils, but she spends little time with them outside of these activities.

Although the girls' parents are quite pleased with their adjustment to a new culture and schools, they also have several concerns. Their family always has been very close and deeply religious. They believe that Morena is spending far too much time with her friends and not enough time at home with her family or devoted to her studies. They know little about her new friends and worry that Morena easily could be pressured into doing things of which they disapprove, such as drinking or experimenting with drugs, because she is eager to be accepted. In addition, her parents have been surprised by some of the recent changes that they have observed in Morena's clothing and music choices, as well as her impulsive decisions. Although they have fewer concerns about Emilia's progress, they worry that she has become more self-conscious, moody, and withdrawn lately. She often retreats to her bedroom in the evening and seems to have only one close friend with whom she spends time.

## Ask Yourself

- Do you think the developmental changes exhibited by the girls are typical, or should they be cause for concern?
- How could the girls' parents determine if their concerns are justified or nothing to worry about?
- In what ways may differences in cultural expectations be contributing to the parents' worries?

# Thirteen- to Nineteen-Year-Olds

Adolescence marks a period of dramatic transitions, confusion, and uncertainty for children, their families, and teachers alike. Bodily changes and emerging feelings of sexuality can lead to increased self-consciousness, self-doubt, and a readjustment of self-identity. Children who were once spontaneous, cooperative, and fun-loving may become moody, questioning, and, at times, rebellious teenagers. They resent being treated as children, yet they are not ready to assume full responsibility for decisions governing their own behavior until near the end of this stage. Although they may challenge adult authority and demand independence, adolescents truly want and need their families to care and to set reasonable limits that help protect them from harmful consequences (e.g., substance abuse, sexually transmitted diseases, pregnancy, or crime). Is it any wonder that few adults want to relive their adolescence, or that parents have mixed emotions as their children enter their teenage years?

Although it is easy to dwell on the negative aspects of adolescence, it is more important to remember that most children are "good kids," even those who may be difficult to manage at times (Figure 9-1). They possess many positive intellectual and personal qualities: They are eager to learn, curious, capable, industrious, inventive, and interested in making a difference. They are able to think in abstract terms, use logic to solve problems, and communicate complex thoughts with adultlike sophistication (Kleibeuker, De Dreu, & Crone, 2013). They begin to dream about career options during the early adolescent years and later pursue the training that ultimately will help to achieve their goals. They embrace technology, are active participants in social networking, and rely on instant messaging to stay connected with friends and family (Liu, Ang, & Lwin, 2013).

**Did You Know**

...that adolescents make up 20 percent of the world's population, and approximately 85 percent of them live in developing countries?

Figure 9-1  Most adolescents are "good kids" who have many positive qualities.

Why does the adolescent show such a contrast in personalities? Recent medical research has provided some clues. It has long been thought that brain development was complete by the time children reached their teen years. However, new findings based upon analyses of brain images reveal that structural changes in the cortex (i.e., increased white matter, thinning of gray matter, and sensitivity to brain chemicals) and reorganization (i.e., the formation of new **neural connections**) continue well into the early twenties (Miller & Halpern, 2014; Pokhrel et al., 2013). The brain centers most affected by these changes include those that regulate emotion, decision making, memory, social and sexual behavior, and impulsivity, which may help explain the adolescent's often unpredictable and questionable behavior choices (Figure 9-2). These responses should not be viewed as negative qualities, but rather as behaviors that eventually enable adolescents to understand themselves better, determine how they fit into a society, make sound decisions, and, ultimately, to achieve adult maturity. What adolescents need most during these turbulent years are caring adults who provide patience, understanding, consistency, and nurturing support.

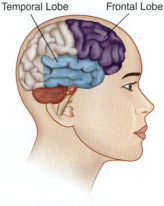

Figure 9-2  Areas where developmental changes occur in the adolescent brain include the temporal and frontal lobes.

# Thirteen- and Fourteen-Year-Olds (Early Adolescence)

Thirteen- and fourteen-year-olds are confronted with countless new feelings, experiences, and expectations which, at times, may prove to be overwhelming. How these events are perceived and handled is influenced by the adolescents' and families' unique cultural, social, and environmental beliefs and conditions. As thirteen-year-olds transition to junior high or middle school, they often face a host of fears and uncertainties: "Will I have any friends?" "What if the classes are too hard?" "What if the teachers

**neural connections** Organized linkages formed between brain cells as a result of learning.

don't like me?" They also begin to discover a multitude of new interests and activities—organized sports, arts, academic subjects, etc.—and want to try them all, but they must make tough choices due to time constraints. Early adolescents are extremely curious, able to think hypothetically, and readily accepting of intellectual challenge. However, concerns about physical appearance begin to raise feelings of insecurity as hormones trigger troublesome weight gain, acne, facial hair, menstruation, voice changes, and extremities that grow at uneven rates. In some cultural groups, these changes signal an important transition from childhood to adulthood and are celebrated as a "coming of age." Despite the fact that thirteen-year-olds may consider themselves to be grown up and perceive rules and limits as overly confining and restrictive, they need consistent nurturing and guidance now more than ever.

Although thirteen-year-olds experience some loss of self-confidence as they adjust to the many physical and psychological changes occurring in their lives, their sense of self-identity quickly returns the following year. Fourteen-year-olds conduct themselves with greater self-assurance and emotional control, become more outgoing, have an improved (positive) outlook on life, and consider friendships more important. Their time outside of classes is often spent with same-gender peers—participating in extra-curricular activities of mutual interest (e.g., school council, chess or glee club, theater, organized athletics, church groups, 4-H, computer gaming, etc.), gathering at a local hangout, talking on cell phones, texting, blogging, or engaging in other social networking platforms. Advancements in social and moral development are evident in the fourteen-year-olds' emerging interests in civic responsibility (giving back) and participation in community service or service learning projects. In other words, fourteen-year-olds are beginning to show significant signs of maturing.

## Developmental Profiles and Growth Patterns

### Growth and Physical Characteristics

- Weight gain varies by individual based on food intake, physical activity, and genetics.
- Continues to grow taller; boys, especially, begin to experience rapid growth spurts. Girls may experience small increases, but most have already reached their adult height by this time.
- Head size and facial features are adultlike; the arms, legs, and feet often appear large and out of proportion to the rest of the body.
- Has a full set of permanent teeth, except for the second and third molars (wisdom teeth).
- Tires easily, especially after vigorous activity, but quickly regains energy following a brief rest.
- Has blood pressure that approximates adult values (approximately 110/80); varies with the child's weight, activity, emotional state, and ethnicity (some racial groups are prone to higher blood pressure) (Anyaegbu & Dharnidharka, 2014).
- Develops facial blemishes due to hormonal changes.
- Continues to experience bodily changes associated with puberty; girls begin having regular monthly periods; boys develop facial hair, voice changes, and nocturnal emissions.
- Complains of blurred vision or fatigue while reading; should have eyes examined to rule out any acuity problem if complaints persist.

## Developmental Profiles and Growth Patterns *(continued)*

### Motor Development

- Has movements that are often awkward and uncoordinated due to irregular and rapid growth.

- Engages in purposeful activity; spends less time "just fooling around."

- Is able to sit quietly for longer periods, but still needs frequent outlets to relieve excess energy.

- Exhibits greater speed and agility, especially girls; boys have better strength and endurance.

- Develops new interests in individual sports (e.g., swimming, golf, or gymnastics) and team athletics (e.g., softball, soccer, basketball, football, or hockey) (Figure 9-3).

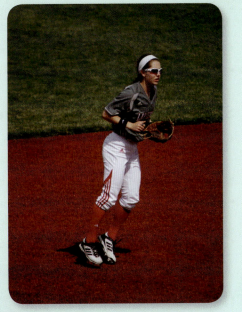

**Figure 9-3** **New interests in sports reflect improved motor abilities at this stage.**

### Perceptual-Cognitive Development

- Uses more advanced thought processes (e.g., theoretical, rational, and logical) to formulate opinions.

- Begins to analyze problems from multiple perspectives before arriving at a solution; first makes a prediction (hypothesis) and then considers multiple variables or options one at a time before arriving at a conclusion. (Piaget referred to this process as **formal operational thinking**.)

- Is able to understand and learn advanced material; thinks abstractly about complex issues, but still lacks the experience necessary to make sound decisions at all times.

- Likes school and academic challenge: arrives early; is eager to explore new academic subjects and extracurricular activities; feels overwhelmed at times by schoolwork, tests, and expectations (Berry & LaVelle, 2013).

- Fascinated with technology; uses the Internet for homework, entertainment, and communication purposes; has difficulty determining if media content is truthful, and therefore reliable.

- Spends considerable time in self-reflection; often retreats to the bedroom to think and to communicate with friends (Wang et al., 2013).

- Plans and organizes activities without adult assistance.

- Begins to make some plans for the future, but most attention is focused on the present.

### Speech and Language Development

- Is articulate in expressing ideas and thoughts; word comprehension and fluency have nearly reached adult levels.

- Pauses and thinks before responding.

**formal operational thinking** Piaget's fourth stage of cognitive development; the period when children are capable of using abstract thought to predict, test, and reason to arrive at a logical conclusion.

## Developmental Profiles and Growth Patterns *(continued)*

- Answers questions in a direct and concise manner; is less likely to engage in spontaneous conversation with family members than during earlier years.

- Spends endless time texting, emailing, and talking on the phone with friends.

- Understands irony, sarcasm, and metaphors when used in conversation.

### Social-Emotional Development

- Has unpredictable periods of moodiness (usually related to hormonal changes); may act out when frustrated or faced with new or stressful challenges.

- Develops firm moral viewpoints about what is right and wrong.

- Is often opinionated and questions parental decisions; although this may result in hurt feelings, it is an important step in becoming independent.

- Embarrassed by displays of adult affection in public (e.g., father putting his arm around son's shoulder, mother hugging daughter good-bye).

- Begins to display signs of adolescent **egocentrism**; becomes increasingly self-conscious and sensitive to criticism; compares self to an **imaginary audience** (e.g., friends, movie stars, rock musicians, and fashion models in magazines) and attempts to mimic their image; often expresses dissatisfaction with own body appearance (especially girls) and personal achievements.

**Figure 9-4** Friends and friendships become more important than spending time with family.

- Spends increasing time with friends rather than family (Figure 9-4).

- Has strong desire for peer acceptance; makes an effort to fit in through choice of clothes, behavior, music, and mutual-interest activities (Somerville et al., 2013).

- Has mixed feelings about sexual relationships, although may begin to engage in exploratory behaviors and discussions with peers. Family dysfunction and minority affiliation increase the risk for early sexual activity (Kaplan et al., 2013).

- Is developing a stronger sense of self-identity, but still wavers between feeling confident and independent one moment and insecure and needing reassurance the next.

**egocentrism** Adolescents' belief in their own self-importance.

**imaginary audience** A component of egocentrism whereby adolescents believe that others care about and notice their behavior and appearance.

**▶❚❚ TeachSource Video Connections**

© 2015 Cengage Learning®

### Understanding Adolescent Emotions

New experiences, conflicts, and challenges can be intimidating and sometimes lead to emotions that adolescents find difficult to understand and control. Respond to the following questions after you have watched the learning video *Social-Emotional Development: Understanding Adolescents:*

1. Why would holding a group meeting with these adolescent boys be an effective way to help them address their anger?

2. What positive strategies were the boys able to identify that allowed them to deal with their anger and stress?

3. Why is it important that adults take time to establish rapport with adolescents and listen to their side of the story?

## DAILY ROUTINES

### Eating

- Continues to have a hearty appetite (especially boys); increased consumption often precedes an impending growth spurt.

- Arrives home from school in need of a snack; often eats while studying, watching television, and before bedtime; food choices are not always the most nutritious.

- Concerns about weight may lead to self-imposed food restriction and unhealthy diets, especially among girls; nutritious, well-balanced meals should be provided and children's food intake observed carefully. (*Note:* Avoid drawing too much attention to eating behaviors or making negative comments about weight).

- May show an increased interest in cooking and preparing meals for themselves and others.

### Personal Care and Dressing

- Manages own bathing and care routines but may need gentle reminders at times.

- Begins to shave or trim facial hair (boys); girls may shave legs and underarms.

- Takes pride in appearance; has definite clothing preferences.

- Prefers to select and may help purchase some of own clothing items; choices often reflect what is considered to be "in style" with peers.

**13 and 14 year olds**

## DAILY ROUTINES *(continued)*

### Sleeping

- Stays up later at night: studies, finishes homework, watches television, or plays computer games; often has difficulty waking up in the morning (Koulouglioti et al., 2014).

- Insufficient sleep in adolescents has been linked to depression, poor academic performance, and substance abuse (Shochat, Cohen-Zion, & Tzischinsky, 2014).

### Social Activities

- Relies on friends for companionship. Girls form a close social bond with one or two same-gender friends and confide in them about personal matters. Boys prefer doing things together with several friends or as a group and are less likely to share personal information.

- Shows some interest in casual dating; attends school dances, parties, and other social events; goes to the movies as a couple or with other couples in a group.

- Meets and communicates often with friends through texting and social networking sites (Quinn & Oldmeadow, 2013).

## learning activities to promote **brain development**

The world of possibilities is beginning to open up for thirteen- and fourteen-year-olds. They need continued support and encouragement to explore new opportunities and activities. This is also an important time to emphasize and reinforce healthy lifestyle habits, personal safety, and wise decision making.

### Developmentally appropriate applications for families and teachers

- Encourage children to explore a variety of academic subjects and extracurricular activities; refrain from criticizing or making children feel guilty if they decide to opt out after giving it their best effort.

- Support children's interest in civic responsibility; help them to identify opportunities for volunteering (e.g., animal shelter, local library, neighborhood or school garden, and mentoring younger children), fund-raising for a local cause, or participating in community service projects.

- Designate one evening each week as a "family night." Plan and cook a meal together, make popcorn and watch a movie, play box or electronic games, take a walk, ride bikes, swim, or engage in some other activity together. Time spent with one another strengthens communication and family ties.

- Promote children's interests in the environment and social responsibility: challenge them to design alternative energy devices, such as a solar stove, wind generator, or water heater.

- Foster adolescents' creative literacy: help them to compose a short novel, write and produce a play, make and edit a movie, or initiate a neighborhood newsletter.

- Interest children in researching and organizing a collection: coins, shells, baseball cards, bumper stickers, pencils, maps, insects, or travel souvenirs.

## learning activities *(continued)*

- Challenge children to try a new sport (e.g., track, Frisbee golf, swimming, basketball, table tennis, soccer, handball, bowling, or volleyball). Reinforce the importance of being physically active every day to maintain fitness and health (physical and mental).

- Assign tasks that children are responsible for completing on a regular basis (e.g., feeding and walking the dog, folding and putting away laundry, setting out the recycling containers, vacuuming, or mowing the lawn).

**TeachSource Digital Download**

## developmental alerts

Check with a health-care provider or child development specialist if, by the fifteenth birthday, the child does *not:*

- Make friends and socialize with them; show little interest in activities that were once enjoyable; maintain reasonable eating and sleeping habits. Sudden or prolonged behavioral changes may indicate an emotional problem that needs to be addressed.

- Continue to grow or experience physical changes associated with puberty.

- Demonstrate an ability to think in the abstract; consider more than one solution when solving a problem.

- Read with understanding; express ideas so they are meaningful to others.

- Look forward to school and attend on a regular basis (e.g., makes frequent excuses to stay home or skips school without parents' knowledge).

- Abide by family rules and expectations on most occasions, even if it's under protest.

- Demonstrate moral reasoning or the ability to distinguish right from wrong (e.g., engages in risky behaviors such as drinking, drugs, sexting, or petty crime).

**Note:** Cultural differences may alter the timetable when some developmental skills are acquired. Expanded Developmental Alerts Checklists appear in Appendix A and are also available as digital downloads.

## safety concerns

Continue to implement the safety practices described for the previous stages. Always be aware of new safety issues as the child continues to grow and develop.

### Sports

- Make sure that children are healthy and have medical clearance to play organized sports.
- Insist that appropriate safety equipment be worn at all times, even during practice. Check the condition of any equipment periodically to make sure it is intact, the correct size for the child using it, and adjusted properly.

**13 and 14 year olds**

- Be familiar with the quality of supervision or coaching that children receive. Are children positively reinforced to perform? Are injuries handled properly? Are rest breaks offered? Are adults trained to administer cardiopulmonary resuscitation (CPR) and first aid?

### Suicide/Depression

- Note sudden or significant changes in children's moods (e.g., increased or unusual irritability, aggression, withdrawal, or sadness), eating routines, sleep patterns, or any combination of the three. Depression and suicide thoughts often peak during early adolescence; professional help should be sought if any signs are observed (Verboom et al., 2014; Pisani et al., 2013).
- Monitor adolescents' social networking and Internet use; let them know to alert an adult if they are ever the target of cyberbullying.
- Maintain an open, nonjudgmental dialogue with teens; encourage them to discuss their concerns with a trusted adult (e.g., parent, family friend, teacher, or coach) (Figure 9-5).

### Media Exposure

- Talk with children about online safety: chat-room guidelines; adult-content sites; data-mining by marketers; not accepting messages from unknown persons; telling an adult if they receive inappropriate content; not posting personal information.
- Locate computers in a public area where the child's online activity can be monitored more easily, not in the child's bedroom.
- Limit the amount of time that children spend online, on a tablet, computer, cell phone, or other handheld device.

### Risky Behaviors

- Provide adolescents with
- information to help them make sound decisions regarding sexual activity, alcohol consumption, illicit drugs, prescription medication abuse, tattoos, and body piercings.
- Note early behavioral and emotional signs of a potential eating disorder: consuming less food, skipping meals, weight loss, prolonged dissatisfaction with body image, vomiting, excessive exercising, depression, or any combination of these.
- Establish a plan to know where adolescents are at all times: when to call, where they are going, and when they can be expected to return.

© Cengage Learning

**Figure 9-5** **Adolescents should feel comfortable talking to a trusted adult.**

## Spotlight on Brain Development

### Self-Control and the Adolescent Brain

Parents often describe the task of raising teenagers as one of their most significant challenges. They find children's behavior puzzling at times, and wonder how the morals and values they have instilled to this point seem to vanish when adolescents are making important decisions. Apparent contradictions in their behavior cause many parents to question if, how, or should they have taken a different approach.

Throughout adolescence, children may be more easily tempted, impulsive, and less likely to control their desires in situations that require them to think before they act. Recently, scientists have discovered that significant structural and functional changes occur in the brain's prefrontal cortex during the adolescent years (Burgaleta et al., 2014; Miller & Halpern, 2014). This particular region is responsible for regulating emotional control and sensitivity to rewards. These findings have contributed to an enhanced understanding of adolescents' behavior and their tendency to exhibit reduced self-control and increased participation in high-risk activities (Casey & Caudle, 2013).

Other study results have identified specific pleasure-producing areas within the brain's cerebral cortex that are responsible for receiving and interpreting information. These areas appear to be especially sensitive to peer-related feedback, thrill-seeking, and immediate gratification during adolescent brain maturation (Albert, Chein, & Steinberg, 2013; Peake et al., 2013). The act of engaging in risky behaviors (e.g., binge drinking, driving fast, drug use, unprotected sexual activity, violence, and aggression) may produce significant excitement and reward for some teens (Luna et al., 2013; Somerville, 2013). Teens who engage in such high-risk activities are also more likely to seek out peers who share similar risk-taking interests. Additionally, brain neurochemical alterations have been shown to increase the adolescent's vulnerability and sensitivity to the effects of drugs and alcohol and, thus, may raise the potential for abuse (Spear, 2014).

Although these developments occur at a time when more time is spent with friends than with family, only a small percentage of adolescents ultimately engage in extreme thrill-seeking behaviors. Individual differences in temperament, biological makeup, family expectations and support, social and cultural values, and religious beliefs have a strong influence on how these behaviors are expressed. Most adolescents are able to manage relative self-control and to make reasonable decisions during these critical years.

### What are the connections?

1. What brain-based explanation could you offer to a distraught parent of a fifteen-year-old who was caught drinking at his friend's house?
2. Are fourteen-year-olds mature enough to begin driving a vehicle? Explain your response from a brain development perspective.
3. Why do so many drug prevention programs offered in secondary schools fail? How might they use the current knowledge about adolescent brain development to design effective programs?

# Fifteen and Sixteen-Year-Olds (Middle Adolescence)

Behavioral contrasts continue to be evident during middle adolescence. However, the ways in which they are experienced and expressed often vary due to differences in family, social, religious, and cultural values. Typical fifteen-year-olds exhibit

**15 and 16 year olds**

many developmental traits that are similar to those of thirteen-year-olds. Once again, they become more introspective, indifferent, rebellious, and intent on gaining autonomy. Friends (one on one and in groups) gradually replace family as a source of comfort, security, and personal information. Fifteen-year-olds either like school and work hard to achieve good grades, or they become disengaged and uninterested. They find convenient reasons (e.g., school activities, errands, and social events) not to stay home and, when they are at home, often retreat to their room and immerse themselves in computer games, online chatting, listening to music, daydreaming, or watching television. Although most fifteen-year-olds enjoy excellent health, they may experience considerable stress and tension from daily occurrences (e.g., test taking, team tryouts, feelings of sexuality, or friendships) (Rudolph et al., 2014; Somerville, 2013).

Many positive qualities begin to return as adolescents approach their sixteenth birthday. They develop a renewed sense of self-confidence, respect, emotional control, tolerance, and self-determination. Friends are important and continue to play a vital role. Relationships are formed on the basis of common interests, are relatively stable, and are intimate in some cases. Sexual identity is well established, although some adolescents are reluctant to acknowledge or to discuss concerns about homosexual tendencies or gender confusion (Russell et al., 2014; Bregman et al., 2013). This can interfere with the adolescent's sense of acceptance or belonging and lead to significant depression (Mustanski et al., 2013).

Sixteen-year-olds have developed more advanced cognitive and analytical skills that enable **deductive reasoning**, improved decision making, and planning ahead for the future (Kleibeuker, Koolschijn, & Jolles, 2013). They continue to explore and experiment with everything from clothing styles and interpersonal relationships to technology, philosophical ideas, and vocational interests (Figure 9-6). In other words, sixteen-year-olds are well on their way to becoming independent thinkers and doers.

**Figure 9-6** Adolescents continue to refine their self-identity by exploring and experimenting with everything from technology to interpersonal relationships.

**deductive reasoning**
A process of considering hypothetical alternatives before reaching a conclusion.

# Developmental Profiles and Growth Patterns

## Growth and Physical Characteristics

15 and 16 year olds

- Weight gain varies by individual and depends on food intake, physical activity, and genetics.
- Continues to grow taller; boys, especially, experience rapid growth spurts. Girls have reached their approximate adult height; males will do so by the end of this stage.
- Wisdom teeth (third molars) may erupt.
- Still tires easily, especially following vigorous activity.
- Experiences fewer skin eruptions (acne) as hormone levels stabilize.
- Continues to undergo gradual body changes associated with puberty.
- The arms, legs, hands, and feet still may appear large and out of proportion to the rest of the body.
- Continues to add muscle mass, especially for boys, but also for girls who are athletically active.

## Motor Development

- Motor coordination, speed, and endurance have reached their peak in girls; boys begin to surpass girls in these abilities and continue to improve until age twenty.
- Hand–eye coordination becomes more precise and controlled.
- Appears awkward and uncoordinated (clumsy) during periods of rapid growth; prone to more injuries during these times.

## Perceptual-Cognitive Development

▶❙❙ **TeachSource** Video Connections

© 2015 Cengage Learning®

### Technology and Learning

Technology has revolutionized our daily lives and changed the way that students learn. Innovative instructional programs offer enriched opportunities for exploring and understanding complex information. Respond to the following questions as you watch the learning video *Integrating Technology to Improve Student Learning: A High School Science Simulation:*

1. What perceptual-cognitive skills are fifteen- and sixteen-year-olds developing that enable them to grasp complex ideas, such as technology and genetics?
2. In what ways are the students using scientific reasoning to explain genetic differences?
3. Why would the use of instructional technology appeal to adolescents?
4. What examples of the adolescent's ability to focus attention on multiple activities at the same time can be observed in this video?

- Solves abstract problems using deductive reasoning; is able to visualize or recall a concept, place, or thing without actually seeing or experiencing it at the time.
- Plans ahead; considers the pros and cons of several weekend activities before deciding on a final choice; makes hypothetical plans for the summer break; thinks about future career options.
- Uses **scientific reasoning** to solve increasingly complex problems; combines knowledge, experience, and logic to arrive at a solution or outcome.

**scientific reasoning** Critical thinking skills (identify, analyze, and conclude) used to achieve a solution.

# Developmental Profiles and Growth Patterns *(continued)*

- Becomes aware of a much larger world; is curious, eager for academic challenge, and interested in trying new things.
- Is able to focus attention on several activities at the same time: listens to music on headphones or watches television while doing homework.
- Recognizes that not all information is trustworthy; evaluates an information source before accepting it as reliable.

## Speech and Language Development

- Experiences modest gains in vocabulary; girls continue to score higher than boys on tests of verbal ability.
- Is capable of learning additional languages, but it requires more time and effort than when younger (an important consideration for schools given the numbers of non-English-speaking children) (DeKeyser, 2013).
- Adjusts language and communication style according to the situation: conversing on the phone with friends, discussing a project with teachers, or texting in cyber slang.
- Uses increasingly complex grammar and sentence constructions to express ideas.
- Spends considerable time engaged in social networking and communicating with friends; uses technology (e.g., texts, cell phone, Internet, Facebook, "tweeting," Skyping, taking and posting "selfies").
- Understands and engages in adult humor.

## Social-Emotional Development

- Establishes friendships with peers of both genders; having friends and being "popular" are important (Perry et al., 2014; Rowsell et al., 2014). (Figure 9-7).
- Continues to struggle with self-identity issues, especially if there are real or perceived differences from one's peers (e.g., religious beliefs, biracial, sexual orientation, adopted, ethnicity, or special needs); is sensitive to peer comments.
- Develops an interest in forming serious romantic relationships. This is an important step in refining one's self-identity and self-image, determining sexual orientation, establishing personal values related to intimacy and sexual behavior, and learning about the qualities desired in a partner.

...that teens send approximately 50 text messages a day (1,500 per month)? Girls send and receive an average of 80 messages per day, boys approximately 30, and most messages focus on friends or school-related activities.

Figure 9-7 **Adolescents begin to take an interest in forming romantic relationships.**

- Has a strong drive to achieve autonomy from the family; dislikes parental authority and limits placed on activities.
- Is caring, cooperative, and responsible much of the time; temperamental, moody, and rebellious on occasion, especially when wishes are not granted.
- Adopts clothing styles and behavior of peer group; may also experiment with risky behaviors (e.g., illicit drugs, tattoos, body piercings, sexual activity, tobacco, and alcohol) to make a statement or to gain acceptance.
- Recognizes right from wrong, but makes some irresponsible decisions that contradict this understanding (Albert, Chein, & Steinberg, 2013; Euser et al., 2013).

## DAILY ROUTINES

### Eating

- Continues to have a healthy appetite, but is less likely to participate in family meals; often eats when hungry or convenient due to time conflicts with school or extracurricular activities.

- Shows interest in food-weight-health connections; may severely restrict food intake to control weight gain. Eating disorders (e.g., anorexia, bulimia, etc.) and severe dieting are more common among both genders during this period and can lead to serious health problems (Ferreiro, Seoane, & Senra, 2014; Wooldridge, & Lytle, 2014).

- Explores new foods and alternative dietary practices (e.g., eating vegetarian meals or organic foods, restricting carbohydrates, eliminating processed foods, and lowering fat intake), but may have less interest in cooking (Fulkerson et al., 2014).

### Personal Care and Dressing

- Takes pride in personal grooming and appearance; girls often apply makeup; boys shave facial hair.

- Bathes or showers daily; washes hair frequently.

- Usually quite particular about clothing choices; prefers items that reflect current styles and fashion trends.

### Sleeping

- Requires approximately nine hours of uninterrupted nighttime sleep to maintain health and attention. Sleep deprivation can interfere with learning, diminish alertness, and contribute to moodiness, irritability, and behavior problems (Shochat, Cohen-Zion, & Tzischinsky, 2014).

- Stays up late at night; biological changes during adolescence cause a shift in wake/sleep rhythms (toward a later bedtime); may fail to get adequate sleep due to school activities, employment, homework, socializing with friends, or all of these.

### Social Activities

- Prefers spending time alone when home; often goes to own bedroom and closes the door.

- Develops new friendships; may spend more time with friends than with family; friends provide an important source of companionship, feedback, and emotional support, especially among girls.

- Enjoys challenge and competition; explores and participates in a variety of social and extracurricular activities; some adolescents may also hold down part-time jobs.

## learning activities to promote **brain development**

Although fifteen- and sixteen-year-olds are becoming more independent, they also want reassurance that adults care and are available if needed. Times spent together provide opportunities for adolescents to talk about subjects that are important to them. Continue to do activities together, have family meals, and guide children's evolving interests.

### Developmentally appropriate applications for families and teachers

- Provide opportunities for privacy; respect adolescents' need and preference for spending time alone; knock before entering their room.

- Encourage and support children's interest in developing leadership skills and assuming leadership roles at school or in local organizations.

**15 and 16 year olds**

## learning activities *(continued)*

- Offer to help arrange small social gatherings where teens can mingle in a safe setting (e.g., pool party, sleepover, watching a movie at home with friends, youth group meetings, or roller skating).

- Support interests in new activities (e.g., singing, theater, art, playing a musical instrument, hunting, robotics, golf, yoga, astronomy, cooking, or hiking).

- Assist teens in locating volunteer opportunities or occasional part-time work (e.g., babysitting, mowing lawns, shoveling snow, pet sitting, or raking leaves).

- Plan trips centered on a learning theme (e.g., space museum, aquarium, national park, working ranch, adventure camp, historical place, snorkeling, or an exposure to a different cultural experience).

- Organize a book club; have teens take turns selecting a book for the group to read and discuss.

- Interest teens in learning about genealogy, researching their family background, and developing a family tree.

- Continue to discuss high-risk behaviors and preventive measures; provide educational reading materials and encourage teens to ask questions.

- Teach time management and organizational skills; encourage teens to set up a digital calendar where due dates for homework, tests, and activities can be noted; create a quiet area for studying and storing school materials.

- Prepare teens to handle difficult situations (e.g., being offered drugs or alcohol, being pressured to have sex, etc.); role-play strategies for avoiding involvement.

**TeachSource Digital Download**

## developmental alerts

Check with a health-care provider or child development specialist if, by the seventeenth birthday, the child does *not*:

- Have or keep friends; is not included in group activities.

- Remember or plan ahead on most occasions.

- Maintain reasonable interest in personal hygiene and daily activities, including school; sudden apathy or failing grades may be signs of depression or other mental health disorders.

- Use language correctly to express thoughts and requests; interpret or respond appropriately to nonverbal behavior.

- Grasp humor, jokes, or puns.

- Confront new situations with a relative degree of self-confidence.

- Avoid involvement in harmful behaviors (e.g., drugs, alcohol abuse, bullying, promiscuous sex, crime, and truancy).

**Note:** Cultural differences may alter the timetable when some developmental skills are acquired. Expanded Developmental Alerts Checklists appear in Appendix A and are also available as digital downloads.

## safety **concerns**

Continue to implement the safety practices described for the previous stages. Always be aware of new safety issues as the child continues to grow and develop.

### Sporting Activities

- Insist that proper protective gear be worn when participating in sporting activities: paintball (goggles); biking (helmet); skateboarding (helmet, protective knee and elbow pads); hunting (earplugs, goggles, reflective vest); baseball and softball (helmet, mouth and shin guards), boating (life jacket).
- Seek medical evaluation for any head injury; prevent teens from returning to the sporting activity until given medical clearance.

### Media Exposure

- Monitor adolescents' Internet use (e.g., social networking sites, movies, computer games, and music) at home; make it a point to know what teens are accessing when alone or spending time with friends.
- Educate teens about potential risks involved in an online presence: urge caution about giving out or posting personal information; report cyberbullying and "sexting" to an adult; never agree to meet an online "friend" unless in a public area, with trusted friends, and after informing an adult.

### Dating

- Educate teens about dating, setting personal limits, and maintaining healthy relationships.
- Discuss dating violence; talk about the warning signs and what to do if teens find themselves in an abusive relationship.
- Provide teens with information about pregnancy and sexually transmitted disease (STD) prevention to help them make informed decisions.

### Travel

- Insist that seat belts be worn when riding in a vehicle with family or friends.
- Educate teens about refusing to ride with a drunk or reckless driver and to report the individual.
- Have teens call when they leave and arrive at their destination; let them know that this rule isn't about trust— rather, it has to do with your concerns about their safety.
- Make sure that teens have emergency contact information with them, such as parents' cell phone numbers.

**17 and 18 year olds**

# Seventeen- and Eighteen-Year-Olds (Late Adolescence)

The remaining years of adolescence are characterized by minimal developmental changes that are either dramatic or significant in number. Girls have completed their physical and reproductive growth, whereas boys will continue to experience small gains in height and muscle mass well into their early twenties. Cognition, social-emotional capacity, speech and language, and motor abilities are well established by now and undergo only minor refinement during late adolescence. Seventeen- and eighteen-year-olds have established a clear sexual identity and are usually comfortable with themselves, self-reliant, more emotionally stable, and philosophical about life. They are now able to shift their interests and energies from skill acquisition and peer acceptance to contemplating the future (Figure 9-8): "What plans do I have following high school?" "What are my long-range career goals, and what must I do to achieve them?"

**17 and 18 year olds**

**Figure 9-8** Much thought is devoted during late adolescence to making future plans and researching career options.

Figure 9-8 Much thought is devoted during late adolescence to making future plans and researching career options.

© iStockphoto.com/stray_cat

"Am I interested in an intimate relationship or long-term commitment?" "How do I plan on supporting myself financially?"

How adolescents ultimately make these decisions is strongly influenced by their cultural, economic, social, and family values (Cheung et al., 2013). In some cultural and social groups, for example, adolescents are expected to continue living with their family and to contribute financially until they marry. By contrast, it is presumed that adolescents in many Western societies will leave home and establish their independence once they have completed school.

And so, the journey through childhood nears an end as adolescents approach their nineteenth birthday. Most are ready to begin the next chapter of life and to face a host of new challenges, decisions, and opportunities as they become young adults.

## Developmental Profiles and Growth Patterns

### Growth and Physical Characteristics

- Undergoes few changes in basic physical development; has almost reached adult maturity.
- Experiences small increases in height, weight, and bone mass; males continue to grow taller until their early twenties; girls have achieved their full adult height.
- Enjoys good health and few illnesses in most cases.
- Experiences a relatively high rate of injury, death, and disability due to irrational decisions, impulsive behavior, and carelessness.

### Motor Development

- Reaches peak muscle mass.
- Continues to develop muscular strength into the early twenties, especially males.

## Developmental Profiles and Growth Patterns *(continued)*

- Achieves precise finger dexterity and hand–eye coordination; manipulates computer and video games with skill.

- Has movements that are now coordinated and controlled.

### Perceptual-Cognitive Development

- Uses recall, logic, and abstract thinking to solve complex problems.

- Begins to rely on **analytical thinking** when planning and problem solving more often than in the past; identifies and evaluates potential solutions, although does not always reach a rational decision (Figure 9-9).

Figure 9-9 **On the brink of adulthood, older adolescents now are capable of solving complex problems based on analytical thinking.**

© iStockphoto.com/Christopher Futcher

17 and 18 year olds

- Shows some gender differences in cognitive abilities: girls tend to achieve greater verbal skills; boys may excel in science and mathematics. However, these differences are becoming less significant as more opportunities and support are equalizing skill acquisition across genders (Miller & Halpern, 2014).

- Continues to make impulsive decisions and illogical choices that sometimes make adults wonder. Remember that adolescent brains still are undergoing development and maturation in the areas responsible for emotional control and decision making (Spear, 2013).

### Speech and Language Development

- Uses correct grammar and more elaborate sentence structure; is able to critique own written work.

- Articulates complex ideas, varying the style according to the situation.

- Continues to expand vocabulary; adds words that are more advanced, sophisticated, and abstract.

- Participates heavily in social networking; uses Internet slang and shortcuts masterfully to converse (via texting) with friends ("b/c," because; "g2g," got to go; "sbrd," so bored; "meh," whatever; "PAW," parents are watching) (Figure 9-10).

- Understands and uses **figurative language**: "He jumped as high as the sky," "She was as quiet as a mouse," "The walls have ears."

Figure 9-10 **Teens spend a good deal of time engaged in social networking and staying in touch with friends.**

© iStockphoto.com/GlobalStock

**analytical thinking** A cognitive process used when attempting to solve problems or make plans; identifying and evaluating the pros and cons of alternative solutions.

**figurative language** Words or statements that have meanings other than their literal definitions.

## Developmental Profiles and Growth Patterns *(continued)*

### Social-Emotional Development

**17 and 18 year olds**

- Is becoming more open and receptive to adult advice; may actually request it on occasion (Telzer et al., 2013).

- Continues to refine a self-identity based more on realistic goals and cultural ideals and less on idealistic notions ("I want to be a famous musician, but it's going to take a lot of hard work and dedication.")

- Has more self-confidence; is less likely to be influenced by peers or to rely on them for approval.

- Sees oneself as part of a much larger world; continues to redefine personal values and beliefs about social roles and civic responsibilities; seeks out opportunities to become involved in community programs (Crone, 2013).

- Has better emotional control, but still exhibits a range of moods and occasional impulsive behavior.

- Seeks intimate relationships based more on shared interests than pure romantic desire.

- Understands and is more likely to accept responsibility for own behavior.

**Did You Know**

...that many high school students give back to their communities by volunteering? They account for more than 25 percent of all volunteers and most often participate in civic events that address homelessness, hunger, fund-raising, community cleanup, animal care, and mentoring children in recreational activities.

---

▶❚❚  **TeachSource Video Connections**

© 2015 Cengage Learning®

### Peer Influence

Friendships and peers play an essential role in adolescent development. However, the nature of these relationships changes over time. Respond to the following questions as you watch the learning video *12–18 Years: Peers and Domain Influences in Development:*

1. What is meant by "domain-specific peer influence"?

2. What developmental areas are parents most likely to influence?

3. Why do seventeen- and eighteen-year-olds value the input of peers and parents differently?

4. Why do they appear to be more receptive to adult advice at this point in their development?

## DAILY ROUTINES

### Eating

- Continues to have important nutritional needs (e.g., protein, calcium, vitamins, iron, zinc, etc.) that must be satisfied to assure optimum growth, health, and performance.
- Eating patterns may become more erratic as activities and schedules compete with mealtimes; skips occasional meals, overeats following vigorous workouts or during stressful periods.
- Makes independent decisions about food choices; eats with friends and away from home more often.
- Weight concerns and emotional problems may lead to unhealthy diets, eating disorders, or both.

### Personal Care and Dressing

- Is self-sufficient in managing personal care responsibilities.
- Chooses clothes that are "popular" with peers or that express individuality.

### Sleeping

- Requires approximately nine hours of uninterrupted nighttime sleep.
- May nap following vigorous activity or if up late the night before; napping too long can delay falling asleep at night.
- Stress, medications, and mental health disorders such as depression may interfere with sleep patterns (sleeping too much or too little).

### Social Activities

- Has learned to drive and may transport self to school activities and events.
- Juggles school, homework, and employment so that there is still time to take in a movie with friends, attend a sporting event or party, go out on a date, or simply join friends for something to eat.
- Has more friends of the opposite gender, some of whom the adolescent may be dating; friendships are formed on the basis of personalities and common interests, with fewer concerns about popularity.
- Spends considerable time staying in touch with friends through social networks, instant messaging, or phone calls.
- Continues to develop and experiment with new interests and activities, such as surfing, skiing, or bowling; learning another language; playing a musical instrument; discovering religion; taking up yoga; repairing cars; practicing martial arts.

**17 and 18 year olds**

## learning activities to promote **brain development**

Maintaining a respectful relationship with teens is important at this stage. Encourage healthy eating and sleep habits, set realistic expectations, and support their interests in planning for the future.

### Developmentally appropriate applications for families and teachers

- Continue to discuss risky behaviors and safety considerations; role-play strategies for resisting negative peer pressure.
- Offer guidance with experiences that may be new to the adolescent, such as opening a checking account, applying for admission to college, purchasing a first car, or obtaining employment.

- Help adolescents learn healthy stress and anger management techniques.
- Encourage and support the adolescent's interest in volunteering or becoming involved in community service activities.
- Motivate adolescents to follow a healthy diet and engage in physical activity.
- Create opportunities that give adolescents responsibility and acknowledge their efforts and contributions.
- Talk about and practice time management skills (these will be helpful as they continue their education and seek employment).
- Locate first aid and CPR classes and urge adolescents to complete the training.

**TeachSource Digital Download**

**17 and 18 year olds**

## developmental **alerts**

Check with a health-care provider or child development specialist if, by the nineteenth birthday, the child does *not*:

- Maintain usual eating and sleeping routines; sudden or prolonged changes may signal substance abuse or mental health problems.
- Show interest and initiative in achieving independence from family.
- Link moral reasoning to behavioral choices; take responsibility for own behavior and learn from experience.
- Exhibit self-confidence and positive self-esteem in most daily activities.
- Attend school on a regular basis.
- Use reasonable judgment in regulating emotions.
- Grasp and process information when making decisions.
- Achieve functional literacy (reading and writing skills).
- Make and keep friends that have a positive influence on behavior.

**Note:** Cultural differences may alter the timetable when some developmental skills are acquired. Expanded Developmental Alerts Checklists appear in Appendix A and are also available as digital downloads.

## safety **concerns**

Continue to implement the safety practices described for the previous stages. Always be aware of new safety issues as the child continues to grow and develop.

### Health and Well-being

- Reinforce the importance of consuming a healthy diet and maintaining an active lifestyle.
- Continue to talk with adolescents about the risks of pregnancy and sexually transmitted infections.
- Recognize the signs of undue stress; encourage teens to talk about things that are making them feel anxious; be a patient listener and provide nonjudgmental support; reinforce healthy coping skills (e.g., tackling challenges in small steps; seeing the positive side of a problem; and making time for fun and relaxation by listening to music, taking a walk, talking with friends, or reading a book).

## safety concerns *(continued)*

### Unintentional Injury

- Continue to emphasize safe driving; motor vehicle accident and fatality rates are highest among older teens, especially males (Asemota et al., 2013) (Figure 9-11). Teens tend to believe that they are invincible!
- Prohibit the use of cell phones and texting while driving or driving under the influence of drugs or alcohol (a legal offense). Many states have passed laws banning texting or talking on a cell phone while driving.
- Urge caution when participating in recreational activities such as weight lifting, hunting, riding all-terrain vehicles (ATVs), jogging, and swimming. Make sure that proper equipment, training, and supervision are provided.
- Educate adolescents about the risk and warning signs of concussions (traumatic brain injury, or TBI) that may be sustained during athletic activity. Stress the importance of seeking medical attention and clearance before the activity is resumed.
- Ensure that adolescents complete appropriate safety training if they use firearms for hunting or target practice.

### Violence (Suicide, Homicide)

- Recognize the early warning signs of depression, mood disorders, sexual abuse, and potential suicide; adolescents' sexual orientation increases the likelihood of malicious harassment and bullying (Flett & Hewitt, 2013).

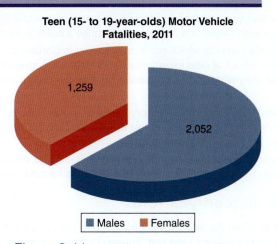

**Teen (15- to 19-year-olds) Motor Vehicle Fatalities, 2011**

1,259

2,052

■ Males  ■ Females

**Figure 9-11** **Adolescent motor vehicle fatalities.**

Source: National Highway Traffic Safety Administration (NHTSA). *Fatality analysis reporting system encyclopedia (FARS)*. Retrieved on February 13, 2014 from http://www.nhtsa.gov/FARS.

17 and 18 year olds

- Educate adolescents about their increased vulnerability to the effects of drugs and alcohol; maturational changes in brain structure and function can interfere with rational thought, intensify sensitivity to substances, and increase the probability of addiction (Spear, 2014).
- Know who the adolescent's friends are, where they hang out, and what they do when they are together.
- Foster resilience and empower teens to resist peer pressure; continue to strengthen the adolescent's communication skills, self-esteem, and healthy mentoring relationships with caring adults.

## positive behavior guidance

Behavioral guidance and limit-setting remain important adult responsibilities. However, the expectations and way in which these roles are performed are highly influenced by a person's social and cultural background. Adolescents who are raised in societies where parent–child relationships demand respect and obedience are less likely to experience conflict than their counterparts in countries where autonomy is strongly encouraged. Teens need and want continued adult support, protection, respect, and guidance in making sound decisions (even if they seem to object). At the same time, adults can promote adolescents' quest for autonomy by gradually relinquishing parental control and involving them in responsible decision making.

### Thirteen- and fourteen-year-olds

- Let teens know that you are available to talk (in a nonjudgmental manner); encourage them to discuss concerns with family or a trusted adult; make a point to spend time together as a family.
- Choose your battles; decide which conflicts are most important to address. Adolescents face a host of new experiences and must learn how to make responsible choices. Understand that they won't always make the right decisions but the hope is that they will learn from their mistakes.
- Listen to the adolescent's side of the story; learn why she chose to violate a rule. It isn't necessary to agree, but it is important to respect her opinion, build a healthy relationship, and help her understand why the rule was necessary.
- Involve adolescents in establishing rules, responsibilities, and consequences for unacceptable behavior. Enforce rules consistently to build respect and accountability.

### Fifteen- and sixteen-year-olds

- Make an effort to know the adolescent's friends and the values they share; meet them at school functions; invite them over to hang out. Friends can be a source of positive social-emotional support or the basis for negative peer pressure.
- Never hit, humiliate, or call the adolescent sarcastic names. Overreacting, disciplining when you are angry, or using physical force sets a poor example and teaches negative ways of handling a situation.
- Negotiate to reduce frequent disagreements and help adolescents understand the rational for establishing a rule; involve your teen in defining the behavior in question, identifying reasonable solutions, arriving at a mutual decision, implementing, enforcing, and monitoring how well the solution is working.
- Use logical consequences: take the cell phone away if too much time is spent talking or texting with friends or if homework is ignored; set a curfew thirty minutes earlier if the teen was thirty minutes late.
- Acknowledge and reinforce responsible behavior; teens want adults to notice and to be proud of their accomplishments.
- Address harmful or risky behaviors in a direct, firm, and consistent manner. Let adolescents know that their poor choices indicate a lack of readiness to make mature decisions.

### Seventeen- and eighteen-year-olds

- Continue to provide a safe, structured environment; maintain and enforce reasonable limits.
- Convey a sense of trust and respect, even though teens may make occasional mistakes in judgment. Encourage them to talk about and learn from mistakes.
- Give adolescents increased responsibility for handling their own affairs (e.g., checking account, laundry, scheduling, bill payments, or clothing purchases) and acknowledge their efforts. Take time to help adolescents learn from their mistakes.
- Let adolescents know that you are available to talk; they continue to need support and reassurance as they encounter new and challenging experiences.

17 and 18 year olds

## Summary

9-1  Changes associated with puberty and brain development require periods of major reorganization and readjustment.

- Structural modifications that occur in the brain's cortex region during adolescence require new neural connections to be formed.
- Emotion, decision making, and memory are regulated by the cortex.

continued on following page

# Summary

**9-2**  Thirteen- and fourteen-year-olds begin to experience numerous physical and psychological changes associated with puberty. These hormone-driven changes can cause children to lose self-confidence while they gradually comprehend, reexamine, and adjust to a new identity.

**9-3**  Fifteen- and sixteen-year-olds continue to value friendships and consider them to be important for companionship, emotional support, information, and an opportunity for sharing common interests. Friendships also provide a forum for learning about oneself and feelings toward others.

**9-4**  Seventeen- and eighteen-year-olds have achieved a level of relative maturity and independent thought. They generally understand who they are, how and where they fit in, and what they want in life. They begin to accept responsibility for their behavior and are less likely to act on impulse.

# Key Terms

neural connections **p. 213**      egocentrism **p. 216**          scientific reasoning **p. 223**

formal operational                 imaginary audience **p. 216**   analytical thinking **p. 229**

  thinking **p. 215**        deductive reasoning **p. 222**  figurative language **p. 229**

# Apply What You Have Learned

## A.  Case Study Connections

*Reread the developmental sketch about Morena and Emilia presented at the beginning of this chapter and answer the following questions:*

1.  What social-emotional behaviors are characteristic of most typical thirteen- and fourteen-year-olds?

2.  How do friendships and the nature of their importance differ for thirteen-year-olds and sixteen-year-olds? Would you consider Morena's and Emilia's relationships with friends to be typical for their age?

3.  What factors may account for the differences in the girls' personalities?

4.  What age-appropriate issues should Morena and Emilia's parents be discussing with them to protect their safety and well-being?

## B.  Review Questions

1.  What physical changes are thirteen- and fourteen-year-olds likely to experience?

2.  What cognitive advantages does formal operational thinking give the adolescent?

3.  Describe the nature of peer relationships and the role that they play in the lives of fifteen- and sixteen-year-olds.

4.  How would you respond to parents who ask why their once-well-behaved child is now acting impulsively and making questionable choices as an adolescent?

5.  Why do adolescents prefer to stay up late at night? What are the consequences of sleep deprivation?

6. Explain, from a developmental standpoint, why adolescents seem to devote so much time to instant messaging and social networking.

7. What is egocentrism? What adolescent behaviors would illustrate this concept?

## C. Your Turn: Chapter to Practice

1. Interview a teen from each of the age divisions described in this chapter (13–14, 15–16, 17–18 years). Ask them to identify two or three concerns that they find particularly challenging at this time. In what ways are the concerns similar and different among the age groups? What conclusions can you draw from these findings?

2. Visit with a school truancy officer. What is the school's policy regarding truancy? What reasons are cited most often for student truancy? In what ways does the school work with students and families to prevent repeat truancy?

3. Develop a rationale based on the information in this chapter to explain why the legal drinking age in most countries is set at eighteen years.

4. Stroll through a local shopping mall and note what strategies (e.g., merchandise, marketing, ambience, and salespersons' age and gender) retailers use to attract and appeal to adolescents. Discuss why these methods work based on your understanding of adolescents' developmental characteristics.

# Online Resources

## American Institutes for Research (AIR)

This international organization is one of the largest nonprofit research groups to focus on behavioral and social science. Extensive resource information for teachers across all grade levels and in specialty areas (e.g., English-language learners [ELL], after-school programs, special education, girls' education, health, assessment, child development, and reading) is provided on the website.

## International Multicultural Institute

The mission of this global organization is to address emerging diversity issues and to promote improved multicultural understanding and education. Multicultural case studies, training exercises, and a gender diversity quiz can be accessed here.

## Talking with Kids About Tough Issues

The Henry J. Kaiser Family Foundation and Children Now have partnered to encourage and support families in their effort to discuss challenging issues (e.g., alcohol, sex, violence, HIV/AIDS, and drug abuse) with children. Research-based information, pamphlets, and links to additional resource sites are provided.

## WiredSafety

This site is dedicated to the promotion of online safety education and the elimination of harassment and cybercrime. Special information sections are provided for families, educators, and teens.

# References

Albert, D., Chein, J., & Steinberg, L. (2013). The teenage brain. Peer influences on adolescent decision making. *Current Directions in Psychological Science*, 22(2), 114–120.

Anyaegbu, E., & Dharnidharka, V. (2014). Hypertension in the teenager. *Pediatric Clinics of North America*, 61(1), 131–151.

Asemota, A., George, B., Bowman, S., Haider, A., & Schneider, E. (2013). Causes and trends in traumatic brain injury for United States adolescents. *Journal of Neurotrauma*, 30(2), 67–75.

Berry, T., & LaVelle, K. (2013). Comparing socioemotional outcomes for early adolescents who join after school for internal or external reasons. *Journal of Early Adolescence*, 33(1), 77–103.

Bregman H., Malik, N., Page, M., Makynen, E., & Lindahl, K. (2013). Identity profiles in lesbian, gay, and bisexual youth: The role of family influences. *Journal of Youth and Adolescence*, 42(3), 417–430.

Burgaleta, M., Johnson, W., Waber, D., Colom, R., & Karama, S. (2014). Cognitive ability changes and dynamics of cortical thickness development in healthy children and adolescents. *NeuroImage*, 84, 810–819.

Casey, B., & Caudle, K. (2013). The teenage brain: Self-control. *Current Directions in Psychological Science*, 22(2), 82–87.

Cheung, F., Wan, S., Fan, W., & Leong, F. (2013). Collective contributions to career efficacy in adolescents: A cross-cultural study. *Journal of Vocational Behavior*, 83(3), 237–244.

Crone, E. (2013). Considerations of fairness in the adolescent brain. *Child Development Perspectives*, 7(2), 97–103.

DeKeyser, R. (2013). Age effects in second language learning: Stepping stones toward better understanding. *Language Learning*, 63(Supp.1), 52–67.

Euser, A., Evans, B., Greaves-Lord, K., Huizink, A., & Franken, I. (2013). Parental rearing behavior prospectively predicts adolescents' risky decision-making and feedback-related electrical brain activity. *Developmental Science*, 16(3), 409–427.

Ferreiro, F., Seoane, G., & Senra, C. (2014). Understanding the role of body dissatisfaction in the gender differences in depressive symptoms and disordered eating: A longitudinal study during adolescence. *Journal of Adolescence*, 37(1), 73–84.

Flett, G., & Hewitt, P. (2013). Disguised distress in children and adolescents "flying under the radar." *Canadian Journal of School Psychology*, 28(1), 12–27.

Fulkerson, J., Larson, N., Horning, M., & Neumark-Sztainer, D. (2014). A review of associations between family or shared meal frequency and dietary and weight status outcomes across the lifespan. *Journal of Nutrition Education and Behavior*, 46(1), 2–19.

Kaplan, D., Jones, E., Olson, E., & Yunzal-Butler, C. (2013). Early age of first sex and health risk in an urban adolescent population. *Journal of School Health*, 83(5), 350–356.

Kleibeuker, S., De Dreu, C., & Crone, E. (2013). The development of creative cognition across adolescence: Distinct trajectories for insight and divergent thinking. *Developmental Science*, 16(1), 2–12.

Kleibeuker, S., Koolschijn, P., & Jolles, D. (2013). Prefrontal cortex involvement in creative problem solving in middle adolescence and adulthood. *Developmental Cognitive Neuroscience*, 5, 197–206.

Koulouglioti, C., Cole, R., Moskow, M., & McQuillan, B. (2014). The longitudinal association of young children's everyday routines to sleep duration. *Journal of Pediatric Health Care*, 28(1), 80–87.

Liu, C., Ang, R., & Lwin, M. (2013). Cognitive, personality, and social factors associated with adolescents' online personal information disclosure. *Journal of Adolescence*, 36(4), 629–638.

Luna, B., Paulsen, D., Padmanabhan, A., & Geier, C. (2013). The teenage brain: Cognitive control and motivation. *Current Directions in Psychological Science*, 22(2), 94–100.

Miller, D., & Halpern, D. (2014). The new science of cognitive sex differences. *Trends in Cognitive Sciences*, 18(1), 37–45.

Mustanski, B., Birkett, M., Greene, G., Rosario, M., Bostwick, W., & Everett, B. (2013). The association between sexual orientation identity and behavior across race/ethnicity, sex, and age in a probability sample of high school students. *American Journal of Public Health*, 104(2), 237−244.

Peake, S., Dishion, T., Stormshak, E., & Moore, W. (2013). Risk-taking and social exclusion during adolescence: Neural mechanisms underlying peer influences on decision-making. *NeuroImage*, 82, 23–34.

Perry, R., Braun, R., Cantu, M., Dudovitz, R., & Sheoran, B. (2014). Associations among text messaging, academic performance, and sexual behaviors of adolescents. *Journal of School Health*, 84(1), 33–39.

Pisani, A., Wyman, P., Petrova, M., Schmeelk-Cone, K., Goldston, D., & Xia, Y. (2013). Emotion regulation difficulties, youth-adult relationships, and suicide attempts among high school students in underserved communities. *Journal of Youth and Adolescence*, 42(6), 807–820.

Pokhrel, P., Herzog, T., Black, D., Zaman, A., Riggs, N., & Sussman, S. (2013). Adolescent neurocognitive development, self-regulation, and school-based drug use prevention. *Prevention Science*, 14(3), 218–228.

Quinn, S., & Oldmeadow, J. (2013). The martini effect and social networking sites: Early adolescents, mobile social networking, and connectedness to friends. *Mobile Media & Communication*, 1(2), 237–247.

Rowsell, H., Ciarrochi, J., Heaven, P., & Deane, F. (2014). The role of emotion identification skill in the formation of male and female friendships: A longitudinal study. *Journal of Adolescence*, 37(2), 103–111.

Rudolph, K., Gary, S., Stuart, E., Glass, T., Marques, A., Duncko, R., & Merikangas, K. (2014). The association between cortisol and neighborhood disadvantage in a U.S. population-based sample of adolescents. *Health Place* (January 25), 68–77. doi: 10.1016/j.healthplace.2013.11.001.

Russell, S., Everett, B., Rosario, M., & Birkett, M. (2014). Indicators of victimization and sexual orientation among adolescents: Analyses from Youth Risk Behavior Surveys. *American Journal of Public Health*, 104(2), 255−261.

Shochat, T., Cohen-Zion, M., & Tzischinsky, O. (2014). Functional consequences of inadequate sleep in adolescents: A systematic review. *Sleep Medicine Reviews*, 18(1), 75–87.

Somerville, L. (2013). The teenage brain. Sensitivity to social evaluation. *Current Directions in Psychological Science*, 22(2), 121–127.

Somerville, L., Jones, R., Ruberry, E., Dyke, J., Glover, G., & Casey, B. (2013). The medial prefrontal cortex and the emergence of self-conscious emotion in adolescence. *Psychological Science*, 24(8), 1554–1562.

Spear, L. (2013). The teenage brain: Adolescents and alcohol. *Current Directions in Psychological Science,* 22(2), 152–157.

Spear, L. (2014). Adolescents and alcohol: Acute sensitivities, enhanced intake, and later consequences. *Neurotoxicology and Teratology,* 41, 51–59.

Telzer, E., Fuligni, A., Lieberman, M., & Galvan, A. (2013). Meaningful family relationships: Neurocognitive buffers of adolescent risk taking. *Journal of Cognitive Neuroscience,* 25(3), 374–387.

Verboom, C., Sijtsema, J., Verhulst, F., Penninx, B., & Ormel, J. (2014). Longitudinal associations between depressive problems, academic performance, and social functioning in adolescent boys and girls. *Developmental Psychology,* 50(1), 247–257.

Wang, J., Rubin, K., Laursen, B., Booth-LaForce, C., & Rose-Krasnor, L. (2013). Preference-for-solitude and adjustment difficulties in early and late adolescence. *Journal of Clinical Child & Adolescent Psychology,* 42(6), 834–842.

Wooldridge, T., & Lytle, P. (2014). An overview of anorexia nervosa in males. *Eating Disorders,* 20(5), 368–378.

## Learning Objectives

*After reading this chapter, you will be able to:*

**10-1** Discuss at least five legislative acts passed on behalf of children with exceptionalities and their families.

**10-2** Describe several factors that can complicate the process of determining if a child is or is not developing typically.

**10-3** Defend this statement: Observing and recording a child's behavior is an essential first step in determining if there is a developmental problem.

**10-4** Discuss the developmental team's role in the assessment and intervention process.

## naeyc NAEYC Standards Linked to Chapter Content

**1a and 1b:** Promoting child development and learning

**2a and 2b:** Building family and community relationships

**3a, 3b, 3c, and 3d:** Observing, documenting, and assessing to support young children and families

**4a:** Using developmentally effective approaches

**6b and 6e:** Becoming a professional

Amita's parents recently moved to a new community where her father would begin working on a graduate degree at the local university. Her family's initial concern was to find a suitable child care program for four-year-old Amita, who was bilingual but spoke only limited English. A neighbor suggested they contact the Head Start program located on campus to see if they had an opening. Fortunately for Amita and her parents, the Head Start director was able to offer a space that had been vacated just days before.

The teachers' supportive attention helped ease Amita's transition into the program. They quickly discovered that she understood more English words than she was able to speak. However, Amita's teachers became concerned about her overall development in the weeks and months that followed. She seemed to have difficulty acquiring additional words, frequently looked puzzled when spoken to, and often failed to respond appropriately when given directions. Amita seldom interacted with the other children despite their urgings, instead choosing simply to stand and observe. The teachers also expressed concern about her inability to stay engaged in an activity for more than two or three minutes at a time. There was one exception: Amita enjoyed painting and would remain at the easel until the teachers gently guided her to another activity.

When asked about Amita's health history, her mother spoke vaguely of earaches and "runny ears," "hot spells," and "twitches." Amita's mother, who recently celebrated her twenty-first birthday, is a thin, pale woman, midway into her second pregnancy. She works full time in the university cafeteria and is the family's sole breadwinner.

Amita's mother displays genuine warmth and concern for her daughter but apparently does not understand the importance of seeking medical care for herself or her family. The Head Start teachers have recommended that Amita be evaluated by a physician and also have her hearing tested. However, Amita's parents have no family doctor or health insurance to help cover expenses. They also seem reluctant to accept that there may be anything wrong with Amita, believing instead that "she is only four and will eventually grow out of these problems."

## Ask Yourself

- What behaviors have caused Amita's teachers to be concerned about her developmental progress?
- What environmental factors may have contributed to Amita's developmental delays?

Is my child all right? Most parents, at one time or another, have asked this question during their children's early and growing-up years (Figure 10-1) (Turygin et al., 2014; Deakin-Bell, Walker, & Badawi, 2013). Many caregivers and teachers ask a similar question about a child who seems "different" from other children with whom they work. Such questions are a positive sign because they indicate awareness and concern. Children, as emphasized in Chapters 1 and 2, are unique and can vary greatly in their development. Many factors, including genetics, culture, family structure and values, nutrition, health, and poverty influence the rate and nature of children's developmental progress. It is the rare child who is truly typical in every way. Some children who have developmental irregularities of one kind or another do not experience any long-term negative effects. Other children who have irregularities that do not appear significant may be at considerable developmental risk. In both instances, it is important that the child be seen by a health care professional or child development specialist and perhaps referred for evaluation and intervention services.

# Public Policy and Social Attitudes

Supporting children's optimal development has become a major social and legislative focus. Much of the initial impetus came in the 1960s as part of the antipoverty movement (often referred to as the "war on poverty"). Many precedent-setting research studies provided conclusive evidence that developmental disabilities in infants and young children could be reduced significantly through early intervention. As a result, several major strategies have evolved since then. One is based on the prevention of atypical development through improved prenatal care and maternal nutrition. Another is the early identification of children with, or at risk for, developmental problems. Both methods are associated with noteworthy improvements in reducing the incidence and long-term effects of childhood disabilities through a family systems approach (Polisenska &Kapalkova, 2014; Guevara et al., 2013).

## Legislation Supporting Optimum Development

The passage of legislation in the 1960s established several precedent-setting programs that supported child and family health. These developments marked one of the first large-scale efforts aimed at reducing developmental risks and disabilities:

Figure 10-1 Families often wonder if their child is developing "normally."

- **PL 88-452 Head Start (1965)** This act, part of the antipoverty movement, established the Head Start program and its supplemental services, including developmental screening, medical and dental care, nutrition, parent training, and early education for income-eligible children three to five years of age. Amendments in 1972 and 1974 mandated Head Start to serve children with disabilities as well. Reauthorization in 1994 created Early Head Start programs, which extended services to infants and toddlers from income-eligible families.

- **PL 101-239 Early and Periodic Screening, Diagnosis, and Treatment Act (EPSDT) (1967)** This national program was added to Medicaid and continues to serve the health and developmental needs (diagnosis and treatment) of income-eligible children who are deemed to be at risk.

- **PL 94-105 Supplemental Nutrition Program for Women, Infants, and Children (WIC) (1975)** The primary goal of this program is aimed at improving the health of at-risk mothers during their pregnancy in order to promote full-term fetal development and increase newborn birth weight. Medical supervision, food vouchers, and nutrition education are provided to low-income pregnant and nursing women and their children under age five to ensure a healthy start.

Legislation that specifically addressed the needs of children who have developmental differences has also been enacted, including the following:

- **PL 89-10 Elementary and Secondary Education Act (ESEA) (1965)** This act established federal requirements and funding for U.S. public schools (K–12). Additional funds and resources were authorized for schools and districts (preschool through high school) serving a high proportion of children from low-income families; these programs are designated as Title I programs.

- **PL 90-538 Handicapped Children's Early Education and Assistance Act (HCEEAA) (1968)** This law provided funding for the establishment of model classrooms to serve preschool children who had confirmed disabilities.

**Did You Know**

...that more than 30 million children, birth to 5 years, have participated in the Head Start program since it was established in 1965? Several of its famous alumni include the athlete Shaquille O'Neal; U.S. Congresswoman Loretta Sanchez; Anna Maria Chavez, CEO, Girl Scouts of America; and actors Chris Rock and Brandon Adams.

▶❚❚ **TeachSource** Video Connections

## Including Children with Developmental Disabilities

Schools are experiencing many changes in their educational practices as a result of legislative directives—some of these changes are considered to be improvements, while the long-term outcome of others is yet to be determined. Respond to the following questions after you have watched the learning video *No Child Left Behind*:

1. What is the ultimate goal of NCLB?
2. Are these expectations reasonable for all students?
3. In what ways does a school benefit from a state waiver?
4. Why have many educators criticized the NCLB requirements?

- **PL 94-142 Education for All Handicapped Children Act (EHA) (1975)**  This landmark law required states to provide comprehensive evaluation, "free and appropriate" education, and intervention services for all children ages three to five years who have, or are at risk for, developmental disabilities. The law was amended in 1990 and 1997 and renamed the Individuals with Disabilities Education Act (IDEA) (PL 101-476), described below.

- **PL 99-457 Education of the Handicapped Act Amendments (1986)**  Because the original initiative (PL 94-142) had proven so successful, it was amended to extend early intervention services to infants, toddlers, and their families through the Individualized Family Service Plan (IFSP). This portion of the bill (now known as Part C of IDEA) is not mandated or fully funded; therefore, it is not available in all communities. Additional features of this act include an emphasis on multidisciplinary assessment, a designated service coordinator, a family-focused approach, and a system of service coordination

- **PL 101-336 Americans with Disabilities Act (ADA) (1990)**  This national civil rights law protects persons of all ages against discrimination on the basis of a disability. The intent is to remove barriers that interfere with full inclusion in education, employment, and public services. The law's implications for children and their families are clear. Child care programs and schools cannot refuse to enroll children who have a disability; they must modify their settings and programs to accommodate all children.

- **PL 101-476 Individuals with Disabilities Education Act (IDEA) (1990)**  This law amended the original Education for All Handicapped Children Act (PL 94-142) and updated the language and service provisions. It established Part B special education services for children 3 to 21 years old and Part C services for infants, toddlers, and their families. The law was again amended in 1997 (as PL105-17) and emphasized the role of students and their families in the educational process and improved children's access to a general education curriculum.

- **PL 108-446 Individuals with Disabilities Education Improvement Act of 2004**  This law increased accountability for children's educational outcomes, improved identification methods, enhanced family involvement, and reduced the amount of required paperwork . It also established guidelines for the appropriate discipline of students with disabilities.

- **PL 107-110 No Child Left Behind Act (NCLB) (2002)**  This legislation, a reauthorization of the ESEA, attempted to address the problems of academic inequity and failure in this country. The intended goal was to hold schools and teachers accountable for quality improvements in educational opportunities for *all* children and, in turn, increase academic success rates or lose federal funding. Although many positive changes have resulted, the law also triggered a number of unintended consequences (e.g., undue emphasis on standardized testing and

© 2015 Cengage Learning®

test scores, unethical testing practices, incompatible goals of IDEA and NCLB, and school budgetary crises). In 2012, the Obama administration began granting waivers to states that requested exemption from having to meet all NCLB regulations if they agreed to establish high grade-level standards, invest in teachers to improve their effectiveness, and be held more accountable. Full reauthorization of ESEA (including NCLB) currently has been put on hold.

# Early Identification and Intervention Programs

Legislative and public policy changes have established several avenues for getting children with suspected developmental problems into appropriate evaluation and early intervention programs.

# Infants and Children at Medical Risk

Family physicians and pediatricians are becoming increasingly aware of the importance of evaluating infants and young children for developmental and behavioral problems (Rose, Herzig, & Hussey-Gardner, 2014) (Figure 10-2). Many pediatric practices today ask families to complete a developmental screening tool such as the Abbreviated Denver Developmental Screening Test, the Revised Parent Developmental Questionnaire, or the Ages and Stages Questionnaire® during each office visit so that children's progress can be monitored closely (Windham et al., 2014; Deakin-Bell, Walker, & Badawi, 2013). Physicians are also beginning to note deviations in infants' neurological development that could indicate an irregularity and are referring families to genetic, neurological, and child development specialists for evaluation. These trends have contributed to the earlier detection of high-risk conditions, such as autism, hearing impairments, or delayed language or motor skills, that are often associated with a failure to achieve important developmental milestones.

Infants who are discharged from premature nurseries and neonatal intensive care units, including those from multiple births, comprise another group of children known to experience a high rate of developmental problems. Many communities in urban areas now have follow-up clinics where the developmental progress of these children can be monitored on a regular basis. Appropriate intervention services can be secured when disabilities or delays are identified in their earliest stages and, thus, lessen the potentially harmful effects that they otherwise may have on children's developmental progress.

Medical conditions such as diabetes, hearing loss, communicable diseases, cancer, and arthritis can also have a negative effect on a child's development. Children's energy and interest in learning may be affected negatively by the conditions and unpleasant side effects of medications or medical procedures. For this reason, it is important to monitor these children closely and note any behavioral changes. Patience, caring support, and appropriate intervention services can help children continue to make developmental progress through difficult times.

Figure 10-2 Developmental delays associated with certain medical conditions and syndromes are better understood today.

ECE Library

# Community Screening

The majority of young children who will benefit from early identification and intervention do not always come from medically high-risk groups. These children may be located most effectively through a variety of community screening services.

Screening programs are designed to identify children who have or might be at risk for developmental problems. The primary emphasis is on evaluating a child's hearing and vision, general health, speech and language, cognition, motor skills, and overall developmental progress. Most screening tests are easily administered locally to large numbers of children. Often they can be accessed through local public health departments, Head Start programs, community colleges and universities, clinics, public schools, and early education programs. Teachers and volunteers can be trained to conduct certain types of screenings, such as measurements of children's height, weight, and vision. Advanced training usually is required to administer other forms of assessment such as hearing, speech and language, and developmental progress. Careful consideration should be given to obtaining data from multiple assessment sources before arriving at any conclusions. Early screening and detection of developmental disabilities permit children to receive intervention services before they reach school age. Delays in providing needed therapies and educational services can reduce the chances of successfully improving or overcoming some conditions.

**Child Find** is a nationwide system of screening programs mandated by IDEA and administered by individual states (Edwards, Gallagher, & Green, 2013). Its purpose is twofold. One is to raise public awareness about developmental disabilities and to locate eligible infants and young children who have undiagnosed developmental problems or are at risk for the onset of such problems. The second purpose is to help families locate appropriate diagnostic screenings and intervention programs and services. The IDEA law requires all states to establish a Child Find system, identify eligibility criteria, and develop service guidelines.

---

**Spotlight on Brain Development**

## Premature Birth and Cognitive Development

Each year, one in every eight infants in the United States is born prematurely (CDC, 2013). Premature (less than 40 weeks gestation) and late-term (34–36 weeks gestation) infants experience a high rate of sensory and neurological disorders that can result in vision and hearing problems, delayed motor skill development, learning and behavior problems, and respiratory conditions (Chau et al., 2013; Kugelman & Colin, 2013). Premature birth is also the leading cause of infant death in the United States and worldwide. These complications primarily are attributed to an incomplete development of the infant's major organ systems, including the brain, which typically undergo rapid growth and maturation during the final weeks of a mother's pregnancy. Premature birth interrupts this process.

A majority of premature infants experience some degree of cognitive impairment. New medical technologies have made it possible for scientists to pinpoint specific areas in the infant's brain that are adversely affected (Rose et al., 2014). They have discovered that preterm infants often have a smaller cerebral volume (white matter) and neural structure abnormalities (connectivity) that are responsible for various developmental disabilities and delays (Ball et al., 2013; Clark et al., 2013). Leppanen et al. (2014) compared the development of infants who were born prematurely (32 weeks) with those born at very low birth weight (less than 3.31 pounds). They found a positive correlation between growth failure (height

---

**Child Find** A screening program designed to locate children who have developmental problems through improved public awareness.

and head circumference) before age 5 years and delayed cognitive development and lower IQ in both groups. Similar studies have also shown that children born prematurely experience persistent cognitive abnormalities, especially those related to memory, language, and mathematical abilities (Farooqi, Hagglof, & Serenius, 2013; Hutchinson et al., 2013).

Efforts to understand better the causes of premature birth and options for its prevention remain a national and international priority. In the meantime, early identification and targeted intervention services show promise for improving the developmental outcomes of children who may be at risk because they were born prematurely.

### What are the connections?

1. Why should countries be concerned about their premature birth rates?
2. What potential effects can premature birth have on a child's development?
3. Why are cognitive disabilities commonly associated with preterm birth?

# Is There a Problem?

Deciding whether a developmental delay or irregularity is of serious concern is not always easy. The signs can be so subtle, so hard to pinpoint, that it is often difficult to distinguish clearly between children who have a definite problem (the definite *yeses*), and those who definitely do not have a problem (the definite *nos*). Identifying the *maybes*—is there a problem or not?—can be an even more complex issue.

In determining whether a delay or deviation is of real concern, several factors may complicate the matter, such as the following:

- Children who exhibit signs of developmental problems in certain areas often continue to develop like a typical child in every other way; such children present a confusing developmental profile. (See the Developmental Checklists in Appendix A.)
- The range of an individual child's achievements within developmental areas can vary greatly as a result of different maturation rates and environmental conditions. Both factors are interacting continuously to exert a strong influence on every aspect of a child's development.
- Family beliefs, values, and cultural background exert a direct influence on child-rearing practices (Trawick-Smith, 2013). Developmental milestones are not predetermined, nor are they universal; the way they are perceived varies from culture to culture and from family to family. Thus, respect for diverse family and community beliefs and practices always must be considered when gathering and interpreting information about a child's development (Figure 10-3).

Figure 10-3 Diversity of family and community values, beliefs, and cultural differences must be considered and treated with respect and dignity.

© GFOW/Cengage Learning

- Developmental delays or problems may not be immediately apparent. Many children learn to compensate for a deficiency. For example, children who have a mild to moderate hearing loss might position themselves closer to the teacher during story time so they can hear. Children who experience difficulty learning to read might depend on other cognitive strategies to overcome their limitations. Sometimes deficiencies are not apparent until the child is placed in structured situations that demand a certain level of performance (as in a first-grade reading or mathematics class) (Allen & Cowdery, 2014).

- Intermittent health problems can affect children's performance. For example, a child may have severe and recurring bouts of **otitis media** (middle-ear infection) that improve temporarily or completely resolve between episodes. A hearing test administered when the child is free of infection may reveal no hearing loss, although the same child may be quite deaf during an acute infection. Periods of intermittent hearing loss, sometimes lasting a week or more, can cause some children to develop considerable language and cognitive delays, as well as troublesome behaviors (Everitt, Hannaford, & Conti-Ramsden, 2013). Misbehavior or the apparent disregard of requests or instruction may occur simply because children cannot hear. Too often, these behaviors are misinterpreted as defiance or willfulness instead of recognizing them as a medical problem that is interfering with a child's ability to learn.

## When to Seek Help

At what point should a hunch or an uncomfortable feeling about a child's development or behavior necessitate a call for action? The answer is clear: whenever families or teachers have a concern! Any uneasiness needs to be discussed with a pediatrician, health care provider, or child development specialist sooner rather than later.

Concern about a developmental irregularity also demands immediate investigation anytime that it interferes with a child's participation in everyday activities. Repeated occurrences or repetitions of a troublesome behavior are often a reliable sign that professional help should be sought. However, seldom is a single incidence of a questionable behavior cause for concern. What is of concern is a child's *continuing* reluctance to attempt a new skill or to acquire a basic developmental skill fully. For example, a ten-month-old who tries to sit alone but still must use both hands for support may or may not have a problem. On the other hand, clusters of developmental differences are always significant—a ten-month-old who is not sitting without support, not smiling, and not babbling in response to others is likely to be at developmental risk.

What should teachers and caregivers do when a family fails to express concern or denies the possibility of a problem? Although it may be difficult, it is the teacher's responsibility to discuss any concerns about a child's development in a straightforward and objective manner with the family. It is important that teachers report only what has been observed and what they would expect to see based on the child's developmental stage. They must refrain from making a diagnosis or labeling the child's behavior. For example, a teacher should say, "Danesha avoids eye contact and often responds inappropriately to questions," rather than "Danesha is probably autistic." Once this information has been shared, teachers should work closely with the family to help them understand and accept the child's need for further evaluation. *Under no circumstances should a teacher or administrator bypass family members and make referrals without their permission.* When families are offered support and assistance in making the necessary arrangements, they are more likely to follow through with any recommendations.

**otitis media** An infection of the middle ear.

# Information Gathering

A comprehensive developmental evaluation requires that information be obtained from multiple sources: observation and recording, screening, and diagnostic assessment. Diagnostic assessment includes in-depth testing and clinical interpretation of all results. Clinicians from various disciplines should participate in the diagnostic process. It is their responsibility to provide detailed information about the specific nature of the child's problems, as well as recommended treatments. For example, a four-year-old's delayed speech might be observed by family members and noted during routine screening procedures. Subsequent diagnostic testing by clinicians may pinpoint several other conditions: a moderate, **bilateral** hearing loss, poor production of many letter sounds, and an expressive vocabulary typical of a three-year-old. These clinical findings can be translated into specific educational strategies and intervention procedures that ultimately will benefit the child's overall development.

## Observing and Recording

The evaluation process always begins with systematic observation (see Chapter 1). Noting and recording various aspects of a child's behavior enables the evaluator—whether a family member, a teacher, or a clinician—to focus on what is actually occurring. In other words, observations yield objective information about what the child can and cannot do at the time of the observation.

An effective evaluation is also based on multiple observations, conducted over a period of days and in a variety of natural settings that are familiar to the child. Direct observation often confirms or rules out impressions or suspicions regarding a child's abilities (Nelson et al., 2013; Wang et al., 2013). For example, a child might not count to five when asked to do so in a testing situation. That same child, however, may be observed counting seven or eight objects spontaneously and correctly while playing in the block area. A child thought to have attention deficit hyperactivity disorder (ADHD) might be observed sitting quietly for five to ten minutes when given more interesting and challenging activities, thereby ruling out concerns about hyperactivity. *Note:* The term *hyperactive* is greatly overused and misused. A child should not be so labeled unless specifically diagnosed by a multidisciplinary team. Focusing on a child at play, alone or with other children, can be particularly revealing. Again, no evaluation is valid without direct and objective observations of a child in familiar surroundings.

A family's observations are an especially valuable component of the assessment process (Figure 10-4). Family members often are able to provide information that is not available from other sources. Their observations also provide insight into unique family attitudes, perceptions, and expectations concerning the child. Involving families in the observation phase of evaluation can also be beneficial in terms of reducing their

© 2015 Cengage Learning®

**▶❚❚ TeachSource Video Connections**

### Children with Developmental Disabilities in the Classroom

The importance of identifying children's developmental disabilities early and arranging appropriate intervention services has been stressed throughout the book. The lives of many children have benefitted as a result of the improved awareness, knowledge, and dedication of families, teachers, and clinicians. Respond to the following questions after you have watched the learning video *5–11 Years: Developmental Disabilities in Middle Childhood:*

**1.** Why must first-person language always be used when referring to children who have a disability?

**2.** How would you justify the importance of early identification, early intervention, and inclusionary practices after watching this video?

**3.** What social skills does each child in the video have that are similar to typically developing counterparts? How do they differ?

**bilateral** Affecting both sides, as in loss of hearing in both ears.

Figure 10-4 Families
contribute information that
adds insight and meaning to
the evaluation process.

© 2015 Cengage Learning®

anxieties. Furthermore, direct observation often reveals a child's previously unrecognized abilities. When family members have an opportunity to see their children engaged in appropriate activities, they may be encouraged to focus more on the children's strengths and positive qualities than on their limitations.

## Screening Tests

Screening tests are useful for gathering general information about children's developmental problems and determining whether more comprehensive evaluation is needed. They are designed to assess a child's current abilities, as well as potential delays in fine and large motor skills, cognition, speech and language development, and personal and social responsiveness.

If problems or suspected problems are noted during an initial screening, further in-depth clinical assessment by a child development specialist is needed before a final diagnosis can be reached. *Note:* Results obtained from screening tests are neither conclusive nor diagnostic. They do not predict a child's future abilities or achievement potential and should not be used as a basis for planning intervention programs.

Several questions should be asked when choosing or interpreting a screening instrument:

- Is it appropriate for the child's age?
- Is it free of bias related to the child's economic, geographic, or cultural background (Hurley et al., 2014)?
- Can it be administered in the child's native language (Lowe et al., 2013; Norbury & Sparks, 2013)? If not, is a skilled interpreter available to assist the child and family?
- Is it reliable for identifying children who should be referred for additional testing from those who do not require additional evaluation at this time?

A sample of widely used screening tests and assessment instruments is provided in Appendix B. Included are examples of ecological evaluations for home and school settings. It is essential to gather information about the child's everyday surroundings and to consider it when interpreting test results and planning intervention programs.

## Interpreting Screening Results

The widespread availability of community-based screening programs has contributed significantly to the early identification of children who may have developmental problems. However, the findings are always open to question. In some cases, the screening process itself may have a negative effect on the outcome. Children's attention spans, especially those of young children, are often short and inconsistent from day to day and from task to task. Illness, fatigue, anxiety, hunger, lack of cooperation, irritability, or distractions can also lead to unreliable results. Children may perform poorly if they are unaccustomed to being tested or are unfamiliar with the person who is conducting the test. When children are evaluated in familiar surroundings, such as a classroom or their home setting, they are more likely to cooperate and perform reliably. Consequently, results derived from screening assessments must be regarded with caution. The following points are intended as reminders for both families and teachers:

- Avoid conclusions based on limited information or a single test score. The results may not be an accurate representation of the child's actual development or developmental potential. Only repeated and periodic observations will provide a comprehensive picture of the child's developing abilities (Johnson et al., 2014).

- Never underestimate the influence of home and family on a child's performance (Baker, 2014; Mulligan et al., 2013). Newer screening procedures make a greater effort to promote family participation and to evaluate family concerns, priorities, and resources. There is also an increasing emphasis on screening in familiar or naturalistic environments where children feel more secure and at ease.

- Recognize the dangers of labeling a child as having a learning disability, intellectual deficiency, speech impairment, or behavior disorder, especially on the basis of the results of a single test. Labels can have a negative effect on expectations for the child and the way in which adults respond to the child unless they have been validated through appropriate testing channels (Figure 10-5).

- Question test scores. Test results can be easily misinterpreted. One test might suggest that a child has a developmental delay when actually nothing is wrong. Such conclusions are called *false positives*. The opposite conclusion can also be reached. A child may have a developmental problem that does not show up in the screening process and so might be identified incorrectly as normal. This is a *false negative*. The first situation leads to unnecessary anxiety and disappointment and may change the way that the family responds to their child. The latter situation can lull a family into not seeking further help and lead to a worsening of the child's developmental problems. Both situations can be avoided through careful interpretation of test scores.

**TeachSource Video Connections**

© 2015 Cengage Learning®

### Assessing Children's Development

Ongoing and comprehensive evaluation of children's developmental progress is essential. Data gathered in naturalistic environments and from multiple sources yields an objective picture of the child's developmental progress. This information allows teachers and families to tailor interventions that address children's current learning needs. Respond to the following questions as you watch the learning video *Observing and Monitoring Perceptual-Cognitive Development in Kindergartners: The Importance of Assessment*:

1. Why is it important to assess children's perceptual-cognitive development?

2. What are the advantages of evaluating children in their natural environments?

3. How did the teacher use her observational data to facilitate children's learning?

4. In what ways does family involvement help children achieve learning goals?

Figure 10-5 Labels are inappropriate unless a disability has been documented.

ECE Library

- Understand that the results of screening tests do *not* constitute a diagnosis. Additional information must be collected and in-depth clinical testing completed before a diagnosis is provided or confirmed (Gellert & Elbro, 2013). Even then, errors can occur. There are many reasons for misdiagnosis, such as inconsistent and rapid changes in a child's growth or changing environmental factors such as divorce, military deployment, the birth of a sibling, or family relocation.

- Do not use failed items on a screening test as curriculum items or skills to be taught; a test item is simply one isolated example of a broad range of skills to be expected in a given developmental area at an approximate age. For example, a child who is unable to stand on one foot for five seconds will not overcome a developmental problem by being taught to stand on one foot for a given amount of time. *Screening test items are not a suitable basis for the construction of curriculum activities.*

- Recognize that test results do not predict the child's developmental future, nor do they necessarily correlate with subsequent testing (Watkins & Smith, 2013). There is always the need for *ongoing* observation, assessment, and in-depth clinical diagnosis when screening tests indicate potential problems or delays.

## IQ Tests: Are They Appropriate for Young Children?

Intelligence tests, such as the Wechsler Intelligence Scale for Children (WISC) and the Stanford Binet Intelligence Scales, were not designed or intended to be used as screening instruments (Mindes, 2010). Neither are they regarded by most developmental specialists as appropriate to use with young children for any purpose. IQ tests administered during the early years are not valid predictors of future (or even current) intellectual performance (Burgaleta et al., 2014), nor do they predict subsequent academic performance. IQ tests do not take into account the opportunities that a child has had to learn, the quality of those learning experiences, or what the dominant culture says a child should know at a given age. Children raised in poverty or in non-English-speaking homes often do not have the same opportunities to acquire specific kinds of information represented by the test items (Calvo & Bialystok, 2014). For example, studies have identified maternal education as an important predictor of children's academic achievement, especially among ethnically diverse and low-income families (Lawson et al., 2014). Therefore, an IQ test score used as the sole determinant of a child's cognitive or intellectual development certainly must be challenged.

## Achievement Tests

The administration of formal **achievement tests** in elementary and secondary schools has become a widespread practice since the passage of NCLB (Figure 10-6). These tests are designed to measure how much the child has learned in school about specific subject areas (Haertel, 2013). Depending on the results, each child is assigned a percentile ranking, based on a comparison with other children of the same grade level. For example, a child in the 50th percentile in mathematics is doing as well as 50 percent of the children in the same grade. Test results are increasingly being used to determine children's placement, assess teacher performance, and evaluate a school's overall academic effectiveness

**achievement tests** Tests used to measure a child's academic progress (what the child has learned).

(Bullough, Hall-Kenyon, & MacKay, 2014; Levine & Levine, 2013). Again, test scores should be supported with observational data and samples of children's work (portfolios) before they can have a valid meaning.

# Diagnosis and Referral

Information obtained from authentic assessment, including direct observations and samples of children's products combined with screening test results, provides the basis for the next question: Are comprehensive diagnostic procedures required? Not all children will require an in-depth clinical assessment, but many will if they and their family are to receive the best possible referral for intervention services. Families can be directed to early childhood intervention programs (Child Find) in their community for evaluation and services offered under Part B for preschool-age children and Part C for infants and toddlers. Evaluation and assessment services are available to school-age children through their local school system. An interdisciplinary team approach that combines the input of clinicians, child development specialists, and the child's family is always essential for achieving effective and meaningful diagnoses and referrals.

**Figure 10-6** Achievement tests often are administered to assess student learning.

## The Developmental Team

Federal law (PL 105-17, IDEA) requires families to be involved in all phases of the assessment and intervention process. They become important members of the child's **developmental team** when they work collaboratively with educators and multidisciplinary professionals. A family-centered approach improves information sharing and enables family members to learn and implement therapy recommendations at home (Kingsley & Mailloux, 2013; Nelson et al., 2013). Sustained interest and participation in the child's intervention program can be achieved when the developmental team:

- Keeps families informed
- Explains rationales for treatment procedures
- Uses terms that families can understand and takes the time to explain those that may not be familiar
- Emphasizes the child's progress and helps families to note improvements
- Teaches family members how to work with their child at home
- Provides families with positive feedback and supports their continued efforts and advocacy on the child's behalf

Best practice suggests that the pooling of knowledge and multidisciplinary expertise—in other words, a team approach—is required to manage children's developmental disabilities effectively. For example, a team effort provides the most accurate picture of how a delay in one area can affect development in other areas, just as progress in one area supports progress in others. A two-year-old with a hearing loss could experience delays in language as well as in the areas of cognitive and social-emotional development. Thus, appropriate intervention strategies for this child might require the services of an audiologist, speech and language therapist, early childhood teacher, nurse, and, perhaps,

> **Did You Know**
>
> …that approximately 6.5 million children between 3 and 21 years of age receive services annually through Part B of IDEA? More than 700,000 are children aged 3 to 5 years.

> **developmental team** A team of qualified professionals, such as special educators, speech-language pathologists, occupational therapists, social workers, audiologists, nurses, and physical therapists, who evaluate a child's developmental progress and together prepare an intervention plan that addresses the child's special needs.

social worker. If a team approach is to benefit the child's overall development, effective communication and cooperation among specialists, service providers, and the family is essential. This process is facilitated by the inclusion of an IFSP for infants and toddlers, or an Individualized Educational Plan (IEP) for preschool through school-age children.

## Service Coordinator

Many families do not understand the significance of children's developmental problems or find themselves overwhelmed by the process of approaching multiple agencies and dealing with bureaucratic red tape (Jennings & Hanline, 2013). As a result, they often fail or are unable to complete the necessary service arrangements unless they receive assistance. This supportive role was viewed as so crucial to successful intervention that the position of **service coordinator** was written into federal legislation (PL 99-457, Part C) to help families address their infants' and toddlers' developmental problems. A service coordinator or case manager works closely with families, matching their needs and their child's needs with appropriate community services and educational programs. The coordinator also assists the family in establishing initial contacts and provides continued support.

## Referral

The referral process involves a multiple-step approach. As described earlier, the child's strengths, weaknesses, and developmental skills are evaluated. The family's needs and resources (e.g., financial, psychological, physical, and transportation) must also be taken into consideration. For example, if a family cannot afford special services, has no knowledge of financial assistance programs, and does not own a car, it is unlikely that they will be able to follow through on professional recommendations. However, such problems are seldom insurmountable. Most communities have individuals and social service agencies available to assist families in meeting these needs and arranging for intervention services.

Placement in an appropriate educational setting frequently is recommended as part of the intervention plan. In these settings, classroom teachers, child development specialists, and other members of the developmental team conduct ongoing assessments of the child's progress (Figure 10-7). In addition, the developmental team continuously

**Figure 10-7** Collaboration among teachers, families, and service providers is essential to an effective intervention plan.

**service coordinator** An individual who serves as a family's advocate and assists them with identifying, locating, and making final arrangements with community services.

ECE Library

reviews the appropriateness of the placements, special services, and progress toward meeting preestablished goals to determine if the child's and family's needs are being met. This step is especially critical with infants and toddlers because their development progresses so quickly. Throughout, there must be effective communication and support among teachers, practitioners, and families to ensure that the child is receiving individually appropriate services and benefiting from the prescribed program.

# Summary

**10-1** Legislative acts have established a number of programs that address prevention, early identification, intervention services, or all three for children who have or are at risk for developmental problems. Several of the laws discussed in this chapter include:

- PL 88-452; Head Start
- PL 101-239; Early and Periodic Screening, Diagnosis, and Treatment Act (EPSDT)
- PL 94-105; Supplemental Nutrition Program for Women, Infants, and Children (WIC)
- PL 89-10; Elementary and Secondary Education Act (ESEA)
- PL 90-538; Handicapped Children's Early Education and Assistance Act (HCEEAA)
- PL 94-142 (1975); Education for All Handicapped Children Act (EHA)
- PL 99-457; Education of the Handicapped Act Amendments
- PL 101-336; Americans with Disabilities Act (ADA)
- PL 101-476; Individuals with Disabilities Education Act Amendment
- PL 105-17; Individuals with Disabilities Education Act Amendment
- PL 108-446; Individuals with Disabilities Education Improvement Act (IDEA)
- PL 107-110; No Child Left Behind Act (NCLB)

**10-2** Several challenges may be encountered when attempting to identify children who have a developmental disability or delay:

- A family may decide to ignore or delay seeking a diagnosis.
- Some developmental irregularities can be subtle in nature and difficult to observe.
- Maturational and environmental changes may cause temporary fluctuations in a child's development.
- Family values, beliefs, and cultural practices influence what is perceived to be a developmental problem.
- Children may learn to compensate for a developmental irregularity.
- Intermittent health conditions may interfere temporarily with a child's developmental progress.

**10-3** The initial step in determining if a child has a developmental problem always involves conducting multiple observations. Data collected from these observations provide a starting point for deciding what additional forms of screening or evaluation are appropriate.

continued on following page

## Summary

**10-4** A multidisciplinary team works cooperatively to obtain a well-rounded, unbiased overview of a child's developmental progress. Individual professionals administer screening tests, interpret and share results with other team members, recommend appropriate services, monitor a child's progress, and inform and support families to assure a successful outcome for the child.

## Key Terms

Child Find **p. 244**

otitis media **p. 246**

bilateral **p. 247**

achievement tests **p. 250**

developmental team **p. 251**

service coordinator **p. 252**

## Apply What You Have Learned

### A. Case Study Connections

*Reread the developmental sketch about Amita and her family presented at the beginning of this chapter and answer the following questions.*

1. Prior to holding a first conference with Amita's mother, what observations and information should her teachers gather and prepare?

2. Why is it imperative that the teachers' initial evaluation of Amita's development include a series of firsthand observations (and recorded notes) conducted in a familiar setting such as the classroom and play yard?

3. Describe three pieces of legislation discussed in this chapter that could be of benefit to a high-risk family such as Amita's.

4. What role might a service coordinator play for Amita's family, and what forms of assistance might this person provide?

### B. Review Questions

1. Identify and discuss three concerns that might prevent families from seeking help for their child.

2. What three features must be considered when determining if a screening test is appropriate for an individual child?

3. Identify and discuss three reasons why it is important to encourage family involvement in a child's intervention program.

4. Describe three factors that may complicate the early identification of a developmental problem.

5. Describe three reasons why screening test results should be interpreted with caution.

### C. Your Turn: Chapter to Practice

1. Observe a child (any age) for approximately 15 minutes with a partner. Focus on a specific behavior and use a frequency count to record your observations. Determine the reliability of your results by comparing them with your partner's.

2. Arrange to sit in on an IEP or IFSP meeting. Briefly describe the purpose of the meeting, the disciplines of team members who were present, how productive you thought the meeting was in terms of achieving the stated objectives, and your reactions to the experience.

3.  Write a public service announcement for a local television or radio station informing families of the importance of early developmental screening and where evaluations can be obtained.

4.  Select one of the screening instruments described in Appendix B and administer it to one or two children. Describe your experience, including any challenges that you encountered.

# Online Resources

## Family and Advocates Partnership for Education (FAPE)

Although funding for the FAPE project has ended, its website remains active so that families, educators, policymakers, and service providers can access information to improve outcomes for children who have disabilities. Links to new federal discipline policies and bully prevention (U.S. Department of Education) programs can be accessed here.

## Global Autism Collaboration (GAC)

More than 100 nonprofit organizations worldwide are collaborating to improve the care and intervention treatments for children and adults who experience autism spectrum disorders. Especially valuable are the overview of autism and new research studies sections posted on the website.

## National Center on Secondary Education and Transition (NCSET)

Extensive resources and technical assistance are available to help educators at the secondary and collegiate levels with supporting youth who experience disabilities. Links to national policies, research studies, a special section for youth, and additional resource organizations are provided.

## Iris Center

Anyone who works with children who have disabilities or teaches special education courses will find a wealth of resources accessible on this website, including syllabi, videos, case studies, and evidence-based practices that address important topics ranging from assessment to instructional and intervention strategies.

# References

Allen, K. E., & Cowdery, G. (2014). *The exceptional child: Inclusion in early childhood education.* 8th Ed. Belmont, CA: Wadsworth Cengage Learning.

Baker, C. (2014). African American fathers' contributions to children's early academic achievement: Evidence from two-parent families from the Early Childhood Longitudinal Study-Birth Cohort. *Early Education & Development,* 25(1), 19–35.

Ball, G., Srinivasan, L., Aljabar, P., Counsell, S., Durighel, G., Hajnal, J., ..., & Edwards, A. (2013). Development of cortical microstructure in the preterm human brain. *Proceedings of the National Academy of Sciences of the United States of America,* 110(23), 9541–9546.

Bullough, R., Hall-Kenyon, K., & MacKay, K. (2014). Head Start and the intensification of teaching in early childhood education. *Teaching and Teacher Education,* 37, 55–63.

Burgaleta, M., Johnson, W., Waber, D., Colom, R., & Karama, S. (2014). Cognitive ability changes and dynamics of cortical thickness development in healthy children and adolescents. *Neuroimage,* 84, 810–819.

Calvo, A., & Bialystok, E. (2014). Independent effects of bilingualism and socioeconomic status on language ability and executive functioning. *Cognition,* 130(3), 278–288.

Centers for Disease Control & Prevention (CDC). (2013). National prematurity awareness month. Accessed on January 23, 2014, from http://www.cdc.gov/features/prematurebirth/.

Chau, V., Synnes, A., Grunau, R., Poskitt, K., Brant, R., & Miller, S. (2013). Abnormal brain maturation in preterm neonates associated with adverse developmental outcomes. *Neurology,* 81(24), 2082–2089.

Clark, C., Fang, H., Espy, K., Filipek, Pl, Juranek, J., Bangert, B., ..., & Taylor, H. (2013). Relation of neural structure to persistently low academic achievement: A longitudinal study of children with differing birth weights. *Neuropsychology,* 27(3), 364–377.

Deakin-Bell, N., Walker, K., & Badawi, N. (2013). The accuracy of parental concern expressed in the Ages and Stages Questionnaire to predict developmental delay. *Journal of Paediatrics & Child Health*, 49(2), e133–e136.

Edwards, N., Gallagher, P., & Green, K. (2013). Existing and proposed Child Find initiatives in one state's Part C program. *Rural Special Education Quarterly*, 32(1), 11–19.

Everitt, A., Hannaford, P., & Conti-Ramsden, G. (2013). Markers for persistent specific expressive language delay in 3–4-year-olds. *International Journal of Language & Communication Disorders*, 48(5), 534–553.

Farooqi, A., Hagglof, B., & Serenius, F. (2013). Behaviours related to executive functions and learning skills at 11 years of age after extremely preterm birth: A Swedish national prospective follow-up study. *Acta Paediatrica*, 102(6), 625–634.

Gellert, A., & Elbro, C. (2013). Do experimental measures of word learning predict vocabulary development over time? A study of children from grade 3 to 4. *Learning and Individual Differences*, 26(1), 1–8.

Guevara, J., Gerdes, M., Localio, R., Huang, Y., Pinto-Martin, J., Minkovitz, C., …, & Pati, S. (2013). Effectiveness of developmental screening in an urban setting. *Pediatrics*, 131(1), 30–37.

Haertel, E. (2013). How is testing supposed to improve schooling? *Measurement: Interdisciplinary Research & Perspectives*, 11(1–2), 1–18.

Hurley, J., Warren, R., Habalow, R., Weber, L., & Tousignant, S. (2014). Early childhood special education in a refugee settlement community: Challenges and innovative practices. *Early Child Development and Care*, 184(1), 50–62.

Hutchinson, E., De Luca, C., Doyle, L., Roberts, G., & Anderson, P. (2013). School-age outcomes of extremely preterm or extremely low-birth-weight children. *Pediatrics*, 131(4), e1053–e1061, doi:10.1542/peds.2012-2311.

Jennings, D., & Hanline, M. (2013). Developmental referrals: Child and family factors that predict referral completion. *Topics in Early Childhood Special Education*, 33(2), 102–111.

Johnson, S., Hollis, C., Marlow, N., Simms, V., & Wolke, D. (2014). Screening for childhood mental health disorders using the Strengths and Difficulties Questionnaire: The validity of multi-informant reports. *Developmental Medicine & Child Neurology*. Published online on January 11, 2014, doi: 10.1111/dmcn.12360.

Kingsley, K., & Mailloux, Z. (2013). Evidence for the effectiveness of different service delivery models in early intervention services. *American Journal of Occupational Therapy*, 67(4), 431–436.

Kugelman, A., & Colin, A. (2013). Late preterm infants: Near term but still in a critical developmental time period. *Pediatrics*, 132(4), 741–751.

Lawson, G., Duda, J., Avants, B., Wu, J., & Farah, M. (2013). Associations between children's socioeconomic status and prefrontal cortical thickness. *Developmental Science*, 16(5), 641–652.

Leppanen, M., Lapinleimu, H., Lind, A., Matomaki, J., Lehtonen, L., Haataja, L., & Rautava, P. (2014). Antenatal and postnatal growth and 5-year cognitive outcome in very preterm infants. *Pediatrics*, 133(1), 63–70.

Levine, M., & Levine, A. (2013). Holding accountability accountable: A cost-benefit analysis of achievement test scores. *American Journal of Orthopsychiatry*, 83(1), 17–26.

Lowe, J., Nolen, T., Vohr, B., Adams-Chapman, I., Duncan, A., & Watterberg, K. (2013). Effect of primary language on developmental testing in children born extremely preterm. *Acta Paediatrica*, 102(9), 896–900.

Mindes, G. (2010). *Assessing young children*. 4th Ed. Upper Saddle River, NJ: Prentice Hall.

Mulligan, A., Anney, R., Butler, L., O'Regan, M., Richardson, T., Tulewicz, E., …, & Gill, M. (2013). Home environment: Association with hyperactivity/impulsivity in children with ADHD and their non-ADHD siblings. *Child: Care, Health, and Development*, 39(2), 202–212.

Nelson, B., Chung, P., Forness, S., & Pillado, O. (2013). Developmental and health services in Head Start preschools: A tiered approach to early intervention. *Academic Pediatrics*, 13(2), 145–151.

Norbury, C., & Sparks, A. (2013). Difference or disorder? Cultural issues in understanding neurodevelopmental disorders. *Developmental Psychology*, 49(1), 45–58.

Polisenska, K., & Kapalkova, S. (2014). Language profiles in children with Down syndrome and children with language impairment: Implications for early intervention. *Research in Developmental Disabilities*, 35(2), 373–382.

Rose, L., Herzig, L., & Hussey-Gardner, B. (2014). Early intervention and the role of pediatricians. *Pediatrics in Review*, 35(1), e1–e10.

Rose, J., Vassar, R., Cahill-Rowley, K., Guzman, X., Stevenson, D., & Barnea-Goraly, N. (2014). Brain microstructural development at near-term age in very-low-birth-weight preterm infants: An atlas-based diffusion imaging study. *Neuroimage*, 86(1), 244–256.

Trawick-Smith, J. (2013). *Early childhood development: A multicultural perspective*. 6th Ed. Upper Saddle River, NJ: Prentice Hall.

Turygin, N., Matson, J., Williams, L., & Belva, B. (2014). The relationship of parental first concerns and autism spectrum disorder in an early intervention sample. *Research in Autism Spectrum Disorders*, 8(2), 53–60.

Wang, P., Morgan, G., Hwang, A., & Liao, H. (2013). Individualized behavioral assessments and maternal ratings of mastery motivation in mental age-matched toddlers with and without motor delay. *Physical Therapy*, 93(1), 79–87.

Watkins, M., & Smith, L. (2013). Long-term stability of the Wechsler Intelligence Scale for Children—Fourth Edition. *Psychological Assessment*, 25(2), 477–483.

Windham, G., Smith, K., Rosen, N., Anderson, M., Grether, J., Coolman, R., & Harris, S. (2014). Autism and developmental screening in a public, primary care setting primarily serving Hispanics: Challenges and results. *Journal of Autism and Developmental Disorders*, doi 10.1007/s10803-014-2032-y.

# Appendix A

## Developmental Checklists

A simple checklist, one for each child, can be a useful tool for observing and recording children's developmental progress. Questions on the checklists that follow can be answered during the course of a child's everyday activities and over a period of one week or more. "No" answers signal that further investigation may be in order; several "No" answers indicate that additional investigation is a necessity.

The "Sometimes" category is also important. It suggests what the child can do at least part of the time or under some circumstances. The "Sometimes" category includes space where brief notes and comments about how and when a behavior occurs can be recorded. In many instances, a child just may need more practice, incentive, or adult encouragement. Hunches often provide an effective starting point for working with the child. Again, if "Sometimes" is checked a number of times, additional evaluation is recommended.

The observation checklists may be duplicated and used as part of the assessment process. They are based on detailed information provided in each of the preceding chapters. The items represent a sampling of developmental milestones associated with each approximate age. When completed, a checklist contains information that members of a developmental team will find useful in evaluating a child's progress and determining appropriate intervention strategies. However, it is important to interpret these findings cautiously and consider cultural, linguistic, and family background variations that may influence children's development.

Child's Name _____    Age _____
Observer _____    Date _____

# DEVELOPMENTAL CHECKLIST

| BY 4 to 6 MONTHS<br><br>Does the child . . . | Yes | No | Sometimes |
|---|---|---|---|
| Show continued gains in height, weight, and head circumference? | | | |
| Exhibit a blink reflex? | | | |
| Begin to roll from stomach to back? | | | |
| Raise up on hands and knees? Begin to crawl? | | | |
| Babble, coo, and imitate sounds (*ba, ba; da, da*)? | | | |
| Turn to locate the source of a sound? | | | |
| Focus on an object and follow its movement vertically and horizontally? | | | |
| Rise up on arms, lifting head and chest, when placed on stomach? | | | |
| Sit with minimal support? | | | |
| Stop crying and relax when held and cuddled? | | | |
| Recognize and respond to familiar faces? | | | |
| Reach for toys or objects when they are presented? | | | |
| Transfer objects from one hand to the other? Put toys in mouth? | | | |
| Use a pincer grip to pick up food pieces and small items? | | | |
| Smile, babble, and laugh out loud? | | | |
| Begin sleeping six to eight hours through the night? | | | |
| Suck vigorously when it is time to eat? | | | |
| Enjoy (splash, coo) playing in water during bath time? | | | |

**Note:** Cultural differences may alter the timetable when some developmental skills are acquired, and should be taken into consideration.

**TeachSource Digital Download**

Child's Name _____   Age _____

Observer _____   Date _____

# DEVELOPMENTAL CHECKLIST

| BY 12 MONTHS<br><br>Does the child . . . | Yes | No | Sometimes |
|---|---|---|---|
| Walk with assistance? | | | |
| Roll a ball in imitation of an adult? | | | |
| Pick objects up with thumb and forefinger? | | | |
| Transfer objects from one hand to the other? | | | |
| Pick up dropped toys? | | | |
| Look directly at an adult's face? | | | |
| Imitate gestures: peek-a-boo, bye-bye, pat-a-cake? | | | |
| Find an object hidden under a cup? | | | |
| Feed himself or herself crackers (munching, not sucking on them)? | | | |
| Hold a cup with two hands; drink with assistance? | | | |
| Smile spontaneously? | | | |
| Turn head or come when name is called? | | | |
| Respond to "no" and "come"? | | | |
| Show hesitation with strangers; want to be picked up only by familiar persons? | | | |
| Respond differently to sounds: vacuum, phone, doorbell? | | | |
| Look at a person who speaks to him or her? | | | |
| Respond to simple directions accompanied by gestures? | | | |
| Make several consonant–vowel combination sounds? | | | |
| Vocalize back to a person who is talking? | | | |
| Use intonation patterns that sound like scolding, asking, exclaiming? | | | |
| Say "da-da" or "ma-ma"? | | | |

**Note:** Cultural differences may alter the timetable when some developmental skills are acquired, and should be taken into consideration.

Child's Name _____    Age _____

Observer _____    Date _____

# DEVELOPMENTAL CHECKLIST

| BY 2 YEARS<br><br>Does the child . . . | Yes | No | Sometimes |
|---|---|---|---|
| Walk alone? | | | |
| Bend over and pick up a toy without falling over? | | | |
| Climb up and sit in a child-size chair? | | | |
| Walk up and down stairs with assistance? | | | |
| Place several rings on a stick? | | | |
| Place five pegs in a pegboard? | | | |
| Turn pages two or three at a time? | | | |
| Hold a marker in a fist and scribble? | | | |
| Follow a one-step direction involving something familiar:<br>    "Give me ___"<br>    "Show me ___"<br>    "Get a ___"? | | | |
| Match familiar objects? | | | |
| Use a spoon with some spilling? | | | |
| Drink from a cup unassisted, holding it with one hand? | | | |
| Take off coat, shoes, socks? | | | |
| Zip and unzip a large zipper? | | | |
| Name and point to self in a mirror? | | | |
| Refer to self by name? | | | |
| Imitate adult behavior in play (e.g., feeds "baby," shaves, cooks)? | | | |
| Help to put things away? | | | |
| Respond to specific words by showing what was named: toy, pet, family member? | | | |
| Ask for desired items by name: ("cookie")? | | | |
| Name an object when asked "What's that?" | | | |
| Make and maintain eye contact when asking or responding to questions? | | | |
| Utter some two-word statements: "Daddy bye-bye"? | | | |

**Note:** Cultural differences may alter the timetable when some developmental skills are acquired, and should be taken into consideration.

Child's Name _____  Age _____

Observer _____  Date _____

# DEVELOPMENTAL CHECKLIST

| BY 3 YEARS | Yes | No | Sometimes |
|---|---|---|---|
| **Does the child . . .** | | | |
| Run with coordination in a forward direction; avoid running into objects or people? | | | |
| Jump in place, two feet together? | | | |
| Walk heel to toe (not on tiptoe)? | | | |
| Throw a ball (but without direction or aim)? | | | |
| Kick a ball forward? | | | |
| String four large beads? | | | |
| Turn pages in book singly? | | | |
| Hold a crayon: imitate circular, vertical, horizontal strokes? | | | |
| Match shapes? | | | |
| Demonstrate number concepts of 1 and 2? (Can select 1 or 2; can tell if there are one or two objects.) | | | |
| Use a spoon without spilling? | | | |
| Drink from a straw? | | | |
| Put on and take off coat? | | | |
| Wash and dry hands with some assistance? | | | |
| Watch other children; play near them; sometimes join in their play? | | | |
| Defend own possessions? | | | |
| Use symbols in play (basket placed on head becomes a helmet, crate turns into a spaceship)? | | | |
| Respond to "Put ___ in the box," "Take the ___ out of the box"? | | | |
| Select the correct item on request (big versus little; one versus two)? | | | |
| Identify objects by their use (show their own shoes when asked "What do you wear on your feet?")? | | | |
| Ask questions and make eye contact? | | | |
| Tell about something with functional phrases that carry meaning ("Daddy go airplane," "Me hungry now")? | | | |

**Note:** Cultural differences may alter the timetable when some developmental skills are acquired, and should be taken into consideration.

Child's Name _____   Age _____

Observer _____   Date _____

# DEVELOPMENTAL CHECKLIST

| BY 4 YEARS | Yes | No | Sometimes |
|---|---|---|---|
| **Does the child . . .** | | | |
| Walk in a straight line? | | | |
| Balance on one foot briefly? Hop on one foot? | | | |
| Jump over an object six inches high and land on both feet together? | | | |
| Throw a ball with direction? | | | |
| Copy circles and Xs? | | | |
| Match six colors? | | | |
| Count to 5? | | | |
| Pour well from a pitcher? | | | |
| Spread butter or jam with a knife? | | | |
| Button and unbutton large buttons? | | | |
| State own gender, age, last name? | | | |
| Use the toilet independently and when needed? | | | |
| Wash and dry hands unassisted? | | | |
| Listen to stories for at least five minutes? | | | |
| Draw the head of a person and at least one other body part? | | | |
| Play with other children? | | | |
| Share and take turns (with some assistance)? | | | |
| Engage in dramatic and pretend play? | | | |
| Respond appropriately to "Put it beside," "Put it under"? | | | |
| Respond to two-step directions: "Give me the sweater and put the shoe on the floor"? | | | |
| Respond by selecting the correct object (hard versus soft object)? | | | |
| Answer "if," "what," and "when" questions? | | | |
| Answer questions about function: "What are books for?" | | | |
| Make and maintain eye contact? | | | |

**Note:** Cultural differences may alter the timetable when some developmental skills are acquired, and should be taken into consideration.

Child's Name _____ Age _____

Observer _____ Date _____

# DEVELOPMENTAL CHECKLIST

| BY 5 YEARS | Yes | No | Sometimes |
|---|---|---|---|
| **Does the child . . .** | | | |
| Walk backward, toe to heel? | | | |
| Walk up and down stairs, alternating feet? | | | |
| Cut on a designated line? | | | |
| Print some letters? | | | |
| Point to and name three shapes? | | | |
| Group common related objects: shoe, sock, and foot; apple, orange, and plum? | | | |
| Demonstrate number concepts to 4 or 5? | | | |
| Cut food with a knife: celery, a sandwich? | | | |
| Lace shoes? | | | |
| Read from a picture storybook (tell a story by looking at pictures)? | | | |
| Draw a person with three to six body parts? | | | |
| Play and interact with other children; engage in dramatic play that is close to reality? | | | |
| Build complex structures with blocks or other building materials? | | | |
| Respond to simple three-step directions: "Give me the pencil, put the book on the table, and put your feet on the floor"? | | | |
| Respond correctly when asked to show a penny, nickel, and dime? | | | |
| Ask "How" questions? | | | |
| Respond verbally to "Hi" and "How are you?" | | | |
| Describe an event using past and future tenses? | | | |
| Use conjunctions to string words and phrases together ("I saw a bear and a zebra and a giraffe at the zoo")? | | | |
| Show interest in trying new things? | | | |
| Dress self with minimal assistance? | | | |

**Note:** Cultural differences may alter the timetable when some developmental skills are acquired, and should be taken into consideration.

Child's Name _____ Age _____

Observer _____ Date _____

# DEVELOPMENTAL CHECKLIST

| BY 6 YEARS<br>Does the child . . . | Yes | No | Sometimes |
|---|---|---|---|
| Walk across a balance beam? | | | |
| Skip with alternating feet? | | | |
| Hop for several seconds on one foot? | | | |
| Cut out simple shapes? | | | |
| Copy his or her own first name? | | | |
| Show well-established handedness; demonstrate consistent right- or left-handedness? | | | |
| Sort objects on one or more dimensions (color, shape, or function)? | | | |
| Name most letters and numerals? | | | |
| Count by rote to 10; know what number comes next? | | | |
| Dress self completely; tie bows? | | | |
| Brush teeth unassisted? | | | |
| Have some concept of clock time in relation to daily schedule? | | | |
| Cross street safely, holding an adult's hand? | | | |
| Draw a person with head, trunk, legs, arms, and features; often add clothing details? | | | |
| Play simple board games? | | | |
| Engage in cooperative play with other children; participate in group decisions, role assignments, and rule observance? | | | |
| Use construction toys such as Legos and blocks to make recognizable structures? | | | |
| Do fifteen-piece puzzles? | | | |
| Use all grammatical structures: pronouns, plurals, verb tenses, conjunctions? | | | |
| Carry on conversations using complex sentences? | | | |

**Note:** Cultural differences may alter the timetable when some developmental skills are acquired, and should be taken into consideration.

**TeachSource Digital Download**

Child's Name _____  Age _____

Observer _____  Date _____

# DEVELOPMENTAL CHECKLIST

| BY 7 YEARS | Yes | No | Sometimes |
|---|---|---|---|
| **Does the child . . .** | | | |
| Continue to grow in height and weight? | | | |
| Exhibit good balance? Walk across a balance beam? | | | |
| Use a pencil and scissors with reasonable skill? | | | |
| Catch a tennis ball? | | | |
| Hit a ball with a bat? | | | |
| Reproduce words and numbers with reasonable skill? | | | |
| Concentrate on completing puzzles and board games? | | | |
| Ask many questions? | | | |
| Use correct verb tenses, word order, and sentence structure in conversation? | | | |
| Correctly identify right and left hands? Days of the week? | | | |
| Make friends easily? | | | |
| Show some control of anger, using words instead of physical aggression? | | | |
| Participate in play that requires teamwork and rule observance? | | | |
| Seek adult approval for efforts? | | | |
| Enjoy reading and being read to? | | | |
| Sleep undisturbed through the night? | | | |
| Plan and carry out simple projects with minimal adult help? | | | |
| Show some understanding of cause-and-effect concepts? | | | |
| Draw pictures with greater detail and sense of proportion? | | | |
| Care for own personal needs with some adult supervision? Wash hands? Brush teeth? Use toilet? Dress self? Tie own shoes? | | | |

**Note:** Cultural differences may alter the timetable when some developmental skills are acquired, and should be taken into consideration.

Child's Name _____   Age _____

Observer _____   Date _____

# DEVELOPMENTAL CHECKLIST

| BY 8 YEARS | Yes | No | Sometimes |
|---|---|---|---|
| **Does the child . . .** | | | |
| Have energy to play? | | | |
| Continue to grow and experience few illnesses? | | | |
| Have a good appetite? Show interest in trying new foods? | | | |
| Use a pencil in a deliberate and controlled manner? | | | |
| Use eating utensils with ease? | | | |
| Express relatively complex thoughts in a clear and logical fashion? | | | |
| Carry out multiple four- or five-step instructions? | | | |
| Become less easily frustrated with his or her own performance? | | | |
| Interact and play cooperatively with other children? | | | |
| Show interest in creative expression (telling stories, jokes, writing, drawing, singing)? | | | |
| Know how to tell time? | | | |
| Read and comprehend the story? | | | |
| Participate in some group activities (games, sports, choir)? | | | |
| Want to go to school? Seem disappointed if he or she must miss a day? | | | |
| Demonstrate beginning skills in reading, writing, and mathematics? | | | |
| Accept responsibility and complete work independently? | | | |
| Handle stressful situations without becoming overly upset or aggressive? | | | |

**Note:** Cultural differences may alter the timetable when some developmental skills are acquired, and should be taken into consideration.

**TeachSource Digital Download**

Child's Name _____   Age _____

Observer _____   Date _____

# DEVELOPMENTAL CHECKLIST

| BY 9 AND 10 YEARS | Yes | No | Sometimes |
|---|---|---|---|
| **Does the child . . .** | | | |
| Continue to gain in height and weight? | | | |
| Exhibit improving coordination (running, climbing, riding a bike, writing)? | | | |
| Handle stressful situations without losing control or becoming overly upset or violent? | | | |
| Construct sentences using reasonably correct grammar (nouns, adverbs, verbs, adjectives)? | | | |
| Understand concepts of time, distance, space, volume? | | | |
| Express thoughts clearly? | | | |
| Understand simple abstract concepts? | | | |
| Have one or two "best friends"? | | | |
| Maintain friendships over time? | | | |
| Approach challenges with a reasonable degree of self-confidence? | | | |
| Play cooperatively and follow group instructions? | | | |
| Begin to show an understanding of moral standards (right from wrong, fairness, honesty, good from bad)? | | | |
| Look forward to and enjoy school most days? | | | |
| Appear to hear well, listen attentively, respond appropriately? | | | |
| Enjoy reasonably good health with few episodes of illness or health-related complaints? | | | |
| Have a good appetite and enjoy mealtimes? | | | |
| Take care of own personal hygiene without assistance? | | | |
| Sleep through the night, waking up refreshed and energetic? | | | |

**Note:** Cultural differences may alter the timetable when some developmental skills are acquired, and should be taken into consideration.

Child's Name _____ Age _____

Observer _____ Date _____

# DEVELOPMENTAL CHECKLIST

| BY 11 AND 12 YEARS | Yes | No | Sometimes |
|---|---|---|---|
| **Does the child . . .** | | | |
| Continue to grow (gain in height and maintain a healthy weight, not too thin or too heavy)? | | | |
| Understand changes associated with puberty or have an opportunity to learn and ask questions? | | | |
| Have good vision or wear glasses; not complain of headaches or blurred vision? | | | |
| Have straight posture (no curving of the spine or other abnormality)? | | | |
| Seem energetic and not chronically fatigued? | | | |
| Remain focused on tasks and complete assignments? | | | |
| Remember and carry out complex instructions? | | | |
| Sequence, order, and classify objects? | | | |
| Use longer and more complex sentence structure? | | | |
| Engage in conversation; tell jokes and riddles? | | | |
| Enjoy playing organized games and team sports? | | | |
| Respond to anger-invoking situations without resorting to violence or physical aggression? | | | |
| Begin to understand and solve complex mathematical problems? | | | |
| Accept blame for actions on most occasions? | | | |
| Participate in, and enjoy, competitive activities? | | | |
| Make and keep friends? | | | |
| Accept and carry out responsibility in a dependable manner? | | | |
| Go to bed willingly and wake up refreshed? | | | |
| Take pride in personal appearance and hygiene? | | | |

**Note:** Cultural differences may alter the timetable when some developmental skills are acquired, and should be taken into consideration.

Child's Name _____ Age _____

Observer _____ Date _____

# DEVELOPMENTAL CHECKLIST

| BY 13 AND 14 YEARS | Yes | No | Sometimes |
|---|---|---|---|
| **Does the child . . .** | | | |
| Continue to experience growth and changes associated with puberty? | | | |
| Have sufficient energy to participate in school and extracurricular activities? | | | |
| Demonstrate improved hand–eye coordination? | | | |
| Think through situations and anticipate the potential outcomes and/or consequences? | | | |
| Like school and show interest in learning new material? | | | |
| Plan and manage time wisely; complete homework and projects on time? | | | |
| Understand right from wrong and accept responsibility for own behavior? | | | |
| Begin to develop empathy and consider others' viewpoints and perspectives? | | | |
| Read and comprehend material? | | | |
| Express thoughts and ideas clearly? | | | |
| Work cooperatively with classmates on projects? | | | |
| Have friends and do things with them outside of school? | | | |
| Understand and engage in humorous antics and interactions? | | | |
| Approach daily activities and unfamiliar tasks with reasonable self-confidence? | | | |
| Get adequate sleep (8–9 hours) and appear well rested? | | | |
| Take pride in personal cleanliness and appearance most of the time? | | | |
| Maintain a healthy weight and consume a nutritious diet? | | | |

**Note:** Cultural differences may alter the timetable when some developmental skills are acquired, and should be taken into consideration.

Child's Name _____    Age _____

Observer _____    Date _____

# DEVELOPMENTAL CHECKLIST

| BY 15 AND 16 YEARS<br><br>Does the child . . . | Yes | No | Sometimes |
|---|---|---|---|
| Continue to gain and exhibit self-confidence? | | | |
| Make and keep friends who have a positive influence on behavior? | | | |
| Set and achieve established goals? | | | |
| Understand complex problems and cause–effect relationships? | | | |
| Communicate and express ideas logically? | | | |
| Take pride in personal accomplishments? | | | |
| Exhibit good hand-eye coordination? | | | |
| Make independent decisions and follow through? | | | |
| Express emotions and resolve conflicts in a healthy manner? | | | |
| Develop improved emotional control and stability? Limit impulsivity and aggression? | | | |
| Show interest in school and extracurricular activities? | | | |
| Experience relatively good health (infrequent illness, energetic, maintain an appropriate weight)? | | | |
| Respect limits and rules set by adults (on most occasions)? | | | |
| Have a trusted and supportive adult with whom to talk? | | | |
| Avoid peer pressure to engage in drugs and alcohol? | | | |
| Use appropriate protective gear when participating in sports, outdoor activities, or work? | | | |

**Note:** Cultural differences may alter the timetable when some developmental skills are acquired, and should be taken into consideration.

**TeachSource Digital Download**

Child's Name _____   Age _____

Observer _____   Date _____

# DEVELOPMENTAL CHECKLIST

| BY 17 AND 18 YEARS | Yes | No | Sometimes |
|---|---|---|---|
| **Does the child . . .** | | | |
| Make independent decisions and assume personal responsibility for outcomes? | | | |
| Set realistic goals and take steps to achieve them? | | | |
| Have and acknowledge a clear sexual identity? | | | |
| Demonstrate effective work and study habits? | | | |
| Use analytical thinking to solve complex problems? | | | |
| Express ideas with clarity and logical thought? Answer questions appropriately? | | | |
| Have a positive outlook on life? | | | |
| Exhibit emotional stability and decreased conflict with family? | | | |
| Seek advice appropriately? | | | |
| Show initiative in achieving independence from family? | | | |
| Maintain a healthy lifestyle (diet, activity, sleep, safety)? | | | |
| Demonstrate moral maturity in social behaviors? | | | |
| Possess problem-solving, communication, and intellectual skills and use them when confronted with adversity? | | | |
| Demonstrate functional reading and writing skills? | | | |
| Attend school consistently? | | | |
| Experience good health and relatively few illnesses? | | | |

**Note:** Cultural differences may alter the timetable when some developmental skills are acquired, and should be taken into consideration.

**TeachSource Digital Download**

# Appendix B

## Selected Screening and Assessment Instruments

## EXAMPLES OF SCREENING TESTS

*Ages and Stages Questionnaires (ASQ-3)* is a monitoring system for assessing children's development in five areas: communication, personal-social, problem-solving, fine motor, and gross motor. Questionnaires are available for children 4, 6, 8, 10, 12, 14, 16, 18, 20, 22, 24, 27, 30, 33, 36, 42, 48, 54, and 60 months of age. Families complete the questionnaires based on their observations, including language development and behaviors that may be early autism indicators. Forms require two to three minutes to score. Versions of the questionnaires are available in Spanish, French, Korean, and other languages.

*GS Early Screening Profiles (ESP)* test children two to seven years of age for cognitive, language, social, self-help, and motor skills; includes information provided by families, teachers, and child care providers.

*Battelle Developmental Screening Test* is a screening tool that includes 96 items from the Battelle Developmental Inventory that can be used to assess children (from birth to eight years) in five domains: communication, cognitive, personal-social, motor, and adaptive. This instrument is effective for assessing typical development, school readiness, and identification of children with disabilities.

*Beck Depression Inventory-Second Edition (BDI-II)* provides a quick screening test for identifying depression in adolescents and adults and rating its severity (number values are assigned to the adolescent's responses).

*Denver Developmental Screening Test (Denver II)* is appropriate for testing children from two weeks to six years of age in four developmental areas: personal-social, language, fine motor, and gross motor. Ratings of the child's behavior during testing can be recorded. Available in English and Spanish.

*Developmental Activities Screening Inventory (DASI II)* screens children from one month to five years old; a nonverbal test especially useful for children with hearing or language disorders; adaptations for children with vision problems are also offered.

*Developmental Indicators for the Assessment of Learning™, 4th Edition (DIAL™-4)* is designed for screening individual children ages three to six years, eleven months, in five developmental domains: motor, concepts, communication, self-help, and social-emotional. The test requires approximately 30 to 45 minutes to administer. A Spanish-language version is available. *Speed DIAL-4* is an abbreviated version of the test that includes items for motor, language, and concept development and can be administered in less than 15 minutes.

*First Steps: Screening Test for Evaluating Preschoolers* can be used with children from two years, nine months to six years, two months on cognitive, communication, and motor skills; an Adaptive Behavior Checklist and a Social-Emotional Scale are included, as well as a Parent–Teacher Scale related to the child's behavior at home and at school. The test takes approximately 15 minutes to administer.

# EXAMPLES OF ASSESSMENT INSTRUMENTS

*APGAR Scoring System* is administered at one minute and again at five minutes after birth; the APGAR assesses muscle tone, respiration, color, heartbeat, and reflexes for a maximum score of 10. The information is used to determine which infants may require special care.

*Assessment, Evaluation, and Programming Systems (AEPS) for Infants and Children, 2nd Edition* (volume 2, birth to three, three to six; volumes 3 and 4, curriculum interventions for birth to three, three to six) is an authentic, family-friendly system for assessing very young children. The activity-based test covers six developmental domains (e.g., fine motor, gross motor, cognitive, social, social-communication, and adaptive) and can be used with children who have disabilities or are at risk for developmental delays. It ties together assessment outcomes and early intervention strategies that are activity-based and family-centered. Test results can be used to determine a child's eligibility for intervention services, establish IEP/IFSP goals, and evaluate intervention effectiveness.

*Audiology*, that is, hearing assessment of infants and children, requires clinical testing by a trained technician. It is *imperative*, however, in terms of early identification, for teachers and families to record and report their observations whenever they suspect a child is not hearing well. Warning signs include:

- Pulling or banging on an ear
- Drainage from the ear canal
- Failing to respond or looking puzzled when spoken to
- Requesting frequent repetitions—What? Huh?
- Speaking in too loud or too soft of a voice
- Articulating or discriminating sounds poorly

*Bayley Scales of Infant and Toddler Development III Assessment®* (Bailey-III®) is used to evaluate all developmental areas: cognitive, motor, language, social-emotional, adaptive, and behavior. The age range has been expanded to cover children from one month to three years, six months.

*Brigance Inventory of Early Development®III (IED-III®)* is a criterion-referenced instrument for assessing children, birth through seven years, in multiple developmental domains: fine and gross motor, speech and language, knowledge and comprehension, self-help, and pre-academic skills (basic reading, mathematics, and writing readiness). Test results can be used for assessing school readiness, goal setting and curriculum planning, and a child's progress toward achieving early learning standards, but they are not intended for determining a child's eligibility for special services.

*Child Behavior Checklist (CBCL)* is a standardized rating scale commonly used to assess children for emotional, social, and behavioral problems (e.g., aggression, defiance, attention deficit, anxious-depressed, or withdrawn). Two versions of the test are available—one for two- to three-year-olds and another for four- to eighteen-year-olds. Parents rate the child on 100 items, which are then scored and used to develop a behavioral profile. A *Teacher's Report Form* and *Youth Self-Report Form* also are available.

*Environmental Rating Scales* are available in four versions: *Early Childhood Environment Rating Scale-Revised (ECERS-R); Infant-Toddler Environmental Scale-Revised (ITERS-R); Family Child Care Environmental Rating Scales-Revised (FCCERS-R);* and *School-Age Care Environmental Rating Scales (SACERS-R).* These well-respected, culturally sensitive assessment tools can be used to evaluate classroom environment quality, including space, materials, learning activities, schedules, health and safety, communication, program structure, and family/staff interaction.

*Hawaii Early Learning Profile (HELP)* is a user- and family-friendly assessment instrument designed for evaluating, developing play-based interventions, and monitoring the developmental progress of children (birth through age three). Developmental milestones for each of the six domains are outlined on an easy-to-read chart. Domains are aligned with Head Start, Office of Special Education, and school readiness goals. HELP fosters an interdisciplinary and family-centered approach.

*Home Observation for Measurement of the Environment (HOME)* is the best-known and most widely used in-home inventory to assess the quality and quantity of stimulation and support a child receives at home. Several versions are available: infant/toddler (0–3 years), early childhood (3–6 years), middle childhood (6–10 years), early adolescent (10–15 years), child care, and disability. Each version assesses the physical environment, as well as the social, emotional, and cognitive support available to the child. A modified version, *Supplement to the HOME for Impoverished Families (SHIF),* is available for assessing the home environment of children who live in poverty.

*Kaufman Assessment Battery for Children, 2nd Edition (KABC-II),* is a "culturally fair" test developed to assess the cognitive abilities of children ages three to eighteen years. Test items are designed to minimize the effects of verbal, gender, and ethnic bias.

*Kaufman Survey of Early Academic and Language Skills (K-SEALS)* is used to assess children's (3–7 years) receptive and expressive language skills, as well as concepts related to numbers, counting, letters, and words. In addition, the test can be used to identify children who are gifted, school readiness, and program effectiveness.

*Learning Accomplishment Profile—Diagnostic Edition (LAP-D)* is a norm-referenced test that can be used to assess children aged two years, six months to six years on fine motor (writing and manipulative skills), gross motor (body and object movement), matching and counting (viewed as cognitive tasks), and language skills (comprehension and object naming). The instrument can be used with children whose development is typical or atypical.

*Learning Accomplishment Profile—Revised (LAP-3)* is a criterion-referenced instrument designed to assess children's development across seven domains (e.g., language, gross motor, fine motor, cognitive, prewriting, self-help, and social-emotional). A modified version, the *Early Learning Accomplishment Profile (E-LAP),* is available for use with children whose functional development ranges from birth to three years.

*Minnesota Multiphasic Personality Inventory®—Adolescent (MMPI®-A)* is used to evaluate adolescents for a variety of mental health disorders, including family conflict, substance abuse, defiant behavior, and depression.

*Neonatal Behavioral Assessment Scale (NBAS),* developed by Dr. T. Berry Brazelton and often referred to simply as the *Brazelton,* is used for evaluating behavioral responses in full-term infants up to two months of age. A significant modification of the NBAS is the *Kansas Supplement (NBAS-K).* It adds a number of critical parameters, as well as assessing the infant's typical behavior (state) and optimal behavior (the only focus of the original NBAS).

*Peabody Developmental Motor Scales (PDMS-2)* are used to evaluate children from birth through five years of age in fine motor (e.g., grasping, eye–hand coordination, and manual dexterity) and gross motor development (e.g., reflexes, balance, locomotion, throwing, and catching). Strategies for remediation are also included.

*Peabody Picture Vocabulary Test, 4th Edition (PPVT-IV),* is a norm-referenced test that can be administered in 10–15 minutes to assess receptive language and verbal ability; appropriate for use with children thirty months and older. A Spanish version is also available.

*Preschool Language Scale-5 (PLS™-5)* can be used to assess the language skills (e.g., auditory comprehension, articulation, grammatical forms, and basic concept development) of children from birth to age seven years and eleven months. A Spanish version based on cultural variations is also available.

*Temperament and Atypical Behavior Scale (TABS)* is a screening instrument that can be used to identify children 11–71 months for potential or existing problematic behaviors related to temperament and/or self-regulation. Test results can be used to determine eligibility for special intervention services, for developing remediation programs, and to help families manage children's challenging behavior.

The *Snellen E* or *Illiterate E* eye test is an instrument commonly used for assessing young children's visual acuity (knowing the alphabet is not required). Observation of the following behavioral indicators also plays an important role in identifying children who may have a vision problem:

- Rubbing eyes frequently, or closing or covering one eye
- Constantly stumbling over or running into things
- Complaining of frequent headaches
- Blinking excessively when looking at books or reading
- Brushing hand over eyes as if trying to get rid of a blur

Healthy eye development has important long-term implications. A nationwide public health program called InfantSEE® was initiated in 2005 to promote early detection and treatment of vision problems. Infants can receive free screening and eye care provided by participating optometrists. The following observations are also useful for noting early signs of potential vision problems:

- Observing the infant's ability to focus on an object
- Watching for uncoordinated eye movements such as crossed or wandering eyes
- Checking for a blink reflex
- Seeing if the infant can visually follow (track) an object, such as a toy, as it is moved in a 180-degree arc

*Woodcock-Johnson® III Normative Update (NU) of Cognitive Abilities* can be used to assess the cognitive abilities of children and adolescents and to identify learning disabilities.

*Work Sampling System®, 4th Edition* (WSS), is a unique approach for documenting authentic and ongoing evaluation of children's developmental progress; it uses a combination of portfolio development (with samples of child's work) and checklists for data collection. Assessments are conducted three times during the course of a year and provide teachers with feedback on effective instructional strategies, as well as on how children are responding; appropriate for children preschool through grade six.

# Appendix C

# Resources for Families and Professionals

Many resources are available to families, teachers, and service providers who work with children. These resources are provided at the community, state, and national levels and fall into two major categories: direct services and information sources.

## DIRECT SERVICES

Developmental screenings are available through a number of local agencies and organizations. In addition, most communities offer an array of services and programs designed to help families cope with and meet the special needs and challenges of caring for a child with developmental disabilities. Some agencies also provide technical assistance to educators and other professionals who are working with these children. Often, the agencies themselves serve as a valuable networking resource because they are familiar with other community-based services, assistance programs, and trained specialists.

### Examples of Community Services and Resources for Families

- Child Find screening programs
- Interagency Coordinating Councils (ICCs)
- Early childhood centers and therapeutic programs for exceptional children
- Public health departments at the city, county, and state levels
- Local public school districts, especially the special services divisions
- Hospitals, medical centers, and well-child clinics
- University-Affiliated Programs (UAPs)
- Head Start and Even Start programs
- Mental health centers
- State-supported, low-cost health insurance for children
- Parent support groups
- Service groups that provide respite care, transportation, or financial assistance
- Marriage counseling programs
- Philanthropic organizations such as the Lion's Club (glasses), Shriners, and Make a Wish Foundation

- Professional practitioners: pediatricians, nurses, psychologists, audiologists, ophthalmologists, early childhood specialists, educators, speech-language therapists, occupational and physical therapists, and social workers

## Examples of National and Professional Organizations

There are also many national organizations that offer extensive information, as well as direct assistance, to children and families with specific needs. Contact information can usually be found in local telephone directories, the *Encyclopedia of Associations* (which you can find at the library), or on the Internet. For example:

- Allergy and Asthma Foundation of America (AAFA)
- American Council of the Blind (ACB)
- American Diabetes Association (ADA)
- American Foundation of the Blind (AFB)
- American Heart Association (AHA)
- American Society for Deaf Children (ASDC)
- Autism Society of America
- Children's Craniofacial Association (CCA)
- Cleft Palate Foundation (CPF)
- Council for Exceptional Children (CEC)
- Epilepsy Foundation of America (EFA)
- National Association for Down Syndrome (NADS)
- National Center for Learning Disabilities (NCLD)
- National Easter Seals
- United States Cerebral Palsy Athletic Association (USCPAA)

## Examples of Technical Assistance Programs

In addition, there are many programs and organizations whose purpose is to provide direct technical assistance to educational programs and agencies serving children with developmental disabilities. Many of these groups also offer instructional material. A sample of such agencies includes:

- *American Printing House for the Blind.* This group produces materials and services for children with visual impairments, including talking books, magazines in Braille, and large-type books, as well as materials intended for educators of blind or visually impaired children.

- *Positive Behavioral Interventions and Supports.* This center, established by the Office of Special Education, assists schools in creating environments that promote positive behavior for all children, especially children who have disabilities. Attention is also focused on providing family support and establishing community advocacy.

- *Head Start Resource Access Projects (RAPs).* Their purpose is to assist Head Start programs in providing comprehensive services to children with developmental problems.

- *National Early Childhood Technical Assistance Center (NECTAC)*. This agency provides many forms of assistance to federally funded early childhood programs serving children with disabilities and helps them implement the services mandated by the Individuals with Disabilities Education Act (IDEA).

- *National Dissemination Center for Children with Disabilities*. This organization serves as a central source for information about disabilities, early intervention, research, law, and parent materials. A bilingual site also is provided.

- *National Technical Assistance Center for Children's Mental Health*. Information, training, and technical assistance are available to programs serving children and youth. The center's goal is to provide assistance to programs in improving mental health outcomes for children and their families.

# INFORMATION SOURCES

Extensive information is also published for families, teachers, and professionals who work with children who have developmental problems. Many professional journals, government publications, CD-ROMs, and reference books are available in public and university libraries. Special-interest groups and professional organizations also offer printed and online material focused on high-risk children and youth who have developmental delays.

## Selected Examples of Information Resources

- Professional journals and periodicals, such as the *Journal of the Division for Early Childhood, Topics in Early Childhood Special Education, Young Exceptional Children, Teaching Exceptional Children, Child Development, Developmental Psychology, Early Childhood Research Quarterly, Early Childhood Digest, Journal of Adolescent Research, Journal of Learning Disabilities,* and *Young Children.*

- Trade magazines for families, such as *Parents of Exceptional Children, Parenting,* and *Parents.*

- Government documents, reports, and pamphlets. These cover almost any topic related to child development, child care, early intervention, nutrition, parenting, and specific developmental problems. Publications can be obtained through the Superintendent of Documents, U.S. Government Printing Office, Washington, D.C., 20401; many are available in local government buildings, in public libraries, and on the Internet.

- Bibliographic indexes and abstracts usually located in university, college, and large public libraries. These are particularly useful to students and practitioners who need to locate information quickly on a specific topic. Examples of these include the following:

  - *Review of Child Development*

  - *Current Topics in Early Childhood Education*

  - Electronic journals and serials, such as *Early Childhood Research & Practice, Child Development Perspectives, Networks* (an online journal for teacher research), *Parent News, Contemporary Issues in Early Childhood, Future of Children, Health Child Care,* and *Bulletin of the World Association of Early Childhood Educators*

## Examples of Professional Organizations that Focus on Child and Adolescent Issues

- American Academy of Pediatrics (AAP)
- American Association on Intellectual and Developmental Disabilities (AAIDD)
- American Public Health Association (APHA)
- American Speech, Language, Hearing Association (ASHA)
- Association for Childhood Education International (ACEI)
- The Arc of the United States
- Center for Effective Collaboration and Practice (CECP)
- Center for Mental Health in Schools (CMHS)
- Child Care Aware®
- Children's Defense Fund (CDF)
- Council for Exceptional Children (CEC)
- Early Childhood Resource Center (ECRC)
- Early Head Start (EHS) National Resource Center
- March of Dimes (MOD)
- National Association for the Education of Young Children (NAEYC)
- National Association for Family Child Care (NAFCC)
- National Center for Cultural Competence (NCCC)
- National Head Start Association (NHSA)
- National Parent Information Network (NPIN)
- Positive Behavioral Interventions and Supports (PBIS)
- Special Olympics

# CONCLUSION

Finding help for children with developmental delays and disabilities is not a simple matter. The issues are often complex; some children present tangles of interrelated developmental problems that tend to become more complex when not addressed during the crucial first five years of life. Therefore, effective intervention must begin early and be comprehensive, integrated, ongoing, and family-centered. It also must take into account multiple developmental areas at the same time. This effort requires teamwork on the part of specialists from many disciplines, service providers, and agencies working cooperatively with the child and family. It also requires an awareness of legislative acts and public policies that affect services for children with developmental problems and their families, as well as available resources and effective means of collaboration. Only then will children and families fully benefit from an early intervention team approach.

# Glossary

## A

**abstract**   The ability to think and use concepts; an idea or theory. *p. 200*

**achievement tests**   Tests used to measure a child's academic progress (what the child has learned). *p. 250*

**amniocentesis**   Genetic-screening procedure in which a needle is inserted through the mother's abdomen into the sac of fluids surrounding the fetus to detect abnormalities such as Down syndrome or spina bifida; usually performed between the twelfth and sixteenth weeks. *p. 55*

**analytical thinking**   A cognitive process used when attempting to solve problems or make plans; identifying and evaluating the pros and cons of alternative solutions. *p. 229*

**anencephaly**   A birth defect resulting in malformation of the skull and brain; portions of these structures might be missing at birth. *p. 52*

**at risk**   A term describing children who may be more likely to have developmental problems due to certain predisposing factors such as low birth weight (LBW), neglect, or maternal drug addiction. *p. 11*

**authentic assessment**   A process of collecting and documenting information about children's developmental progress; data is gathered in children's naturalistic settings and from multiple sources. *p. 13*

**autonomy**   A sense of self as being separate from others. *p. 107*

## B

**bilateral**   Affecting both sides, as in loss of hearing in both ears. *p. 247*

**binocular vision**   Both eyes working together to send a single image to the brain. *p. 147*

**bonding**   The establishment of a close, loving relationship between an infant and adults (usually the mother and father); sometimes called *attachment. p. 75*

**bullying**   Verbal and physical behavior that is hurtful, intentional, and repeatedly directed toward a person or child who is viewed as weaker. *p. 176*

## C

**cephalocaudal**   Refers to bone and muscular development that proceeds from head to toe. *p. 38*

**cervix**   The lower portion of the uterus that opens into the vagina. *p. 60*

**cesarean section (C-section)**   The delivery of an infant through an incision in the mother's abdomen and uterus. *p. 61*

**Child Find**   A screening program designed to locate children who have developmental problems through improved public awareness. *p. 244*

**chorionic villus sampling (CVS)**   A genetic-screening procedure in which a needle is inserted and cells removed from the outer layer of the placenta; performed between the eighth and twelfth weeks to detect some genetic disorders, such as Down syndrome. *p. 55*

**chronological**   Refers to events or dates occurring in sequence over the passage of time. *p. 26*

**cleft lip/cleft palate**   Incomplete closure of the lip, palate (roof of the mouth), or both, resulting in a disfiguring deformity. *p. 52*

**conception**   The joining of a single egg or ovum from the female and a single sperm from the male. *p. 47*

**concrete operational thought**   Piaget's third stage of cognitive development; the period when the concepts of conservation and classification are understood. *p. 192*

**conservation**   The stage in children's cognitive development in which they understand that an object's physical qualities (e.g., weight and mass) remain the same despite changes in its appearance; for example, flattening a ball of play-dough does not affect its weight. *p. 171*

**constructivism**   A learning approach in which a child forms his or her own meaning through active participation. *p. 5*

**continuity**   Developmental progress that gradually becomes increasingly refined and complex. *p. 26*

**cyberbullying**   Sending hurtful, threatening, or harassing messages via the Internet or cell phone. *p. 205*

## D

**deciduous teeth**   The initial set of teeth that eventually fall out; often referred to as *baby teeth. p. 161*

**deductive reasoning**   A process of considering hypothetical alternatives before reaching a conclusion. *p. 222*

**depth perception**    The ability to determine the relative distance of objects from the observer. *p. 89*

**descriptive praise**    Words or actions that describe to a child specifically what she or he is doing correctly or well. *p. 12*

**developmentally appropriate**    A term describing learning experiences that are individualized based on a child's level of skills, abilities, and interests. *p. 11*

**developmental sequence**    A continuum of predictable steps along a developmental pathway of skill achievement. *p. 38*

**developmental team**    A team of qualified professionals, such as special educators, speech-language pathologists, occupational therapists, social workers, audiologists, nurses, and physical therapists, who evaluate a child's developmental progress and together prepare an intervention plan that addresses the child's special needs. *p. 251*

**development**    Refers to an increase in complexity, from simple to more complicated and detailed. *p. 25*

**discontinuity**    Development that occurs in irregular periods or stages; not a smooth, continuous process. *p. 26*

**discrete behaviors**    Actions that can be observed and described clearly, such as hitting, pulling hair, or spitting. *p. 16*

**domains**    Areas of development such as physical, motor, social-emotional, and speech and language. *p. 16*

**dysfluency**    Repetition of whole words or phrases, uttered without frustration and often at the beginning of a statement, such as "Let's go, let's go get some cookies." *p. 120*

## E

**ecology**    In terms of children's development, refers to interactive effects between children and their family, child care situation, school, and everything in the wider community that affects their lives. *p. 35*

**ectopic pregnancy**    Pregnancy that occurs when a fertilized egg attaches itself outside the uterus, most often in one of the fallopian tubes located between the ovaries and uterus. *p. 55*

**egocentricity**    Believing that everything and everyone is there for your benefit. *p. 108*

**egocentrism**    Adolescents' belief in their own self-importance. *p. 216*

**embryo**    The cell mass from the time of implantation through the eighth week of pregnancy. *p. 49*

**emerging literacy**    Early experiences, such as being read and talked to, naming objects, and identifying letters, that prepare a child for later reading, writing, and language development. *p. 159*

**essential needs**    Basic physical requirements such as food, shelter, and safety, as well as psychological needs, including love, security, and trust, which are required for survival and healthy development. *p. 11*

**expressive language**    Words used to verbalize thoughts and feelings. *p. 40, 111*

## F

**figurative language**    Words or statements that have meanings other than their literal definitions. *p. 229*

**fine motor**    Refers to small muscle movements; also referred to as *manipulative skills*; includes the ability to stack blocks, button and zip clothing, hold and use a pencil, and brush teeth. *p. 38*

**fontanels**    Small openings (sometimes called "soft spots") in the infant's skull bones; covered with soft tissue; eventually, they close. *p. 71*

**food jag**    A period when only certain foods are preferred or accepted. *p. 26, 113*

**formal operational thinking**    Piaget's fourth stage of cognitive development; the period when children are capable of using abstract thought to predict, test, and reason to arrive at a logical conclusion. *p. 215*

**functional language**    Language that allows children to get what they need or want. *p. 36*

## G

**gender**    Reference to being either male or female. *p. 136*

**genes**    Genetic material that carries codes, or information, for all inherited characteristics. *p. 47*

**gestational diabetes**    A form of diabetes that occurs only during pregnancy and places the fetus at increased risk; often associated with excess maternal weight gain, a family history of diabetes, and certain ethnicities (e.g., Latina, Native American, African American, Asian, Pacific Islander). *p. 54*

**gross motor**    Refers to large muscle movements such as locomotor skills (walking, skipping, or swimming) and nonlocomotive movements (sitting, pushing and pulling, or squatting). *p. 38*

**growth**    Physical changes leading to an increase in size. *p. 24*

## H

**hand dominance**    Preference for using one hand over the other; most individuals are said to be either right-handed or left-handed. *p. 132*

**hands-on learning**    A curriculum approach that involves children as active participants, encouraging them to manipulate, investigate, experiment, and solve problems. *p. 160*

**head circumference**    Measurement of the head taken at its largest point (across the forehead, around the back of the head, and returning to the starting point). *p. 24*

**holophrastic speech**    Using a single word to express a complete thought. *p. 110*

## I

**imaginary audience**    A component of egocentrism whereby adolescents believe that others care about and notice their behavior and appearance. *p. 216*

**implantation**    The attachment of the blastocyst to the wall of the mother's uterus; occurs around the twelfth day. *p. 49*

**intelligible**    Featuring language that can be understood by others. *p. 110*

**interdependent**    Affecting or influencing development in multiple domains. *p. 37*

**intuition**    A thought or idea based on a feeling or hunch. *p. 192*

**in utero**    Latin term for "in the mother's uterus." *p. 70*

## J

**jargon**    Unintelligible speech; in young children, it usually includes sounds and inflections of the native language. *p. 26*

**jaundice**    A yellow discoloration of the infant's skin and eyes caused by excess bilirubin (a yellow pigment that results when red blood cells are broken down) circulating in the bloodstream. *p. 71*

## L

**linguistic code**    Verbal expression that has meaning to the child. *p. 119*

**logical consequence**    A planned response that is implemented in response to misbehavior. *p. 206*

**logic**    A process of reasoning based on a series of facts or events. *p. 189*

**low birth weight (LBW)**    An infant who weighs less than 5.5 pounds (2,500 grams) at the time of birth. *p. 51*

## N

**natural consequence**    An outcome that occurs as a result of a certain behavior. *p. 206*

**naturalistic settings**    Environments that are familiar and part of children's everyday experiences, such as classrooms, care arrangements, and the home. *p. 13*

**nature vs. nurture**    Refers to whether development is primarily due to biological–genetic forces (heredity–nature) or to external forces (environment–nurture). *p. 3*

**neural connections**    Organized linkages formed between brain cells as a result of learning. *p. 30, 213*

**neurological**    Refers to the brain and nervous system. *p. 28*

**norms**    Age-level expectancies associated with the achievement of developmental skills. *p. 4*

**nurturing**    Refers to qualities of warmth, loving, caring, and attention to physical and emotional needs. *p. 11*

## O

**obesity**    Although no uniform definition exists, experts usually consider a child whose height-weight ratio (otherwise known as body mass index, or BMI) exceeds the 85th percentile for his age to be overweight, and obese if it is greater than the 95th percentile. *p. 180*

**object permanence**    Piaget's sensorimotor stage in which infants understand that an object exists even when it is not in sight. *p. 80*

**otitis media**    An infection of the middle ear. *p. 246*

**ova**    Female reproductive cells (eggs) that contain reproductive materials. *p. 54*

## P

**parallel play**    Playing alongside or near another person, but not involved in that person's activity. *p. 114*

**placenta**    A specialized lining that forms inside the uterus during pregnancy to support and nourish the developing fetus. *p. 49*

**plasticity**    The brain's ability to change and reorganize its structure as a result of learning. *p. 30*

**premature infant**    An infant born before thirty-seven weeks following conception. *p. 51*

**proximodistal**    Refers to bone and muscular development that begins closest to the trunk, gradually moving outward to the extremities. *p. 38*

**pruning**    The process of eliminating unused neurons and neural connections to strengthen those that the child is actively using. *p. 30*

**pupil**    The small, dark, central portion of the eye. *p. 73*

## R

**receptive language**    Understanding words that are heard. *p. 40, 110*

**reciprocal**    Refers to exchanges between individuals or groups that are mutually beneficial (or hindering). *p. 11*

**refinement**    Progressive improvement in the ability to perform fine and gross motor skills. *p. 38*

**reflexive**    Refers to movements resulting from impulses of the nervous system that cannot be controlled by the individual. *p. 38*

## S

**scientific reasoning**    Critical thinking skills (identify, analyze, and conclude) used to achieve a solution. *p. 223*

**self-esteem**    Feelings about one's self-worth. *p. 12*

**sensory information**    Information received through the senses: eyes, ears, nose, mouth, touch. *p. 39*

**sensory**    Refers to the five senses: hearing, seeing, touching, smelling, and tasting. *p. 159*

**service coordinator**    An individual who serves as a family's advocate and assists them with identifying, locating, and making final arrangements with community services. *p. 252*

**sexting**    Sending sexually explicit messages or pictures of yourself or friends via a cell phone. *p. 205*

**solitary play**    Playing alone. *p. 108*

**sonogram**    A visual image of the developing fetus, created by directing high-frequency sound waves (ultrasound) at the mother's uterus; the procedure is used to determine fetal age and physical abnormalities. *p. 55*

**sphincter**    The muscles necessary to accomplish bowel and bladder control. *p. 37*

**spina bifida**    A birth defect caused by a malformation of the baby's spinal column. *p. 52*

**stammering**    To speak in an interrupted or repetitive pattern; not to be confused with stuttering. *p. 26*

**stranger anxiety**    A cross-cultural phenomenon in which infants begin to show distress or fear when approached by persons other than their primary caregivers. *p. 90*

## T

**telegraphic speech**    Uttering two-word phrases to convey a complete thought. *p. 110*

**temperament**    An individual's characteristic manner or style of response to everyday events, including degree of interest, activity level, and regulation of behavior. *p. 47*

**teratogens**    Harmful agents that can cause fetal damage (e.g., malformations, neurological, and behavioral problems) during the prenatal period. *p. 56*

**transactional process**    The give-and-take relationship between children, their primary caregivers, and daily events that influences behavior and developmental outcomes. *p. 35*

**tripod grasp**    A hand position whereby an object, such as a pencil, is held between the thumb and first and second fingers. *p. 132*

**typical**    Refers to the achievement of certain skills according to a fairly predictable sequence, although with many individual variations. *p. 28*

## V

**voluntary**    Refers to movements that can be willed and purposively controlled and initiated by the individual. *p. 38*

## Z

**Zone of Proximal Development**    Vygotsky's term for tasks that initially prove too difficult for children to master by themselves but that they can perform with adult guidance or assistance. *p. 7*

**zygote**    The cell formed as a result of conception; called a *zygote* for the first fourteen days. *p. 47*

# Index

## A

Abstract thinking, 200, 283
Accommodation, 6–7
ACES. *See* Adverse Childhood Experiences
Achievement tests, 250–51, 283
ADA. *See* Americans with Disabilities Act
ADHD. *See* Attention deficit hyperactivity disorder
Adolescents (thirteen- to nineteen-year olds), 211–38. *See also specific ages*
  age divisions for, 41
  brain development in, 31, 213, 221
  case study on, 211–12
  cultural differences in, 214, 228, 233
  developmental checklists for, 269–71
  as percentage of population, 212
  positive behavior guidance for, 233–34
  pregnancy among, 54
Adverse Childhood Experiences (ACES) Study, 168–69
Affection, cultural differences in expressions of, 120
African Americans, breast-feeding among, 86
Age, at time of pregnancy, 54–55
Age divisions, 41–42
Age-level expectancies, 26–27
Alcohol consumption, during pregnancy, 57–58
Ambidexterity, 119
Americans with Disabilities Act (ADA) of 1990, 242
Amnesia, infantile, 141
Amniocentesis, 55, 56, 283
Analytical thinking, 229, 283
Anecdotal notes, 16
Anencephaly, 52, 283
Animals, safety around, 182
Anti-bullying initiatives, 176
Antipoverty movement, 240–41
Apgar scoring system, 62

Aristotle, 3
Assessment
  authentic, 13–14, 283
  examples of instruments for, 274–77
  portfolio, 18
Assimilation, 6–7
At risk children, 35–36
  definition of, 11, 35, 283
  indicators of, 35–36
Attachment, 92
Attention deficit hyperactivity disorder (ADHD)
  observation in evaluation of, 247
  physical activity and, 198
Atypical growth and development, 36. *See also* Developmental delays
Authentic assessment, 13–14, 283
Autism
  early indicators of, 87
  gender and, 121
  research on causes of, 121
Autonomy
  definition of, 107, 283
  in toddlers, 107
Autonomy vs. shame and doubt stage, 5

## B

Baby blues, 62
Baby bottle tooth decay (BBTD), 91
Backpacks, 182
Bandura, Albert, 8
Bathing
  birth to one month, 76
  eight to twelve months, 99
  five-year-olds, 150
  four to eight months, 91
  four-year-olds, 144
  one to four months, 84
  one-year-olds, 113
  three-year-olds, 136
  two-year-olds, 121–22
BBTD. *See* Baby bottle tooth decay
Behavior. *See also specific types of behavior*
  contemporary theories on, 3–13

  management and modification of (*See* Positive behavior guidance)
Behaviorism, 8–9
Bilateral hearing loss, 247, 283
Bilingual children, 130
Binocular vision, 147, 283
Bioecological theory, 9–10
Biological readiness, 3
Biology, in theories of child development, 3–4
Birth. *See* Childbirth
Birth defects, 52–56
Birth to one month, 70–78
  brain development in, 76–77
  daily routines of, 75–76
  developmental alerts for, 77
  development and growth profiles for, 70–75
  positive behavior guidance for, 101
  safety concerns for, 78
Birth to twelve months. *See* Infants; *specific ages*
Blastocysts, 47
Bonding, 75, 283
Brain growth and development, 29–32
  in adolescents, 31, 213, 221
  autism and, 121
  birth to one month, 76–77
  breast-feeding and, 86
  computerized imaging of, 3, 13, 121
  eighteen-year-olds, 231–32
  eight to twelve months, 99–100
  eight-year-olds, 181
  eleven-year-olds, 204
  fifteen-year-olds, 225–26
  five-year-olds, 151–52
  fourteen-year-olds, 218–19
  four to eight months, 92–93
  four-year-olds, 144–45
  history of study of, 13
  in infants, 29, 30–31
  learning activities to promote (*See* Digital Downloads)
  nature vs. nurture in, 3
  nine-year-olds, 196

Brain growth and development
    (continued)
  one to four months, 84–85
  one-year-olds, 114–15
  physical activity and, 197–98
  poverty and, 31–32
  prenatal, 49
  seventeen-year-olds, 231–32
  seven-year-olds, 174–75
  sixteen-year-olds, 225–26
  six-year-olds, 165–66
  sleeping habits and, 139
  ten-year-olds, 196
  thirteen-year-olds, 218–19
  three-year-olds, 137
  toxic stress and, 168–69
  twelve-year-olds, 204
  two-year-olds, 122–23
Breast-feeding, and brain
    development, 86
Bronfenbrenner, Urie, 9–10
Bullying
  anti-bullying initiatives, 176
  cyberbullying, 205, 283
  definition of, 176, 283
  emotional development and, 194
  types of, 176
Burns
  birth to one month, 78
  four to eight months, 94
  four-year-olds, 146
  one to four months, 86
  one-year-olds, 116
  six-year-olds, 168
  three-year-olds, 138
  two-year-olds, 124

C

Case studies
  on adolescents, 211–12
  on child development, 1–2, 23–24
  on early childhood, 129–30,
      158–59, 239–40
  on infants, 69–70
  on middle childhood, 188–89
  on prenatal development, 46–47
  on toddlers, 106–7
Centers for Disease Control and
    Prevention (CDC), 169
Cephalocaudal development, 38, 283
Cerebral cortex, 221

Cervix, 60, 283
Cesarean section (C-section), 61, 283
Checklists, developmental, 17–18,
    257–71
  for adolescents, 269–71
  for early childhood, 261–66
  for infants, 258–59
  for middle childhood, 267–68
Chemicals, and prenatal develop-
    ment, 58–59
Child abuse and neglect, and brain
    development, 168–69
Childbirth
  depression after, 62–63
  process of, 60–62
Child development, 1–22. See also
    specific ages and aspects of
    development
  atypical, 36 (See also
    Developmental delays)
  case studies on, 1–2, 23–24
  contemporary theories of, 3–13
    behaviorism and social learning
      theory, 8–9
    bioecological theory, 9–10
    cognitive-developmental theory,
      5–7
    essential needs theory, 10–13
    maturational theory, 3–4
    psychoanalytic and psychosocial
      theory, 4–5
  data gathering on, 13–15
  history of study of, 2–3
  principles of, 23–45
  public policy on, 240–44
  sequences of, 26–27, 38, 284
  typical, 26–28
Child Find, 244, 283
Choking
  birth to one month, 78
  eight to twelve months, 101
  one to four months, 86
  one-year-olds, 116
  three-year-olds, 138
  two-year-olds, 124
Chorionic villus sampling (CVS),
    55, 283
Chronological events, 26, 283
Chronosystems, 9
Cleft lip/palate, 52, 283
Clothes. See Dressing

Cognitive development, 39–40. See
    also Perceptual-cognitive
    development
  definition of, 39
  poverty and, 31–32
  premature birth and, 244–45
  stages of, 5–6, 40
  theories of, 5–7
Cognitive-developmental theory,
    5–7, 33
Community screening, 243–44, 279–80
Conception, 47, 283
Conceptualization skills, 142, 148
Concrete operational stage of cogni-
    tive development, 6, 40, 171,
    172, 192, 283
Consequences
  logical, 206, 285
  natural, 206, 285
Conservation, 171, 283
Constructivism, 5, 283
Continuity, 26, 283
Contralateral locomotion, 27
Creative thinking, 130, 140
Crossing the midline, 109
Cultural differences
  in adolescents, 214, 228, 233
  in autonomy, development of, 107
  in conceptualization skills, 148
  in culturally responsive teaching, 14
  in displays of affection, 120
  in early childhood, 131, 134, 142,
      144, 148, 171, 179, 180
  and gender identity formation, 33
  in gender stereotypes, 190
  in infants, 25, 87, 90, 94, 98
  and IQ tests, 250
  in language development, 94, 130,
      134, 171, 201
  in math education, 193
  in middle childhood, 190, 196, 201
  in motor skills, 25, 94
  in play and social activities, 144, 180
  in pregnancy and childbirth, 62, 63
  and signs of developmental
      delays, 245
  in sleeping habits, 113, 139
  in social and emotional develop-
      ment, 142, 179
  in stranger anxiety, 90, 98
  teaching children about, 196

in temperament, 120
in toddlers, 107, 113, 120
Culture
in cognitive-developmental theory, 7
in gender identity formation, 33
CVS. *See* Chorionic villus sampling
Cyberbullying, 205, 283

## D

Daily routines
birth to one month, 75–76
eighteen-year-olds, 231
eight to twelve months, 98–99
eight-year-olds, 180
eleven-year-olds, 203–4
fifteen-year-olds, 225
five-year-olds, 150–51
fourteen-year-olds, 217–18
four to eight months, 91
four-year-olds, 143–44
nine-year-olds, 195
one to four months, 84
one-year-olds, 113–14
seventeen-year-olds, 231
seven-year-olds, 173
sixteen-year-olds, 225
six-year-olds, 164–65
ten-year-olds, 195
thirteen-year-olds, 217–18
three-year-olds, 135–36
twelve-year-olds, 203–4
two-year-olds, 121–22
Dangerous objects, and four-year-
olds, 146
Data gathering, 13–15
Dating, safety concerns in, 227
Death, understanding of concept
of, 130
Deciduous teeth, 161, 283
Deductive reasoning, 222, 283
Depression
in adolescence, 220
maternal, 62–63
Depth perception, 89, 284
Descriptive praise, 12, 284
Development. *See also* Child development; Human development
definition of, 25, 284
vs. growth, 24
Developmental alerts
birth to one month, 77
eighteen-year-olds, 232

eight to twelve months, 100–101
eight-year-olds, 181–82
eleven-year-olds, 205
fifteen-year-olds, 226
five-year-olds, 152
fourteen-year-olds, 219
four to eight months, 93
four-year-olds, 145–46
nine-year-olds, 196–97
one to four months, 85
one-year-olds, 115
seventeen-year-olds, 232
seven-year-olds, 175
sixteen-year-olds, 226
six-year-olds, 166–67
ten-year-olds, 196–97
thirteen-year-olds, 219
three-year-olds, 138
twelve-year-olds, 205
two-year-olds, 123–24
Developmental checklists, 17–18,
257–71
for adolescents, 269–71
for early childhood, 261–66
for infants, 258–59
for middle childhood, 267–68
Developmental delays or deviation,
239–56
case study on, 239–40
definition of, 36
diagnosis of and referral for,
251–53
early identification and intervention programs for, 243–44
information gathering for evaluation of, 247–51
public policy and, 240–44
screening for (*See* Screening)
signs of, 245–46
when to seek help for, 246
Developmental domains, 36–41. *See
also specific domains*
definition of, 16, 36, 284
interdependence of, 28–29, 37,
96, 285
Developmentally appropriate experiences, 11, 284
Developmental milestones, 25–26
Developmental sequences, 26–27,
38, 284
Developmental teams, 251–52, 284
Diabetes, gestational, 54, 284

Diet. *See also* Eating
during pregnancy, 51–54
"Difficult" children, 32–33
Digital Downloads: Learning Activities
to Promote Brain Development
birth to one month, 76–77
eighteen-year-olds, 231–32
eight to twelve months, 99–100
eight-year-olds, 181
eleven-year-olds, 204
fifteen-year-olds, 225–26
five-year-olds, 151–52
fourteen-year-olds, 218–19
four to eight months, 92–93
four-year-olds, 144–45
nine-year-olds, 196
one to four months, 84–85
one-year-olds, 114–15
seventeen-year-olds, 231–32
seven-year-olds, 174–75
sixteen-year-olds, 225–26
six-year-olds, 165–66
ten-year-olds, 196
thirteen-year-olds, 218–19
three-year-olds, 137
twelve-year-olds, 204
two-year-olds, 122–23
Direct services, for families and professionals, 279–81
Discontinuity, 26, 284
Discrete behaviors, 16, 284
Disequilibrium, 7
Diversity
bioecological theory and, 10
cultural (*See* Cultural differences)
teaching children about, 196
Doctors, evaluation of infants and
children by, 243
Domains. *See* Developmental
domains
Dressing
birth to one month, 76
eighteen-year-olds, 231
eight to twelve months, 99
eight-year-olds, 180
eleven-year-olds, 203
fifteen-year-olds, 225
five-year-olds, 150
fourteen-year-olds, 217
four to eight months, 91
four-year-olds, 144
nine-year-olds, 195

Dressing *(continued)*
  one to four months, 84
  one-year-olds, 113
  seventeen-year-olds, 231
  seven-year-olds, 173
  sixteen-year-olds, 225
  six-year-olds, 164–65
  ten-year-olds, 195
  thirteen-year-olds, 217
  three-year-olds, 136
  twelve-year-olds, 203
  two-year-olds, 121–22
Drowning. *See* Water safety
Drug abuse. *See* Substance abuse
Drugs, and prenatal development, 58–59
Duration counts, 17
Dysfluencies, 120, 284

**E**

Early adolescence. *See* Fourteen-year-olds; Thirteen-year-olds
Early and Periodic Screening, Diagnosis, and Treatment Act (EPSDT) of 1967, 241
Early childhood (three- to eight-year-olds), 129–87. *See also* specific ages
  age divisions for, 41
  case studies on, 129–30, 158–59, 239–40
  cultural differences in, 131, 134, 142, 144, 148, 171, 179
  developmental checklists for, 261–66
  positive behavior guidance for, 153, 183
Early Head Start programs, 241
"Easy" children, 32
Eating
  birth to one month, 75
  eighteen-year-olds, 231
  eight to twelve months, 98–99
  eight-year-olds, 180
  eleven-year-olds, 203
  fifteen-year-olds, 225
  five-year-olds, 150
  fourteen-year-olds, 217
  four to eight months, 91
  four-year-olds, 143–44
  nine-year-olds, 195
  one to four months, 84
  one-year-olds, 113

  seventeen-year-olds, 231
  seven-year-olds, 173
  sixteen-year-olds, 225
  six-year-olds, 164
  ten-year-olds, 195
  thirteen-year-olds, 217
  three-year-olds, 135
  twelve-year-olds, 203
  two-year-olds, 121
Eating disorders, 203, 220, 225, 231
Ecological factors, examples of, 35
Ecological theory of child development, 9–10
Ecology, definition of, 35, 284
Ectopic pregnancies, 55, 284
Education, impact of poverty on, 36
Education for All Handicapped Children Act (EHA) of 1975, 242
Education of the Handicapped Act Amendments of 1986, 242
Egocentricity, 108, 284
Egocentrism, 216, 284
Ego identity, 5
EHA. *See* Education for All Handicapped Children Act
Eighteen-year-olds, 227–33
  Learning activities to promote brain development in, 231–32
  daily routines of, 231
  developmental alerts for, 232
  developmental checklists for, 271
  development and growth profiles for, 228–30
  positive behavior guidance for, 234
  safety concerns for, 232–33
Eight to twelve months, 94–101
  Learning activities to promote brain development in, 99–100
  daily routines of, 98–99
  developmental alerts for, 100–101
  developmental checklists for, 259
  development and growth profiles for, 95–98
  positive behavior guidance for, 102
  safety concerns for, 101
Eight-year-olds, 176–82
  Learning activities to promote brain development in, 181
  daily routines of, 180
  developmental alerts for, 181–82
  developmental checklists for, 266

  development and growth profiles for, 177–79
  positive behavior guidance for, 183
  safety concerns for, 182
Elementary and Secondary Education Act (ESEA) of 1965, 241
  reauthorization of, 242–43
Eleven-year-olds, 198–206
  Learning activities to promote brain development in, 204
  daily routines of, 203–4
  developmental alerts for, 205
  developmental checklists for, 268
  development and growth profiles for, 199–202
  positive behavior guidance for, 206
  safety concerns for, 205–6
Embryo, 49, 284
Embryonic stage, 49–50
Emerging literacy, 159, 284
Emotional development. *See* Social and emotional development
Entertainment. *See* Media exposure
Environment, in child development theories, 3–13
Environmental Protection Agency (EPA), 53
EPSDT. *See* Early and Periodic Screening, Diagnosis, and Treatment Act
Equilibrium, 7
Equipment safety
  eleven-year-olds, 205
  seven-year-olds, 176
  six-year-olds, 168
  twelve-year-olds, 205
Erikson, Erik, 5, 107
ESEA. *See* Elementary and Secondary Education Act
Essential needs, 11, 284
Essential needs theory, 10–13
Event sampling, 16–17
Exercise. *See* Physical activity
Exosystems, 9
Expressive language, 40, 111, 284

**F**

FAE. *See* Fetal alcohol effect
Falls
  eight to twelve months, 101
  five-year-olds, 152
  four to eight months, 94

four-year-olds, 146
one to four months, 86
one-year-olds, 116
six-year-olds, 168
three-year-olds, 138
False negatives, 249
False positives, 249
Families
in developmental teams, 251–52
observation by, 15, 247–48
resources for, 279–82
FAS. *See* Fetal alcohol syndrome
FASDs. *See* Fetal alcohol spectrum
disorders
Fathers, history of participation in
child care, 112
Fencing position, 73
Fetal alcohol effect (FAE), 58
Fetal alcohol spectrum disorders
(FASDs), 57
Fetal alcohol syndrome (FAS), 57
Fetal stage, 50
Fetus. *See* Prenatal development
Fifteen-year-olds, 221–27
Learning activities to promote
brain development in, 225–26
daily routines of, 225
developmental alerts for, 226
developmental checklists for, 270
development and growth profiles
for, 223–24
positive behavior guidance for, 234
safety concerns for, 227
Figurative language, 229, 284
Fine motor skills, 38–39, 88, 284
Firearm safety
in early childhood, 175
in middle childhood, 197
Fist, rule of, 85
Five-year-olds, 146–53
Learning activities to promote
brain development in, 151–52
daily routines of, 150–51
developmental alerts for, 152
developmental checklists for, 263
development and growth profiles
for, 147–50
positive behavior guidance for, 153
safety concerns for, 152–53
Folic acid, 52–53
Fontanels, 71, 284
Food jags, 26, 113, 284

Forceps, 61
Formal operational stage of cognitive
development, 6, 40, 215, 284
Foster care, toddlers in, 107
Fourteen-year-olds, 213–20
Learning activities to promote
brain development in, 218–19
daily routines of, 217–18
developmental alerts for, 219
developmental checklists
for, 269
development and growth profiles
for, 214–17
positive behavior guidance for, 234
safety concerns for, 219–20
Four to eight months, 87–94
Learning activities to promote
brain development in, 92–93
daily routines of, 91
developmental alerts for, 93
developmental checklists for, 258
development and growth profiles
for, 87–90
positive behavior guidance for, 102
safety concerns for, 94
Four-year-olds, 140–46
Learning activities to promote
brain development in, 144–45
daily routines of, 143–44
developmental alerts for, 145–46
developmental checklists for, 262
development and growth profiles
for, 140–43
positive behavior guidance for, 153
safety concerns for, 146
Frequency counts, 17
Freud, Sigmund, 4–5, 33
Friendships, in early childhood, 150,
160, 179
Frontal lobe, 213
Functional language, 36, 284

**G**

Gender
and autism, 121
definition of, 136, 284
and literacy skills, 200
Gender identity formation, 33–34,
117, 130
Gender stereotypes
in early childhood, 136
in middle childhood, 190

Generativity vs. stagnation stage, 5
Genes, definition of, 47, 284
Genetics
in temperament, 47
in theories of child development,
3–4
Genetic tests during pregnancy, 55, 56
Germinal stage, 47–49
Gesell, Arnold, 3, 4
Gestational diabetes, 54, 284
Gifted and talented children, 11
Glossary, 283–86
Gross motor skills, 38, 133, 284
Growth. *See also* Physical develop-
ment and growth
atypical, 36
definition of, 24, 284
vs. development, 24
typical, 28

**H**

Habituation, 39
Hair, 71
Hand dominance, 119, 132, 284
Handicapped Children's Early
Education and Assistance Act
(HCEEAA) of 1968, 241
Hands-on learning, 160, 285
Head circumference, 24, 71, 285
Head Start program, 241
Health concerns, for adolescents, 232
Hearing, birth to one month, 73
Hearing loss
bilateral, 247, 283
otitis media and, 246, 285
Holophrastic speech, 110, 285
Homicide, 233
Huffing, 206
Human development, Erikson's
stages of, 5. *See also* Child
development
Hyperactive, misuse of term, 247

**I**

IDEA. *See* Individuals with
Disabilities Education Act
Identity vs. confusion stage, 5
IEPs. *See* Individualized Education
Plans
IFSPs. *See* Individualized Family
Service Plans
Imaginary audience, 216, 285

Imaging technologies, 3, 13, 121
Implantation, 49, 285
Inclusion, social, 135
Individualized Education Plans
        (IEPs), 252
Individualized Family Service Plans
        (IFSPs), 242, 252
Individuals with Disabilities
        Education Act (IDEA) of
        1990, 242, 244, 251
Individuals with Disabilities
        Education Improvement Act
        of 2004, 242
Industry vs. inferiority stage, 5
Infantile amnesia, 141
Infants (birth to twelve months),
        69–105. *See also* specific ages
    age divisions for, 41
    assessment of newborn, 61, 62
    birth of, 60–62
    Learning activities to promote
        brain development in, 29,
        30–31 76–77, 84–85, 92–93,
        99–100
    case study on, 69–70
    cultural differences in, 25, 87, 90,
        94, 98
    developmental checklists for,
        258–59
    premature, 51, 244–45, 285
    screening of, 243
    temperament in, 41
Infections, maternal, 59–60
Information gathering, in
        developmental evaluations,
        247–51
Information resources, examples of,
        281–82
Initiative vs. guilt stage, 5
Injuries, to adolescents, 233
Integration, sensory, 39
Integrity vs. despair stage, 5
Intelligence tests, 250
Intelligible speech, 110, 285
Interdependence of developmental
        domains, 28–29, 37, 96, 285
Internet
    cyberbullying on, 205, 283
    safety on, 197, 220, 227
    slang on, 229
Intimacy vs. isolation stage, 5
Intuition, 192, 285

In utero, 70, 285
IQ
    breast-feeding and, 86
    tests of, 250

**J**

Jargon, 26, 285
Jaundice, 71, 285

**K**

Kaiser-Permanente, 169

**L**

Labeling, dangers of, 249
Labor and delivery, 60–62
Landau reflex, 79, 80
Language
    in cognitive-developmental theory, 7
    definition of, 40
    expressive, 40, 111, 284
    figurative, 229, 284
    functional, 36, 284
    receptive, 40, 41, 110, 285
Language and speech development, 40
    in bilingual children, 130
    birth to one month, 74–75
    brain development and, 30–31
    cultural differences in, 94, 130, 134,
        171, 201
    definition of, 40
    eighteen-year-olds, 229
    eight to twelve months, 97
    eight-year-olds, 178
    eleven-year-olds, 200–201
    fifteen-year-olds, 224
    five-year-olds, 148, 149
    fourteen-year-olds, 215–16
    four to eight months, 90
    four-year-olds, 141–42, 143
    nine-year-olds, 193
    observation methods for, 16–17
    one to four months, 82
    one-year-olds, 110–11
    sequence of, 26
    seventeen-year-olds, 229
    seven-year-olds, 171–72
    sixteen-year-olds, 224
    six-year-olds, 163
    ten-year-olds, 193
    thirteen-year-olds, 215–16
    three-year-olds, 133–34
    twelve-year-olds, 200–201

    two-year-olds, 119–20
Language stage, 40
Late adolescence. *See* Eighteen-year-
        olds; Seventeen-year-olds
LBW. *See* Low birth weight
Learning
    before birth, 49
    in early childhood, 160
    hands-on, 160, 285
    individualization of, 160
    by infants, 83
    play-based, 160
    about responsibility, 167
    technology in, 223
Learning Activities to Promote
        Brain Development. *See*
        Digital Downloads
Learning disabilities, prevalence of, 252
Learning needs, 11–12
Legislation, on child development,
        241–43
Lightening, 60
Linguistic code, 119, 285
Linguistic stage, 40
Literacy
    emerging, 159, 284
    gender and, 200
Locke, John, 3
Locomotion, contralateral, 27
Logic, 189, 285
Logical consequences, 206, 285
Low birth weight (LBW), 51, 52,
        54, 285

**M**

Machinery. *See* Equipment safety
Macrosystems, 9
Manipulative skills, 38
Maslow, Abraham, essential needs
        theory of, 10–13
Maternal depression, 62–63
Mathematics, 193
Maturational theory, 3–4
Media exposure
    in adolescence, 220, 227
    in early childhood, 182
    in middle childhood, 197, 205
    in toddlers, 117
Media industry, perceptual
        development in, 39
Medical conditions, developmental
        delays associated with, 243

Memory, long-term, before age four, 141
Mesosystems, 9
Microsystems, 9
Middle adolescence. *See* Fifteen-year-olds; Sixteen-year-olds
Middle childhood (nine- to twelve-year olds), 188–210. *See also specific ages*
  age divisions for, 41
  case studies on, 188–89
  cultural differences in, 190, 196, 201
  developmental checklists for, 267–68
  positive behavior guidance for, 206
Montessori, Marie, 7
Moral development, 179
Motor development, 37–39
  birth to one month, 72–73
  definition of, 37–38
  eighteen-year-olds, 228–29
  eight to twelve months, 95
  eight-year-olds, 177
  eleven-year-olds, 199–200
  fifteen-year-olds, 223
  five-year-olds, 147–48
  fourteen-year-olds, 215
  four to eight months, 88–89
  four-year-olds, 140–41
  nine-year-olds, 192
  one to four months, 79–80, 81
  one-year-olds, 108–9
  principles of, 38–39
  seventeen-year-olds, 228–29
  seven-year-olds, 170
  sixteen-year-olds, 223
  six-year-olds, 161–62
  ten-year-olds, 192
  thirteen-year-olds, 215
  three-year-olds, 131–32
  twelve-year-olds, 199–200
  two-year-olds, 118
Multiculturalism, 14

**N**

National Association for the Education of Young Children (NAEYC)
  cognitive-developmental theory in, 7
  on hands-on learning, 160
  standards of, 1, 23, 46, 69, 106, 129, 158, 188, 211, 239

National organizations, 280
Natural consequences, 206, 285
Naturalistic settings, 13–14, 285
Nature vs. nurture debate, 3, 8, 285
NCLB. *See* No Child Left Behind
Needs, essential, 10–13, 284
Neural connections, 30, 31, 213, 285
Neurocognitive function, physical activity and, 197–98
Neuroimaging, 3, 13, 121
Neurological, definition of, 28, 285
Neurons, 30
Newborns (birth to one month), 70–78
  assessment at birth, 61, 62
  Learning activities to promote brain development in, 76–77
  daily routines of, 75–76
  developmental alerts for, 77
  development and growth profiles for, 70–75
  positive behavior guidance for, 101
  safety concerns for, 78
Nine-year-olds, 190–97
  Learning activities to promote brain development in, 196
  daily routines of, 195
  developmental alerts for, 196–97
  developmental checklists for, 267
  development and growth profiles for, 191–94
  positive behavior guidance for, 206
  safety concerns for, 197
No Child Left Behind (NCLB) Act of 2002, 242–43, 250
Normal development, 28
Norms, 26–27
  definition of, 4, 27, 285
  in screening tools, 4
Notes, anecdotal, 16
Nurturing, definition of, 11, 285
Nutrition. *See also* Eating
  during pregnancy, 51–54

**O**

Obesity
  definition of, 180, 285
  prevalence of, 197
Object permanence, 80, 89, 285
Observation, 13–18
  data gathering through, 13–15, 247–48
  by families, 15, 247–48

methods of, 15–18
  by teachers, 14–18
One to four months, 78–86
  Learning activities to promote brain development in, 84–85
  daily routines of, 84
  developmental alerts for, 85
  development and growth profiles for, 79–83
  positive behavior guidance for, 102
  safety concerns for, 86
One-year-olds, 108–16
  Learning activities to promote brain development in, 114–15
  daily routines of, 113–14
  developmental alerts for, 115
  developmental checklist for, 259
  development and growth profiles for, 108–12
  positive behavior guidance for, 125
  safety concerns for, 116
Organizations, national and professional, 280, 282
Otitis media, 246, 285
Ova, 54, 285

**P**

Parachute reflex, 88
Parallel play, 114, 285
Peer influence, 230
Perceptual-cognitive development, 39
  birth to one month, 73–74
  definition of, 39
  in early childhood, 249
  eighteen-year-olds, 229
  eight to twelve months, 95–97
  eight-year-olds, 177–78
  eleven-year-olds, 200, 201, 202
  fifteen-year-olds, 223–24
  five-year-olds, 148–49
  fourteen-year-olds, 215
  four to eight months, 89–90
  four-year-olds, 141, 142
  nine-year-olds, 192–93
  one to four months, 80–82
  one-year-olds, 109–10, 112
  seventeen-year-olds, 229
  seven-year-olds, 171, 172
  sixteen-year-olds, 223–24
  six-year-olds, 162–63
  ten-year-olds, 192–93

Perceptual-cognitive development
    (continued)
    thirteen-year-olds, 215
    three-year-olds, 132–33
    twelve-year-olds, 200, 201, 202
    two-year-olds, 118–19
Personal care. See also specific types
    eighteen-year-olds, 231
    eight-year-olds, 180
    eleven-year-olds, 203
    fifteen-year-olds, 225
    fourteen-year-olds, 217
    nine-year-olds, 195
    seventeen-year-olds, 231
    seven-year-olds, 173
    sixteen-year-olds, 225
    six-year-olds, 164–65
    ten-year-olds, 195
    thirteen-year-olds, 217
    twelve-year-olds, 203
Personal safety, in early childhood
    five-year-olds, 153
    four-year-olds, 146
    six-year-olds, 168
Pets, safety around, 182
Physical activity
    in early childhood, 162, 171
    importance of, 171, 197–98
    in middle childhood, 197–98
    and neurocognitive function, 197–98
Physical development and growth, 37
    birth to one month, 70–71
    definition of, 37
    eighteen-year-olds, 228
    eight to twelve months, 95
    eight-year-olds, 177
    eleven-year-olds, 199
    fifteen-year-olds, 223
    five-year-olds, 147
    fourteen-year-olds, 214
    four to eight months, 87–88
    four-year-olds, 140
    nine-year-olds, 191
    one to four months, 79
    one-year-olds, 108
    seventeen-year-olds, 228
    seven-year-olds, 170
    sixteen-year-olds, 223
    six-year-olds, 161
    ten-year-olds, 191
    thirteen-year-olds, 214
    three-year-olds, 131

    twelve-year-olds, 199
    two-year-olds, 117
Physical needs, 11
Physicians, evaluation of infants and
    children by, 243
Physiological needs, 10–13
Piaget, Jean, 5–7, 40, 171, 172, 215
Pincer grip, 89
Placenta, 49, 285
Plasticity, 30, 285
Plato, 3
Play
    parallel, 114, 285
    solitary, 108, 112, 286
Play and social activities
    birth to one month, 76
    cultural differences in, 144, 180
    eight to twelve months, 99
    eight-year-olds, 180
    eleven-year-olds, 203–4
    five-year-olds, 151
    four to eight months, 91
    four-year-olds, 144
    nine-year-olds, 195
    one to four months, 84
    one-year-olds, 113–14
    seven-year-olds, 173
    six-year-olds, 165
    ten-year-olds, 195
    three-year-olds, 136
    twelve-year-olds, 203–4
    two-year-olds, 122
Play-based learning, 160
Play environment
    for seven-year-olds, 175–76
    for two-year-olds, 124
Poisoning
    five-year-olds, 153
    four to eight months, 94
    one-year-olds, 116
    three-year-olds, 138–39
    two-year-olds, 124
Portfolio assessment, 18
Portfolios, 18
Positive behavior guidance
    for adolescents, 233–34
    for early childhood, 153, 183
    for infants, 101–2
    for middle childhood, 206
    for toddlers, 125
Postpartum depression (PPD), 63
Poverty

    in bioecological theory, 10
    brain development affected by,
        31–32
    as disease vs. social problem, 31
    education affected by, 36
    and IQ tests, 250
    and motor skills, 25
    and prenatal care, 51
    prevalence of, 32
    war on, 240–41
PPD. See Postpartum depression
Praise, descriptive, 12, 284
Prefrontal cortex, 221
Pregnancy
    age at time of, 54–55
    alcohol consumption during,
        57–58
    depression after, 62–63
    development during (See Prenatal
        development)
    diet during, 51–54
    duration of, 47
    ectopic, 55, 284
    genetic tests during, 55, 56
    infections during, 59–60
    smoking during, 58
    weight gain during, 53–54
Prelanguage phase, 40
Prelinguistic phase, 40
Premature birth
    and cognitive development,
        244–45
    definition of, 51, 285
Prenatal care, 50–51
Prenatal development, 46–68
    case study on, 46–47
    promotion of healthy, 50–55
    stages of, 47–50
    threats to healthy, 56–60
Preoperational stage of cognitive
    development, 6, 40
Preteens. See Middle childhood
Professional organizations, 280, 282
Proximal Development, Zone of, 7,
    8, 286
Proximodistal development,
    38, 285
Pruning, 30, 285
Psychoanalytic theory, 4–5, 33
Psychological needs, 11
Psychosocial theory, 4–5
Puberty, 189–90

Public policy, on child development, 240–44
Pupils, 73, 285

## R

Rating scales, 17–18
Reading. *See* Literacy
Reasoning
    deductive, 222, 283
    scientific, 223, 286
Receptive language, 40, 41, 110, 285
Reciprocal exchanges, 11, 286
Red shirting, 4, 159
Referral process for developmental delays, 252–53
Refinement, 38–39, 286
Reflexive movements, 38, 72–73, 74, 88, 286
Reinforcement, 8
Reorganization, 28
Respect, need for, 12
Responsibility, learning about, 167
Rest, during pregnancy, 54
Risky behaviors, in adolescence, 220, 221
Rubella, 59

## S

Safety
    birth to one month, 78
    eighteen-year-olds, 232–33
    eight to twelve months, 101
    eight-year-olds, 182
    eleven-year-olds, 205–6
    fifteen-year-olds, 227
    five-year-olds, 152–53
    fourteen-year-olds, 219–20
    four to eight months, 94
    four-year-olds, 146
    nine-year-olds, 197
    one to four months, 85
    one-year-olds, 116
    seventeen-year-olds, 232–33
    seven-year-olds, 175–76
    sixteen-year-olds, 227
    six-year-olds, 168
    ten-year-olds, 197
    thirteen-year-olds, 219–20
    three-year-olds, 138–39
    twelve-year-olds, 205–6
    two-year-olds, 124

Sampling methods, 16–17
Schemas, 6
School attendance, age of compulsory, 160
School lunch programs, 13
Scientific reasoning, 223, 286
Screening for developmental delays, 243–44, 248–50
    community, 243–44, 279–80
    examples of instruments for, 273–74
    interpreting results of, 249–50
    selection of instruments for, 248–49
Seafood, 53
Self-centeredness, 108
Self-control, adolescent brain and, 221
Self-directed learning, 7
Self-esteem
    definition of, 12, 286
    need for, 12
Self-talk, 7
Sensorimotor stage of cognitive development, 5–6, 40
Sensory, definition of, 159, 286
Sensory activities
    definition of, 159
    in early childhood, 159–60
Sensory information, 39, 286
Sensory integration, 39
Sensory system, 38
Sequences of development, 26–27, 38, 284
Service coordinators, 252, 286
Seventeen-year-olds, 227–33
    Learning activities to promote brain development in, 231–32
    daily routines of, 231
    developmental alerts for, 232
    developmental checklists for, 271
    development and growth profiles for, 228–30
    positive behavior guidance for, 234
    safety concerns for, 232–33
Seven-year-olds, 169–76
    Learning activities to promote brain development in, 174–75
    daily routines of, 173
    developmental alerts for, 175
    developmental checklists for, 265
    development and growth profiles for, 170–72

positive behavior guidance for, 183
safety concerns for, 175–76
Sexting, 205, 286
Sexual orientation, 34
Sexual orientation, establishment of, 34
Sharp objects, 86
SIDS. *See* Sudden infant death syndrome
Sixteen-year-olds, 221–27
    Learning activities to promote brain development in, 225–26
    daily routines of, 225
    developmental alerts for, 226
    developmental checklists for, 270
    development and growth profiles for, 223–24
    positive behavior guidance for, 234
    safety concerns for, 227
Six-year-olds, 160–68
    Learning activities to promote brain development in, 165–66
    daily routines of, 164–65
    developmental alerts for, 166–67
    developmental checklists for, 264
    development and growth profiles for, 161–64
    positive behavior guidance for, 183
    safety concerns for, 168
Sketches
    on adolescents, 211–12
    on child development, 1–2, 23–24
    on early childhood, 129–30, 158–59
    on infants, 69–70
    on middle childhood, 188–89
    on prenatal development, 46–47
    on toddlers, 106–7
Skin, birth to one month, 70–71
Skinner, B. F., 8
Sleeping
    birth to one month, 76
    cultural differences in, 113, 139
    eighteen-year-olds, 231
    eight to twelve months, 99
    eight-year-olds, 180
    eleven-year-olds, 203
    fifteen-year-olds, 225
    five-year-olds, 151
    fourteen-year-olds, 218
    four to eight months, 91
    four-year-olds, 144
    importance of, 136, 139
    nine-year-olds, 195

Sleeping (continued)
one to four months, 84
one-year-olds, 113
seventeen-year-olds, 231
seven-year-olds, 173
sixteen-year-olds, 225
six-year-olds, 165
ten-year-olds, 195
thirteen-year-olds, 218
three-year-olds, 136
twelve-year-olds, 203
two-year-olds, 122
"Slow-to-warm" children, 32–33
Smoking, during pregnancy, 58
Social activities of adolescents. See also Play and social activities
eighteen-year-olds, 231
fifteen-year-olds, 225
fourteen-year-olds, 218
seventeen-year-olds, 231
sixteen-year-olds, 225
thirteen-year-olds, 218
Social and emotional development, 41
birth to one month, 75
definition of, 41
eighteen-year-olds, 230
eight to twelve months, 97–98
eight-year-olds, 178–79
eleven-year-olds, 201–2
fifteen-year-olds, 224
five-year-olds, 149–50
fourteen-year-olds, 216, 217
four to eight months, 90
four-year-olds, 142–43
nine-year-olds, 193–94
one to four months, 82–83
one-year-olds, 111
seventeen-year-olds, 230
seven-year-olds, 172
sixteen-year-olds, 224
six-year-olds, 164
ten-year-olds, 193–94
thirteen-year-olds, 216, 217
three-year-olds, 134–35
twelve-year-olds, 201–2
two-year-olds, 120
Social attitudes, and child development, 240–44
Social inclusion, 135
Social learning theory, 8–9, 33
Social media. See Media exposure
Solitary play, 108, 112, 286

Sonograms, 55, 56, 286
Special needs. See Developmental delays
Speech
holophrastic, 110, 285
intelligible, 110, 285
telegraphic, 110, 286
Speech development. See Language and speech development
Sphincter muscles, 37, 286
Spina bifida, 52, 286
Sports safety
in adolescence, 219–20, 227
in middle childhood, 205
Spotlight on Brain Development
The Brain-Autism Connection, 121
Breast-feeding and Brain Development, 86
The Importance of Sleep, 139
Learning Before Birth, 49
Physical Activity and Neurocognitive Function, 197–98
Poverty's Toxic Effects, 31–32
Premature Birth and Cognitive Development, 244–45
Self-Control and the Adolescent Brain, 221
Toxic Stress and Abnormal Brain Development, 168–69
Why Do Brain Research, and What Have We Learned?, 13
Stammering, 26, 286
Standards, NAEYC, 1, 23, 46, 69, 106, 129, 158, 188, 211, 239
Stanford Binet Intelligence Scales, 250
Stepping reflex, 72
Stimulus-response, 8
Stranger anxiety, 90, 98, 286
Strangulation
eight to twelve months, 101
four to eight months, 94
one-year-olds, 116
two-year-olds, 124
Stress
during pregnancy, 54
toxic, and abnormal brain development, 168–69
Substance abuse
in middle childhood, 206
and prenatal development, 58–59
Sudden infant death syndrome (SIDS), 76

Suffocation, 77
birth to one month, 78
eight to twelve months, 101
four-year-olds, 146
Suicide risks, in adolescence, 220, 233
Supplemental Nutrition Program for Women, Infants, and Children (WIC), 241
Swallowing reflex, 88

T

Talking. See Language and speech development
Teachers, as classroom observers, 14–18
TeachSource Digital Downloads. See Digital Downloads
TeachSource Video Connections
0–2 Years: Attachment in Infants and Toddlers, 92
0–2 Years: Birth, 61
0–2 Years: Early Learning in Infants and Toddlers, 83
0–2 Years: Fine Motor Development for Infants and Toddlers, 88
0–2 Years: Observation Module for Infants and Toddlers, 111
0–2 Years: Prenatal Assessment, 56
0–2 Years: Temperament in Infants and Toddlers, 41
0–2 Years: The Newborn and Reflex Development, 74
2–5 Years: Gross Motor Development for Early Childhood, 133
2–5 Years: Language Development for Early Childhood, 143
5–11 Years: Developmental Disabilities in Middle Childhood, 247
5–11 Years: Lev Vygotsky, the Zone of Proximal Development and Scaffolding, 8
5–11 Years: Moral Development in Middle Childhood, 179
5–11 Years: Observation Module for Middle Childhood, 202
5–11 Years: Piaget's Concrete Operational Stage, 172
12–18 Years: Peers and Domain Influences in Development, 230
Culturally Responsive Teaching: A Multicultural Lesson for Elementary Students, 14

*Infancy: Brain Development*, 29
*Infants and Toddlers: Cognitive Development and Imaginative Play*, 112
*Integrating Technology to Improve Student Learning*, 223
*Kindergarten Children's Observations about a 100 Chart*, 163
*No Child Left Behind*, 242
*Observing and Monitoring Language Development in Infants*, 97
*Observing and Monitoring Perceptual-Cognitive Development in Kindergartners*, 249
*Observing and Monitoring Physical/Motor Development in Toddlers*, 118
*Portfolio Assessment: Elementary Classroom*, 18
*Preschool: Social Development, Cooperative Learning, and Play*, 149
*School Age: Emotional Development*, 194
*School Age: Guidance*, 167
*Social-Emotional Development: Understanding Adolescents*, 217
*Students Living in Poverty*, 36
Technical assistance programs, 280–81
Technology. *See also* Internet
in learning, 223
Teenagers. *See* Adolescents
Teeth
baby bottle tooth decay, 91
deciduous, 161, 283
Telegraphic speech, 110, 286
Television viewing. *See also* Media exposure
by toddlers, 117
Temperament, 32–33
cultural differences in, 120
definition of, 32, 41, 47, 286
genetics of, 47
in infants and toddlers, 41
Temporal lobe, 213
Ten-year-olds, 190–97
Learning activities to promote brain development in, 196
daily routines of, 195

developmental alerts for, 196–97
developmental checklists for, 267
development and growth profiles for, 191–94
positive behavior guidance for, 206
safety concerns for, 197
Teratogens, 56, 286
Tests
achievement, 250–51, 283
intelligence, 250
screening (*See* Screening)
Text messaging, 205, 224
sexting, 205, 286
Thinking
abstract, 200, 283
analytical, 229, 283
creative, 130, 140
Thirteen-year-olds, 213–20
Learning activities to promote brain development in, 218–19
daily routines of, 217–18
developmental alerts for, 219
developmental checklists for, 269
development and growth profiles for, 214–16
positive behavior guidance for, 234
safety concerns for, 219–20
Three-year-olds, 131–39
Learning activities to promote brain development in, 137
daily routines of, 135–36
developmental alerts for, 138
developmental checklists for, 261
development and growth profiles for, 131–35
positive behavior guidance for, 153
safety concerns for, 138–39
Time sampling, 16–17
TNR. *See* Tonic neck reflex
Tobacco. *See* Smoking
Toddlers (twelve to twenty-four months), 106–28. *See also* One-year-olds; Two-year-olds
age divisions for, 41
case study on, 106–7
cultural differences in, 107, 113, 120
developmental checklists for, 260
positive behavior guidance for, 125
temperament of, 41
Toileting
birth to one month, 76
eight to twelve months, 99

five-year-olds, 150
four to eight months, 91
four-year-olds, 144
one to four months, 84
one-year-olds, 113
three-year-olds, 136
two-year-olds, 121–22
Tonic neck reflex (TNR), 73
Tools. *See* Equipment safety
Toxic stress
and abnormal brain development, 168–69
definition of, 168
Toy safety, in early childhood
eight-year-olds, 182
five-year-olds, 152
four-year-olds, 146
Traffic safety
five-year-olds, 153
nine-year-olds, 197
six-year-olds, 168
ten-year-olds, 197
three-year-olds, 139
Transactional process, 35, 286
Transportation safety, 78
Travel safety, 227
Trimesters, 47
Tripod grasp, 132, 286
Trust vs. mistrust stage, 5
Twelve to twenty-four months. *See* One-year-olds; Toddlers; Two-year-olds
Twelve-year-olds, 198–206
Learning activities to promote brain development in, 204
daily routines of, 203–4
developmental alerts for, 205
developmental checklists for, 268
development and growth profiles for, 199–202
positive behavior guidance for, 206
safety concerns for, 205–6
Twenty-four months. *See* Two-year-olds
Two-year-olds, 116–24
Learning activities to promote brain development in, 122–23
daily routines of, 121–22
developmental alerts for, 123–24
developmental checklists for, 260
development and growth profiles for, 117–20

Two-year-olds *(continued)*
   positive behavior guidance
      for, 125
   safety concerns for, 124
Typical development, 26–28
   definition of, 28, 286
   vs. normal development, 28

## U

Unintentional injuries, to adolescents, 233

## V

Vehicle safety
   for adolescents, 227, 233
   for toddlers, 124
Video Connections. *See* TeachSource
   Video Connections
Vision
   binocular, 147, 283
   birth to one month, 73
   depth perception in, 89, 284
Vitamins, in prenatal development,
   52, 53
Vocabulary development, 148
Voluntary movements,
   38, 286
Volunteering, 230
Vygotsky, Lev, 7, 8

## W

Walking
   average age for, 27
   cultural differences in, 94
Water safety
   eight to twelve months, 101
   eight-year-olds, 182
   nine-year-olds, 197
   one-year-olds, 116
   seven-year-olds, 176
   six-year-olds, 168
   ten-year-olds, 197
   three-year-olds, 138
   two-year-olds, 124
Watson, John B., 8
Wechsler Intelligence Scale for
   Children (WISC), 250
Weight gain, during pregnancy, 53–54
Well-being, of adolescents, 232
What Do You *See*?
   Concept and classification
      development, 142
   Development as biological
      manifestation, 4
   Early motor development, 81
   Friendships, 150, 179
   A healthy pregnancy, 57
   Integration of developmental
      domains, 96

Interest in learning, 201
The interplay of developmental
   domains, 29
Maternal diet and fetal
   development, 53
Motor development, 38
Observing children in naturalistic
   environments, 14
Physical activity, 162
Physical development, 191
Promoting language
   development, 82
Social development, 120
Social inclusion, 135
Toddler development, 112
WHO. *See* World Health
   Organization
WIC. *See* Supplemental Nutrition
   Program for Women, Infants,
   and Children
WISC. *See* Wechsler Intelligence
   Scale for Children
World Health Organization
   (WHO), 197

## Z

Zone of Proximal Development, 7,
   8, 286
Zygote, 47, 286